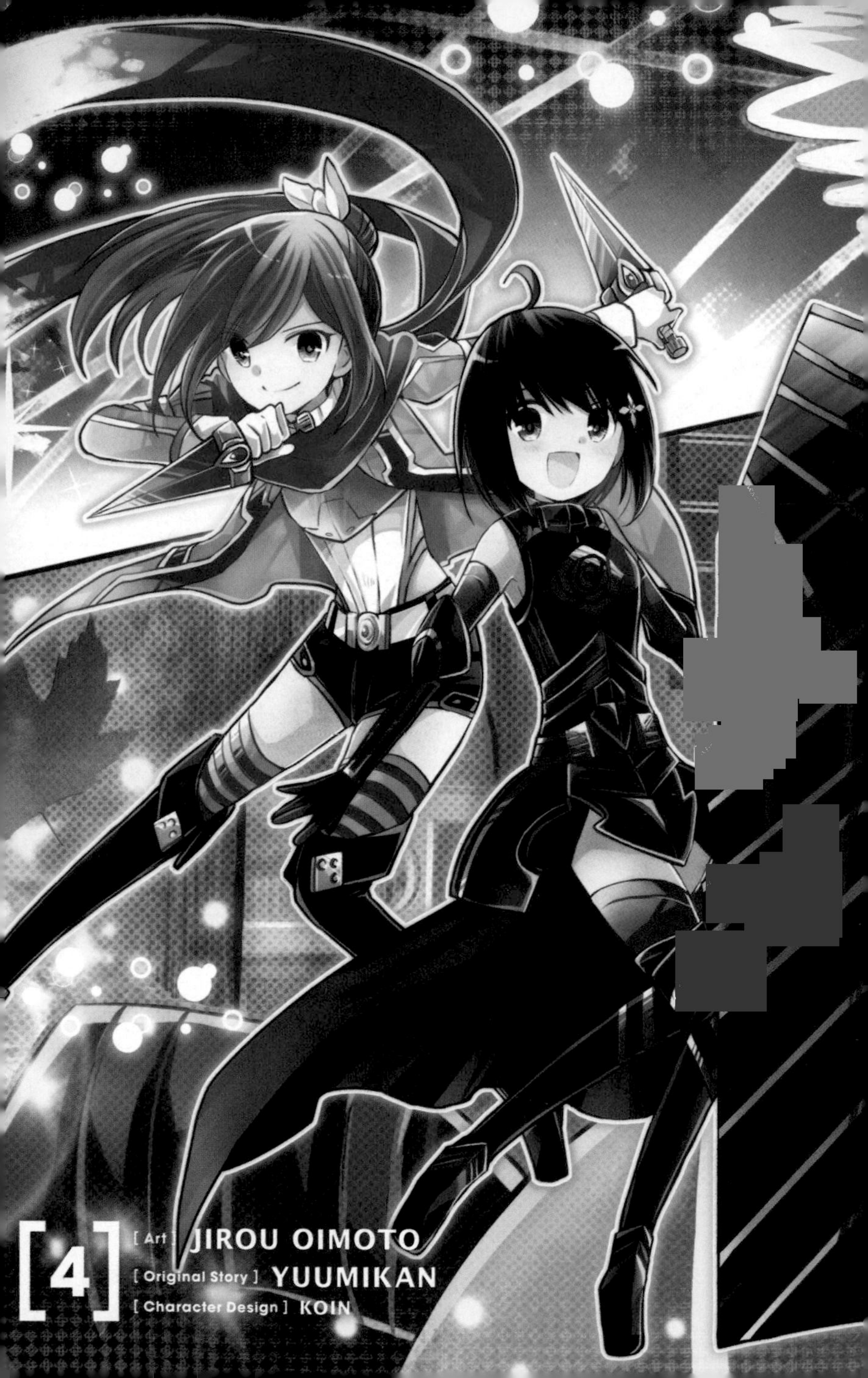
[4]
[Art] JIROU OIMOTO
[Original Story] YUUMIKAN
[Character Design] KOIN

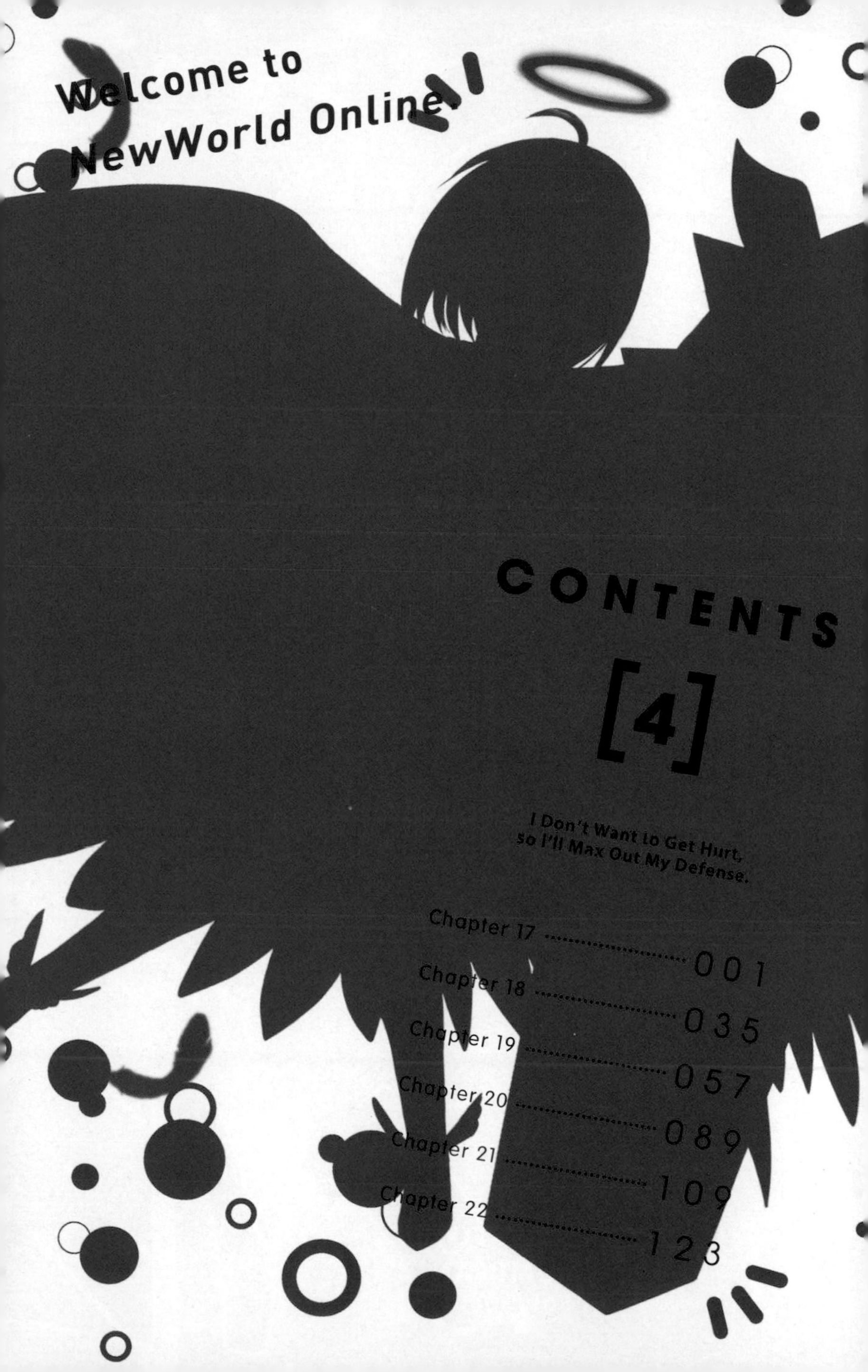

Welcome to NewWorld Online.

CONTENTS

[4]

I Don't Want to Get Hurt, so I'll Max Out My Defense.

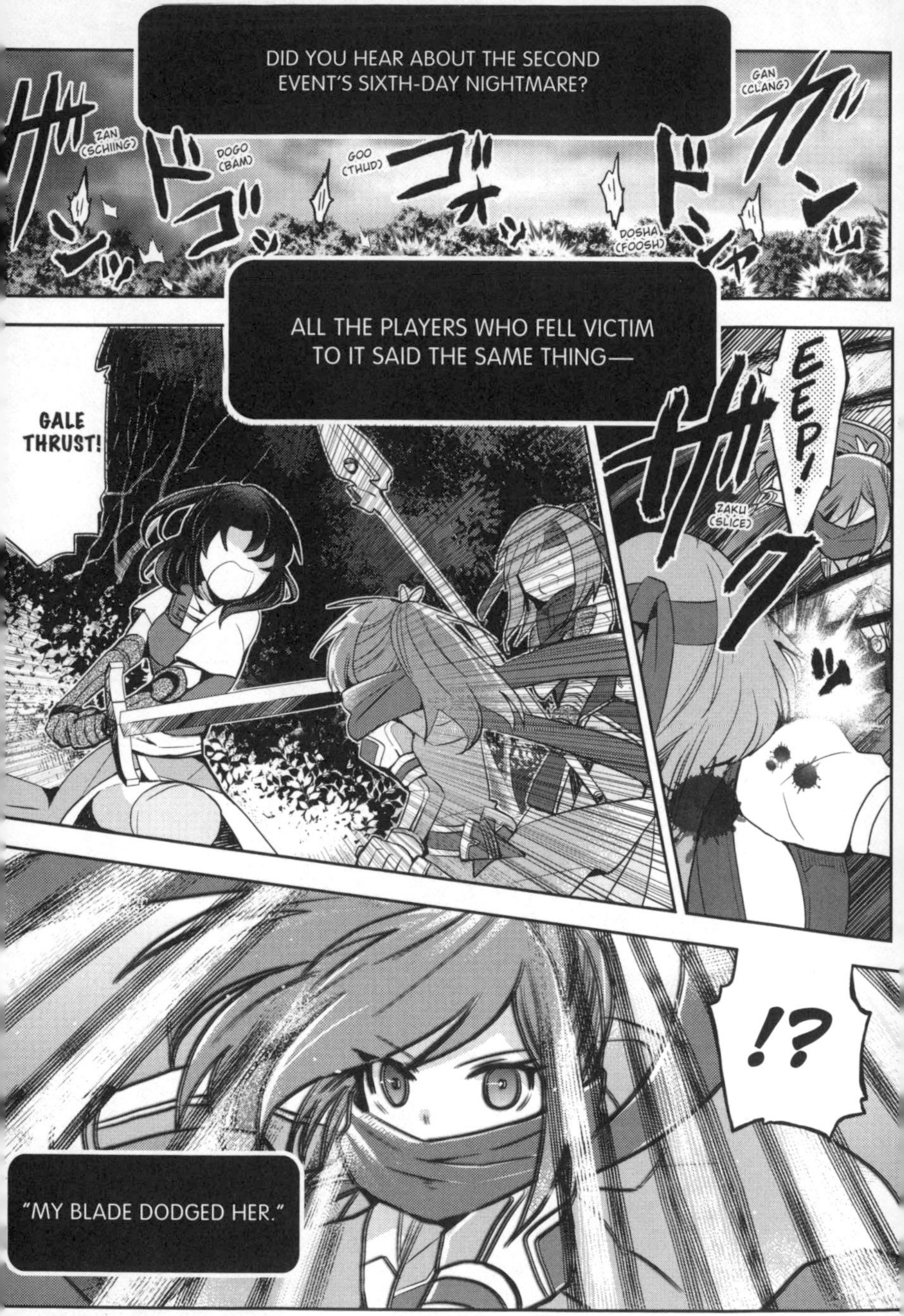
DID YOU HEAR ABOUT THE SECOND EVENT'S SIXTH-DAY NIGHTMARE?
GAN (CLANG)
DOSHA (FOOSH)
GOO (THUD)
DOGO (BAM)
ZAN (SCHIING)
ALL THE PLAYERS WHO FELL VICTIM TO IT SAID THE SAME THING—
EEP!
ZAKU (SLICE)
GALE THRUST!
!?
"MY BLADE DODGED HER."

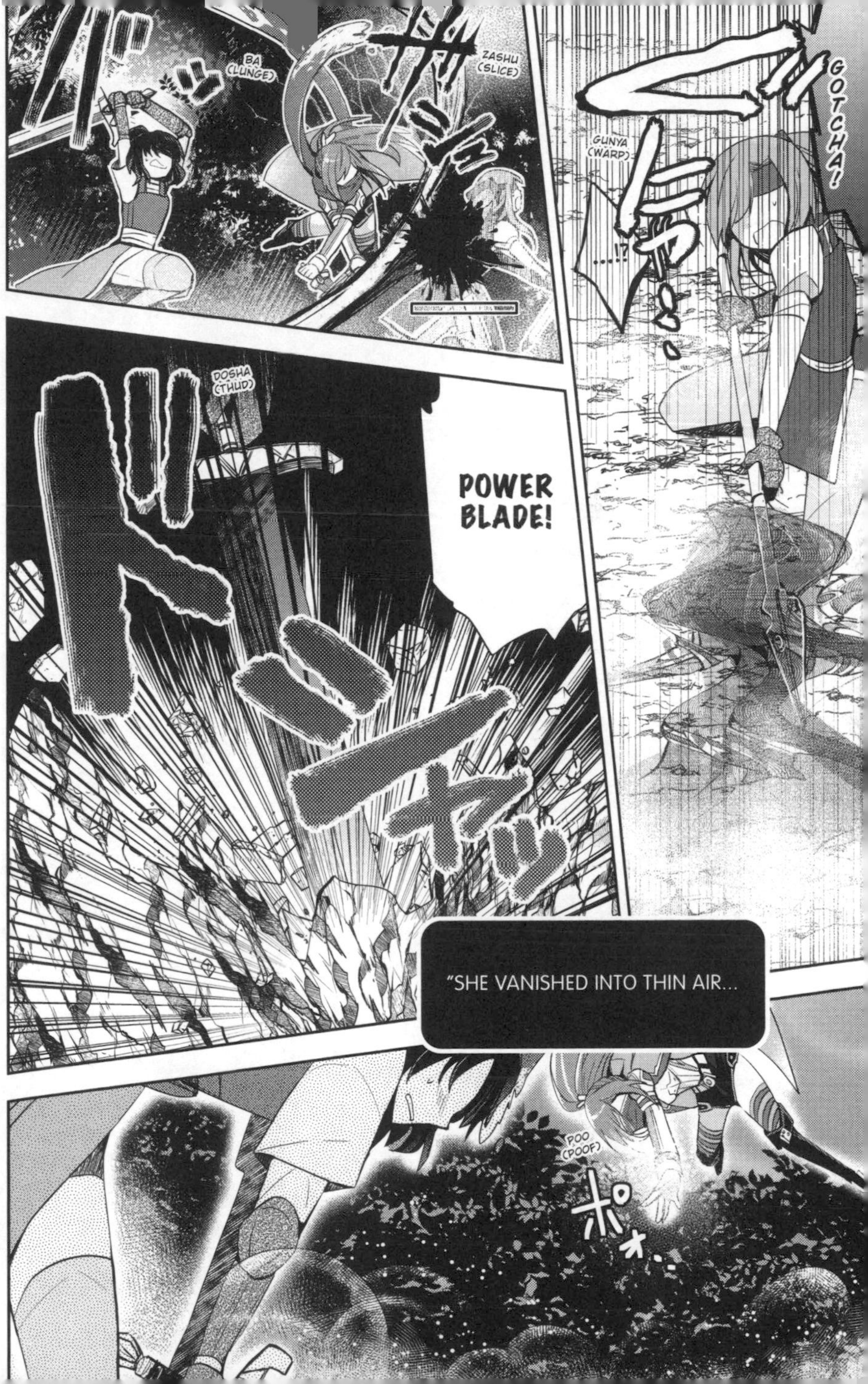
GOTCHA!
GUNYA (WARP)
...!?
ZASHU (SLICE)
BA (LUNGE)
DOSHA (THUD)
POWER BLADE!
"SHE VANISHED INTO THIN AIR...
POO (POOF)

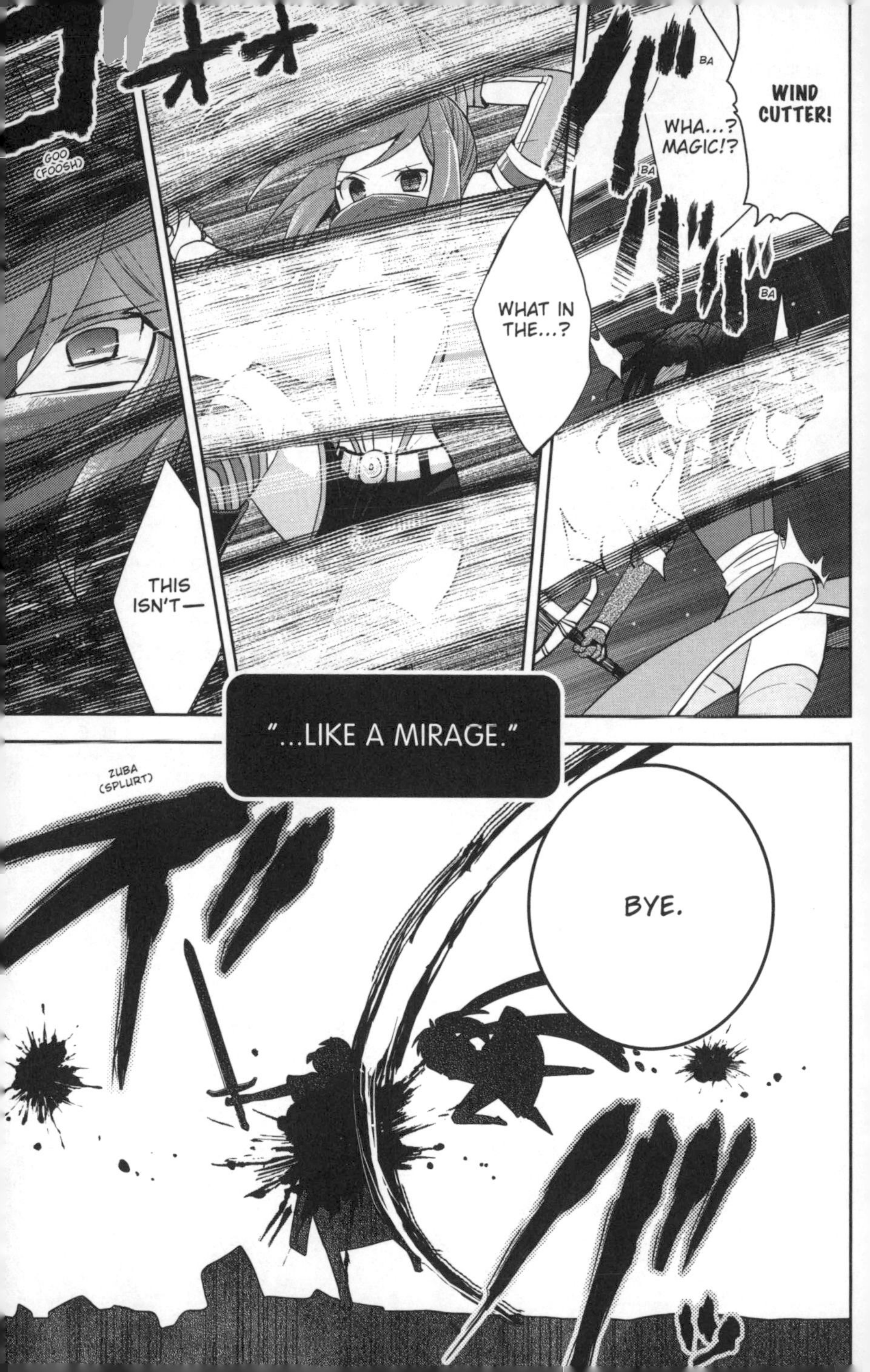
WIND CUTTER!
BA
WHA...? MAGIC!?
BA
BA
WHAT IN THE...?
GOO (FOOSH)
THIS ISN'T—
"...LIKE A MIRAGE."
BYE.
ZUBA (SPLURT)

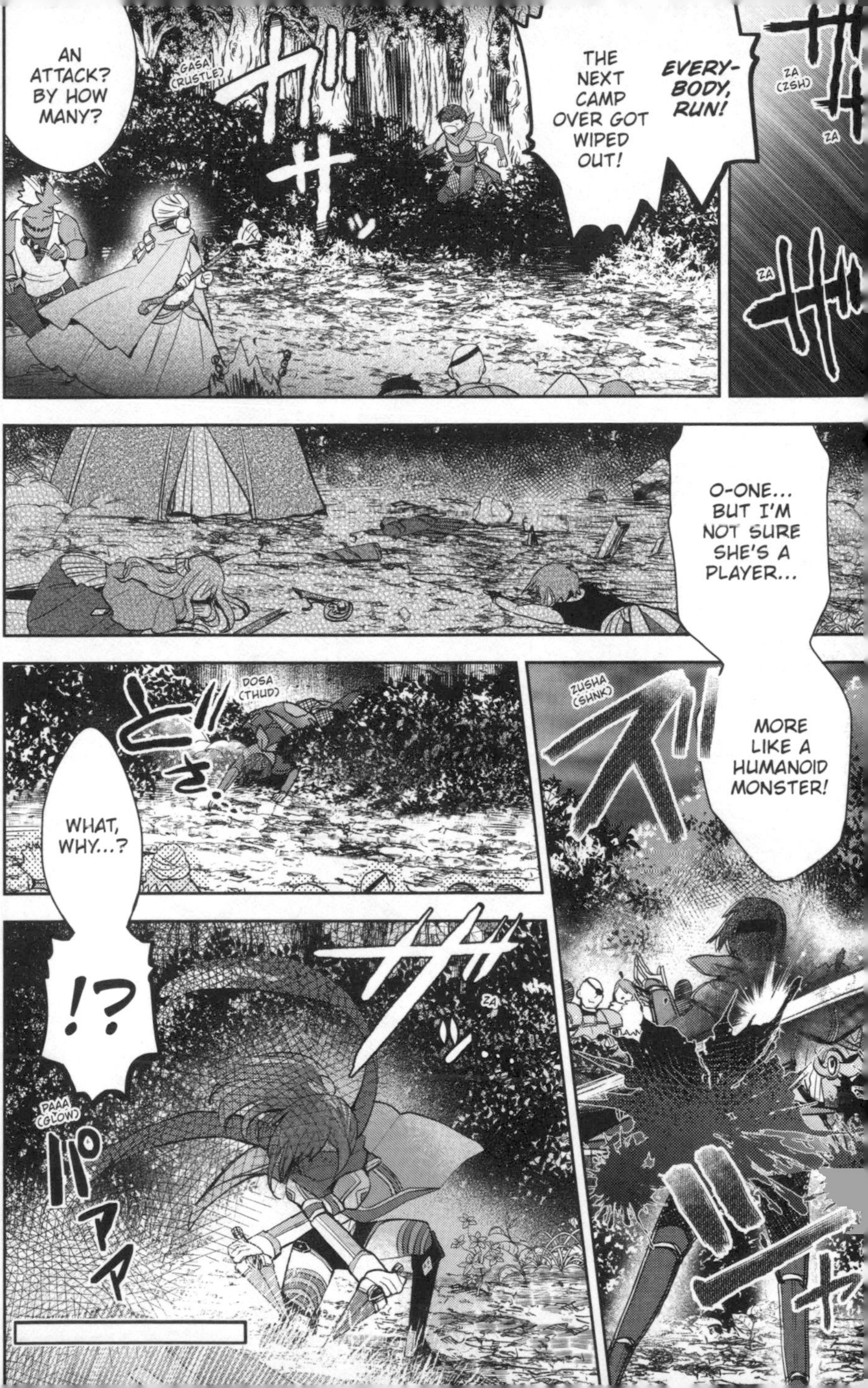
ZA (ZSH)
ZA
ZA
EVERY-BODY, RUN!
THE NEXT CAMP OVER GOT WIPED OUT!
GASA (RUSTLE)
AN ATTACK? BY HOW MANY?
O-ONE... BUT I'M NOT SURE SHE'S A PLAYER...
ZUSHA (SHNK)
MORE LIKE A HUMANOID MONSTER!
DOSA (THUD)
WHAT, WHY...?
ZA
!?
PAAA (GLOW)

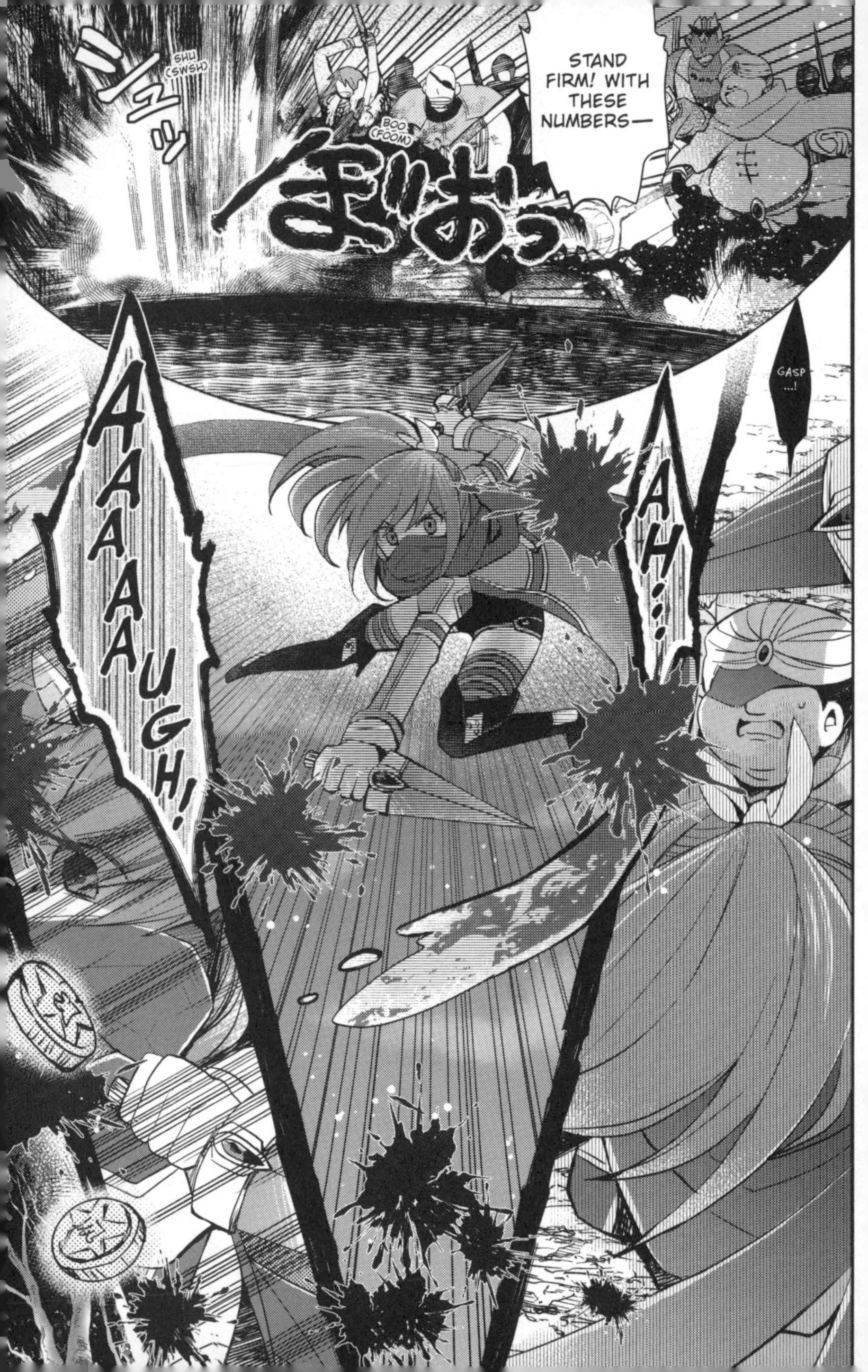
STAND FIRM! WITH THESE NUMBERS—
BOO (FOOM)
SHU (SWSH)
GASP ...!
AH...!
AAAAAUGH!

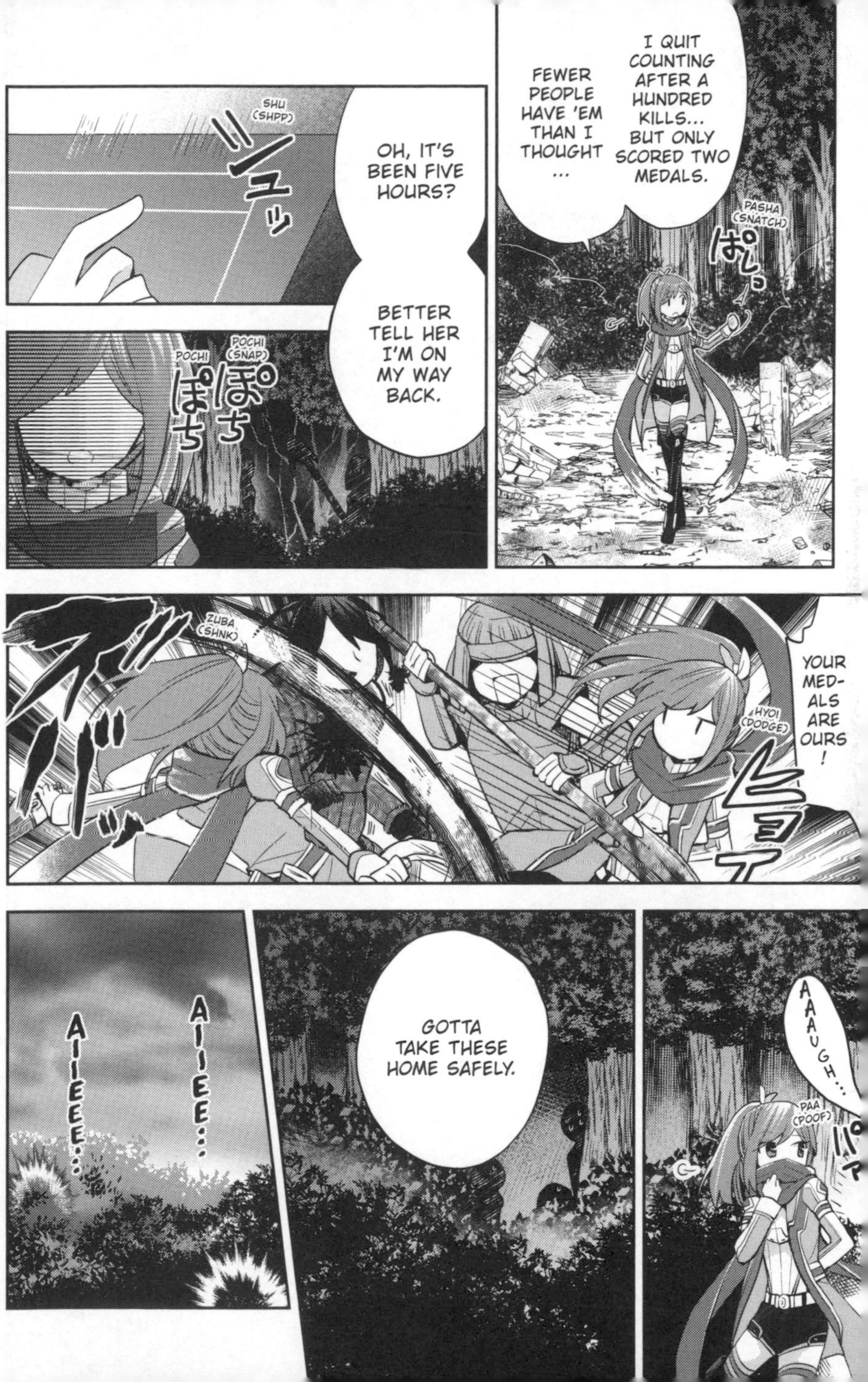
I QUIT COUNTING AFTER A HUNDRED KILLS... BUT ONLY SCORED TWO MEDALS.
FEWER PEOPLE HAVE 'EM THAN I THOUGHT ...
PASHA (SNATCH)
SHU (SHPP)
OH, IT'S BEEN FIVE HOURS?
BETTER TELL HER I'M ON MY WAY BACK.
POCHI (SNAP)
POCHI
YOUR MED-ALS ARE OURS!
HYOI (DODGE)
ZUBA (SHNK)
AAAUGH...
PAA (POOF)
GOTTA TAKE THESE HOME SAFELY.
AIIEEE...
AIIEEEE...

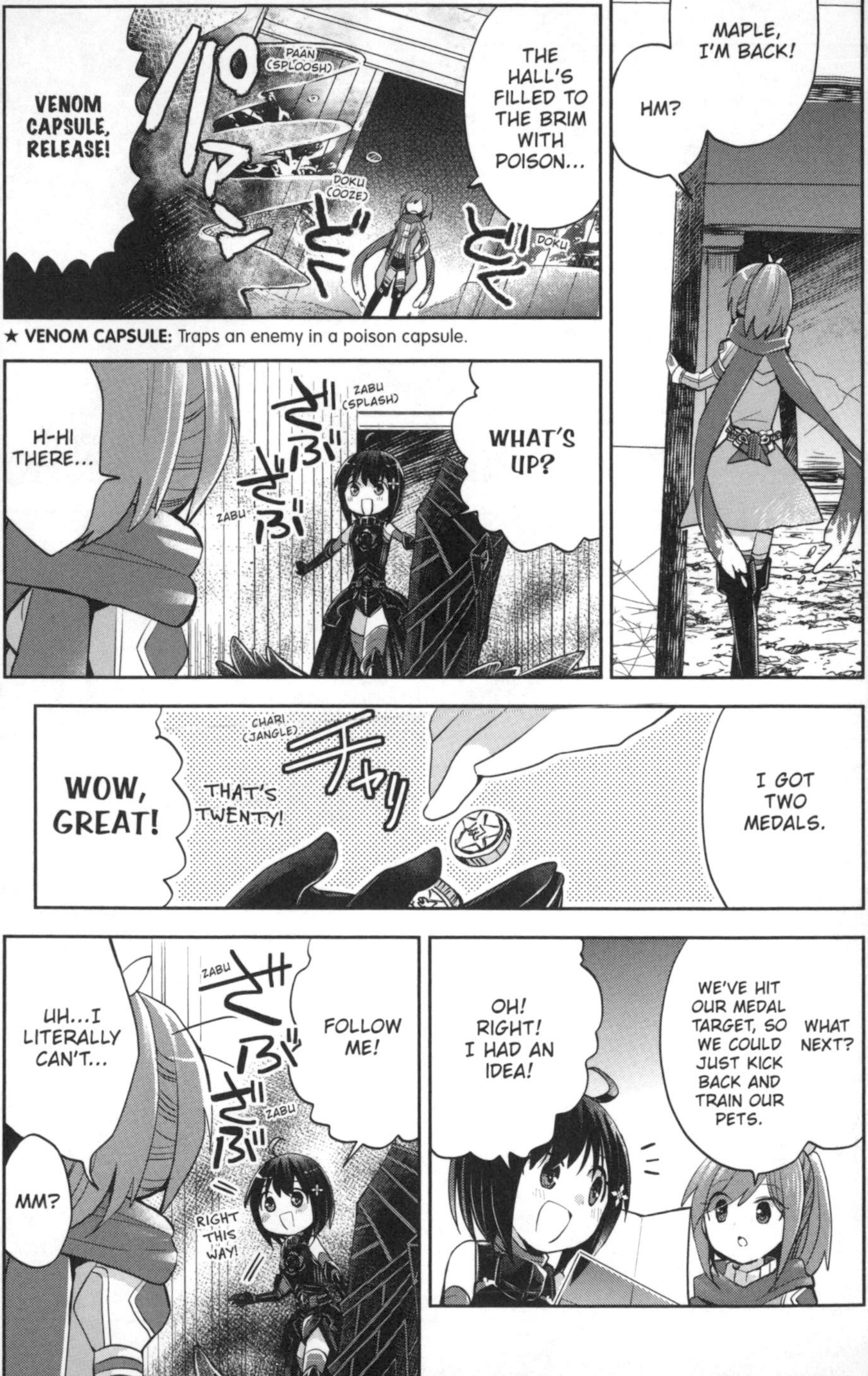
MAPLE, I'M BACK!
HM?
THE HALL'S FILLED TO THE BRIM WITH POISON...
DOKU
DOKU (OOZE)
PAAN (SPLOOSH)
VENOM CAPSULE, RELEASE!
WHAT'S UP?
ZABU (SPLASH)
ZABU
H-HI THERE...
I GOT TWO MEDALS.
CHARI (JANGLE)
THAT'S TWENTY!
WOW, GREAT!
WHAT NEXT?
WE'VE HIT OUR MEDAL TARGET, SO WE COULD JUST KICK BACK AND TRAIN OUR PETS.
OH! RIGHT! I HAD AN IDEA!
FOLLOW ME!
ZABU
ZABU
RIGHT THIS WAY!
UH...I LITERALLY CAN'T...
MM?

★ **VENOM CAPSULE:** Traps an enemy in a poison capsule.

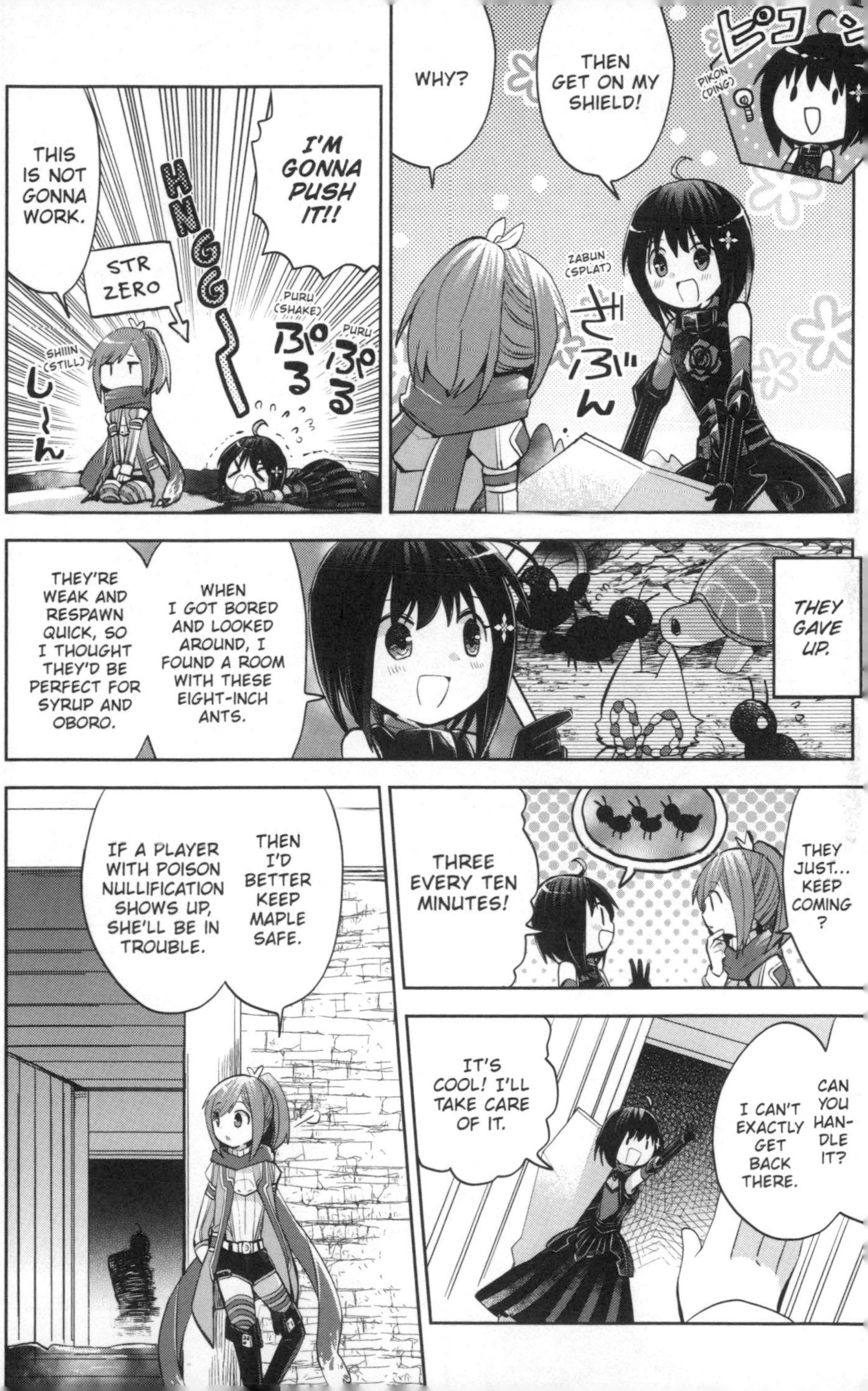

ピコン
PIKON (DING)
THEN GET ON MY SHIELD!
WHY?
ざぶん
ZABUN (SPLAT)
I'M GONNA PUSH IT!!
HNGG~
THIS IS NOT GONNA WORK.
STR ZERO
ぷる
PURU (SHAKE)
ぷる
PURU
しーん
SHIIN (STILL)
THEY GAVE UP.
WHEN I GOT BORED AND LOOKED AROUND, I FOUND A ROOM WITH THESE EIGHT-INCH ANTS.
THEY'RE WEAK AND RESPAWN QUICK, SO I THOUGHT THEY'D BE PERFECT FOR SYRUP AND OBORO.
THEY JUST... KEEP COMING?
THREE EVERY TEN MINUTES!
CAN YOU HANDLE IT?
I CAN'T EXACTLY GET BACK THERE.
IT'S COOL! I'LL TAKE CARE OF IT.
THEN I'D BETTER KEEP MAPLE SAFE.
IF A PLAYER WITH POISON NULLIFICATION SHOWS UP, SHE'LL BE IN TROUBLE.

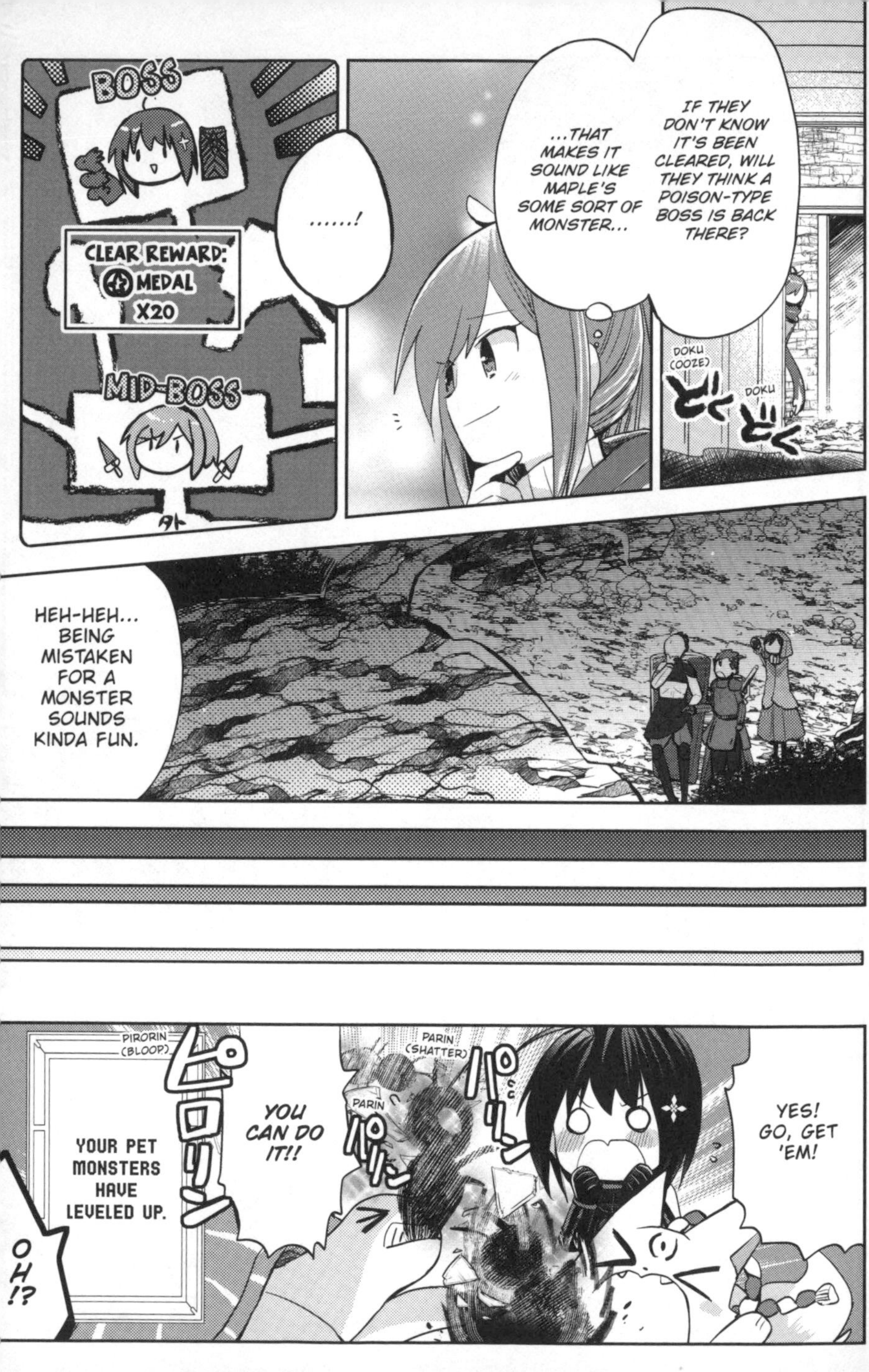
IF THEY DON'T KNOW IT'S BEEN CLEARED, WILL THEY THINK A POISON-TYPE BOSS IS BACK THERE?
DOKU (OOZE)
DOKU
...THAT MAKES IT SOUND LIKE MAPLE'S SOME SORT OF MONSTER...
......!
BOSS
CLEAR REWARD: MEDAL X20
MID-BOSS
HEH-HEH... BEING MISTAKEN FOR A MONSTER SOUNDS KINDA FUN.
YES! GO, GET 'EM!
PARIN (SHATTER)
PARIN
YOU CAN DO IT!!
PIRORIN (BLOOP)
YOUR PET MONSTERS HAVE LEVELED UP.
OH!?

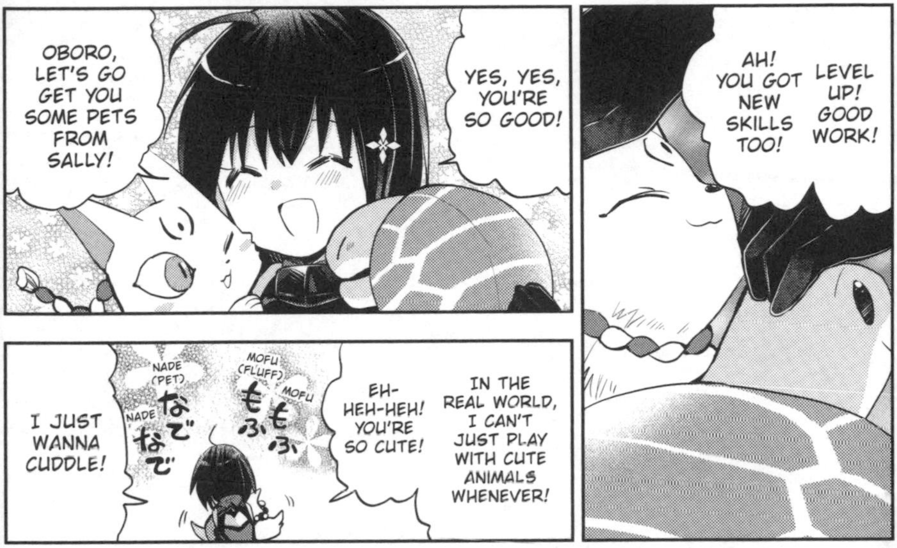
LEVEL UP! GOOD WORK!
AH! YOU GOT NEW SKILLS TOO!
YES, YES, YOU'RE SO GOOD!
OBORO, LET'S GO GET YOU SOME PETS FROM SALLY!
IN THE REAL WORLD, I CAN'T JUST PLAY WITH CUTE ANIMALS WHENEVER!
EH-HEH-HEH! YOU'RE SO CUTE!
MOFU (FLUFF) もふ
MOFU もふ
NADE (PET) なで
NADE なで
I JUST WANNA CUDDLE!

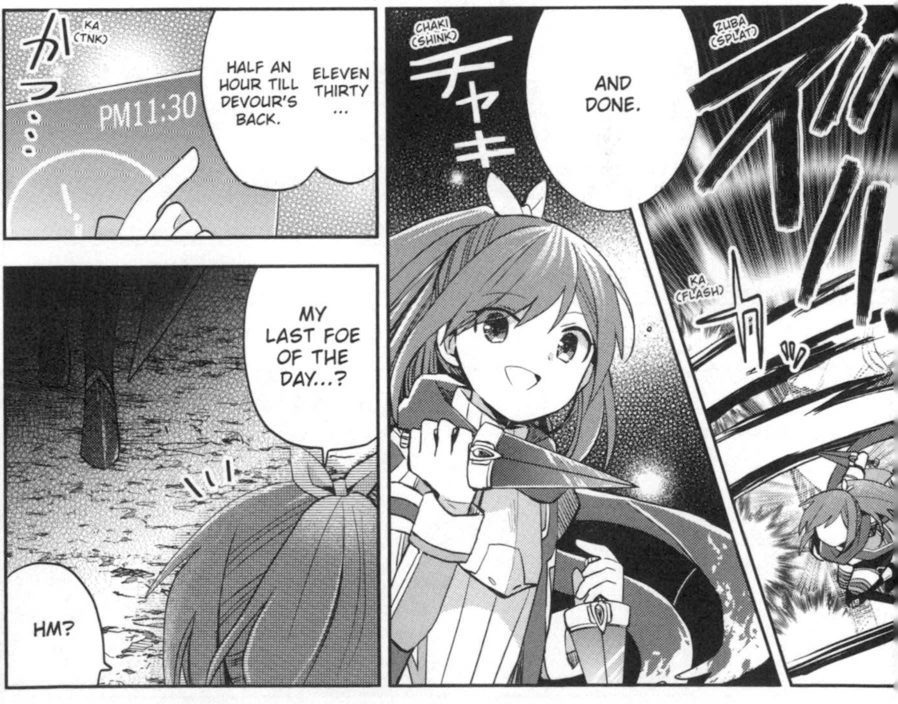
ZUBA (SPLAT)
KA (FLASH)
CHAKI (SHINK) チャキ
AND DONE.
ELEVEN THIRTY ...
HALF AN HOUR TILL DEVOUR'S BACK.
KA (TNK) かつ…
PM11:30
MY LAST FOE OF THE DAY...?
HM?

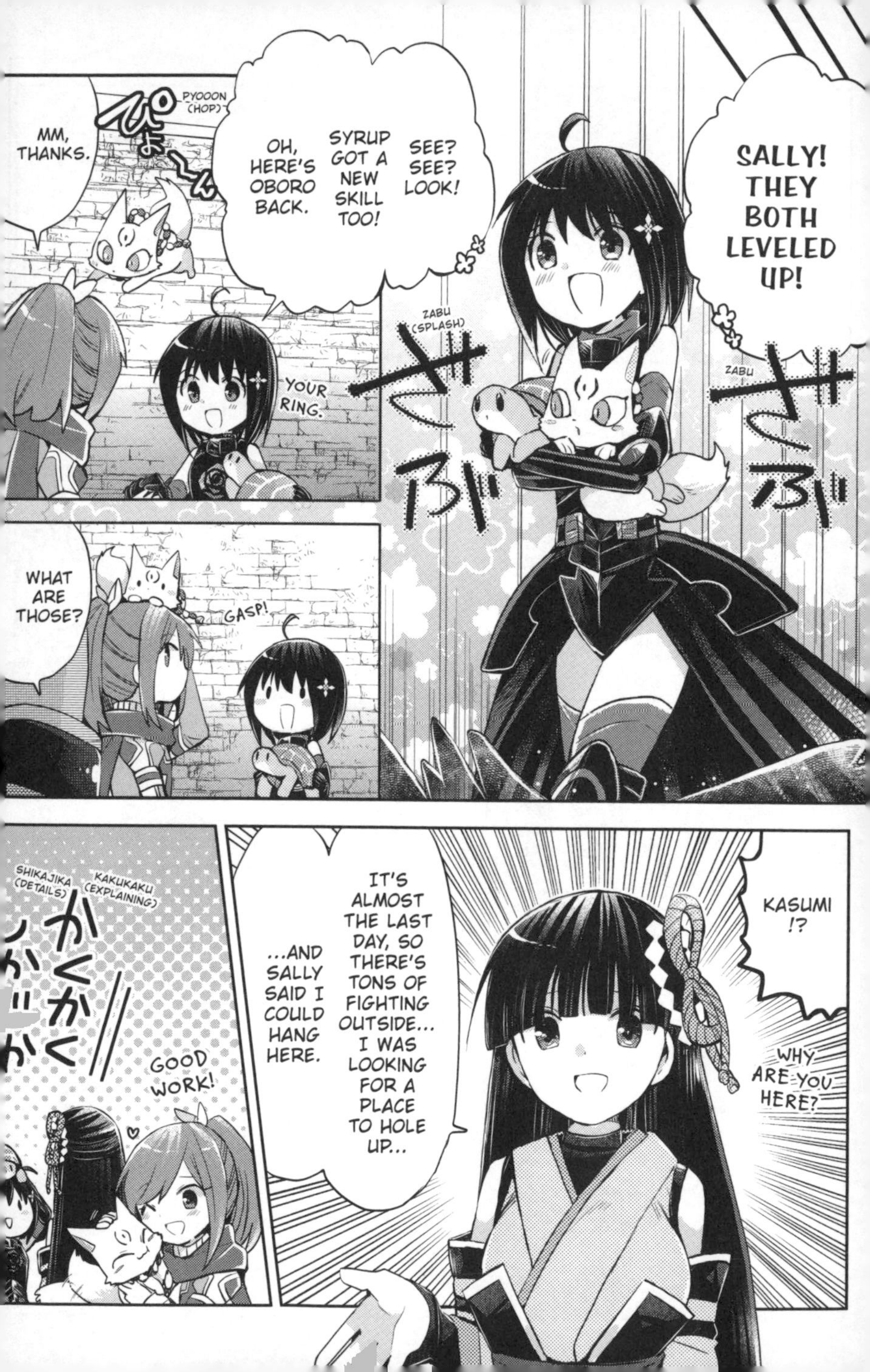
SALLY! THEY BOTH LEVELED UP!
ZABU
ZABU (SPLASH)
OH, HERE'S OBORO BACK. SYRUP GOT A NEW SKILL TOO! SEE? SEE? LOOK!
PYOOON (HOP)
MM, THANKS.
YOUR RING.
GASP!
WHAT ARE THOSE?
KASUMI!?
WHY ARE YOU HERE?
IT'S ALMOST THE LAST DAY, SO THERE'S TONS OF FIGHTING OUTSIDE... I WAS LOOKING FOR A PLACE TO HOLE UP...
...AND SALLY SAID I COULD HANG HERE.
KAKUKAKU (EXPLAINING)
SHIKAJIKA (DETAILS)
GOOD WORK!

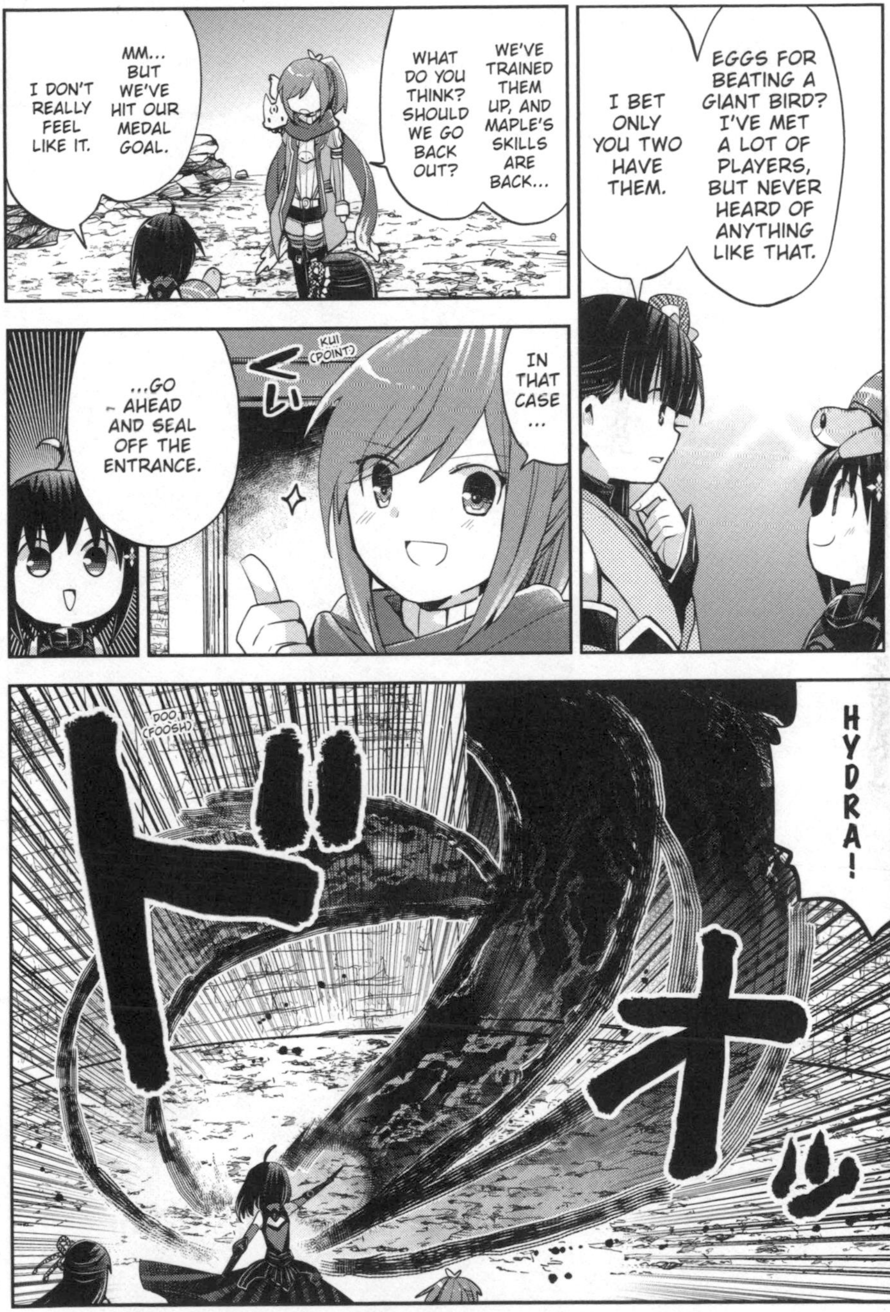
EGGS FOR BEATING A GIANT BIRD? I'VE MET A LOT OF PLAYERS, BUT NEVER HEARD OF ANYTHING LIKE THAT.
I BET ONLY YOU TWO HAVE THEM.
WE'VE TRAINED THEM UP, AND MAPLE'S SKILLS ARE BACK...
WHAT DO YOU THINK? SHOULD WE GO BACK OUT?
MM... BUT WE'VE HIT OUR MEDAL GOAL.
I DON'T REALLY FEEL LIKE IT.
IN THAT CASE...
KUI (POINT)
...GO AHEAD AND SEAL OFF THE ENTRANCE.
HYDRA!
DOO (FOOSH)

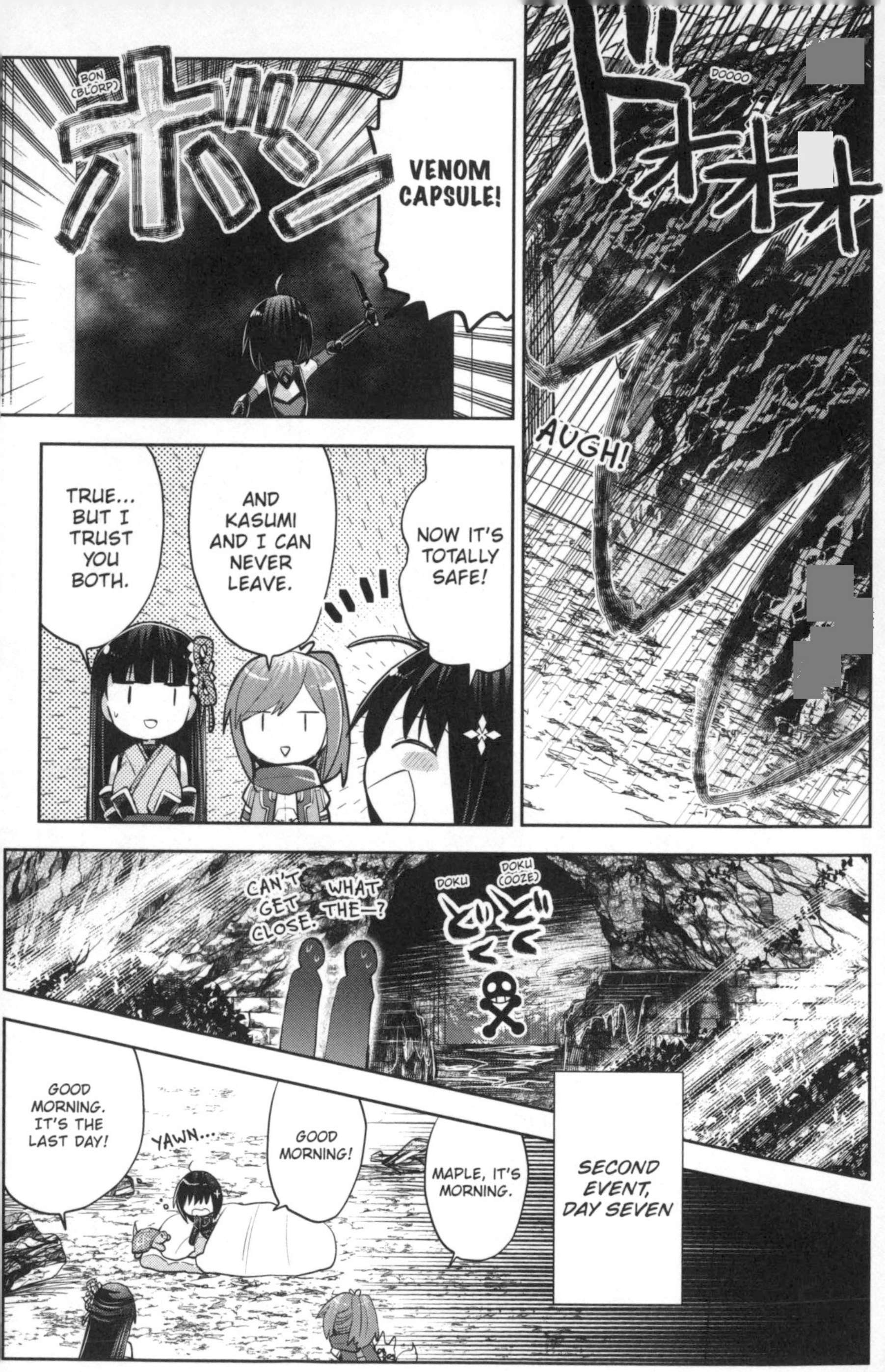
DOOOO
AUGH!
BON (BLORP)
VENOM CAPSULE!
NOW IT'S TOTALLY SAFE!
AND KASUMI AND I CAN NEVER LEAVE.
TRUE... BUT I TRUST YOU BOTH.
DOKU DOKU (OOZE)
WHAT THE—?
CAN'T GET CLOSE.
SECOND EVENT, DAY SEVEN
MAPLE, IT'S MORNING.
GOOD MORNING!
YAWN...
GOOD MORNING. IT'S THE LAST DAY!

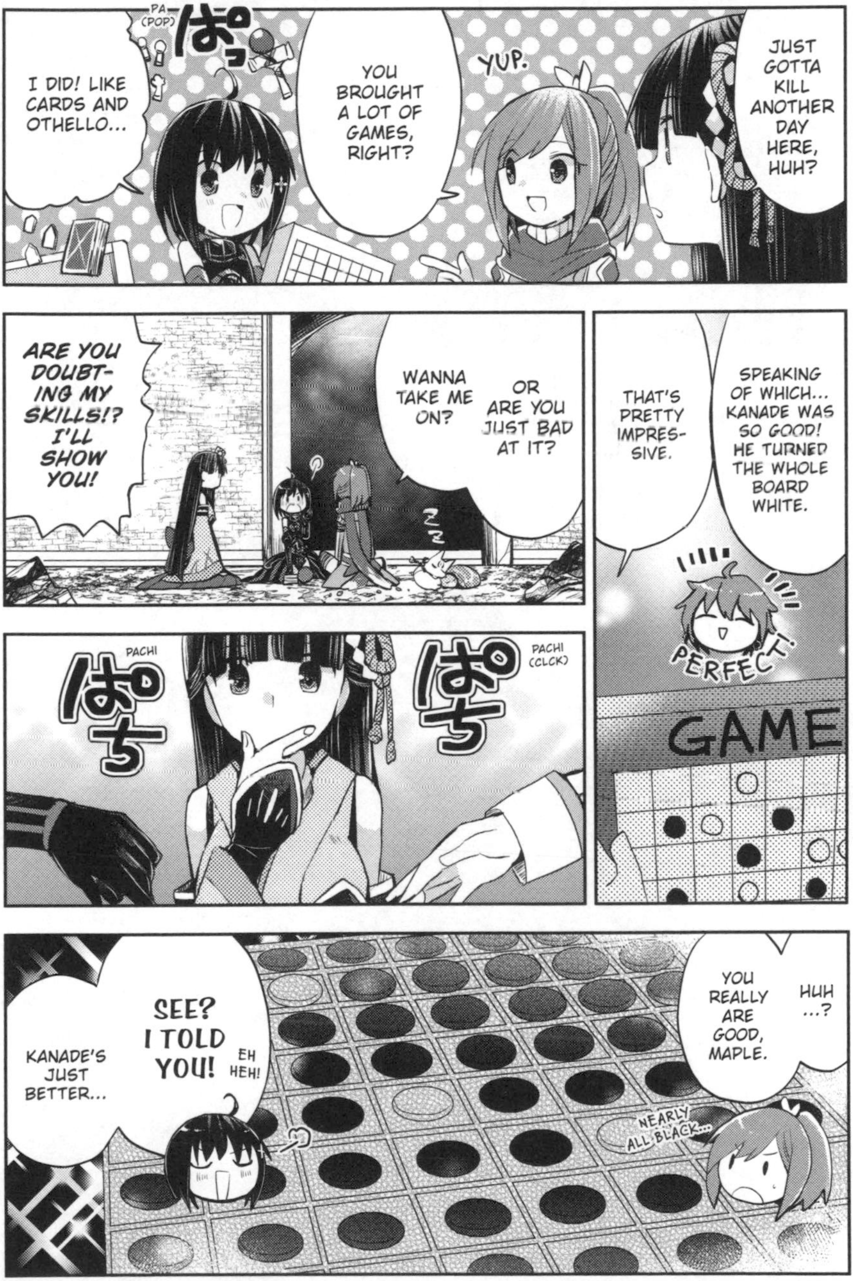
JUST GOTTA KILL ANOTHER DAY HERE, HUH?
YUP.
YOU BROUGHT A LOT OF GAMES, RIGHT?
PA (POP)
I DID! LIKE CARDS AND OTHELLO...
SPEAKING OF WHICH... KANADE WAS SO GOOD! HE TURNED THE WHOLE BOARD WHITE.
THAT'S PRETTY IMPRES-SIVE.
PERFECT!
GAME
OR ARE YOU JUST BAD AT IT?
WANNA TAKE ME ON?
ARE YOU DOUBTING MY SKILLS!? I'LL SHOW YOU!
PACHI (CLCK)
PACHI
HUH ...?
YOU REALLY ARE GOOD, MAPLE.
NEARLY ALL BLACK...
EH HEH!
SEE? I TOLD YOU!
KANADE'S JUST BETTER...

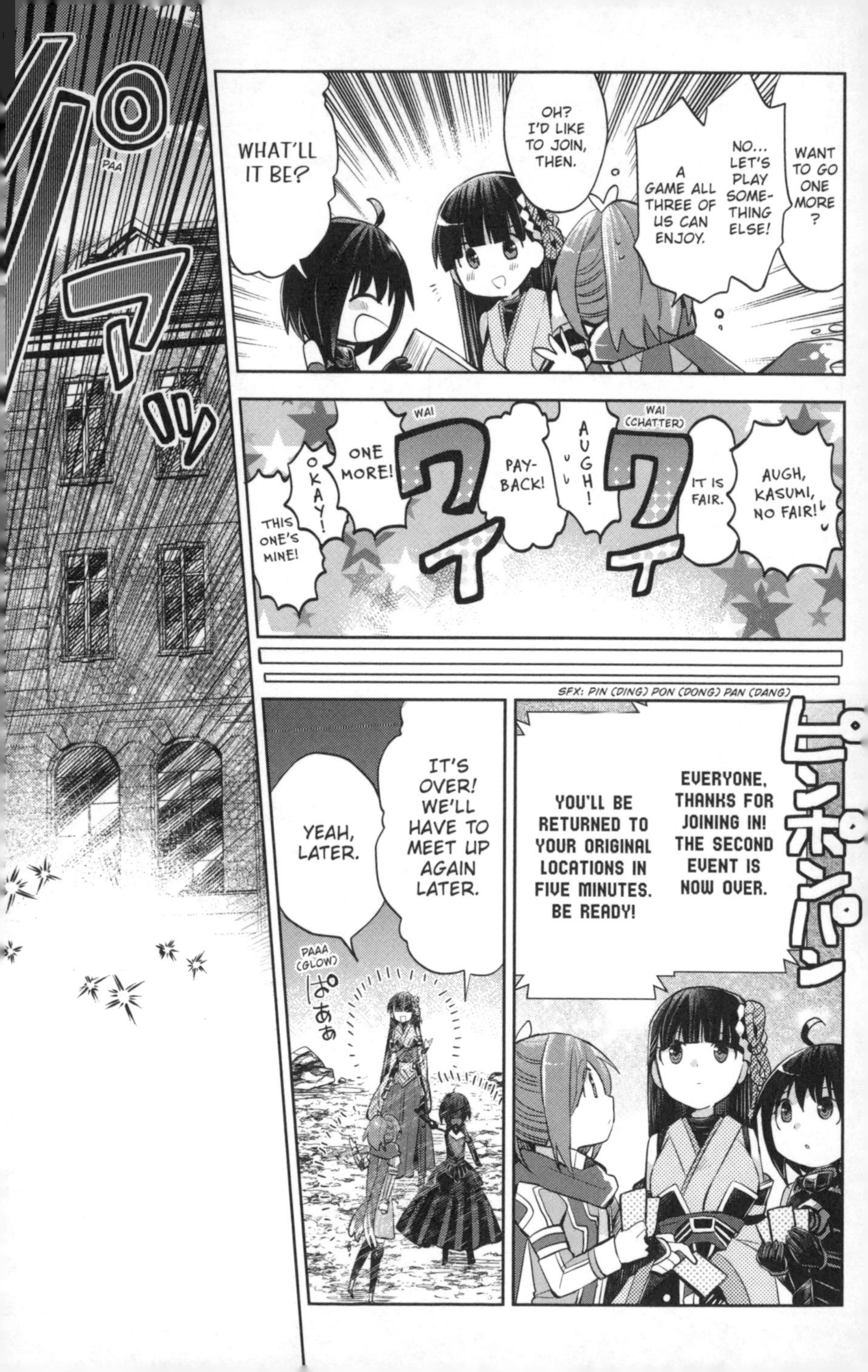
WANT TO GO ONE MORE?
NO... LET'S PLAY SOMETHING ELSE!
A GAME ALL THREE OF US CAN ENJOY.
OH? I'D LIKE TO JOIN, THEN.
WHAT'LL IT BE?
AUGH, KASUMI, NO FAIR!
IT IS FAIR.
WAI (CHATTER)
ワイ
AUGH!
PAY-BACK!
WAI
ワイ
ONE MORE!
OKAY!
THIS ONE'S MINE!
SFX: PIN (DING) PON (DONG) PAN (DANG)
ピンポンパン
EVERYONE, THANKS FOR JOINING IN! THE SECOND EVENT IS NOW OVER.
YOU'LL BE RETURNED TO YOUR ORIGINAL LOCATIONS IN FIVE MINUTES. BE READY!
IT'S OVER! WE'LL HAVE TO MEET UP AGAIN LATER.
YEAH, LATER.
PAAA (GLOW)
ぱぁぁ
パァッ
PAA

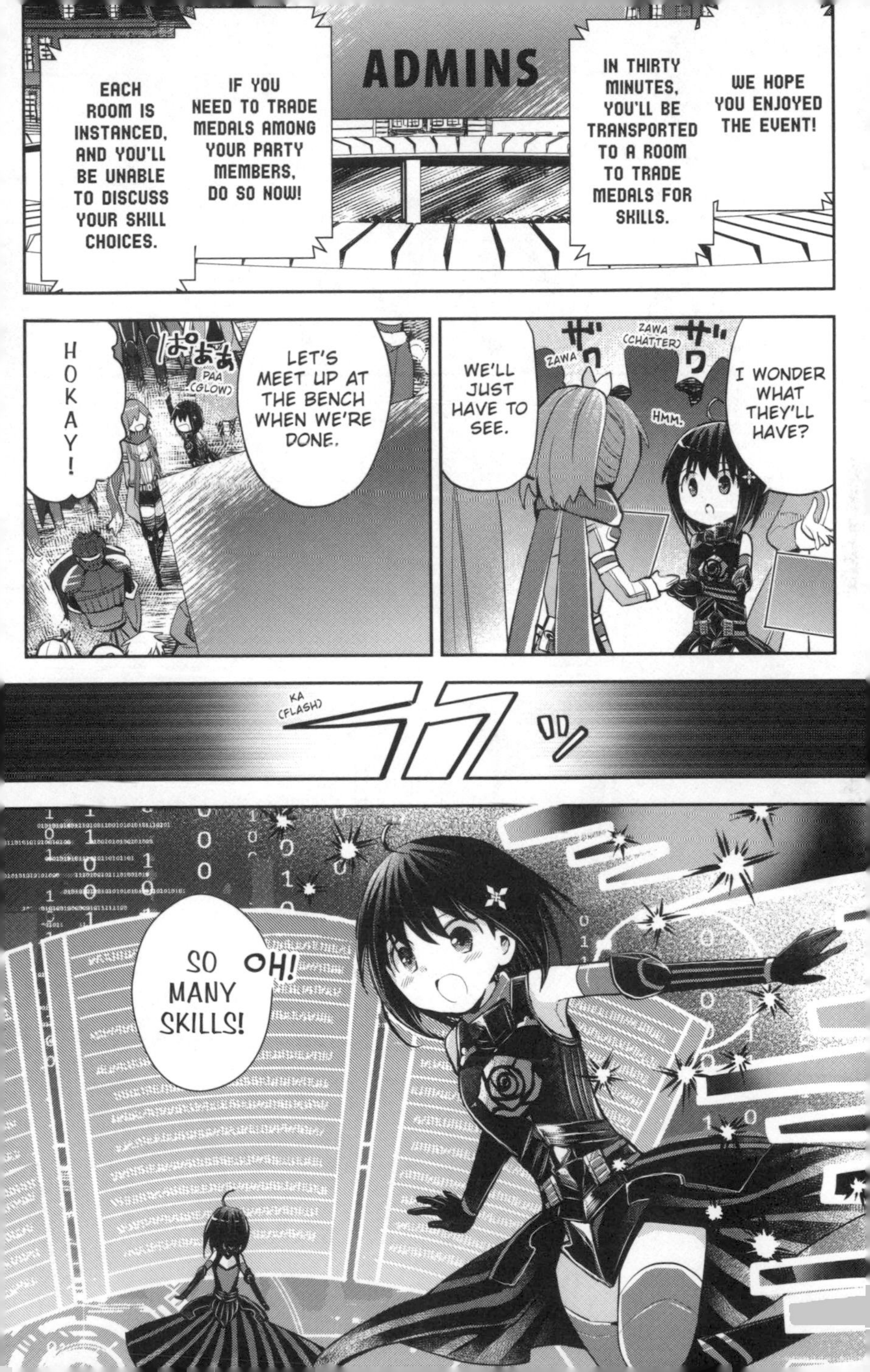
ADMINS
WE HOPE YOU ENJOYED THE EVENT!
IN THIRTY MINUTES, YOU'LL BE TRANSPORTED TO A ROOM TO TRADE MEDALS FOR SKILLS.
IF YOU NEED TO TRADE MEDALS AMONG YOUR PARTY MEMBERS, DO SO NOW!
EACH ROOM IS INSTANCED, AND YOU'LL BE UNABLE TO DISCUSS YOUR SKILL CHOICES.
ザワ ザワ
ZAWA (CHATTER)
ZAWA
I WONDER WHAT THEY'LL HAVE?
HMM.
WE'LL JUST HAVE TO SEE.
LET'S MEET UP AT THE BENCH WHEN WE'RE DONE.
ぱぁあ
PAA (GLOW)
HOKAY!
KA (FLASH)
OH!
SO MANY SKILLS!

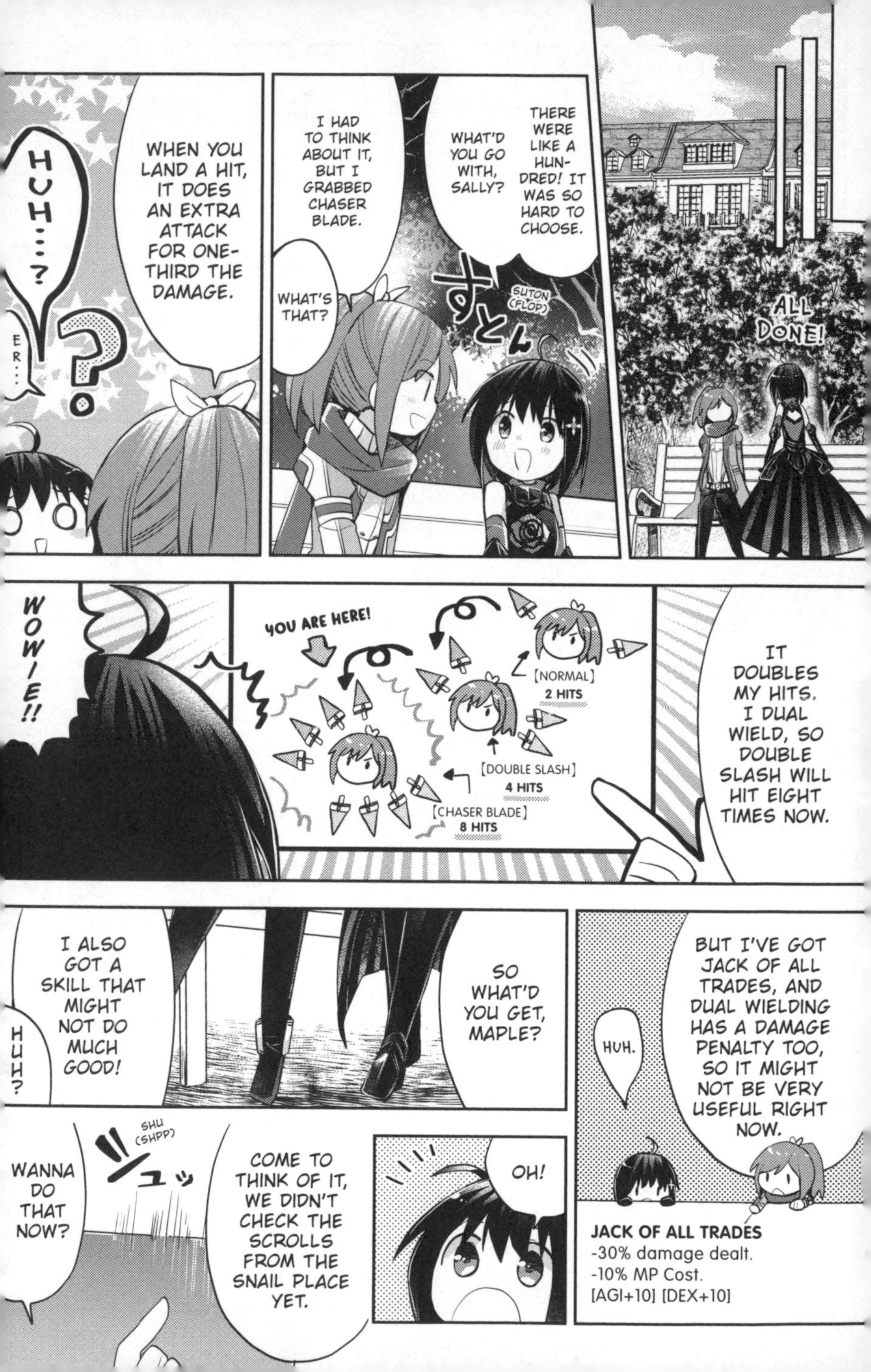
ALL DONE!
THERE WERE LIKE A HUNDRED! IT WAS SO HARD TO CHOOSE.
WHAT'D YOU GO WITH, SALLY?
すとん
SUTON (FLOP)
I HAD TO THINK ABOUT IT, BUT I GRABBED CHASER BLADE.
WHAT'S THAT?
WHEN YOU LAND A HIT, IT DOES AN EXTRA ATTACK FOR ONE-THIRD THE DAMAGE.
HUH...?
ER...
IT DOUBLES MY HITS. I DUAL WIELD, SO DOUBLE SLASH WILL HIT EIGHT TIMES NOW.
YOU ARE HERE!
【NORMAL】 2 HITS
【DOUBLE SLASH】 4 HITS
【CHASER BLADE】 8 HITS
WOWIE!!
BUT I'VE GOT JACK OF ALL TRADES, AND DUAL WIELDING HAS A DAMAGE PENALTY TOO, SO IT MIGHT NOT BE VERY USEFUL RIGHT NOW.
HUH.
JACK OF ALL TRADES
-30% damage dealt.
-10% MP Cost.
[AGI+10] [DEX+10]
SO WHAT'D YOU GET, MAPLE?
I ALSO GOT A SKILL THAT MIGHT NOT DO MUCH GOOD!
HUH?
OH!
COME TO THINK OF IT, WE DIDN'T CHECK THE SCROLLS FROM THE SNAIL PLACE YET.
シュッ
SHU (SHPP)
WANNA DO THAT NOW?

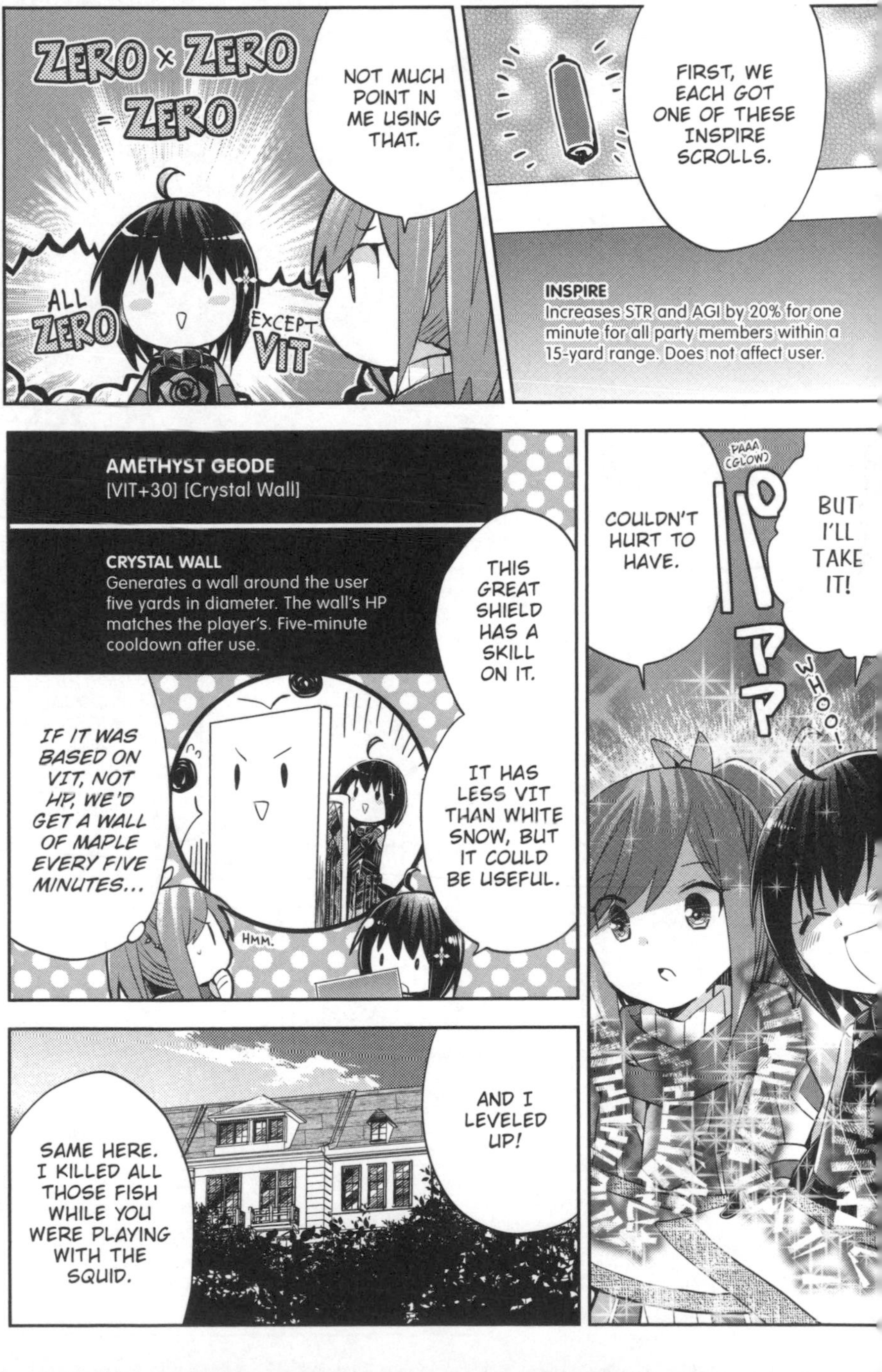
FIRST, WE EACH GOT ONE OF THESE INSPIRE SCROLLS.
INSPIRE
Increases STR and AGI by 20% for one minute for all party members within a 15-yard range. Does not affect user.
NOT MUCH POINT IN ME USING THAT.
ZERO × ZERO = ZERO
EXCEPT VIT
ALL ZERO
PAAA (GLOW)
BUT I'LL TAKE IT!
COULDN'T HURT TO HAVE.
WHOOO!
AMETHYST GEODE
[VIT+30] [Crystal Wall]
CRYSTAL WALL
Generates a wall around the user five yards in diameter. The wall's HP matches the player's. Five-minute cooldown after use.
THIS GREAT SHIELD HAS A SKILL ON IT.
IT HAS LESS VIT THAN WHITE SNOW, BUT IT COULD BE USEFUL.
IF IT WAS BASED ON VIT, NOT HP, WE'D GET A WALL OF MAPLE EVERY FIVE MINUTES...
HMM.
AND I LEVELED UP!
SAME HERE. I KILLED ALL THOSE FISH WHILE YOU WERE PLAYING WITH THE SQUID.

SALLY

Lv.24 HP 32/32 MP 45/45 <+35>
[STR 35 <+20>] [VIT 0] [AGI 85 <+68>]
[DEX 25 <+20>] [INT 30 <+20>]

EQUIPMENT

HEAD: Surface Scarf: Mirage
BODY: Oceanic Coat: Oceanic
RIGHT HAND: Deep Sea Dagger
LEFT HAND: Seabed Dagger
LEGS: Oceanic Clothes
FEET: Black Boots
ACCESSORIES: Bonding Bridge

SKILLS

✦SLASH ✦DOUBLE SLASH
✦GALE SLASH ✦DEFENSE BREAK
✦INSPIRE ✦DOWN ATTACK
✦POWER ATTACK
✦SWITCH ATTACK
✦FIRE BALL
✦WATER BALL
✦WIND CUTTER
✦CYCLONE CUTTER
✦SAND CUTTER
✦DARK BALL
✦WATER WALL
✦WIND WALL
✦REFRESH ✦HEAL
✦AFFLICTION III
✦STRENGTH BOOST (S)
✦COMBO BOOST (S)
✦MARTIAL ARTS V
✦MP BOOST (S)
✦MP COST DOWN (S)
✦MP RECOVERY SPEED BOOST (S)
✦POISON RESIST (S)
✦GATHERING SPEED BOOST (S)
✦DAGGER MASTERY II
✦MAGIC MASTERY II
✦FIRE MAGIC I
✦WATER MAGIC II
✦WIND MAGIC III
✦EARTH MAGIC I
✦DARK MAGIC I
✦LIGHT MAGIC II
✦COMBO BLADE II
✦PRESENCE BLOCK II
✦PRESENCE DETECT II
✦SNEAKY STEPS I
✦LEAP III ✦FISHING
✦SWIMMING X
✦DIVING X
✦COOKING I
✦JACK OF ALL TRADES
✦SUPERSPEED
✦ANCIENT OCEAN
✦CHASER BLADE

MAPLE

Lv.29 HP 40/40 <+160> MP 12/12 <+10>
[STR 0] [VIT 180 <+141>] [AGI 0]
[DEX 0] [INT 0]

EQUIPMENT

HEAD: Empty
BODY: Black Rose Armor
RIGHT HAND: New Moon: Hydra
LEFT HAND: Night's Facsimile: Devour
LEGS: Black Rose Armor
FEET: Black Rose Armor
ACCESSORIES: Bonding Bridge
Toughness Ring
Life Ring

SKILLS

✦SHIELD ATTACK
✦SIDESTEP
✦DEFLECT
✦MEDITATION
✦TAUNT
✦INSPIRE
✦HP BOOST (S)
✦MP BOOST (S)
✦GREAT SHIELD MASTERY IV
✦COVER MOVE I
✦COVER
✦ABSOLUTE DEFENSE
✦MORAL TURPITUDE
✦GIANT KILLING
✦HYDRA EATER
✦BOMB EATER
✦INDOMITABLE GUARDIAN
✦PSYCHOKINESIS
✦FORTRESS

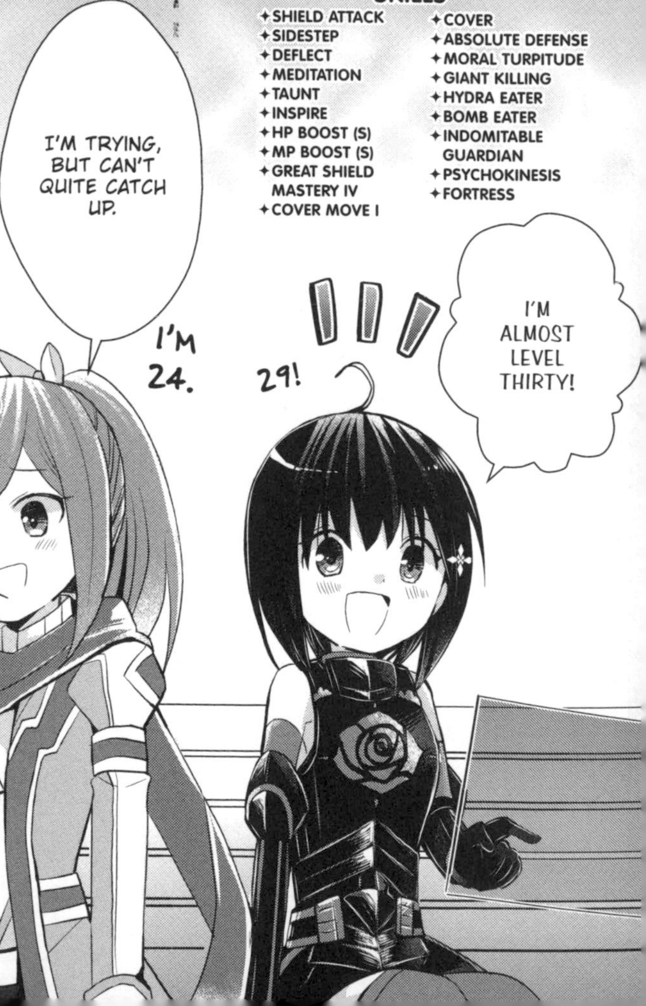

I'M ALMOST LEVEL THIRTY!
29!
I'M 24.
I'M TRYING, BUT CAN'T QUITE CATCH UP.

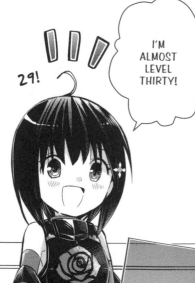

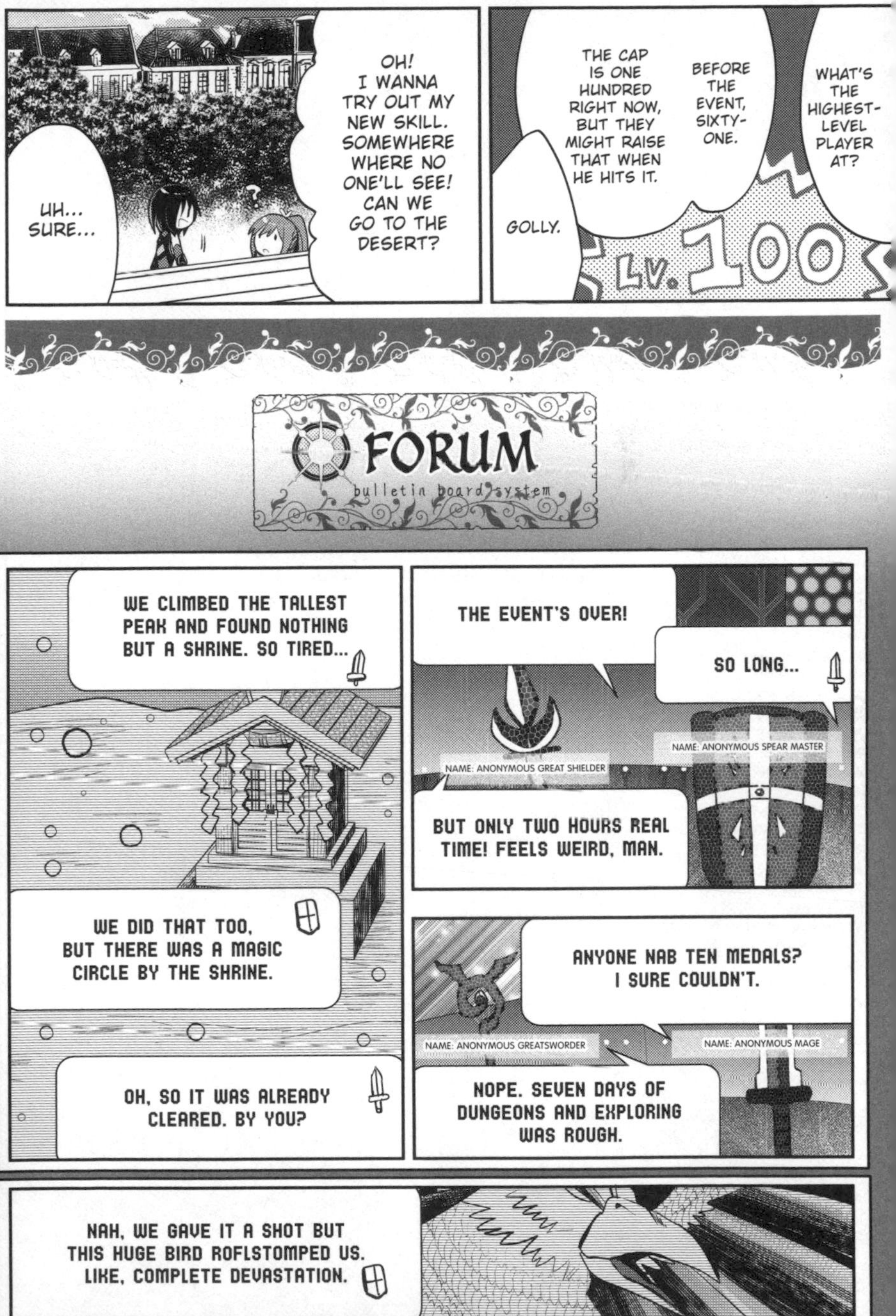
WHAT'S THE HIGHEST-LEVEL PLAYER AT?
BEFORE THE EVENT, SIXTY-ONE.
THE CAP IS ONE HUNDRED RIGHT NOW, BUT THEY MIGHT RAISE THAT WHEN HE HITS IT.
LV. 100
GOLLY.
OH! I WANNA TRY OUT MY NEW SKILL. SOMEWHERE WHERE NO ONE'LL SEE! CAN WE GO TO THE DESERT?
UH... SURE...
FORUM
bulletin board system
THE EVENT'S OVER!
SO LONG...
NAME: ANONYMOUS SPEAR MASTER
NAME: ANONYMOUS GREAT SHIELDER
BUT ONLY TWO HOURS REAL TIME! FEELS WEIRD, MAN.
ANYONE NAB TEN MEDALS? I SURE COULDN'T.
NAME: ANONYMOUS MAGE
NAME: ANONYMOUS GREATSWORDER
NOPE. SEVEN DAYS OF DUNGEONS AND EXPLORING WAS ROUGH.
WE CLIMBED THE TALLEST PEAK AND FOUND NOTHING BUT A SHRINE. SO TIRED...
WE DID THAT TOO, BUT THERE WAS A MAGIC CIRCLE BY THE SHRINE.
OH, SO IT WAS ALREADY CLEARED. BY YOU?
NAH, WE GAVE IT A SHOT BUT THIS HUGE BIRD ROFLSTOMPED US. LIKE, COMPLETE DEVASTATION.

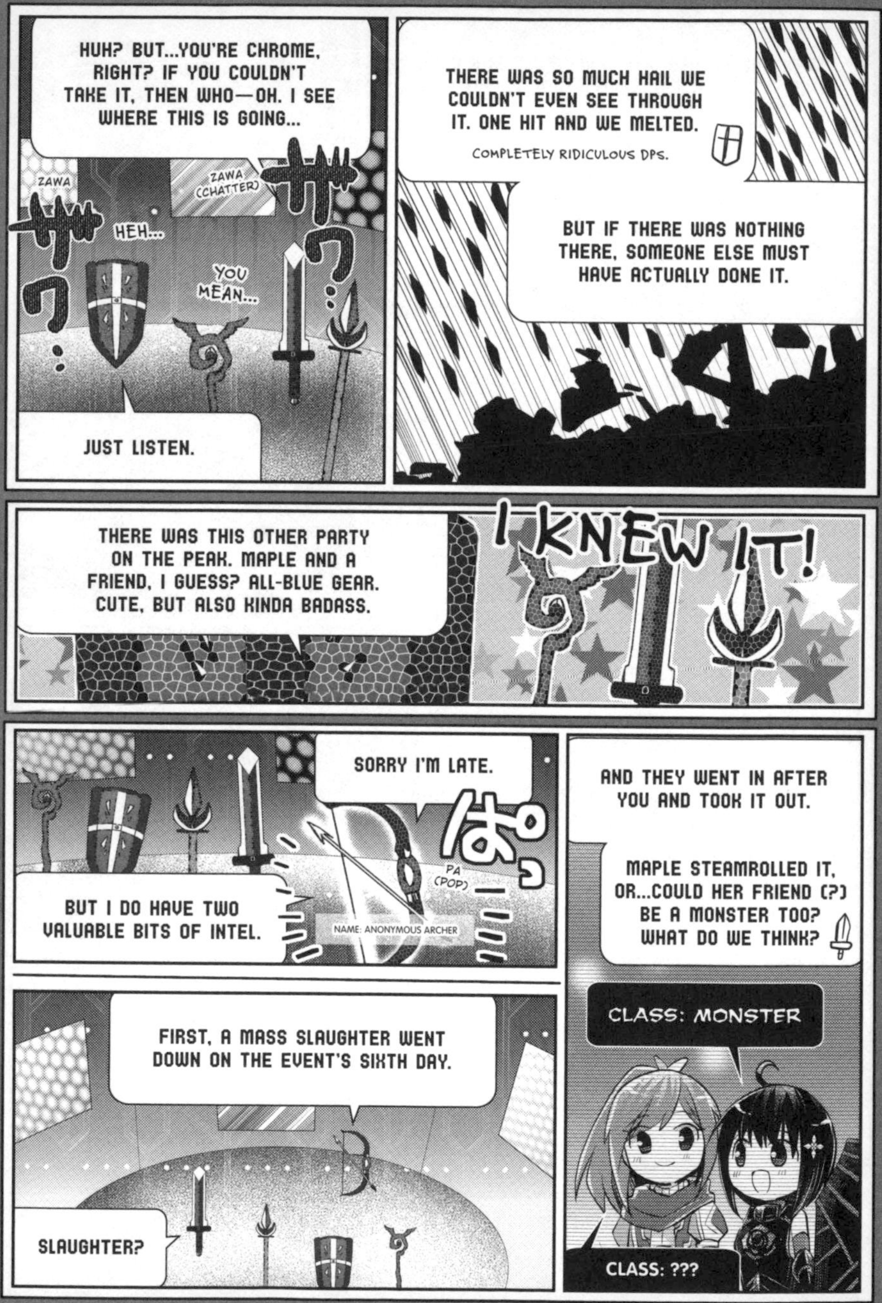
THERE WAS SO MUCH HAIL WE COULDN'T EVEN SEE THROUGH IT. ONE HIT AND WE MELTED.
COMPLETELY RIDICULOUS DPS.
BUT IF THERE WAS NOTHING THERE, SOMEONE ELSE MUST HAVE ACTUALLY DONE IT.
HUH? BUT...YOU'RE CHROME, RIGHT? IF YOU COULDN'T TAKE IT, THEN WHO—OH. I SEE WHERE THIS IS GOING...
ザワ
ZAWA (CHATTER)
HEH...
ザワ
ZAWA
YOU MEAN...
JUST LISTEN.
I KNEW IT!
THERE WAS THIS OTHER PARTY ON THE PEAK. MAPLE AND A FRIEND, I GUESS? ALL-BLUE GEAR. CUTE, BUT ALSO KINDA BADASS.
AND THEY WENT IN AFTER YOU AND TOOK IT OUT.
MAPLE STEAMROLLED IT, OR...COULD HER FRIEND (?) BE A MONSTER TOO? WHAT DO WE THINK?
CLASS: MONSTER
CLASS: ???
SORRY I'M LATE.
ぱっ
PA (POP)
NAME: ANONYMOUS ARCHER
BUT I DO HAVE TWO VALUABLE BITS OF INTEL.
FIRST, A MASS SLAUGHTER WENT DOWN ON THE EVENT'S SIXTH DAY.
SLAUGHTER?

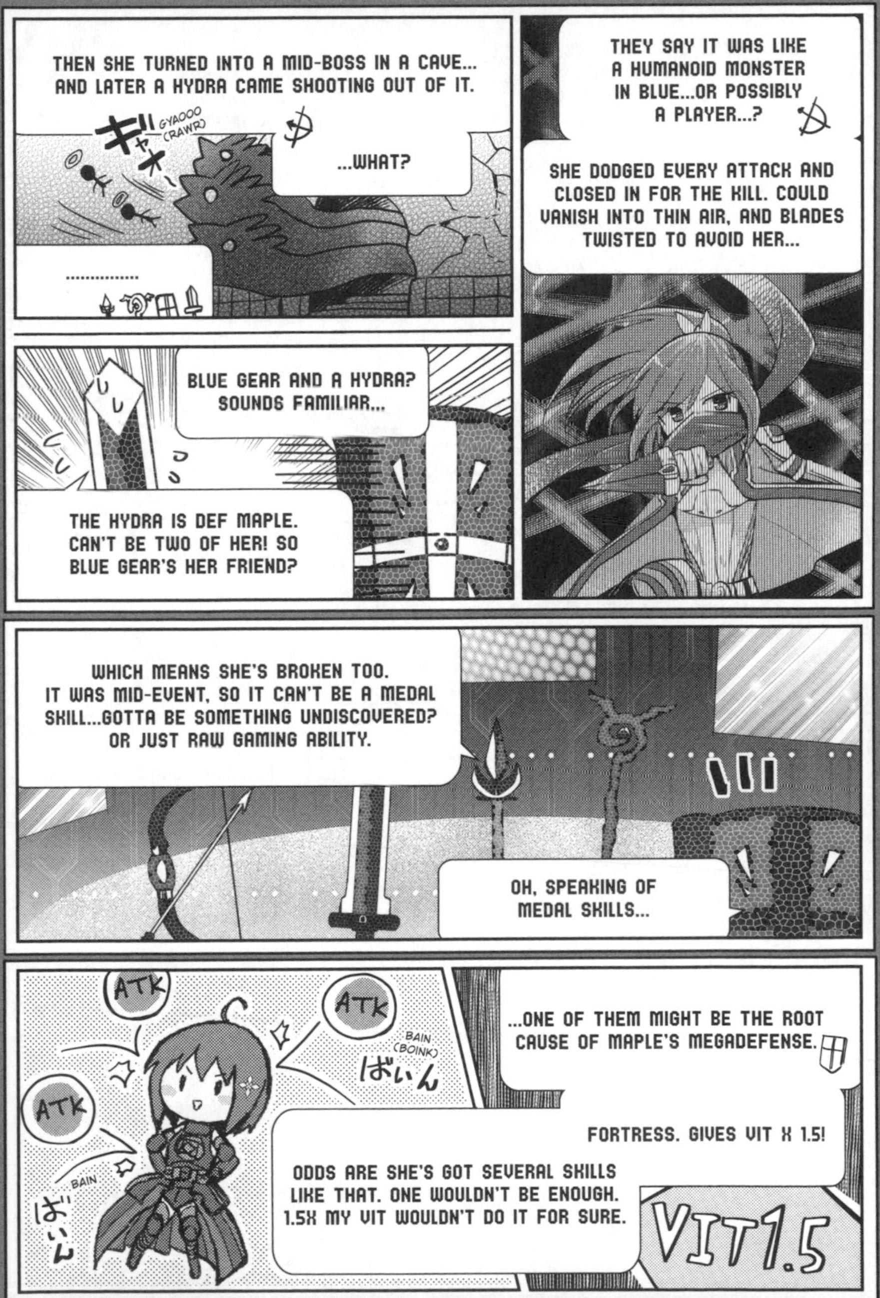
THEY SAY IT WAS LIKE A HUMANOID MONSTER IN BLUE...OR POSSIBLY A PLAYER...?
SHE DODGED EVERY ATTACK AND CLOSED IN FOR THE KILL. COULD VANISH INTO THIN AIR, AND BLADES TWISTED TO AVOID HER...
THEN SHE TURNED INTO A MID-BOSS IN A CAVE... AND LATER A HYDRA CAME SHOOTING OUT OF IT.
GYAOOO (RAWR)
...WHAT?
....
BLUE GEAR AND A HYDRA? SOUNDS FAMILIAR...
THE HYDRA IS DEF MAPLE. CAN'T BE TWO OF HER! SO BLUE GEAR'S HER FRIEND?
WHICH MEANS SHE'S BROKEN TOO. IT WAS MID-EVENT, SO IT CAN'T BE A MEDAL SKILL...GOTTA BE SOMETHING UNDISCOVERED? OR JUST RAW GAMING ABILITY.
OH, SPEAKING OF MEDAL SKILLS...
...ONE OF THEM MIGHT BE THE ROOT CAUSE OF MAPLE'S MEGADEFENSE.
FORTRESS. GIVES VIT X 1.5!
VIT1.5
ATK
ATK
BAIN (BOINK)
ATK
BAIN
ODDS ARE SHE'S GOT SEVERAL SKILLS LIKE THAT. ONE WOULDN'T BE ENOUGH. 1.5X MY VIT WOULDN'T DO IT FOR SURE.

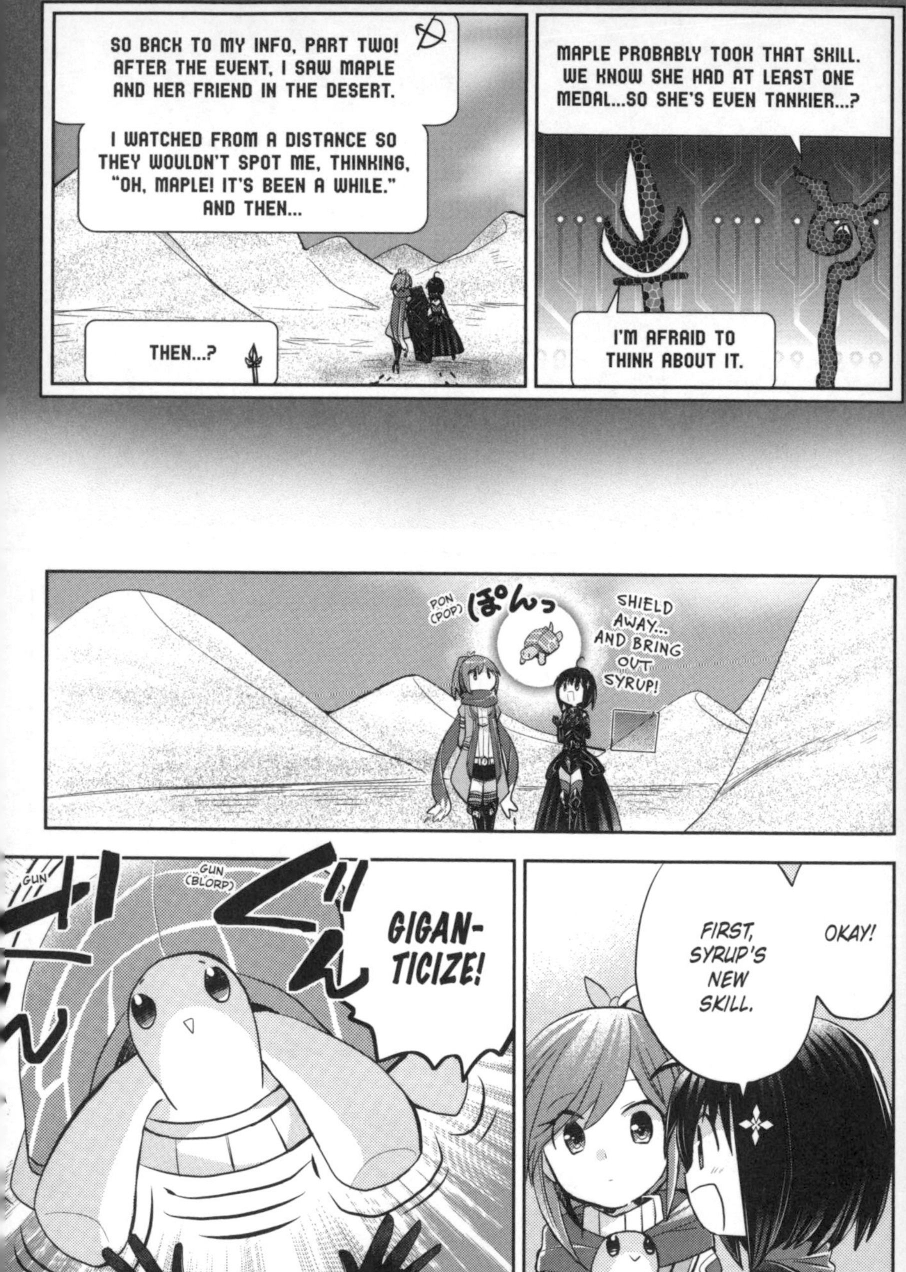
MAPLE PROBABLY TOOK THAT SKILL. WE KNOW SHE HAD AT LEAST ONE MEDAL...SO SHE'S EVEN TANKIER...?
I'M AFRAID TO THINK ABOUT IT.
SO BACK TO MY INFO, PART TWO! AFTER THE EVENT, I SAW MAPLE AND HER FRIEND IN THE DESERT.
I WATCHED FROM A DISTANCE SO THEY WOULDN'T SPOT ME, THINKING, "OH, MAPLE! IT'S BEEN A WHILE." AND THEN...
THEN...?
SHIELD AWAY... AND BRING OUT SYRUP!
PON (POP) ぽんっ
OKAY!
FIRST, SYRUP'S NEW SKILL.
GIGAN-TICIZE!
GUN (BLORP)
GUN

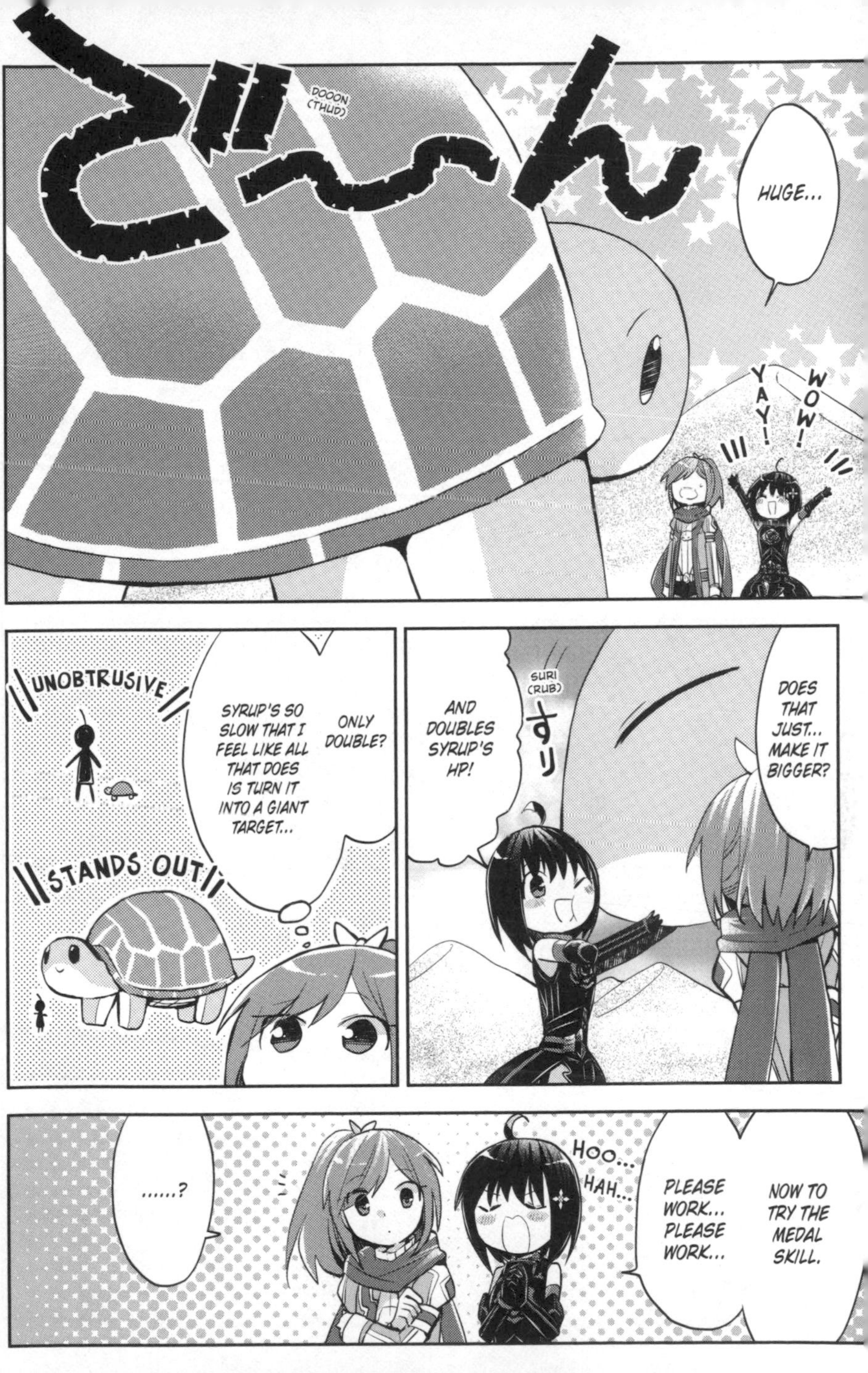
ど〜ん
DOOON (THUD)
HUGE...
WOW!
YAY!
DOES THAT JUST... MAKE IT BIGGER?
AND DOUBLES SYRUP'S HP!
SURI (RUB)
すり
ONLY DOUBLE?
SYRUP'S SO SLOW THAT I FEEL LIKE ALL THAT DOES IS TURN IT INTO A GIANT TARGET...
UNOBTRUSIVE
STANDS OUT
NOW TO TRY THE MEDAL SKILL.
PLEASE WORK... PLEASE WORK...
HOO... HAH...
......?

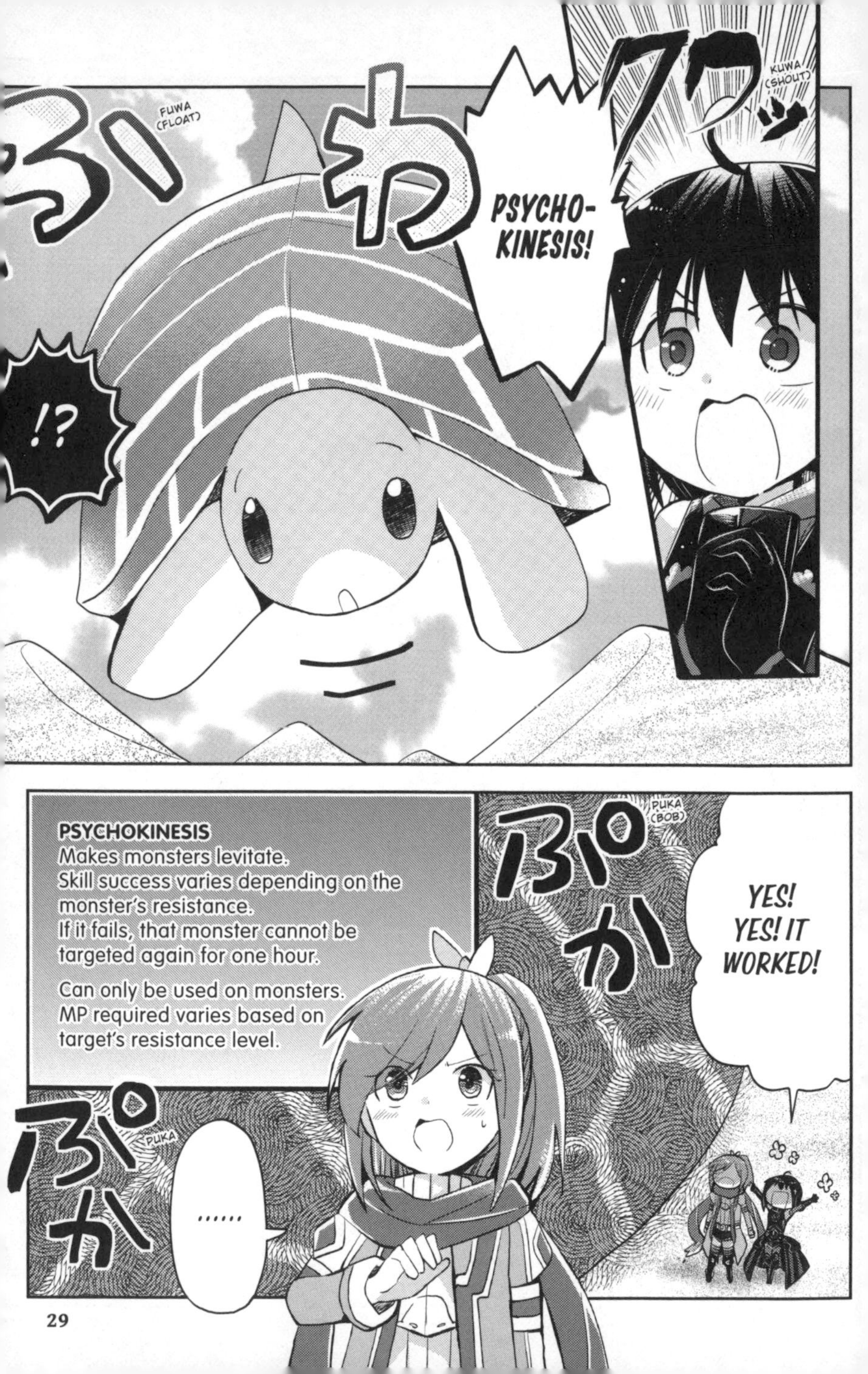
KUWA (SHOUT)
PSYCHO-KINESIS!
FUWA (FLOAT)
!?
PUKA (BOB)
YES! YES! IT WORKED!
PSYCHOKINESIS
Makes monsters levitate.
Skill success varies depending on the monster's resistance.
If it fails, that monster cannot be targeted again for one hour.
Can only be used on monsters. MP required varies based on target's resistance level.
PUKA
......

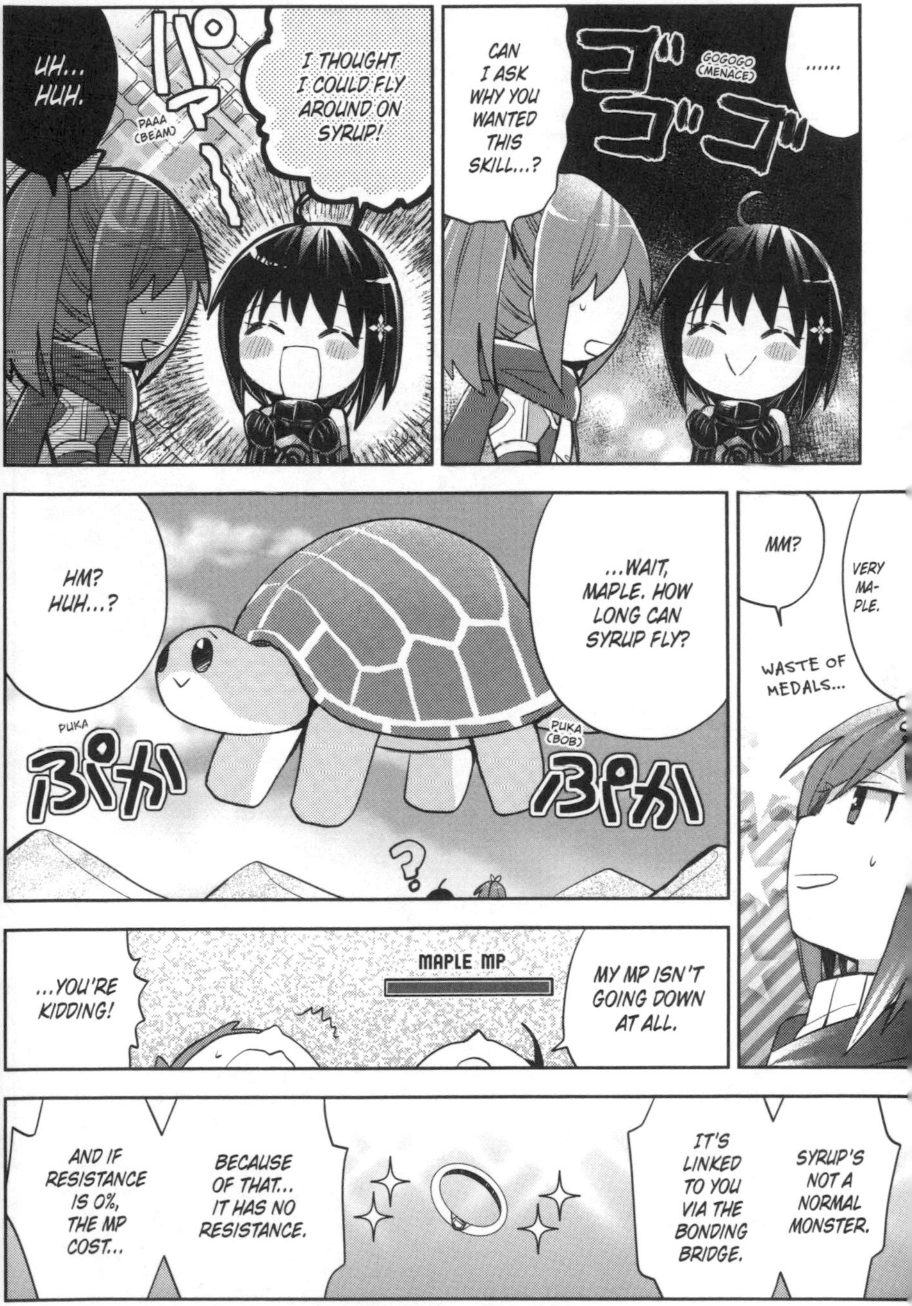
......
GOGOGO (MENACE)
CAN I ASK WHY YOU WANTED THIS SKILL...?
I THOUGHT I COULD FLY AROUND ON SYRUP!
PAAA (BEAM)
UH... HUH.
VERY MA-PLE.
MM?
WASTE OF MEDALS...
...WAIT, MAPLE. HOW LONG CAN SYRUP FLY?
PUKA (BOB)
HM? HUH...?
PUKA
MY MP ISN'T GOING DOWN AT ALL.
MAPLE MP
...YOU'RE KIDDING!
SYRUP'S NOT A NORMAL MONSTER.
IT'S LINKED TO YOU VIA THE BONDING BRIDGE.
BECAUSE OF THAT... IT HAS NO RESISTANCE.
AND IF RESISTANCE IS 0%, THE MP COST...

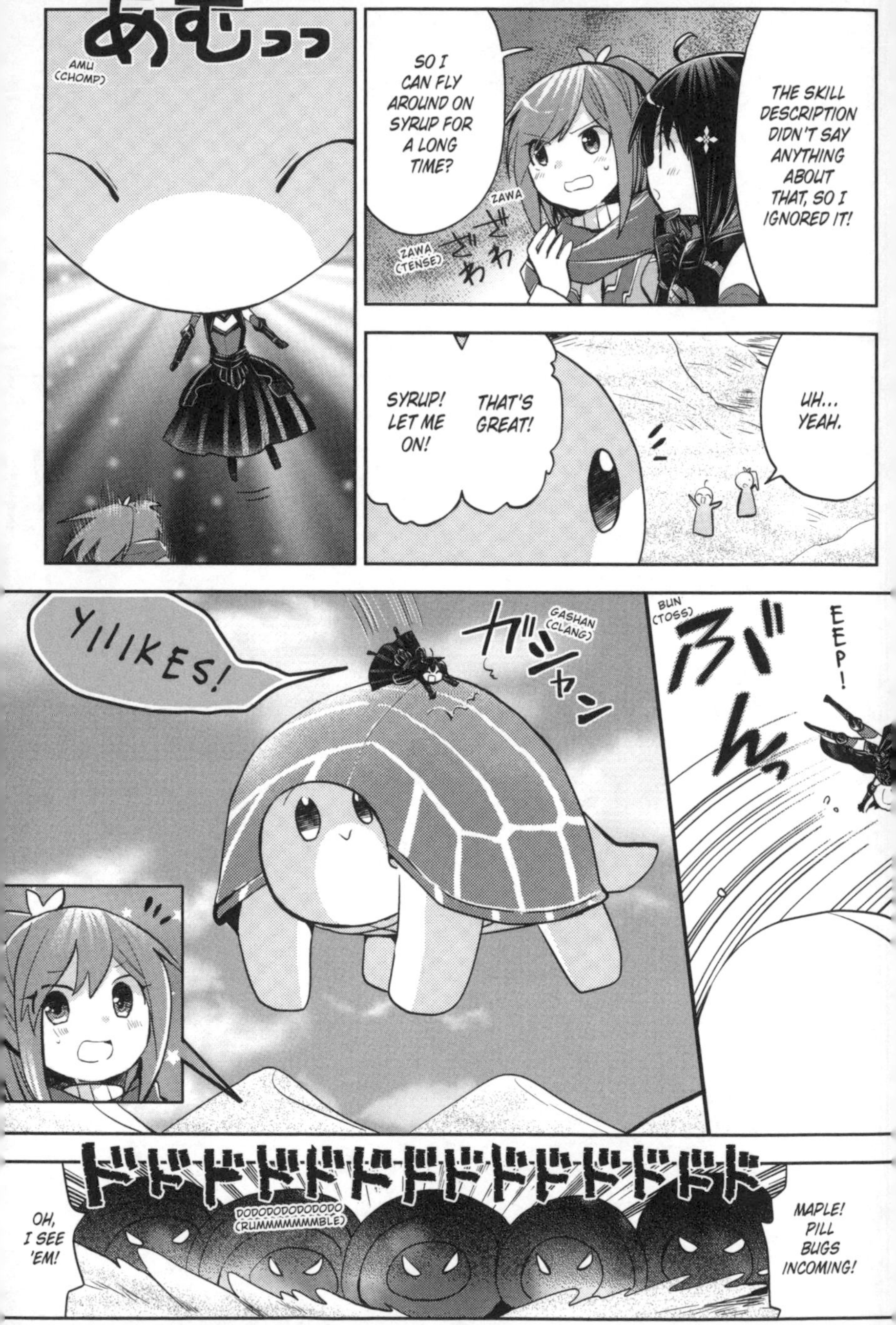
THE SKILL DESCRIPTION DIDN'T SAY ANYTHING ABOUT THAT, SO I IGNORED IT!
SO I CAN FLY AROUND ON SYRUP FOR A LONG TIME?
ざわ ざわ
ZAWA ZAWA (TENSE)
UH... YEAH.
THAT'S GREAT!
SYRUP! LET ME ON!
あむっっ
AMU (CHOMP)
EEEP!
ばんっ
BUN (TOSS)
ガシャン
GASHAN (CLANG)
YIIIKES!
MAPLE! PILL BUGS INCOMING!
ドドドドドドドドドドドドドド
DODODODODODODO (RUMMMMMMMBLE)
OH, I SEE 'EM!

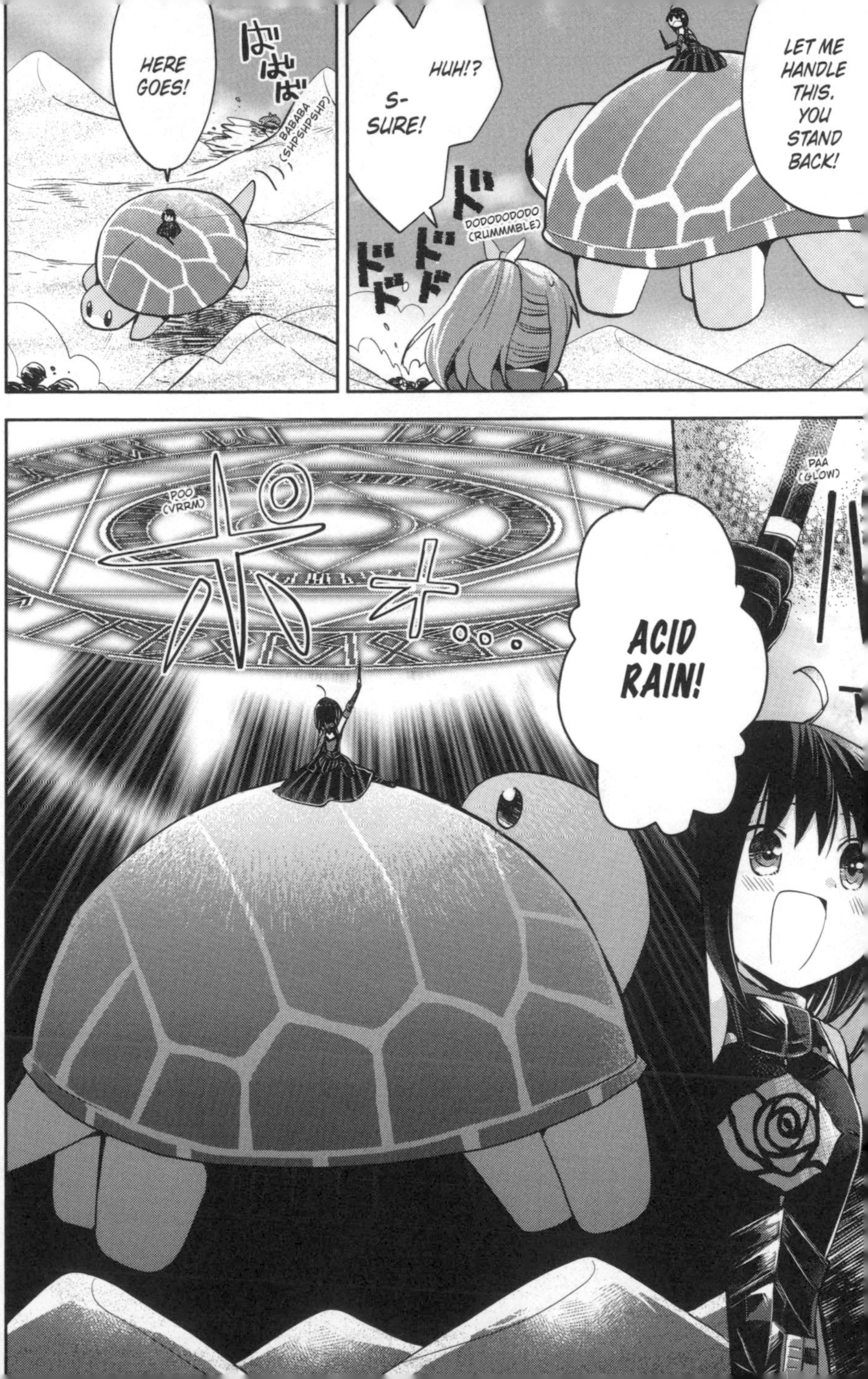
LET ME HANDLE THIS. YOU STAND BACK!
HUH!?
S-SURE!
ドドドドド
DODODODODO (RUMMMBLE)
HERE GOES!
ばばば
BABABA (SHPSHPSHP)
PAA (GLOW)
ACID RAIN!
ポォ…
POO (VRRM)

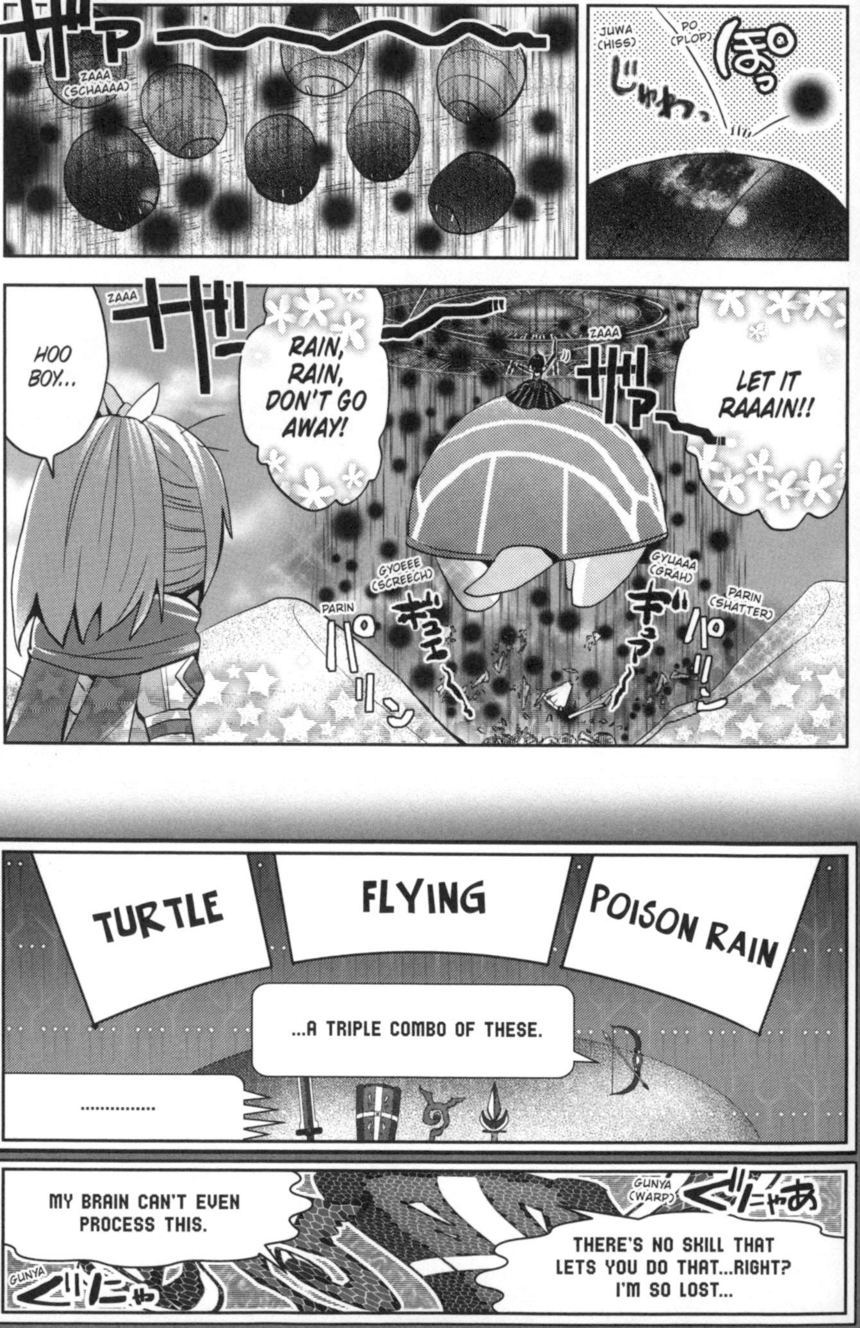
JUWA (HISS)
PO (PLOP)
ZAAA (SCHAAAA)
LET IT RAAAIN!!
ZAAA
RAIN, RAIN, DON'T GO AWAY!
ZAAA
HOO BOY...
PARIN (SHATTER)
GYUAAA (GRAH)
GYOEEE (SCREECH)
PARIN
POISON RAIN
FLYING
TURTLE
...A TRIPLE COMBO OF THESE.
....
GUNYA (WARP)
THERE'S NO SKILL THAT LETS YOU DO THAT...RIGHT? I'M SO LOST...
MY BRAIN CAN'T EVEN PROCESS THIS.
GUNYA

Welcome to
NewWorld Online.

I Don't Want to Get Hurt,

so I'll Max Out My Defense.

presented by: JIROU OIMOTO & YUUMIKAN

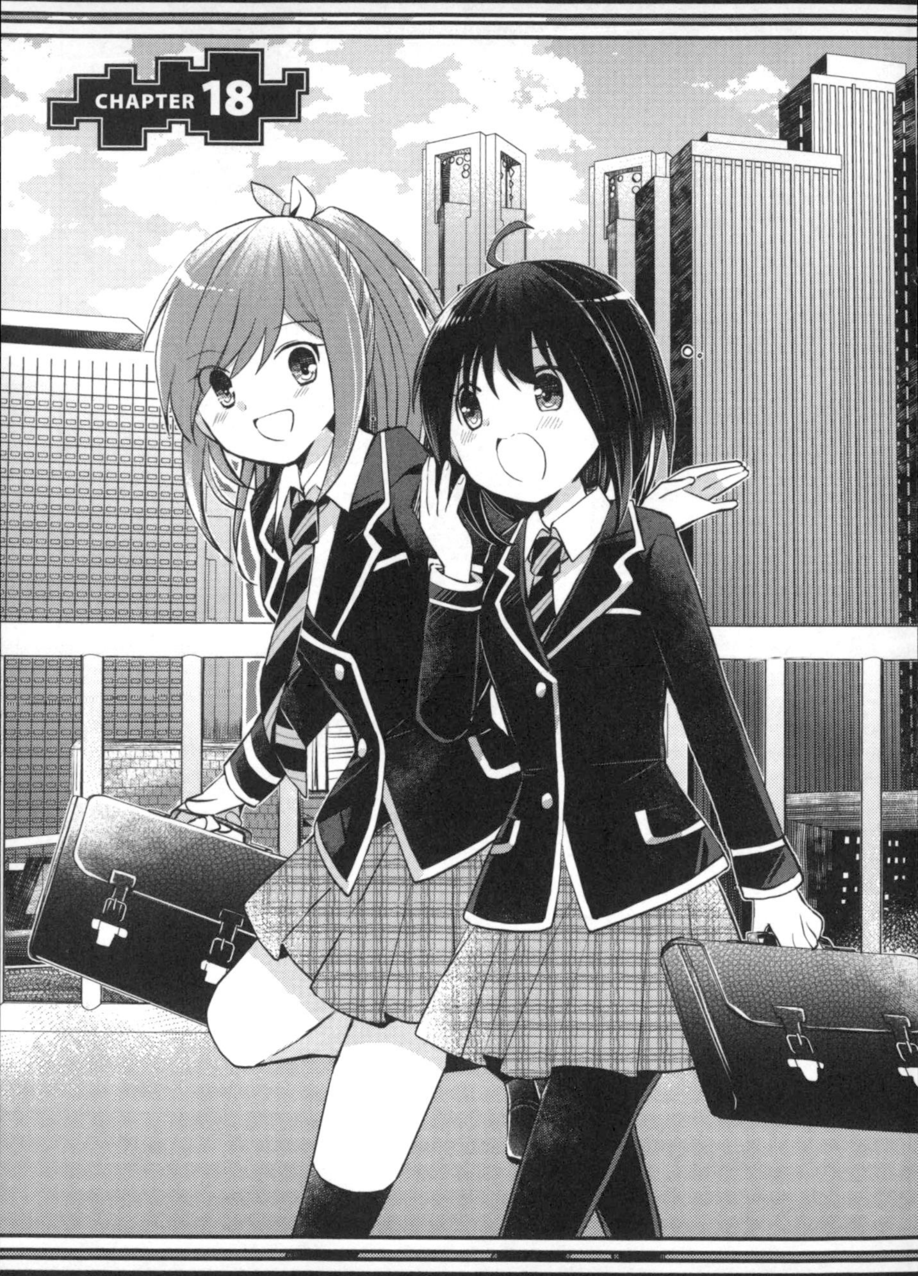
CHAPTER 18

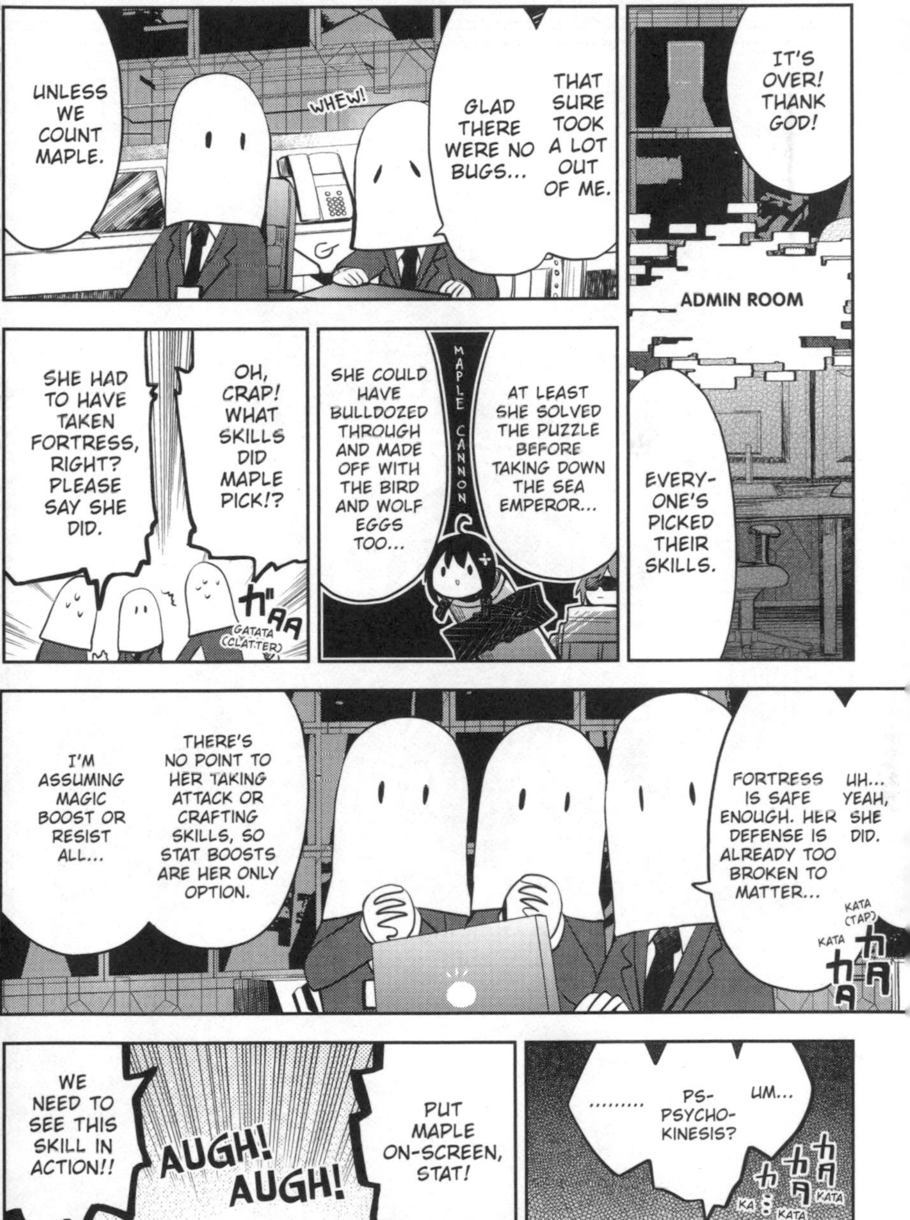
IT'S OVER! THANK GOD!
ADMIN ROOM
THAT SURE TOOK A LOT OUT OF ME.
GLAD THERE WERE NO BUGS...
WHEW!
UNLESS WE COUNT MAPLE.
AT LEAST SHE SOLVED THE PUZZLE BEFORE TAKING DOWN THE SEA EMPEROR...
MAPLE CANNON
SHE COULD HAVE BULLDOZED THROUGH AND MADE OFF WITH THE BIRD AND WOLF EGGS TOO...
EVERYONE'S PICKED THEIR SKILLS.
OH, CRAP! WHAT SKILLS DID MAPLE PICK!?
SHE HAD TO HAVE TAKEN FORTRESS, RIGHT? PLEASE SAY SHE DID.
GATATA (CLATTER)
UH... YEAH, SHE DID.
FORTRESS IS SAFE ENOUGH. HER DEFENSE IS ALREADY TOO BROKEN TO MATTER...
KATA (TAP)
KATA
THERE'S NO POINT TO HER TAKING ATTACK OR CRAFTING SKILLS, SO STAT BOOSTS ARE HER ONLY OPTION.
I'M ASSUMING MAGIC BOOST OR RESIST ALL...
UM...
PS-PSYCHOKINESIS?
....
KATA
KATA
KA
PUT MAPLE ON-SCREEN, STAT!
AUGH! AUGH!
WE NEED TO SEE THIS SKILL IN ACTION!!

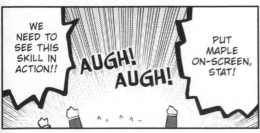

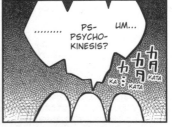

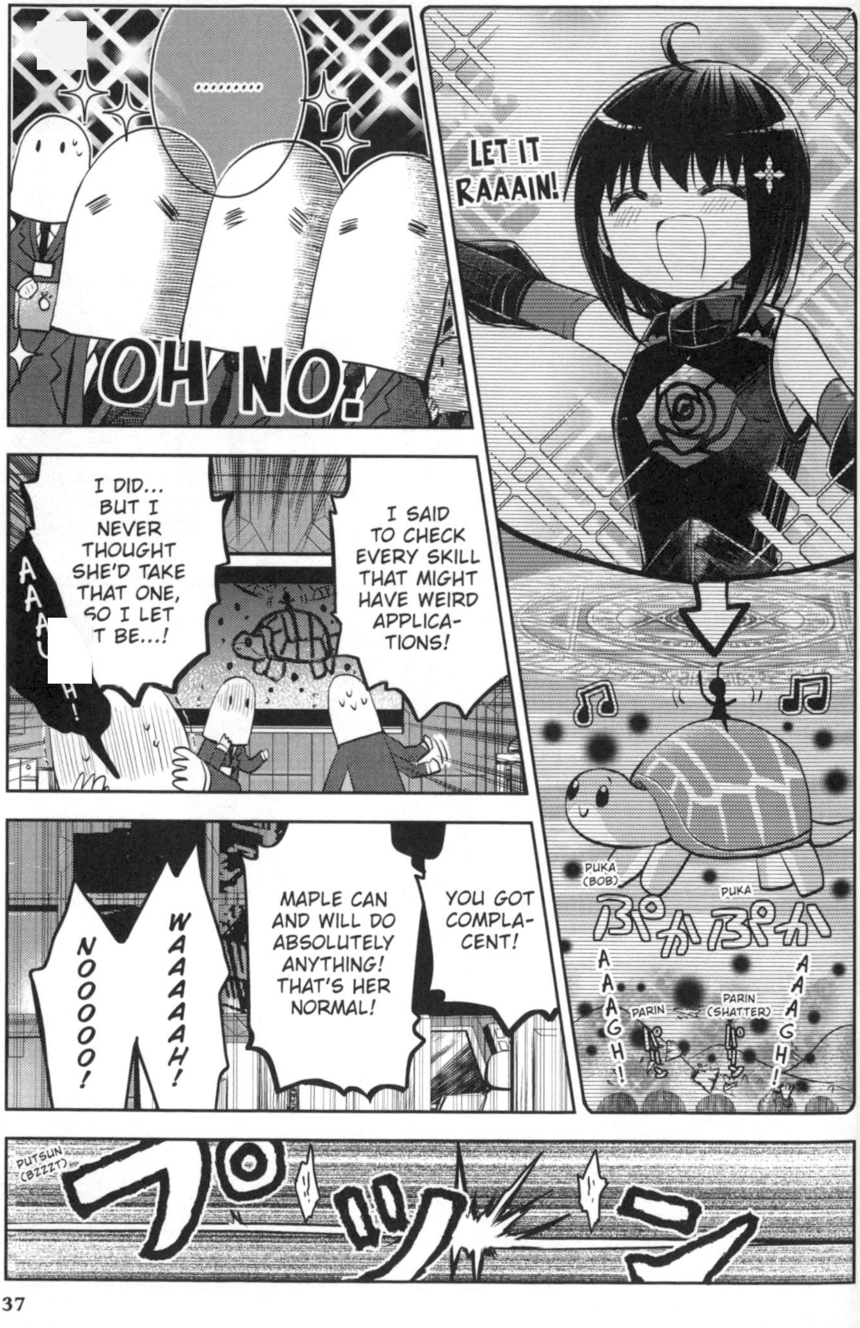
LET IT RAAAIN!
PUKA (BOB)
PUKA
ぷかぷか
AAAGH!
PARIN
PARIN (SHATTER)
AAAGH!
....
OH NO!
I SAID TO CHECK EVERY SKILL THAT MIGHT HAVE WEIRD APPLICATIONS!
I DID... BUT I NEVER THOUGHT SHE'D TAKE THAT ONE, SO I LET T BE...!
YOU GOT COMPLACENT!
MAPLE CAN AND WILL DO ABSOLUTELY ANYTHING! THAT'S HER NORMAL!
WAAAAAAAH!
NOOOOOO!
PUTSUN (BZZZT)

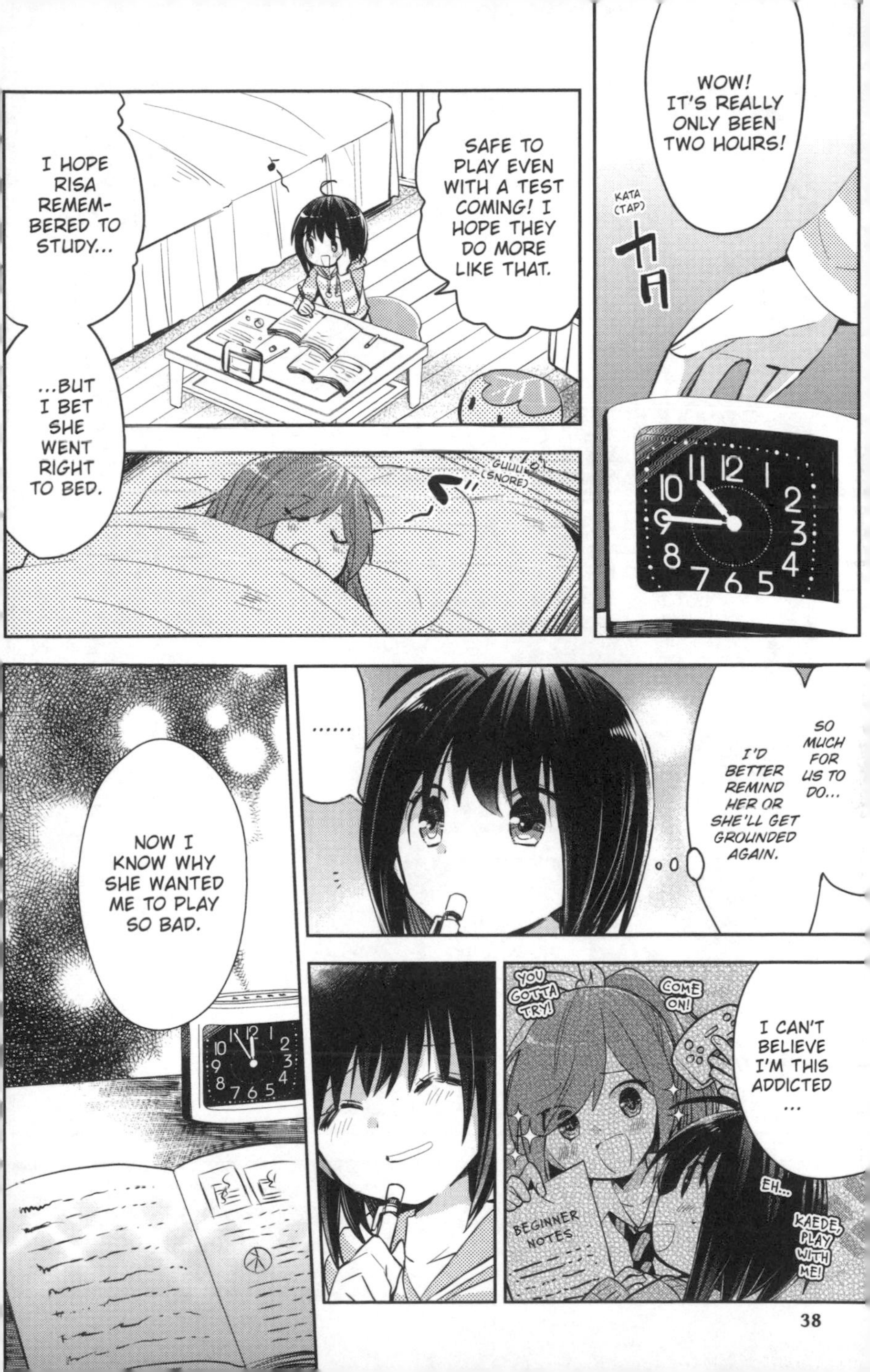

WOW! IT'S REALLY ONLY BEEN TWO HOURS!
KATA (TAP)
SAFE TO PLAY EVEN WITH A TEST COMING! I HOPE THEY DO MORE LIKE THAT.
I HOPE RISA REMEMBERED TO STUDY...
...BUT I BET SHE WENT RIGHT TO BED.
GUUU (SNORE)
SO MUCH FOR US TO DO...
I'D BETTER REMIND HER OR SHE'LL GET GROUNDED AGAIN.
......
I CAN'T BELIEVE I'M THIS ADDICTED...
COME ON!
YOU GOTTA TRY!
BEGINNER NOTES
EH...
KAEDE, PLAY WITH ME!
NOW I KNOW WHY SHE WANTED ME TO PLAY SO BAD.

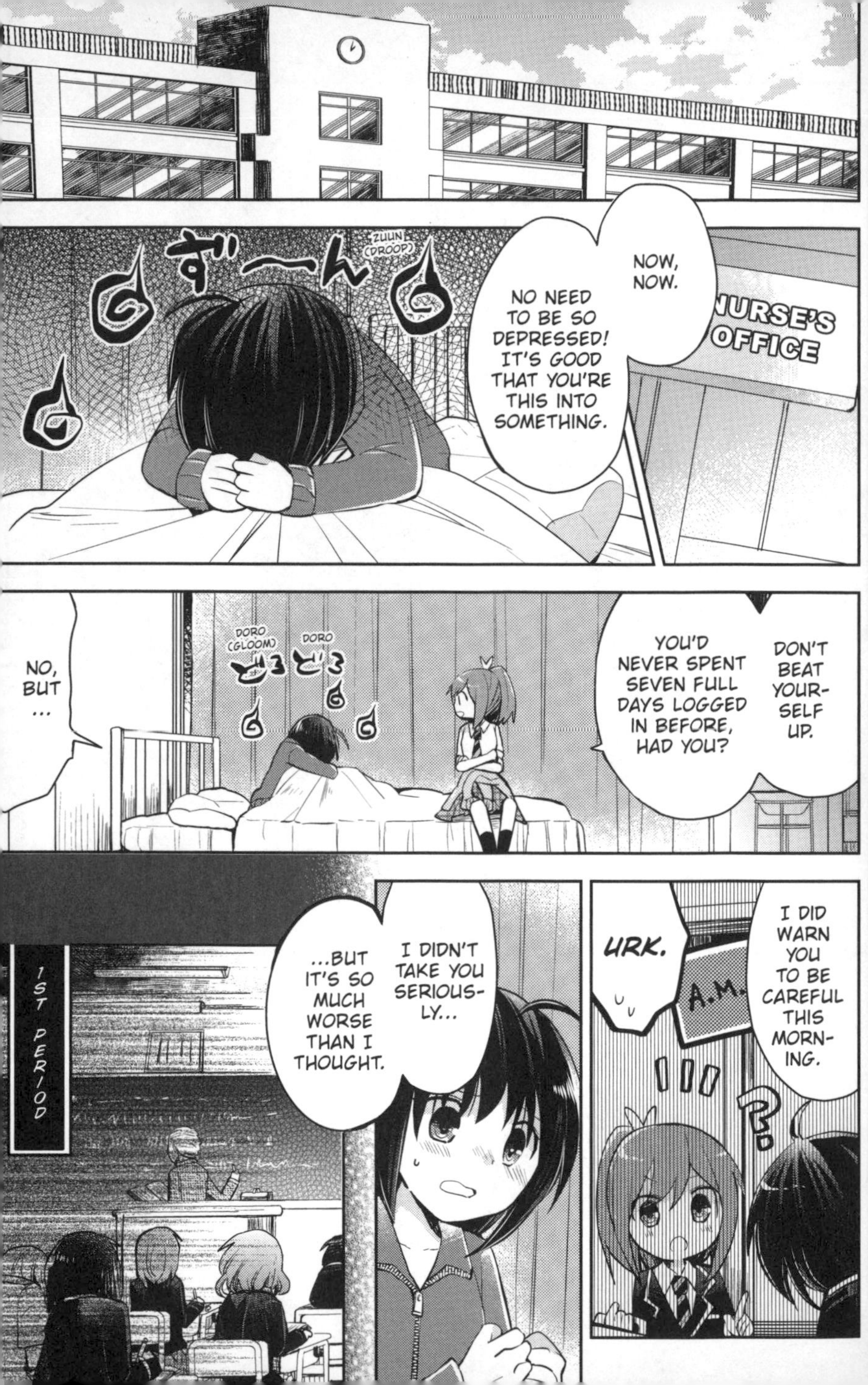
NURSE'S OFFICE
NOW, NOW.
NO NEED TO BE SO DEPRESSED! IT'S GOOD THAT YOU'RE THIS INTO SOMETHING.
ZUUN (DROOP)
DON'T BEAT YOUR-SELF UP.
YOU'D NEVER SPENT SEVEN FULL DAYS LOGGED IN BEFORE, HAD YOU?
DORO DORO (GLOOM)
NO, BUT ...
I DID WARN YOU TO BE CAREFUL THIS MORN-ING.
A.M.
URK.
I DIDN'T TAKE YOU SERIOUS-LY...
...BUT IT'S SO MUCH WORSE THAN I THOUGHT.
1ST PERIOD

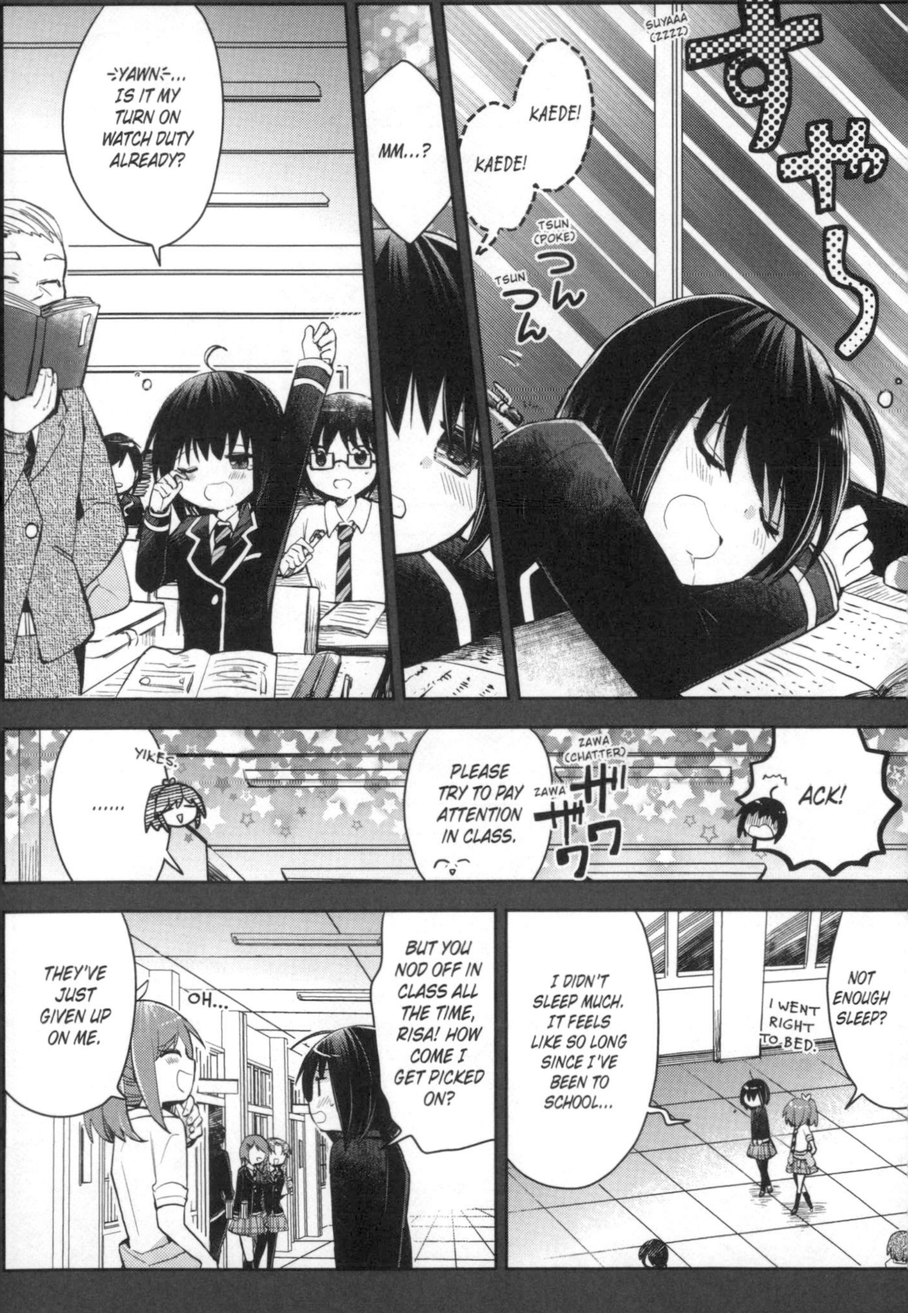
SUYAAA (ZZZZZ)
すやぁ
KAEDE!
KAEDE!
TSUN (POKE)
TSUN
つんつん
MM...?
≈YAWN≈... IS IT MY TURN ON WATCH DUTY ALREADY?
ACK!
ZAWA (CHATTER)
ZAWA
ザワザワ
PLEASE TRY TO PAY ATTENTION IN CLASS.
YIKES.
......
NOT ENOUGH SLEEP?
I WENT RIGHT TO BED.
I DIDN'T SLEEP MUCH. IT FEELS LIKE SO LONG SINCE I'VE BEEN TO SCHOOL...
BUT YOU NOD OFF IN CLASS ALL THE TIME, RISA! HOW COME I GET PICKED ON?
OH...
THEY'VE JUST GIVEN UP ON ME.

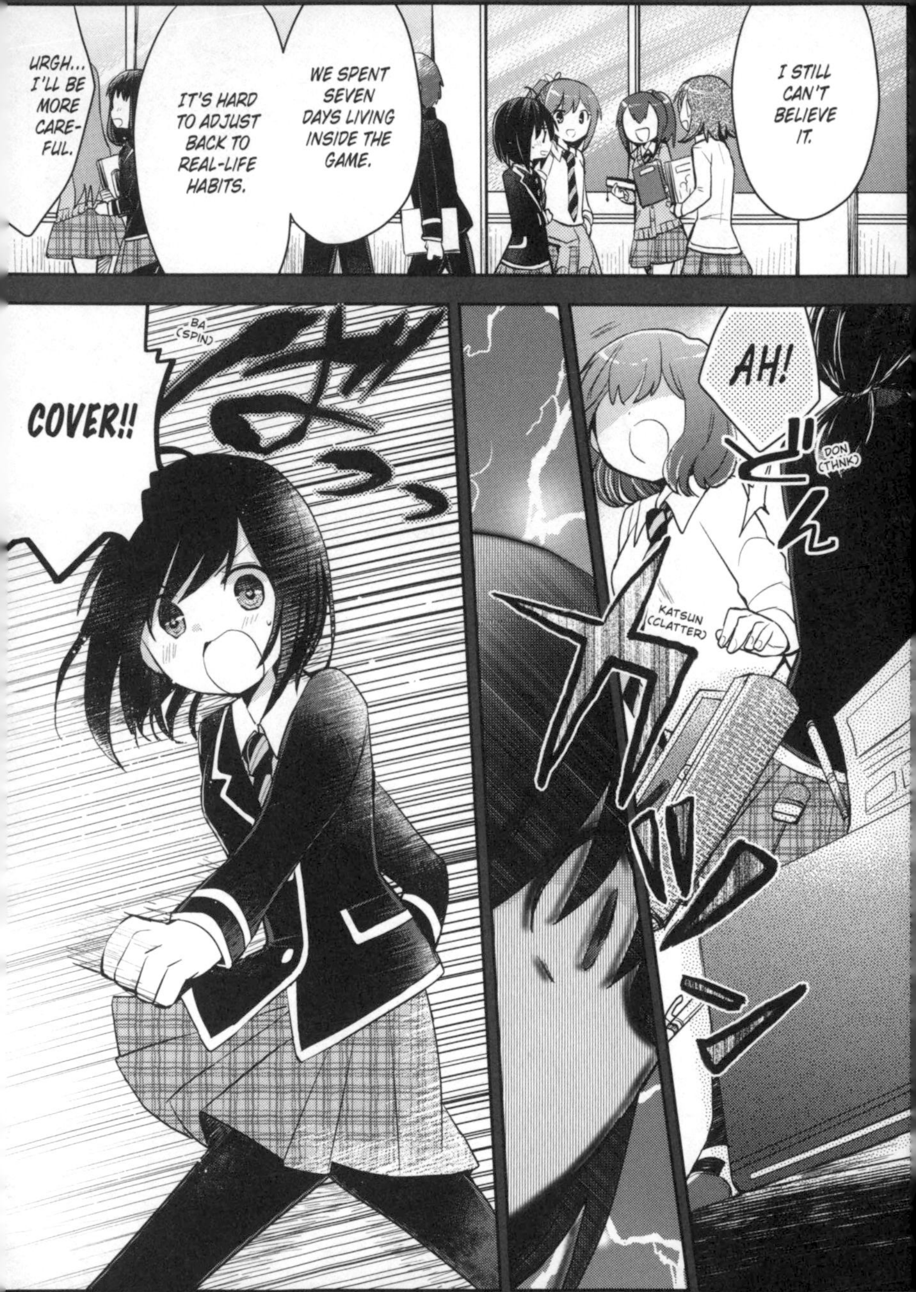
I STILL CAN'T BELIEVE IT.
WE SPENT SEVEN DAYS LIVING INSIDE THE GAME.
IT'S HARD TO ADJUST BACK TO REAL-LIFE HABITS.
URGH... I'LL BE MORE CARE-FUL.
AH!
DON (THINK)
KATSUN (CLATTER)
BA (SPIN)
COVER!!

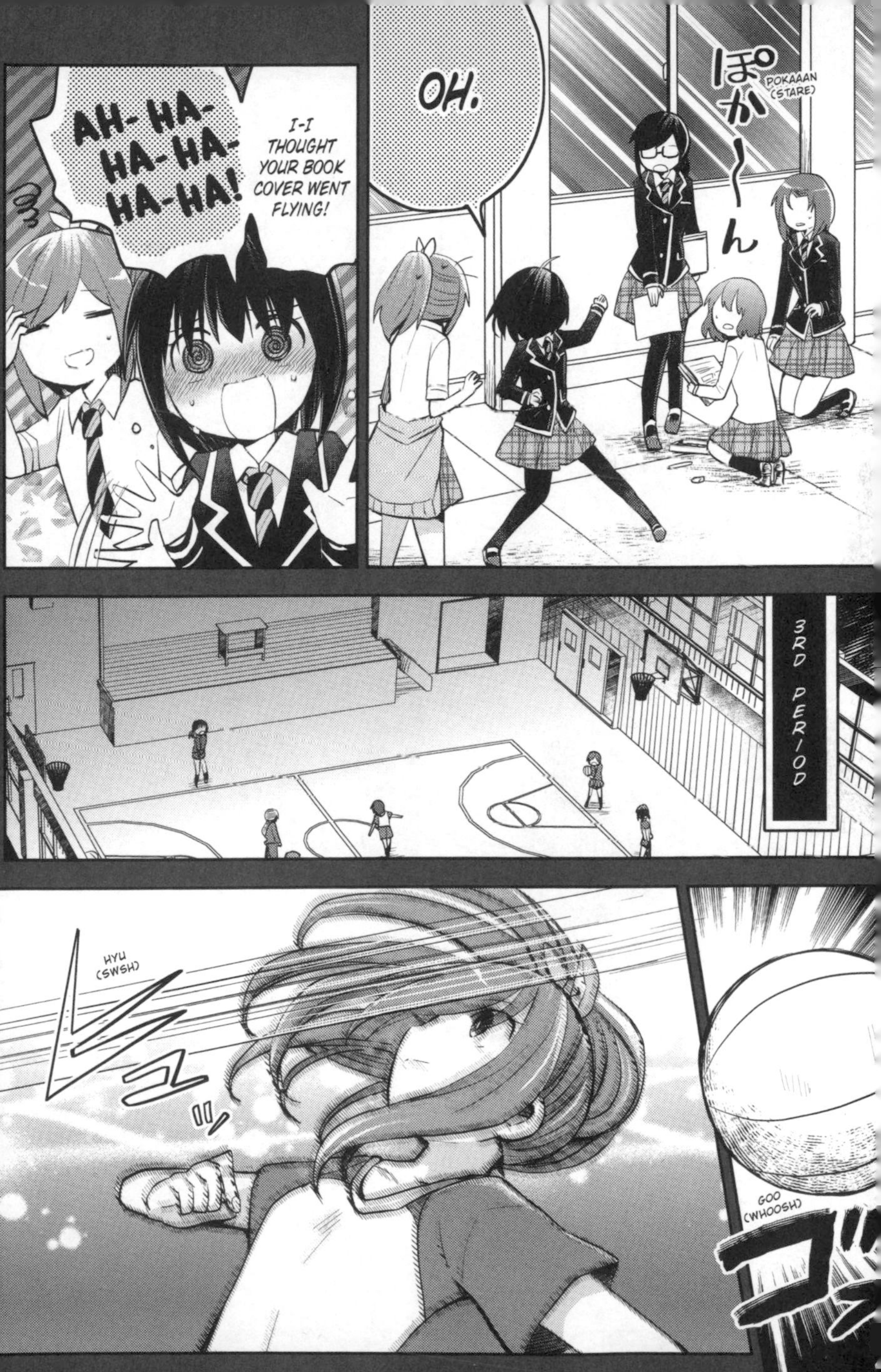
ぽか～ん
POKAAAN (STARE)
OH.
I-I THOUGHT YOUR BOOK COVER WENT FLYING!
AH-HA-HA-HA-HA-HA!
3RD PERIOD
GOO (WHOOSH)
HYU (SWSH)

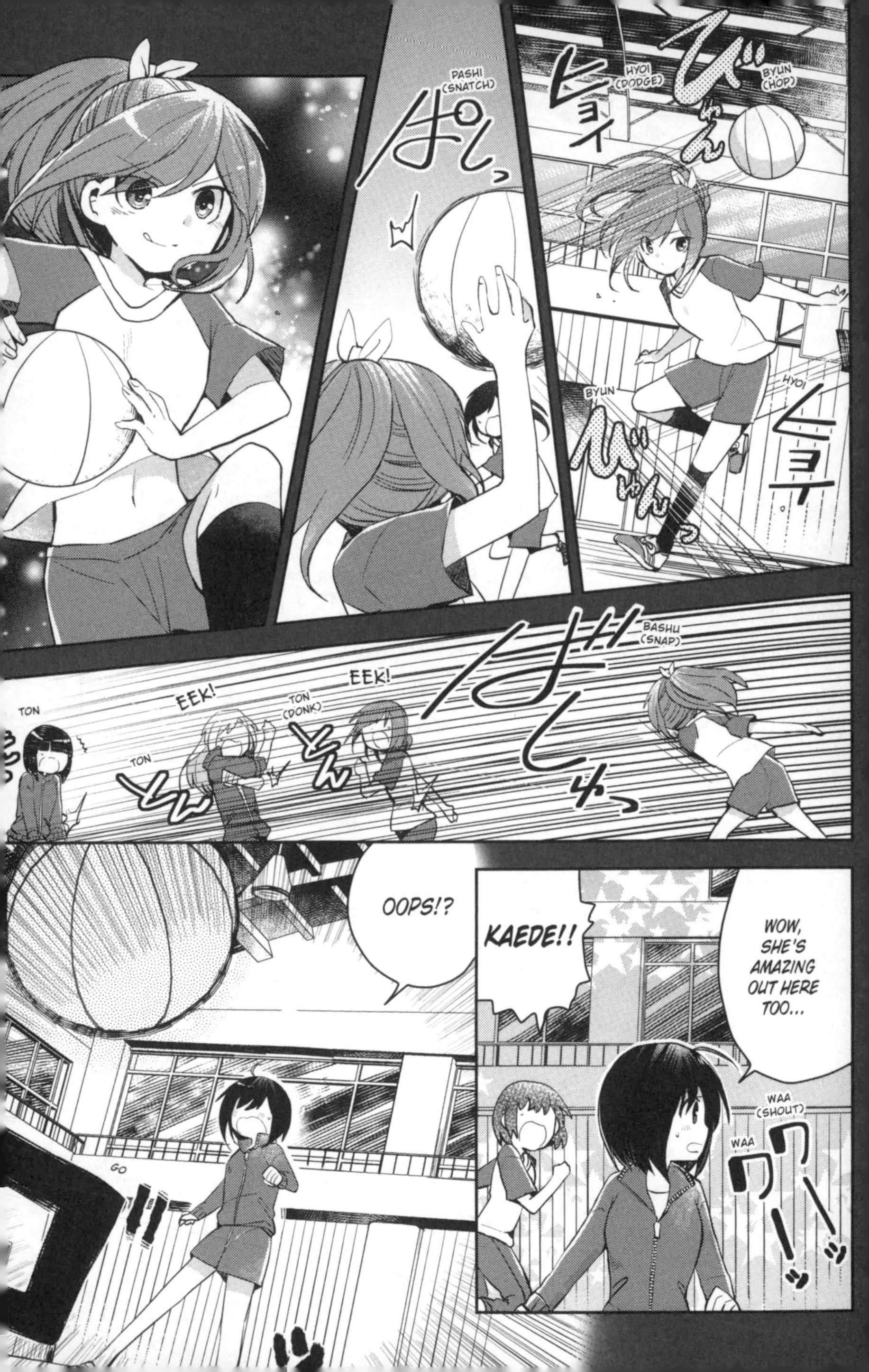
BYUN (HOP)
びゅん
HYOI (DODGE)
ヒョイ
HYOI
ヒョイ
BYUN
びゅんっ
PASHI (SNATCH)
ぱしっ
BASHU (SNAP)
ばしゅっ
EEK!
TON (DONK)
とん
EEK!
TON
とん
TON
WOW, SHE'S AMAZING OUT HERE TOO...
WAA (SHOUT)
WAA
ワーッ
KAEDE!!
OOPS!?
GO

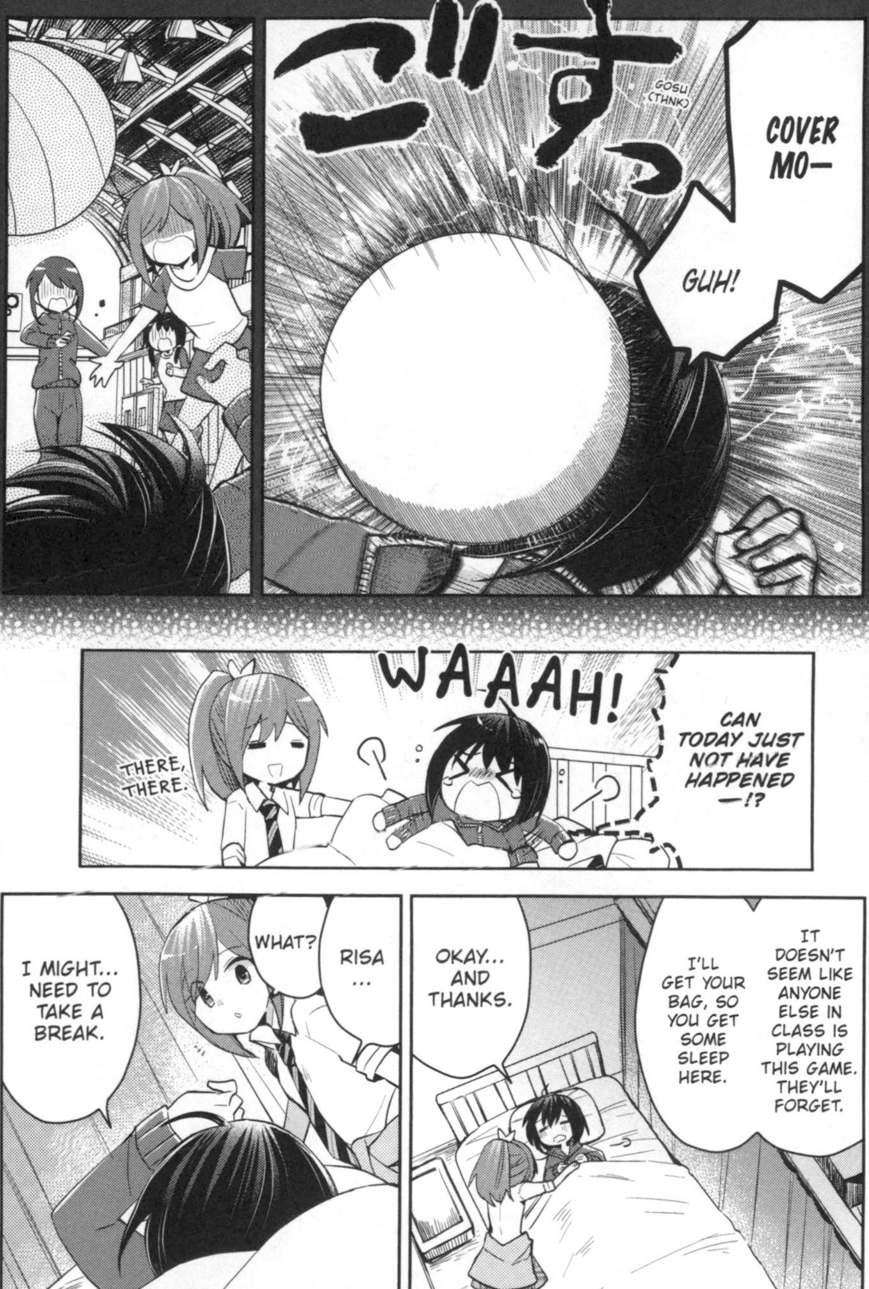
COVER MO—
ごすっ
GOSU (THNK)
GUH!
CAN TODAY JUST NOT HAVE HAPPENED—!?
WAAAH!
THERE, THERE.
IT DOESN'T SEEM LIKE ANYONE ELSE IN CLASS IS PLAYING THIS GAME. THEY'LL FORGET.
I'LL GET YOUR BAG, SO YOU GET SOME SLEEP HERE.
OKAY... AND THANKS.
RISA...
WHAT?
I MIGHT... NEED TO TAKE A BREAK.

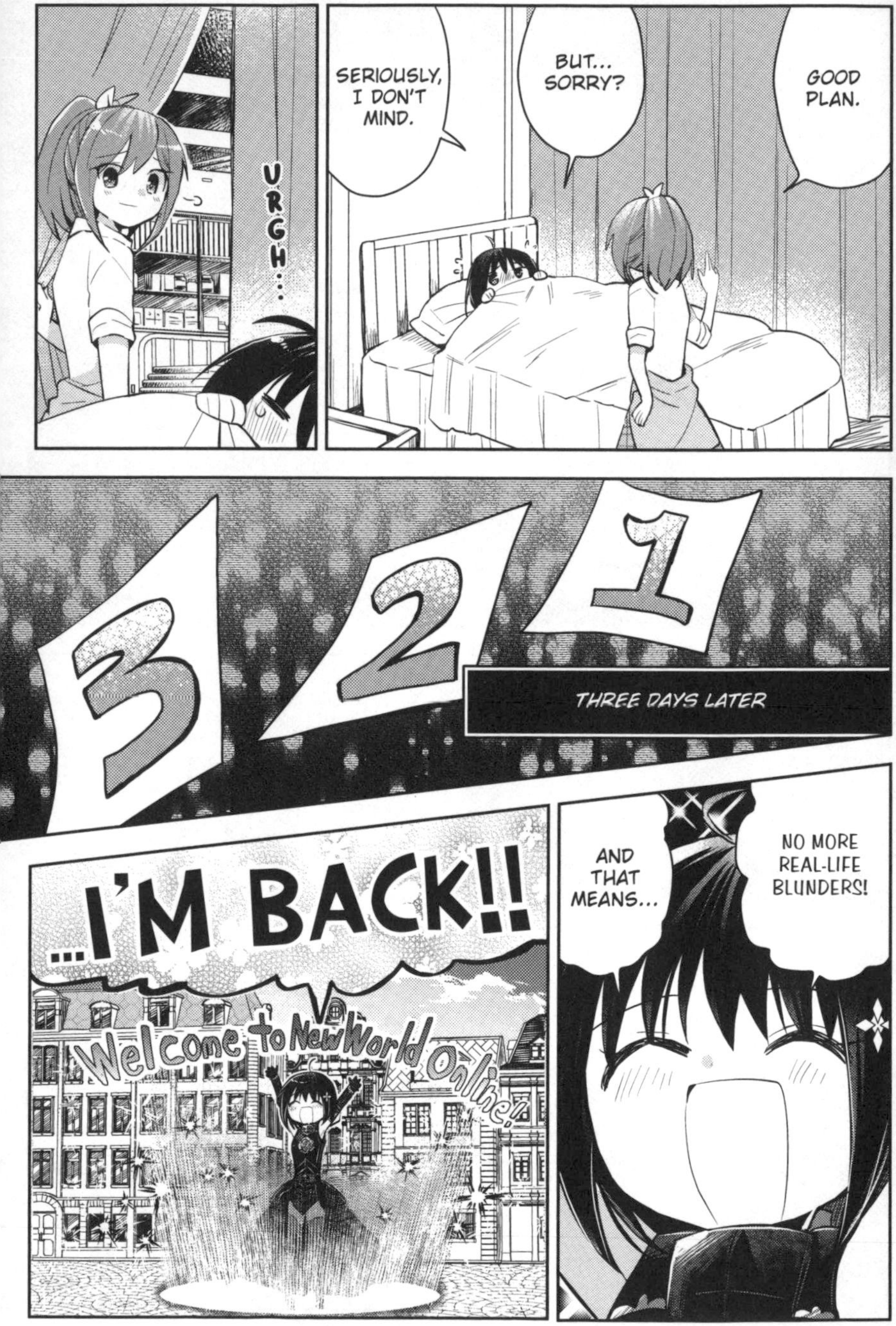
GOOD PLAN.
BUT... SORRY?
SERIOUSLY, I DON'T MIND.
URGH...
3
2
1
THREE DAYS LATER
NO MORE REAL-LIFE BLUNDERS!
AND THAT MEANS...
...I'M BACK!!
Welcome to New World Online!

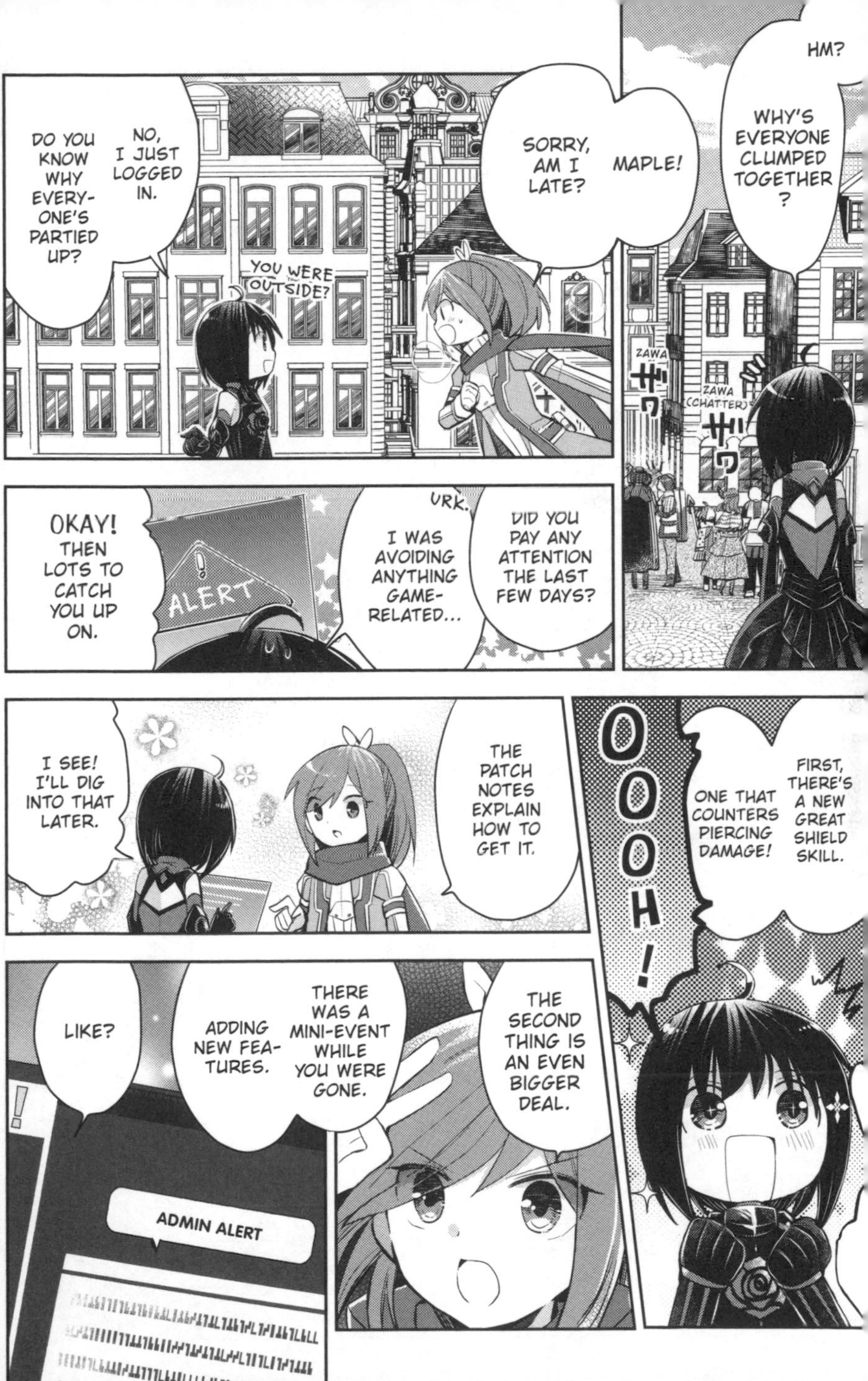
HM?
WHY'S EVERYONE CLUMPED TOGETHER?
ZAWA
ZAWA (CHATTER)
MAPLE!
SORRY, AM I LATE?
YOU WERE OUTSIDE?
NO, I JUST LOGGED IN.
DO YOU KNOW WHY EVERYONE'S PARTIED UP?
DID YOU PAY ANY ATTENTION THE LAST FEW DAYS?
URK.
I WAS AVOIDING ANYTHING GAME-RELATED...
ALERT
OKAY! THEN LOTS TO CATCH YOU UP ON.
FIRST, THERE'S A NEW GREAT SHIELD SKILL.
ONE THAT COUNTERS PIERCING DAMAGE!
OOOOH!
THE PATCH NOTES EXPLAIN HOW TO GET IT.
I SEE! I'LL DIG INTO THAT LATER.
THE SECOND THING IS AN EVEN BIGGER DEAL.
THERE WAS A MINI-EVENT WHILE YOU WERE GONE.
ADDING NEW FEATURES.
LIKE?
ADMIN ALERT

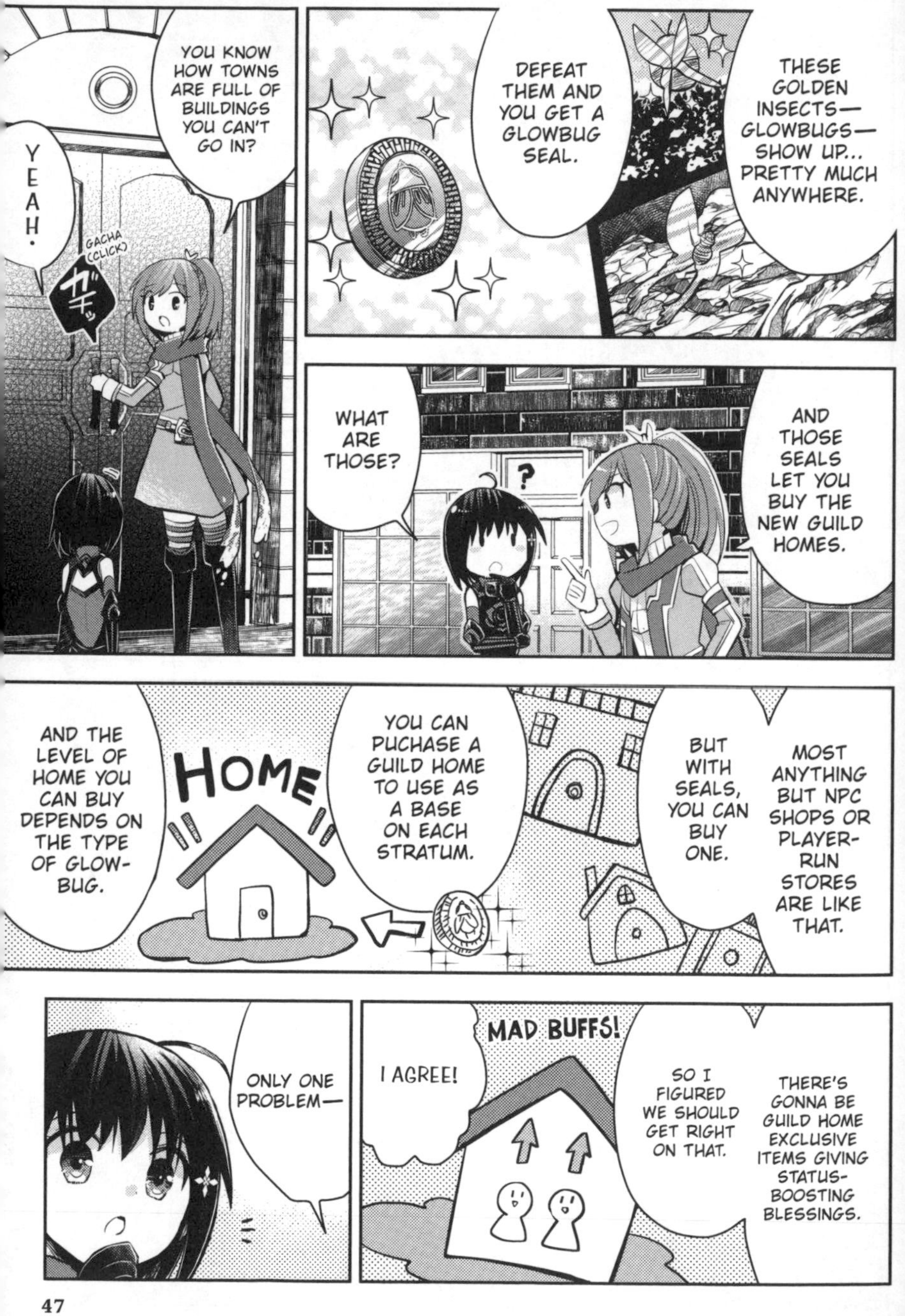
THESE GOLDEN INSECTS—GLOWBUGS—SHOW UP... PRETTY MUCH ANYWHERE.
DEFEAT THEM AND YOU GET A GLOWBUG SEAL.
AND THOSE SEALS LET YOU BUY THE NEW GUILD HOMES.
?
WHAT ARE THOSE?
YOU KNOW HOW TOWNS ARE FULL OF BUILDINGS YOU CAN'T GO IN?
YEAH.
GACHA (CLICK)
MOST ANYTHING BUT NPC SHOPS OR PLAYER-RUN STORES ARE LIKE THAT.
BUT WITH SEALS, YOU CAN BUY ONE.
YOU CAN PUCHASE A GUILD HOME TO USE AS A BASE ON EACH STRATUM.
HOME
AND THE LEVEL OF HOME YOU CAN BUY DEPENDS ON THE TYPE OF GLOW-BUG.
THERE'S GONNA BE GUILD HOME EXCLUSIVE ITEMS GIVING STATUS-BOOSTING BLESSINGS.
SO I FIGURED WE SHOULD GET RIGHT ON THAT.
MAD BUFFS!
I AGREE!
ONLY ONE PROBLEM—

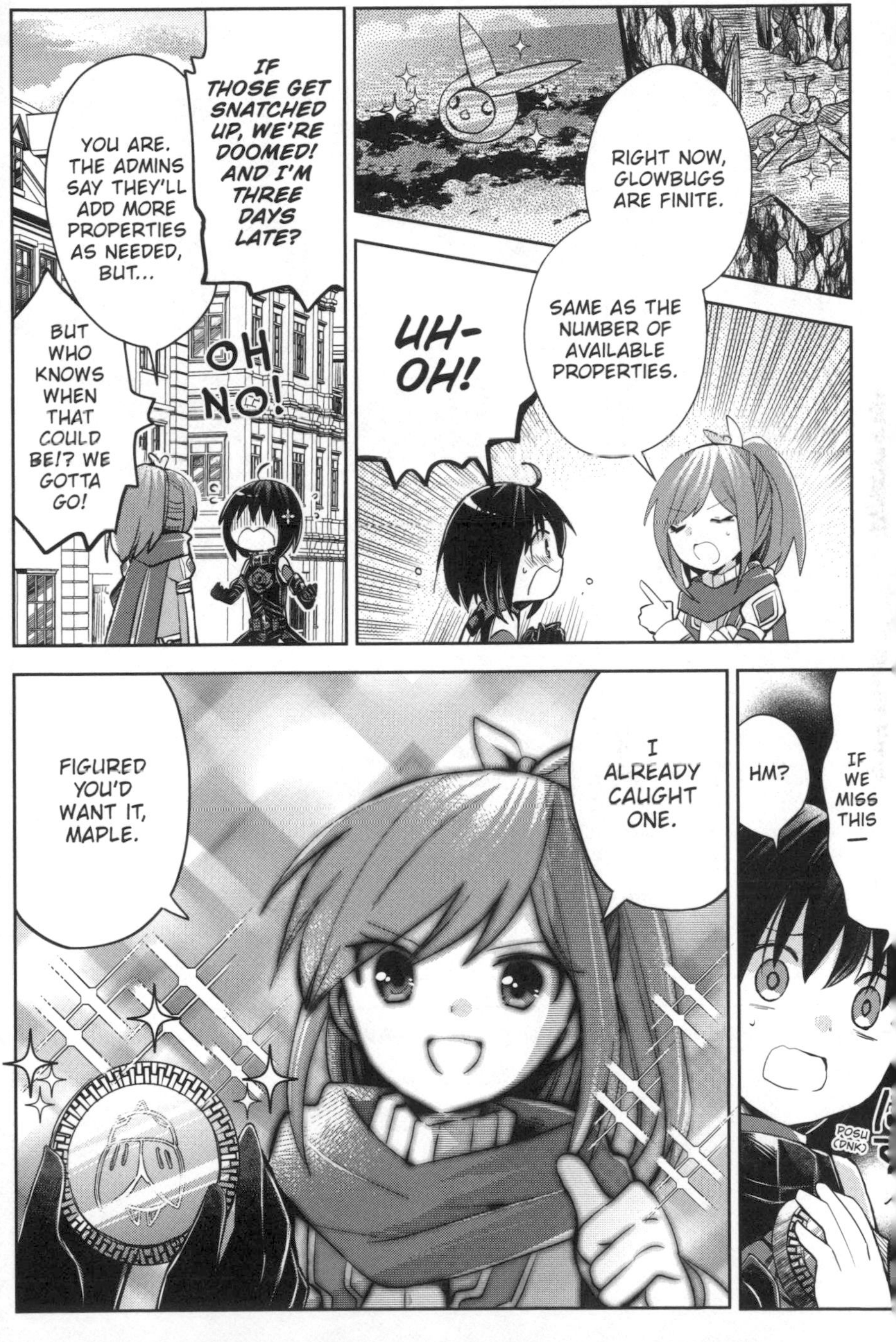
RIGHT NOW, GLOWBUGS ARE FINITE.
SAME AS THE NUMBER OF AVAILABLE PROPERTIES.
UH-OH!
IF THOSE GET SNATCHED UP, WE'RE DOOMED! AND I'M THREE DAYS LATE?
YOU ARE. THE ADMINS SAY THEY'LL ADD MORE PROPERTIES AS NEEDED, BUT...
OH NO!
BUT WHO KNOWS WHEN THAT COULD BE!? WE GOTTA GO!
IF WE MISS THIS—
HM?
POSU (DNK)
I ALREADY CAUGHT ONE.
FIGURED YOU'D WANT IT, MAPLE.

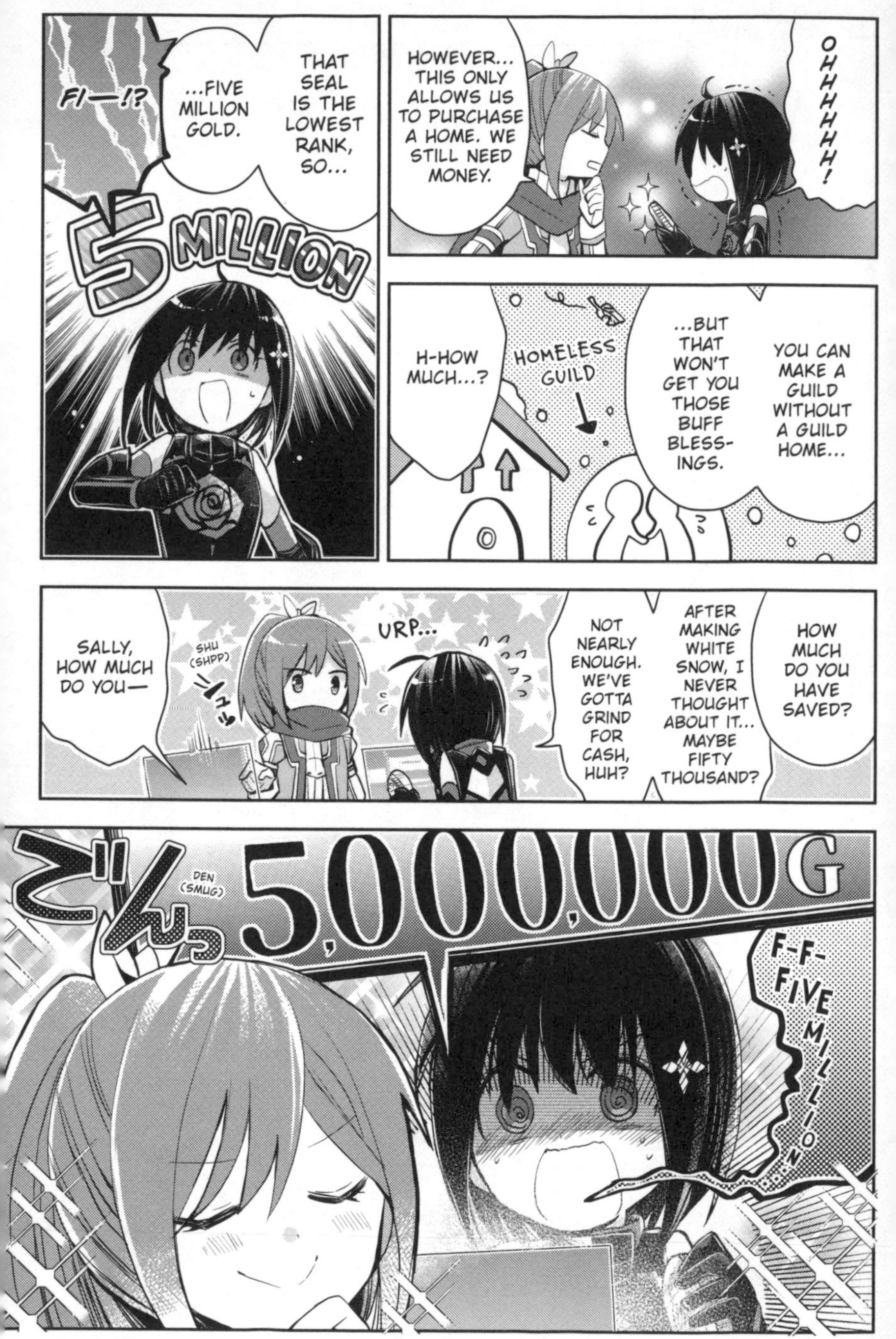
OHHHHHH!
HOWEVER... THIS ONLY ALLOWS US TO PURCHASE A HOME. WE STILL NEED MONEY.
YOU CAN MAKE A GUILD WITHOUT A GUILD HOME...
...BUT THAT WON'T GET YOU THOSE BUFF BLESS-INGS.
HOMELESS GUILD
H-HOW MUCH...?
THAT SEAL IS THE LOWEST RANK, SO...
...FIVE MILLION GOLD.
FI—!?
5 MILLION
HOW MUCH DO YOU HAVE SAVED?
AFTER MAKING WHITE SNOW, I NEVER THOUGHT ABOUT IT... MAYBE FIFTY THOUSAND?
NOT NEARLY ENOUGH. WE'VE GOTTA GRIND FOR CASH, HUH?
URP...
SHU (SHPP)
SALLY, HOW MUCH DO YOU—
F-F-FIVE MILLION...
5,000,000G
DEN (SMUG)

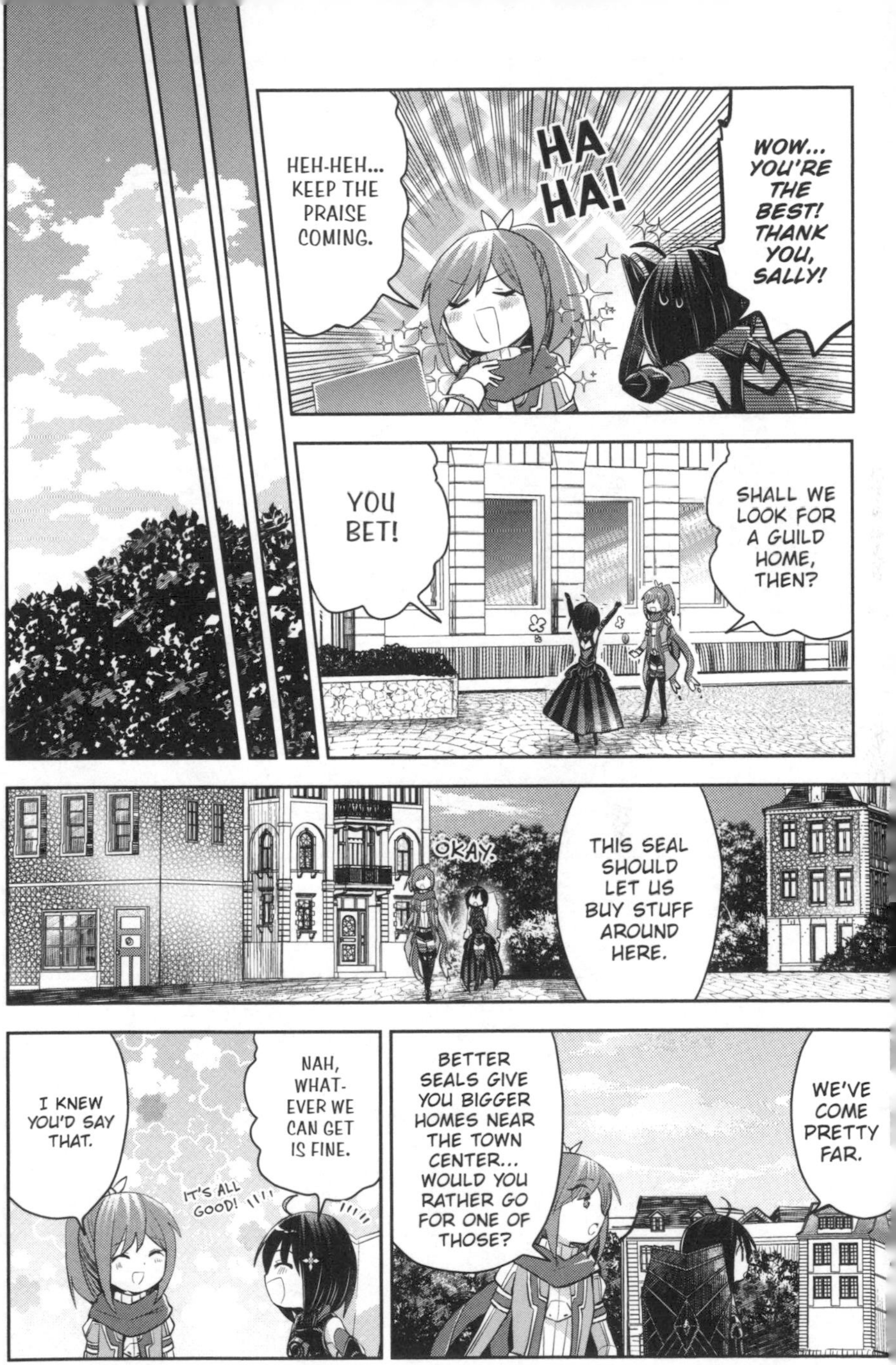
WOW... YOU'RE THE BEST! THANK YOU, SALLY!
HA HA!
HEH-HEH... KEEP THE PRAISE COMING.
SHALL WE LOOK FOR A GUILD HOME, THEN?
YOU BET!
THIS SEAL SHOULD LET US BUY STUFF AROUND HERE.
OKAY.
WE'VE COME PRETTY FAR.
BETTER SEALS GIVE YOU BIGGER HOMES NEAR THE TOWN CENTER... WOULD YOU RATHER GO FOR ONE OF THOSE?
NAH, WHAT-EVER WE CAN GET IS FINE.
IT'S ALL GOOD!
I KNEW YOU'D SAY THAT.

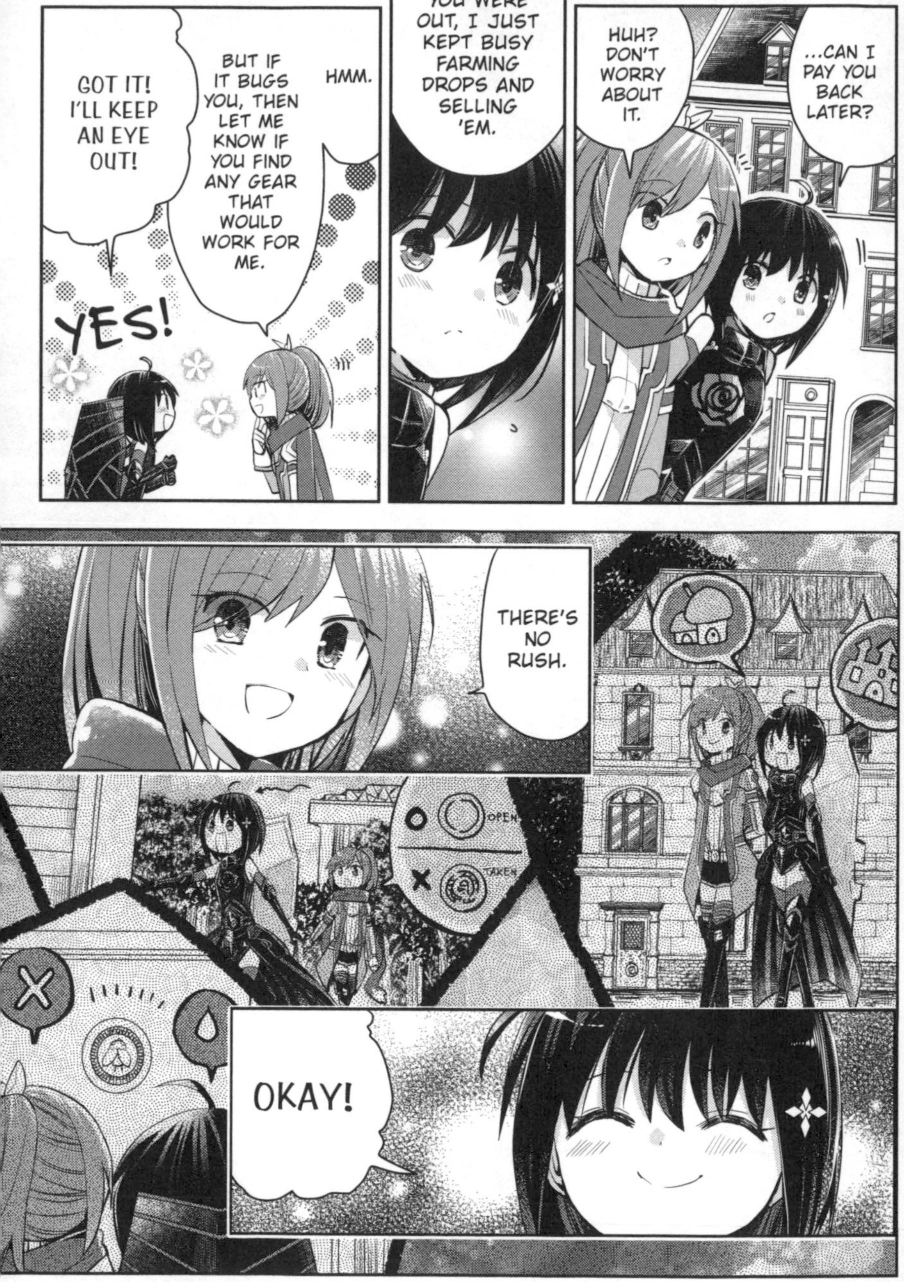
...CAN I PAY YOU BACK LATER?
HUH? DON'T WORRY ABOUT IT.
WHILE YOU WERE OUT, I JUST KEPT BUSY FARMING DROPS AND SELLING 'EM.
HMM.
BUT IF IT BUGS YOU, THEN LET ME KNOW IF YOU FIND ANY GEAR THAT WOULD WORK FOR ME.
GOT IT! I'LL KEEP AN EYE OUT!
YES!
THERE'S NO RUSH.
OPEN
TAKEN
OKAY!

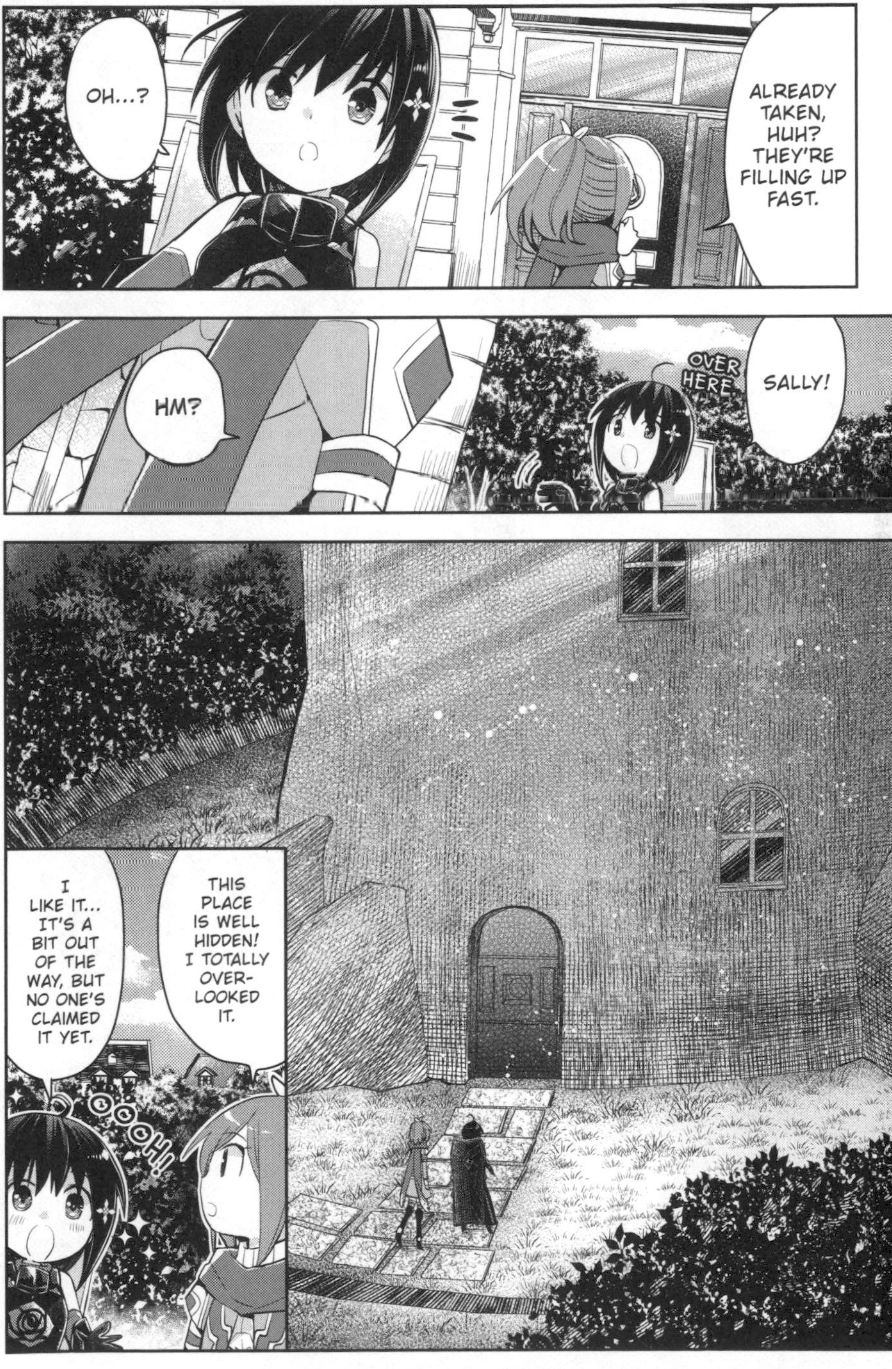
ALREADY TAKEN, HUH? THEY'RE FILLING UP FAST.
OH...?
SALLY!
OVER HERE
HM?
THIS PLACE IS WELL HIDDEN! I TOTALLY OVER-LOOKED IT.
I LIKE IT... IT'S A BIT OUT OF THE WAY, BUT NO ONE'S CLAIMED IT YET.
OOOH!

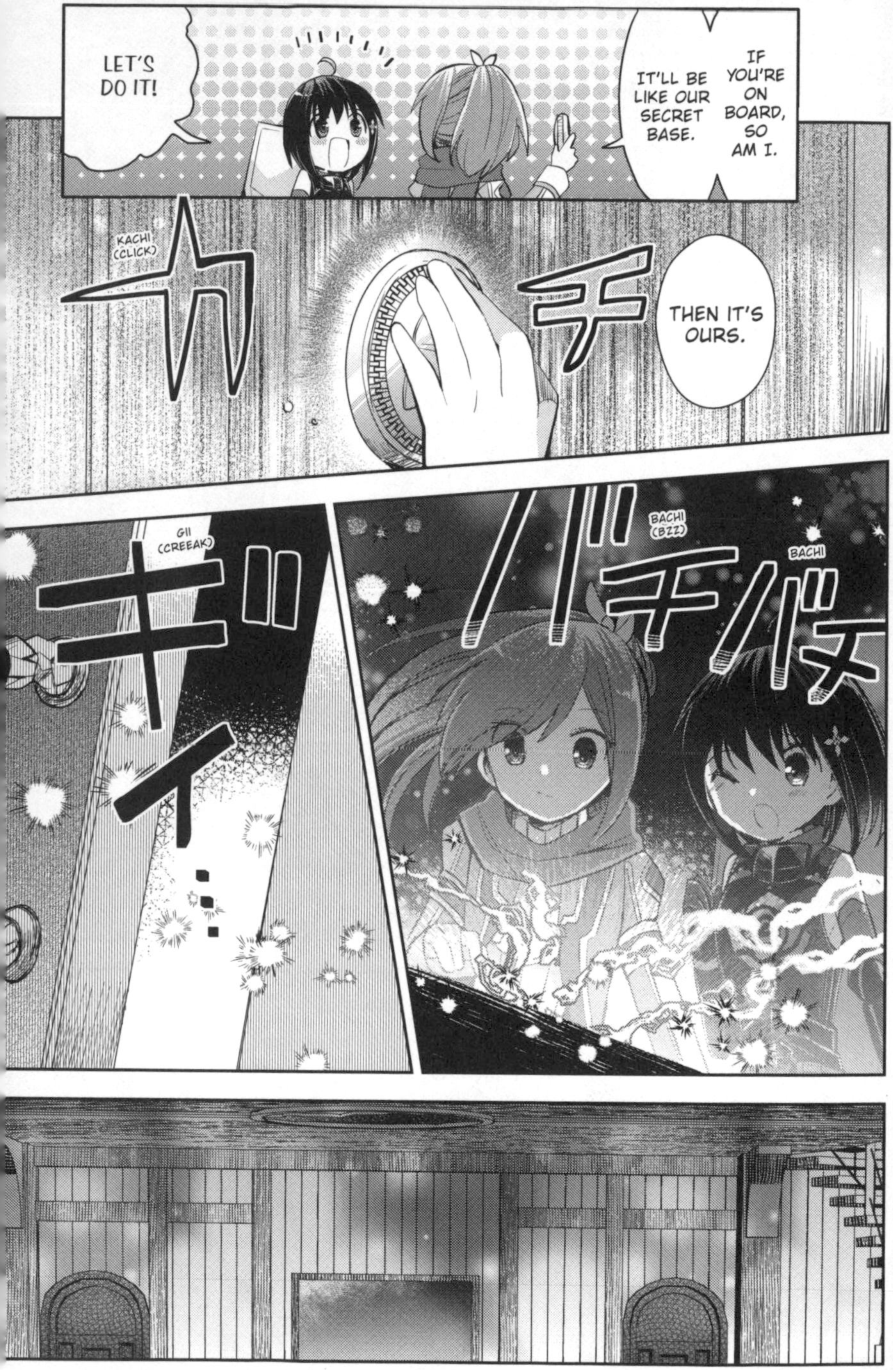
IF YOU'RE ON BOARD, SO AM I.
IT'LL BE LIKE OUR SECRET BASE.
LET'S DO IT!
THEN IT'S OURS.
KACHI (CLICK)
BACHI (BZZ)
BACHI
GII (CREEAK)

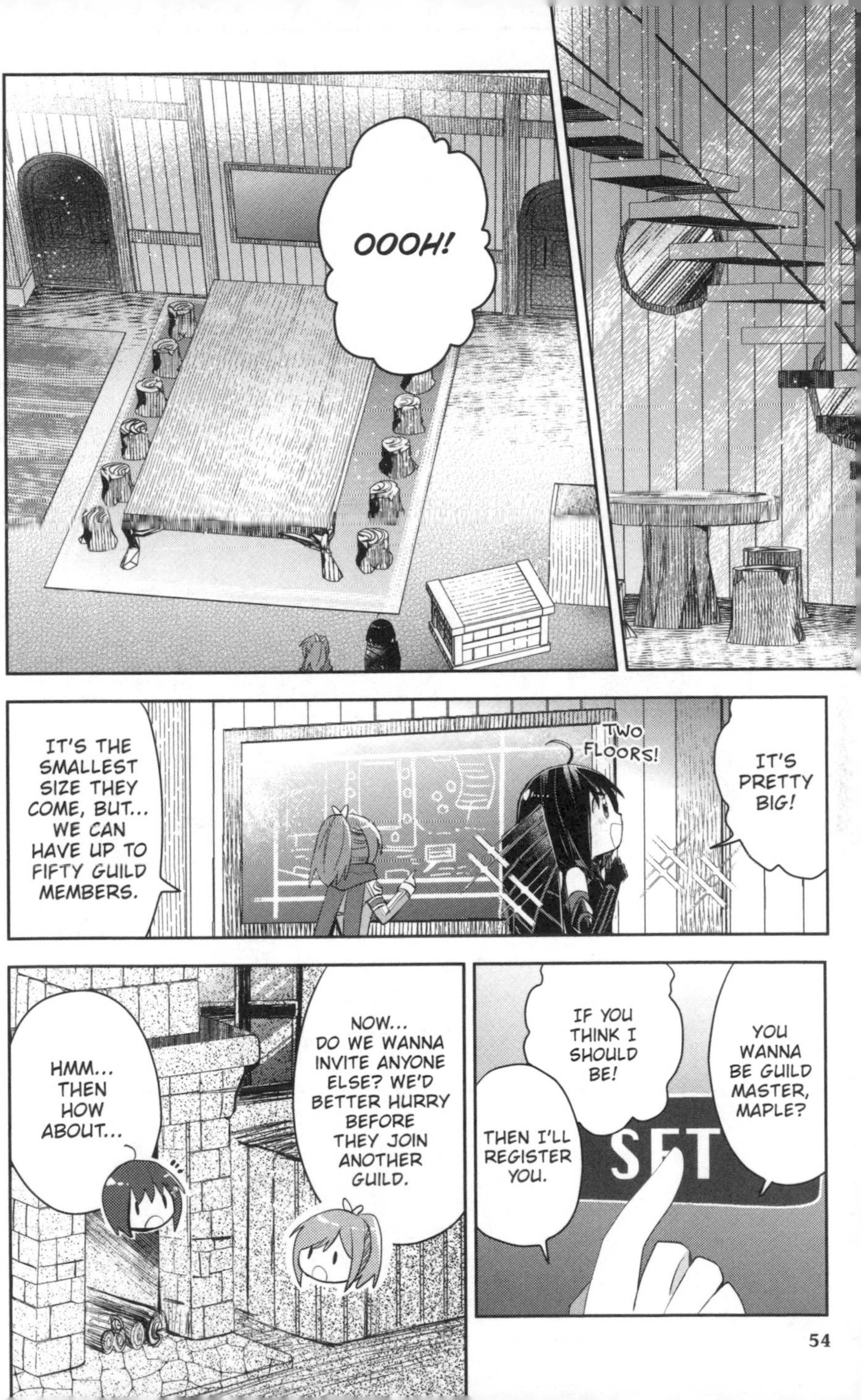
OOOH!
IT'S PRETTY BIG!
TWO FLOORS!
IT'S THE SMALLEST SIZE THEY COME, BUT... WE CAN HAVE UP TO FIFTY GUILD MEMBERS.
YOU WANNA BE GUILD MASTER, MAPLE?
IF YOU THINK I SHOULD BE!
SET
THEN I'LL REGISTER YOU.
NOW... DO WE WANNA INVITE ANYONE ELSE? WE'D BETTER HURRY BEFORE THEY JOIN ANOTHER GUILD.
HMM... THEN HOW ABOUT...

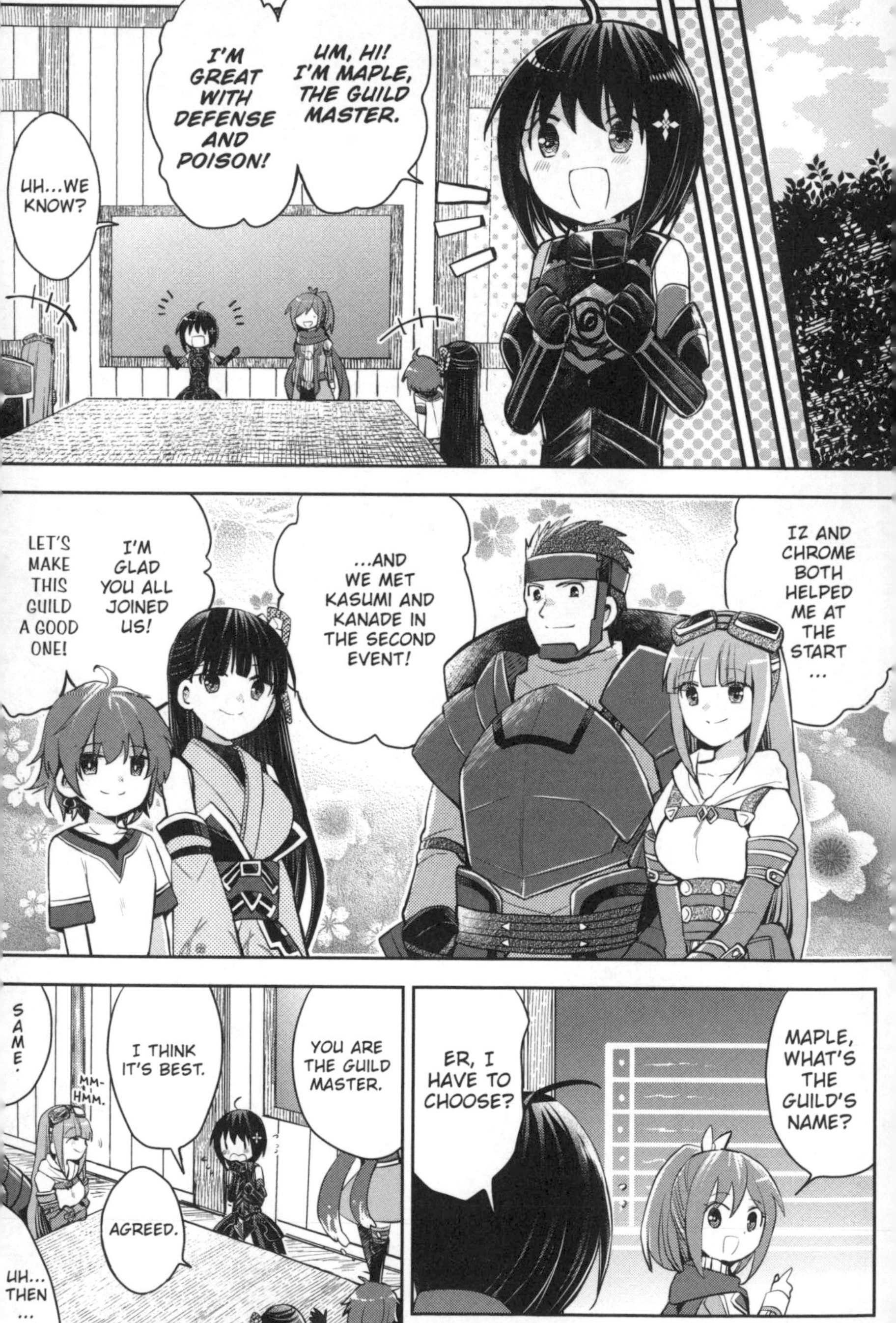
UM, HI! I'M MAPLE, THE GUILD MASTER.
I'M GREAT WITH DEFENSE AND POISON!
UH...WE KNOW?
IZ AND CHROME BOTH HELPED ME AT THE START...
...AND WE MET KASUMI AND KANADE IN THE SECOND EVENT!
I'M GLAD YOU ALL JOINED US!
LET'S MAKE THIS GUILD A GOOD ONE!
MAPLE, WHAT'S THE GUILD'S NAME?
ER, I HAVE TO CHOOSE?
YOU ARE THE GUILD MASTER.
I THINK IT'S BEST.
SAME.
MM-HMM.
AGREED.
UH... THEN...

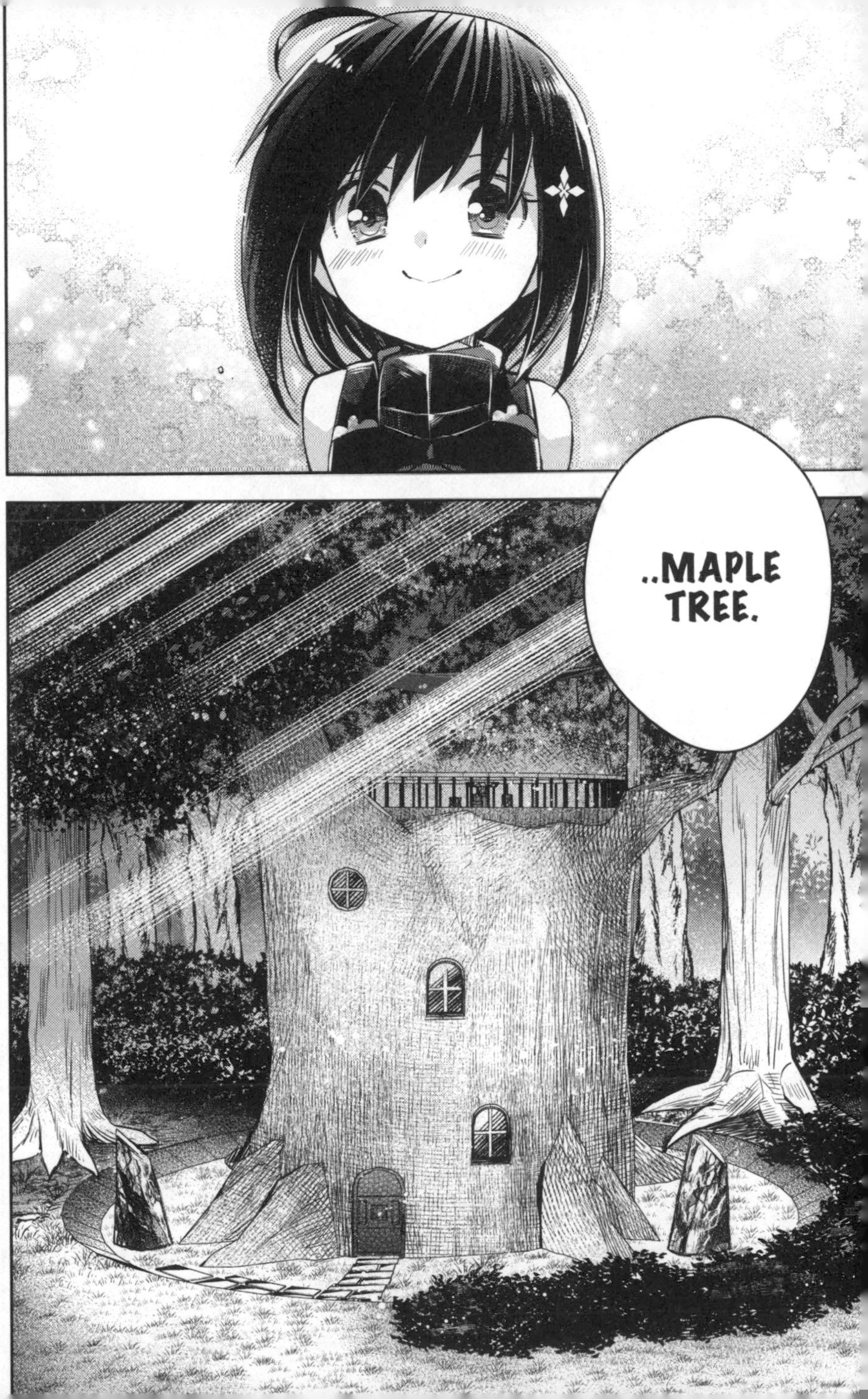
..MAPLE TREE.

CHAPTER 19

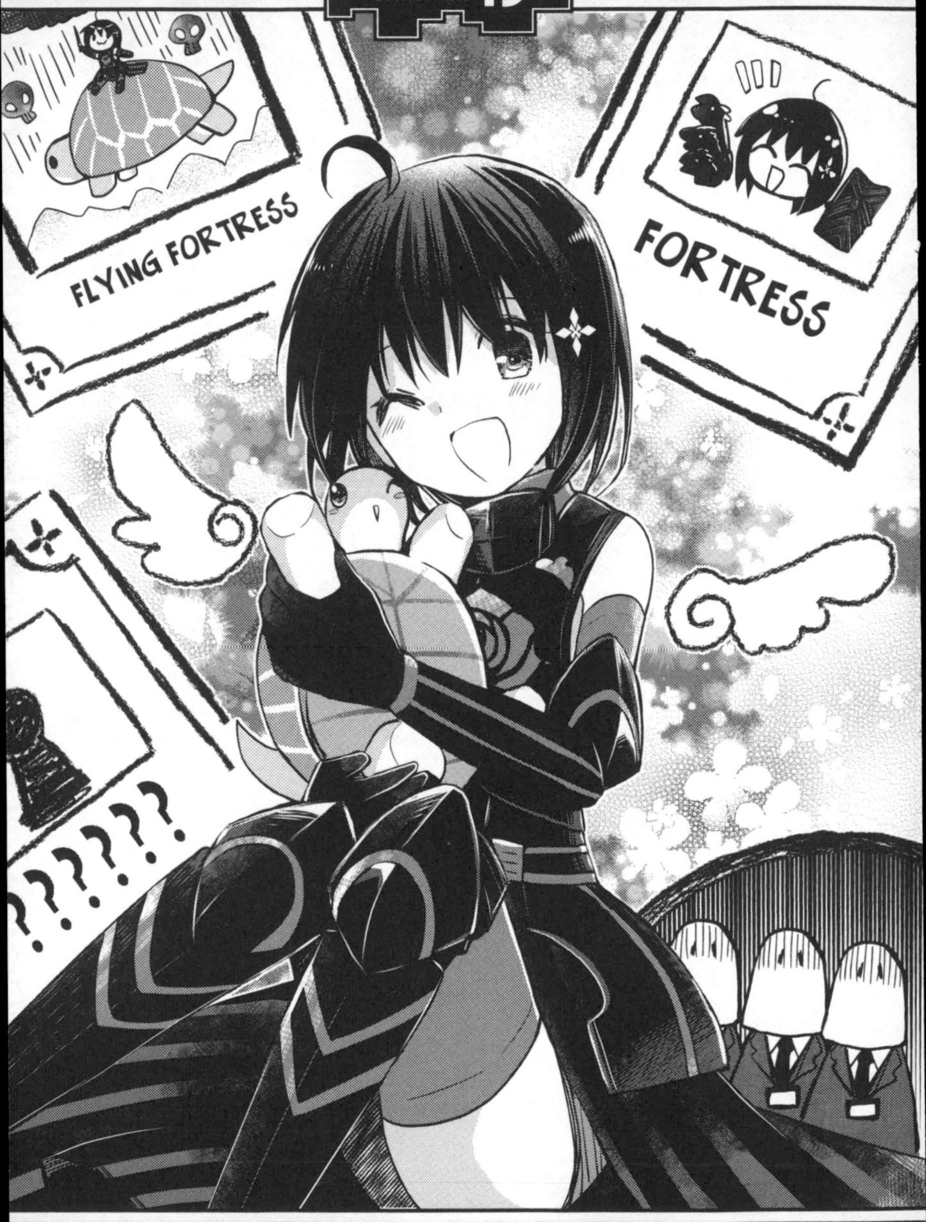
FORTRESS
FLYING FORTRESS
??????

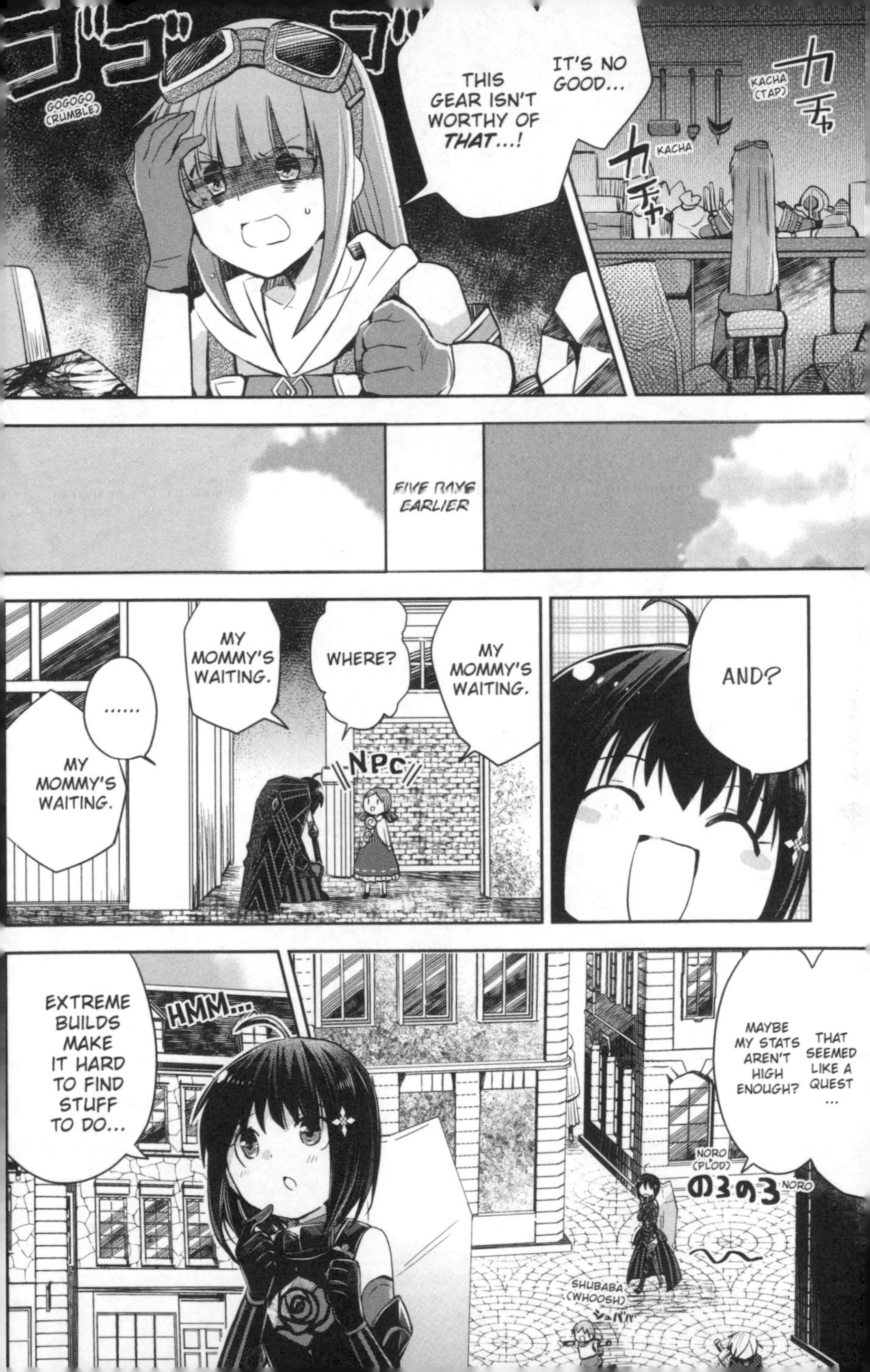
KACHA (TAP)
カチャ
KACHA
カチャ
IT'S NO GOOD...
THIS GEAR ISN'T WORTHY OF THAT...!
GOGOGO (RUMBLE)
FIVE DAYS EARLIER
AND?
MY MOMMY'S WAITING.
WHERE?
MY MOMMY'S WAITING.
NPC
......
MY MOMMY'S WAITING.
THAT SEEMED LIKE A QUEST...
MAYBE MY STATS AREN'T HIGH ENOUGH?
NORO (PLOD)
のろのろ
NORO
SHUBABA (WHOOSH)
HMM...
EXTREME BUILDS MAKE IT HARD TO FIND STUFF TO DO...

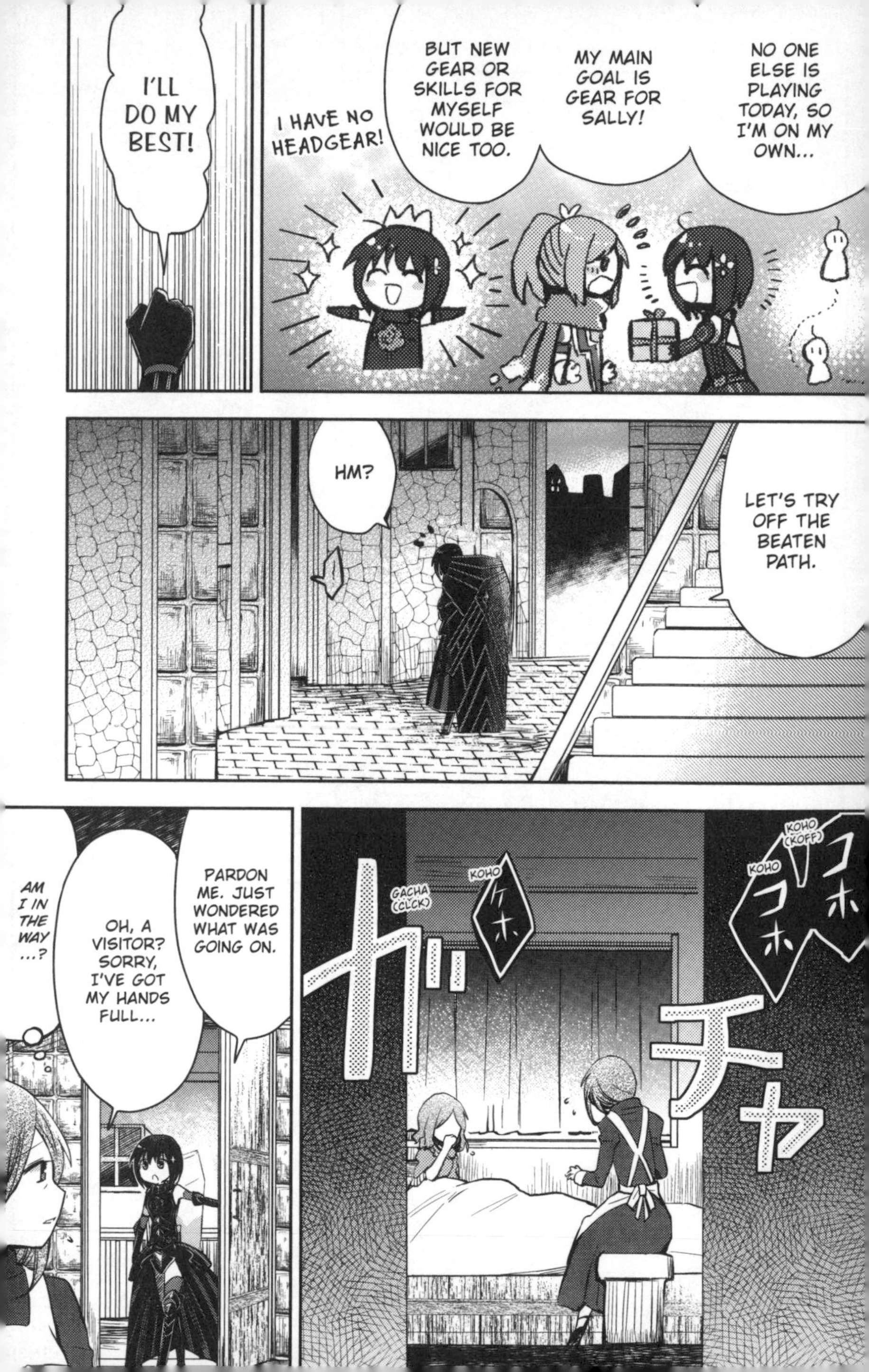
NO ONE ELSE IS PLAYING TODAY, SO I'M ON MY OWN...
MY MAIN GOAL IS GEAR FOR SALLY!
BUT NEW GEAR OR SKILLS FOR MYSELF WOULD BE NICE TOO.
I HAVE NO HEADGEAR!
I'LL DO MY BEST!
LET'S TRY OFF THE BEATEN PATH.
HM?
コホ
KOHO (KOFF)
コホ
KOHO
ケホ
KOHO
ガチャ
GACHA (CLCK)
PARDON ME. JUST WONDERED WHAT WAS GOING ON.
OH, A VISITOR? SORRY, I'VE GOT MY HANDS FULL...
AM I IN THE WAY ...?

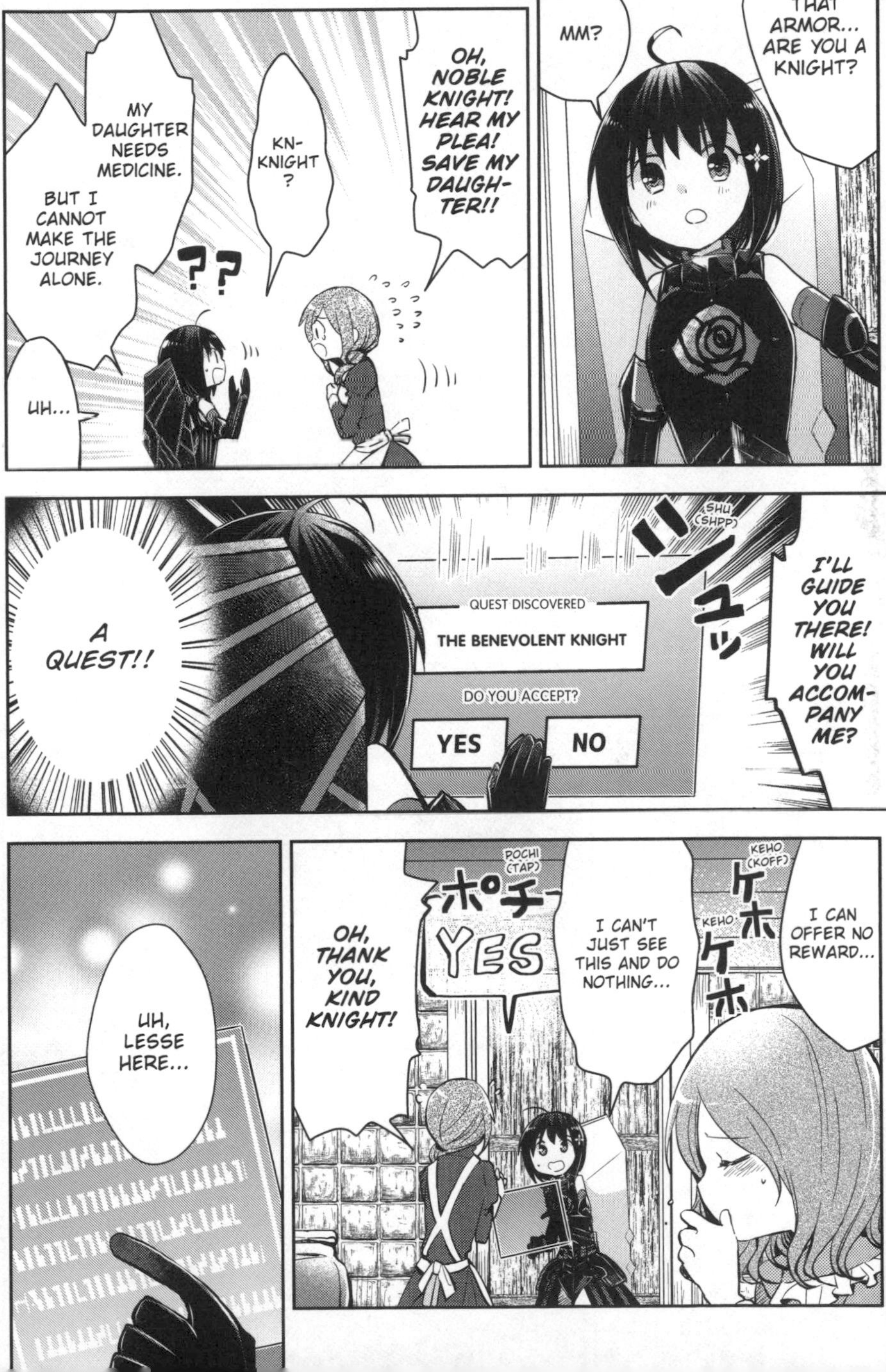
THAT ARMOR... ARE YOU A KNIGHT?
MM?
OH, NOBLE KNIGHT! HEAR MY PLEA! SAVE MY DAUGHTER!!
KN-KNIGHT?
??
MY DAUGHTER NEEDS MEDICINE.
BUT I CANNOT MAKE THE JOURNEY ALONE.
UH...
I'LL GUIDE YOU THERE! WILL YOU ACCOMPANY ME?
SHU (SHPP)
QUEST DISCOVERED
THE BENEVOLENT KNIGHT
DO YOU ACCEPT?
YES
NO
A QUEST!!
I CAN OFFER NO REWARD...
KEHO (KOFF)
KEHO
I CAN'T JUST SEE THIS AND DO NOTHING...
POCHI (TAP)
YES
OH, THANK YOU, KIND KNIGHT!
UH, LESSE HERE...

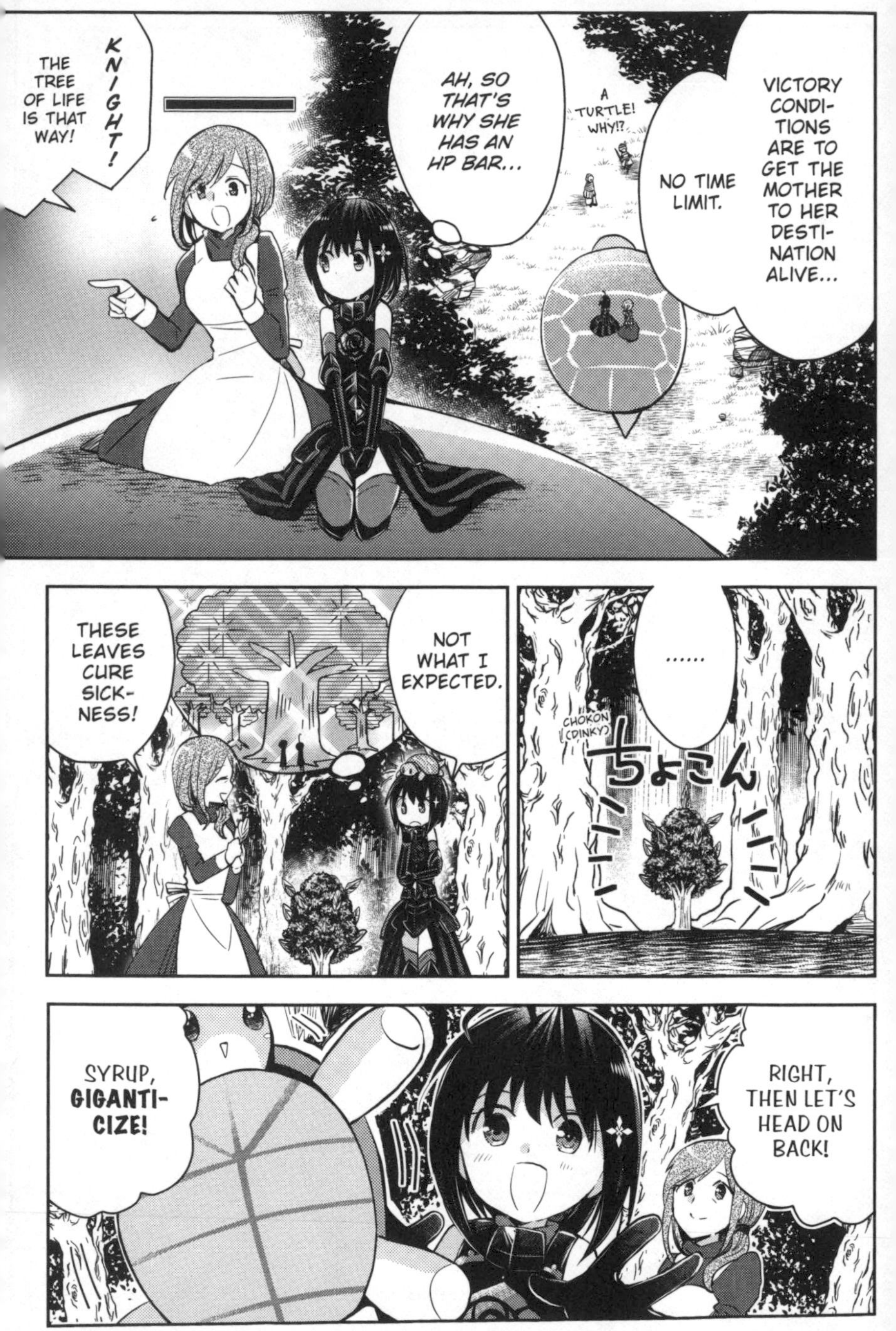
VICTORY CONDITIONS ARE TO GET THE MOTHER TO HER DESTINATION ALIVE...
NO TIME LIMIT.
A TURTLE! WHY!?
AH, SO THAT'S WHY SHE HAS AN HP BAR...
KNIGHT!
THE TREE OF LIFE IS THAT WAY!
......
CHOKON (DINKY)
ちょこん
NOT WHAT I EXPECTED.
THESE LEAVES CURE SICKNESS!
RIGHT, THEN LET'S HEAD ON BACK!
SYRUP, GIGANTICIZE!

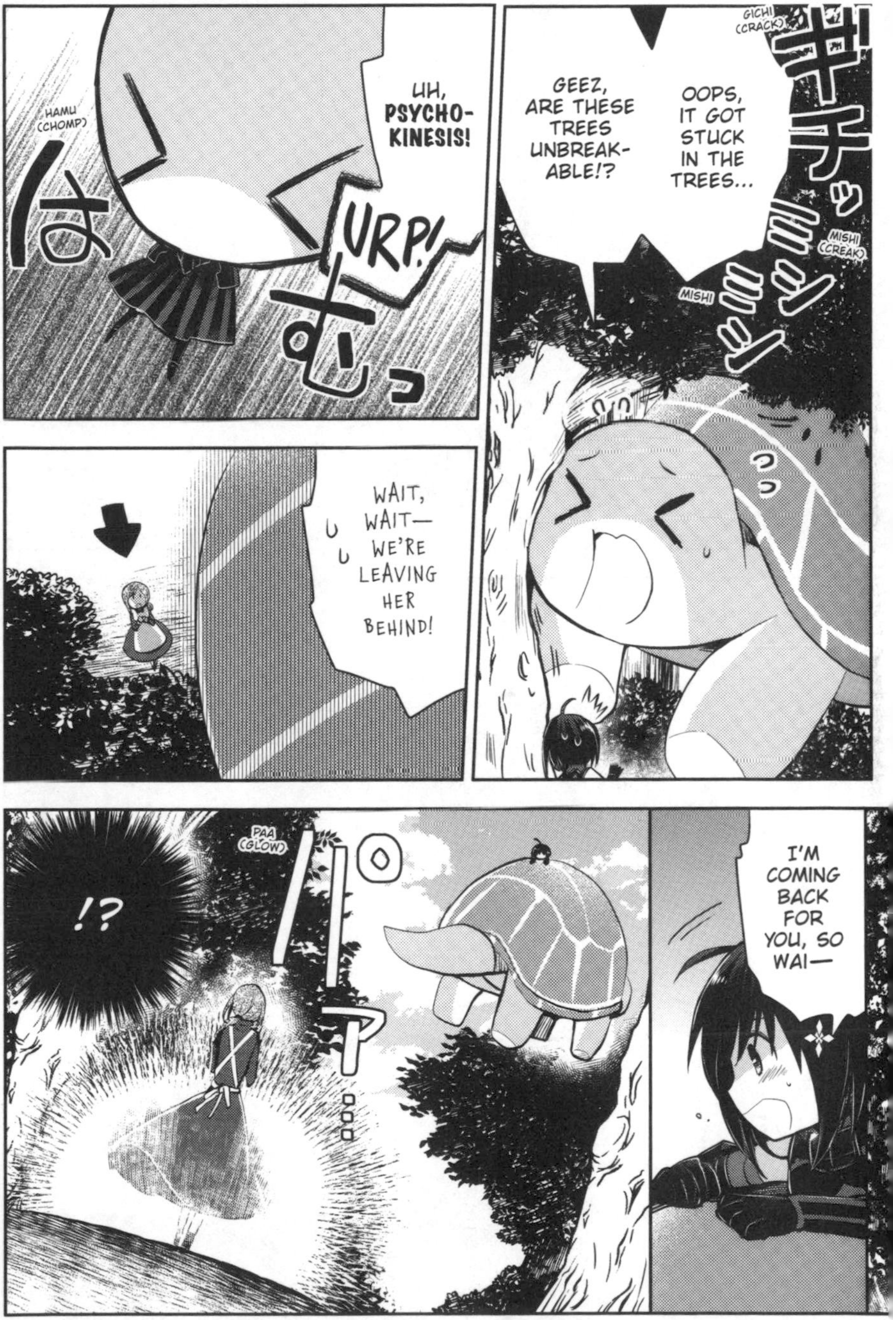
GICHI (CRACK)
OOPS, IT GOT STUCK IN THE TREES...
GEEZ, ARE THESE TREES UNBREAK-ABLE!?
MISHI (CREAK)
MISHI
UH, **PSYCHO-KINESIS!**
HAMU (CHOMP)
URP!
WAIT, WAIT— WE'RE LEAVING HER BEHIND!
I'M COMING BACK FOR YOU, SO WAI—
PAA (GLOW)
!?

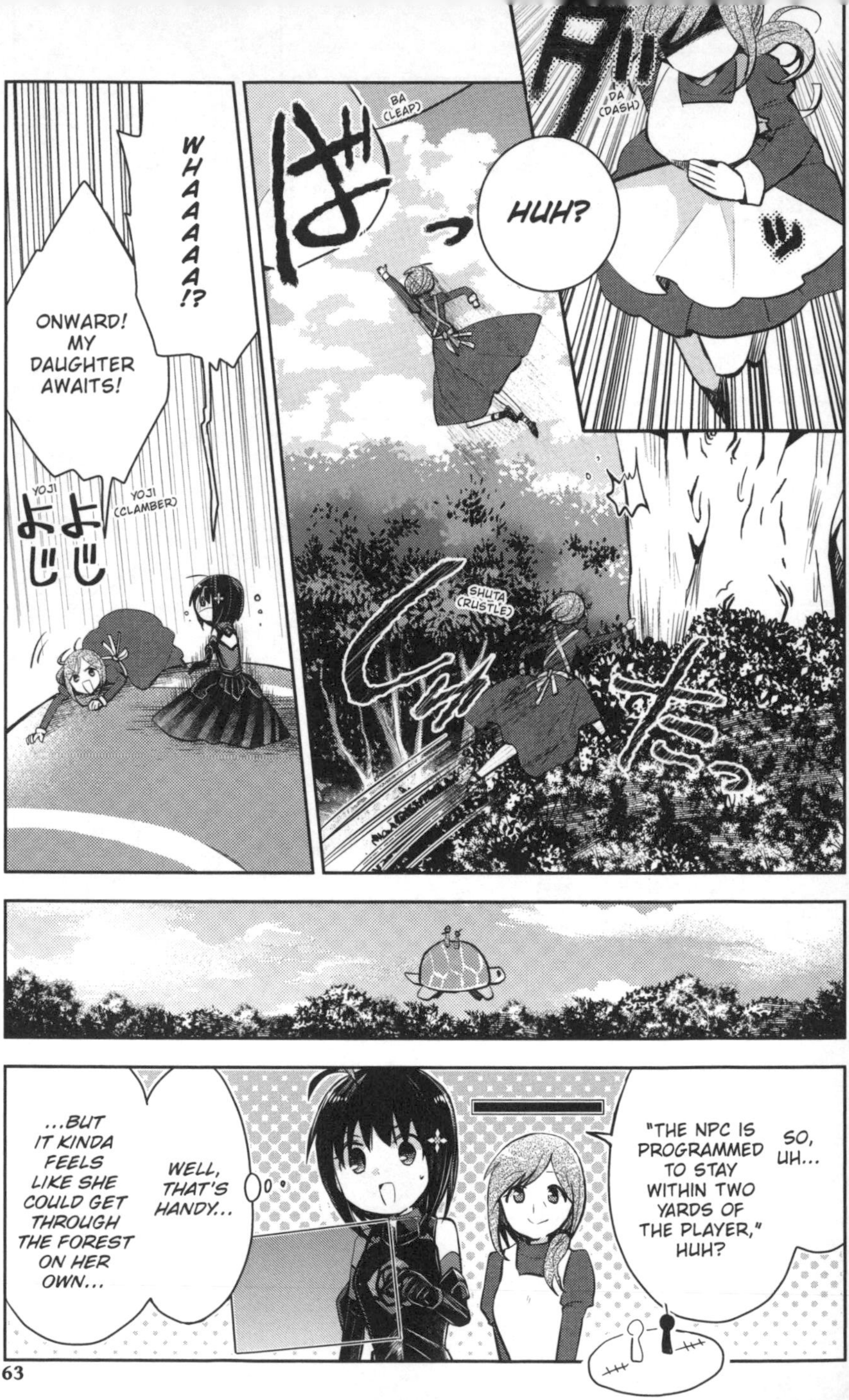
DA (DASH)
HUH?
BA (LEAP)
SHUTA (RUSTLE)
WHAAAAAA!?
ONWARD! MY DAUGHTER AWAITS!
よよじじ
YOJI
YOJI (CLAMBER)
SO, UH...
"THE NPC IS PROGRAMMED TO STAY WITHIN TWO YARDS OF THE PLAYER," HUH?
WELL, THAT'S HANDY...
...BUT IT KINDA FEELS LIKE SHE COULD GET THROUGH THE FOREST ON HER OWN...

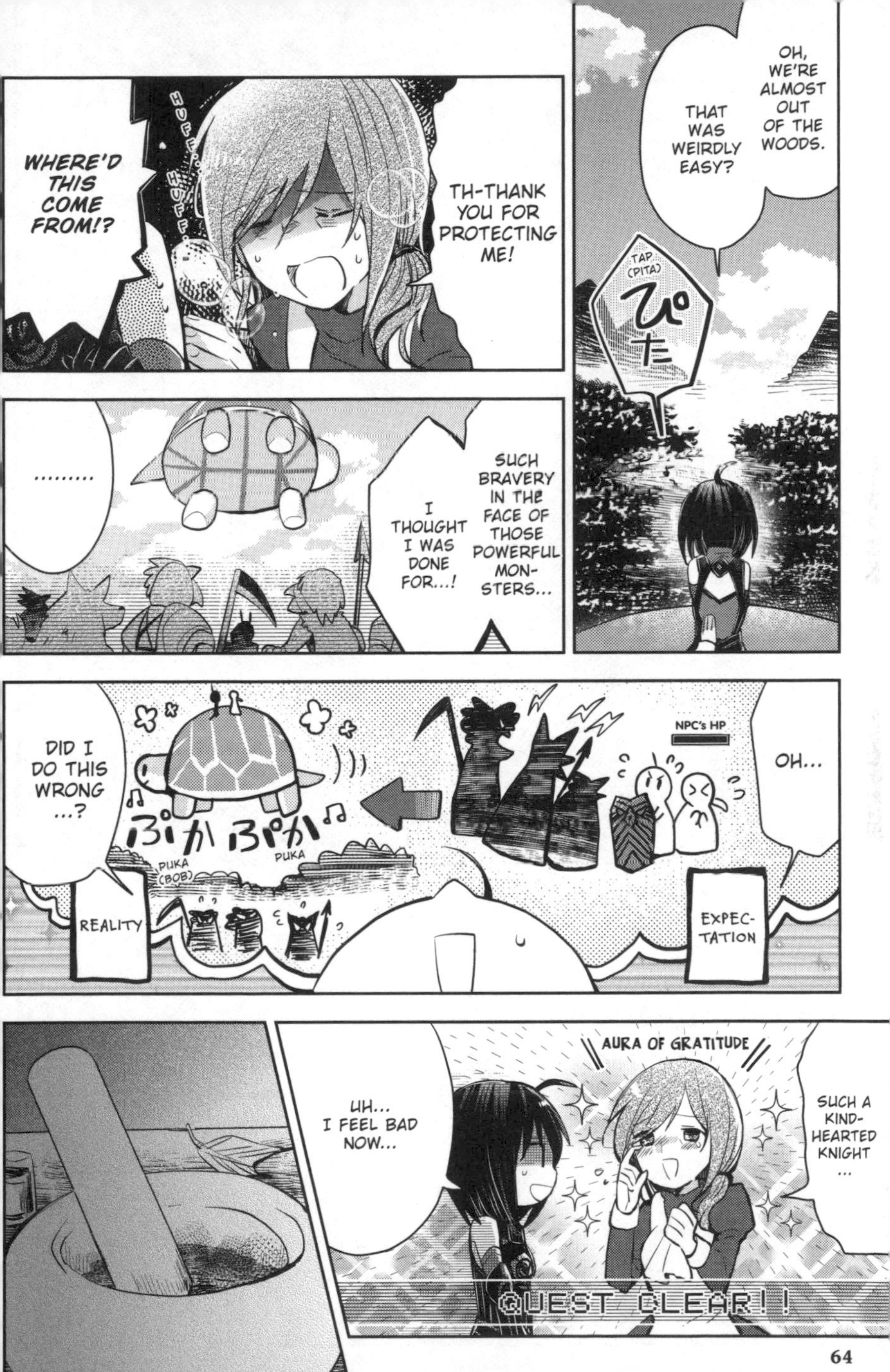
OH, WE'RE ALMOST OUT OF THE WOODS.
THAT WAS WEIRDLY EASY?
TAP (PITA)
ぴた
TH-THANK YOU FOR PROTECTING ME!
HUFF... HUFF...
WHERE'D THIS COME FROM!?
SUCH BRAVERY IN THE FACE OF THOSE POWERFUL MON-STERS...
I THOUGHT I WAS DONE FOR...!
....
OH...
NPC's HP
EXPECTATION
REALITY
ぷかぷか
PUKA (BOB)
PUKA
DID I DO THIS WRONG...?
SUCH A KIND-HEARTED KNIGHT...
AURA OF GRATITUDE
UH... I FEEL BAD NOW...
QUEST CLEAR!!

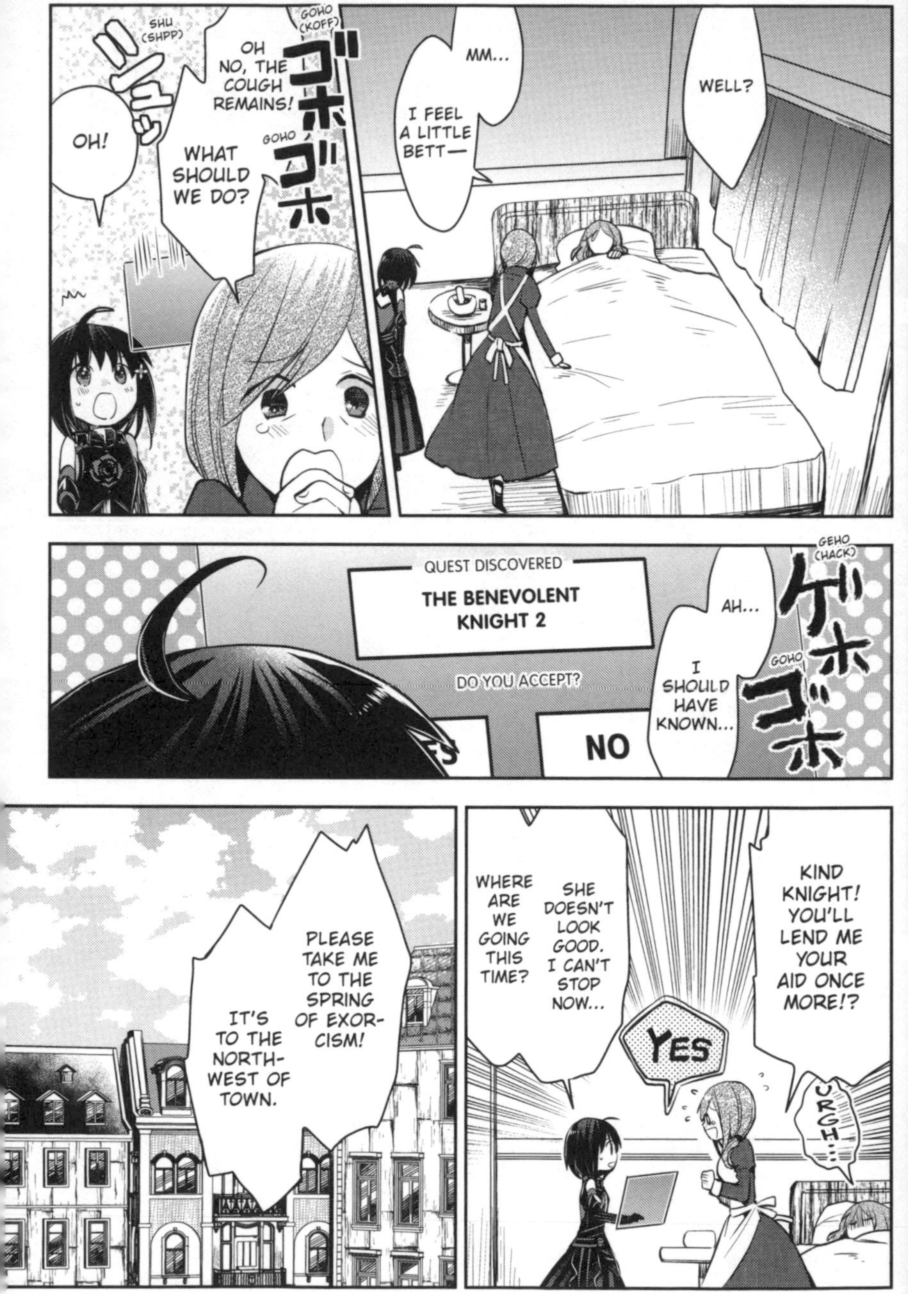
WELL?
MM... I FEEL A LITTLE BETT—
GOHO (KOFF)
OH NO, THE COUGH REMAINS!
GOHO
WHAT SHOULD WE DO?
SHU (SHPP)
OH!
GEHO (HACK)
GOHO
AH... I SHOULD HAVE KNOWN...
QUEST DISCOVERED
THE BENEVOLENT KNIGHT 2
DO YOU ACCEPT?
NO
KIND KNIGHT! YOU'LL LEND ME YOUR AID ONCE MORE!?
SHE DOESN'T LOOK GOOD. I CAN'T STOP NOW...
WHERE ARE WE GOING THIS TIME?
YES
URGH...
PLEASE TAKE ME TO THE SPRING OF EXORCISM!
IT'S TO THE NORTHWEST OF TOWN.

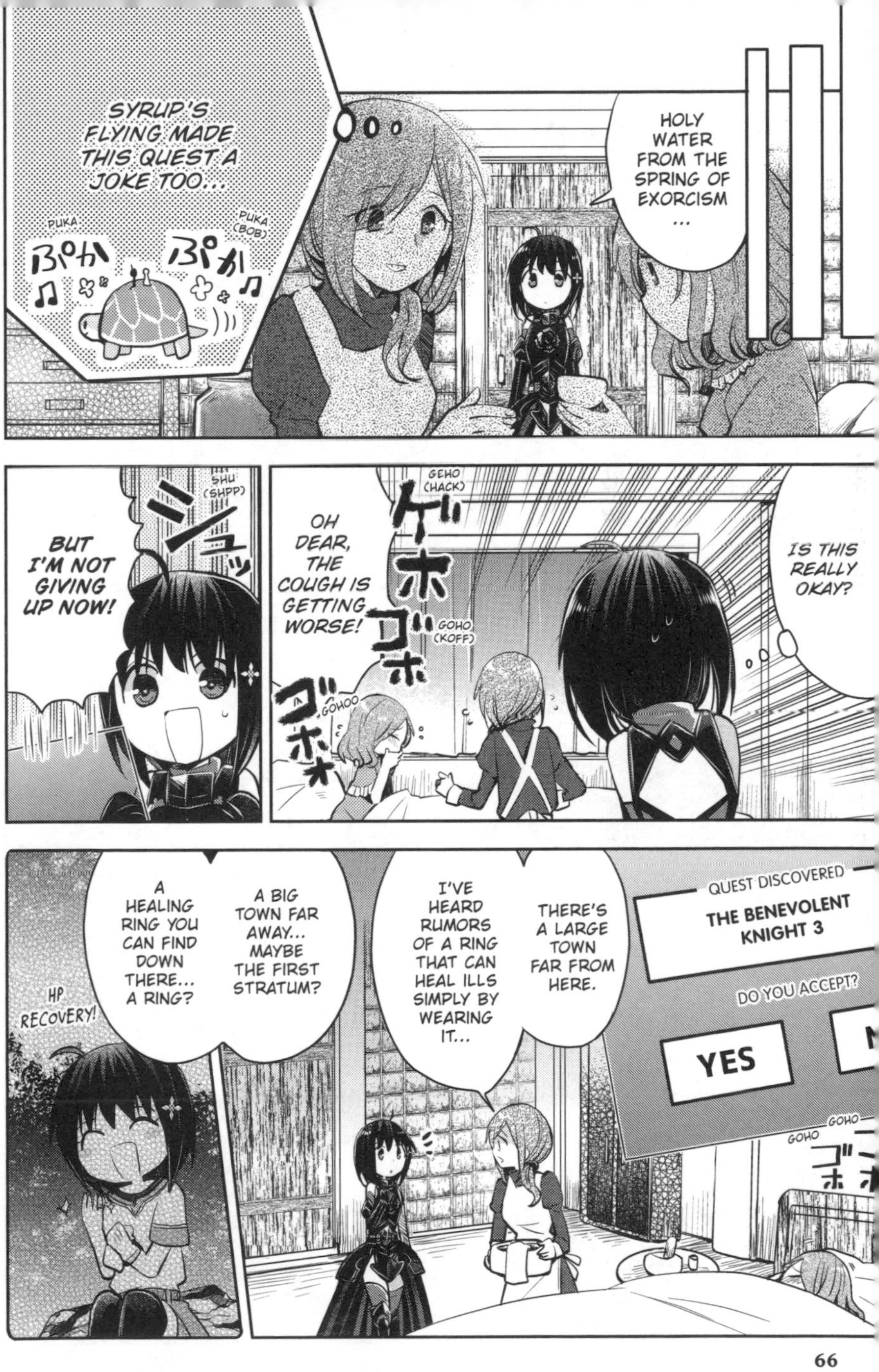
HOLY WATER FROM THE SPRING OF EXORCISM ...
SYRUP'S FLYING MADE THIS QUEST A JOKE TOO...
ぷか PUKA
ぷか PUKA (BOB)
IS THIS REALLY OKAY?
ゲホ GEHO (HACK)
OH DEAR, THE COUGH IS GETTING WORSE!
ゴホ GOHO (KOFF)
ゴホォ GOHOO
シュッ SHU (SHPP)
BUT I'M NOT GIVING UP NOW!
QUEST DISCOVERED
THE BENEVOLENT KNIGHT 3
DO YOU ACCEPT?
YES
THERE'S A LARGE TOWN FAR FROM HERE.
I'VE HEARD RUMORS OF A RING THAT CAN HEAL ILLS SIMPLY BY WEARING IT...
GOHO GOHO
A BIG TOWN FAR AWAY... MAYBE THE FIRST STRATUM?
A HEALING RING YOU CAN FIND DOWN THERE... A RING?
HP RECOVERY!

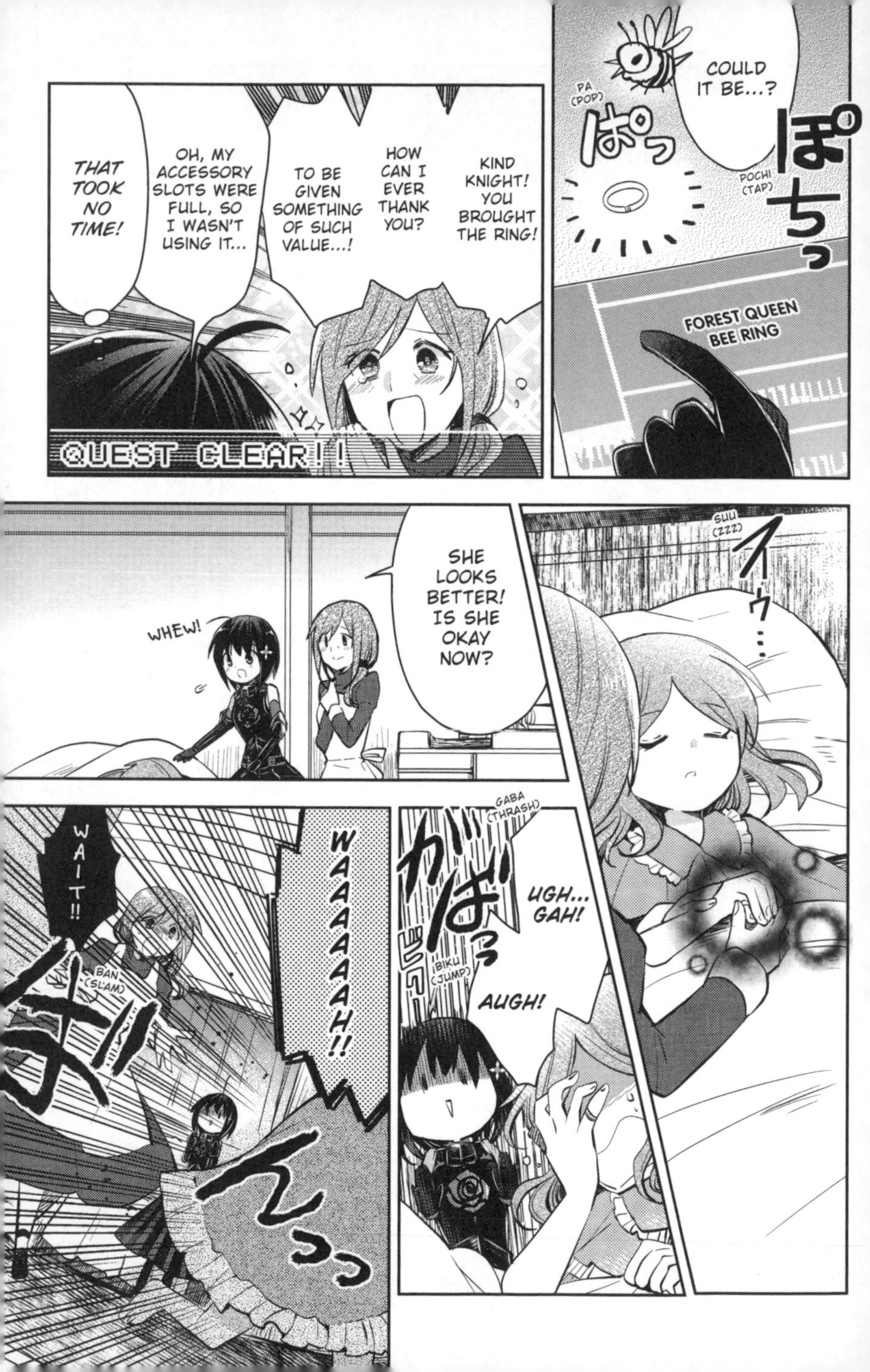
COULD IT BE...?
PA (POP)
ぱっ
POCHI (TAP)
ぽちっ
FOREST QUEEN BEE RING
KIND KNIGHT! YOU BROUGHT THE RING!
HOW CAN I EVER THANK YOU?
TO BE GIVEN SOMETHING OF SUCH VALUE...!
OH, MY ACCESSORY SLOTS WERE FULL, SO I WASN'T USING IT...
THAT TOOK NO TIME!
QUEST CLEAR!!
SUU (ZZZ)
スゥ…
SHE LOOKS BETTER! IS SHE OKAY NOW?
WHEW!
GABA (THRASH)
がばっ
UGH... GAH!
BIKU (JUMP)
ビクッ
AUGH!
WAAAAAAAH!!
WAIT!!
BAN (SLAM)
ばんっ

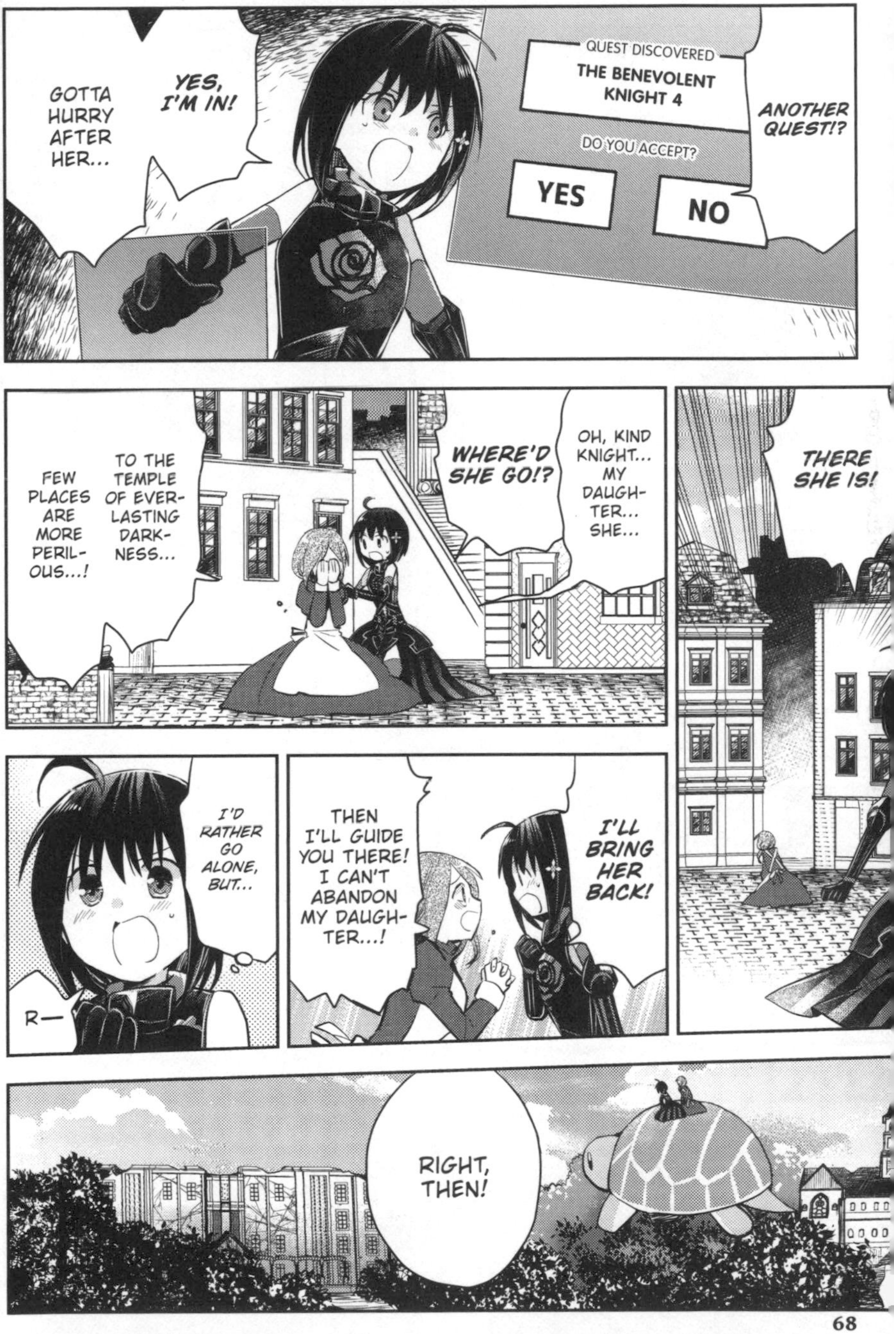
QUEST DISCOVERED
THE BENEVOLENT KNIGHT 4
DO YOU ACCEPT?
YES
NO
ANOTHER QUEST!?
YES, I'M IN!
GOTTA HURRY AFTER HER...
THERE SHE IS!
OH, KIND KNIGHT... MY DAUGHTER... SHE...
WHERE'D SHE GO!?
TO THE TEMPLE OF EVERLASTING DARKNESS...
FEW PLACES ARE MORE PERILOUS...!
I'LL BRING HER BACK!
THEN I'LL GUIDE YOU THERE! I CAN'T ABANDON MY DAUGHTER...!
I'D RATHER GO ALONE, BUT...
R—
RIGHT, THEN!

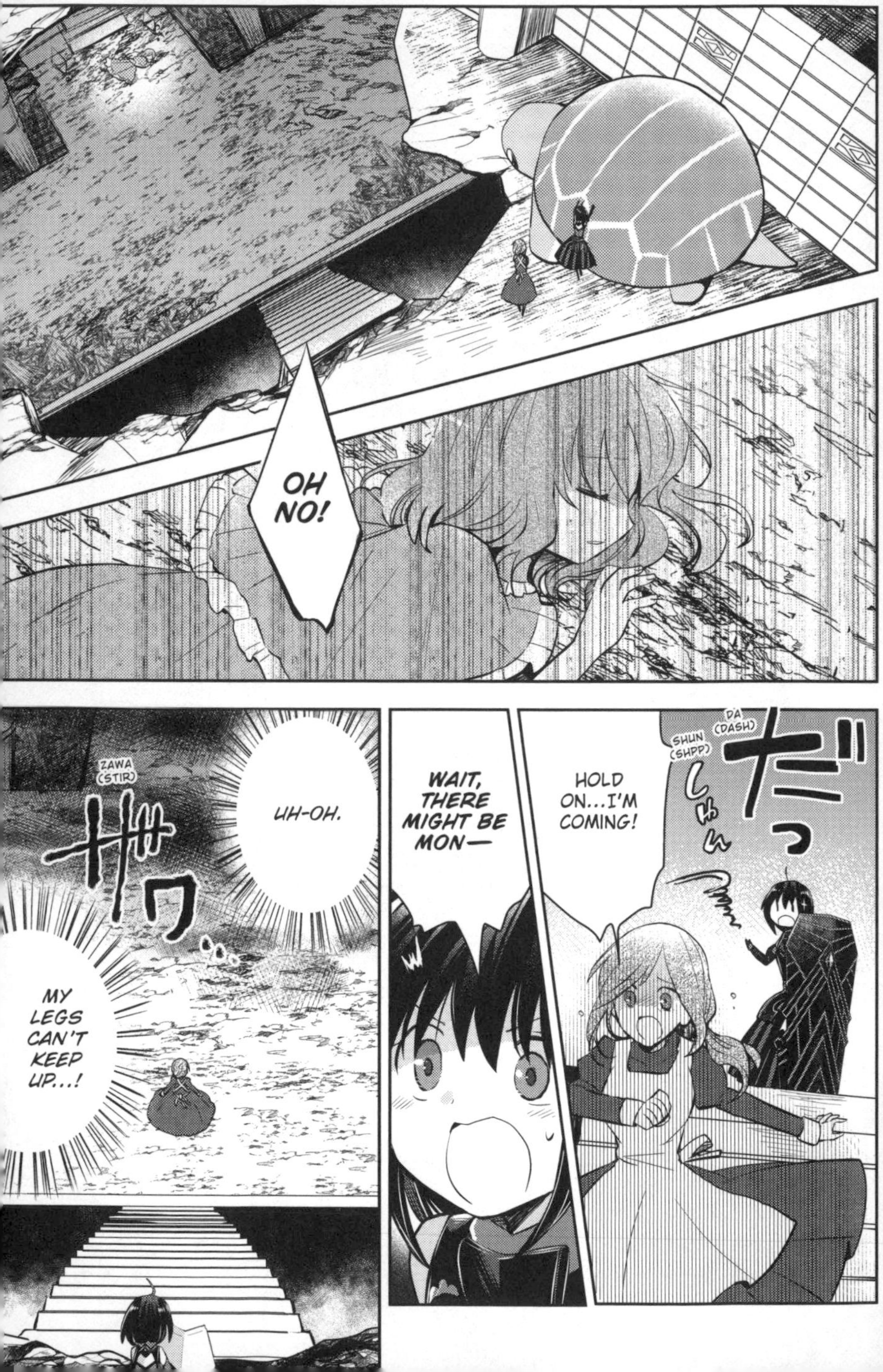
OH NO!
DA (DASH)
だっ
SHUN (SHPP)
しゅん
HOLD ON...I'M COMING!
WAIT, THERE MIGHT BE MON—
ZAWA (STIR)
ザワ
UH-OH.
MY LEGS CAN'T KEEP UP...!

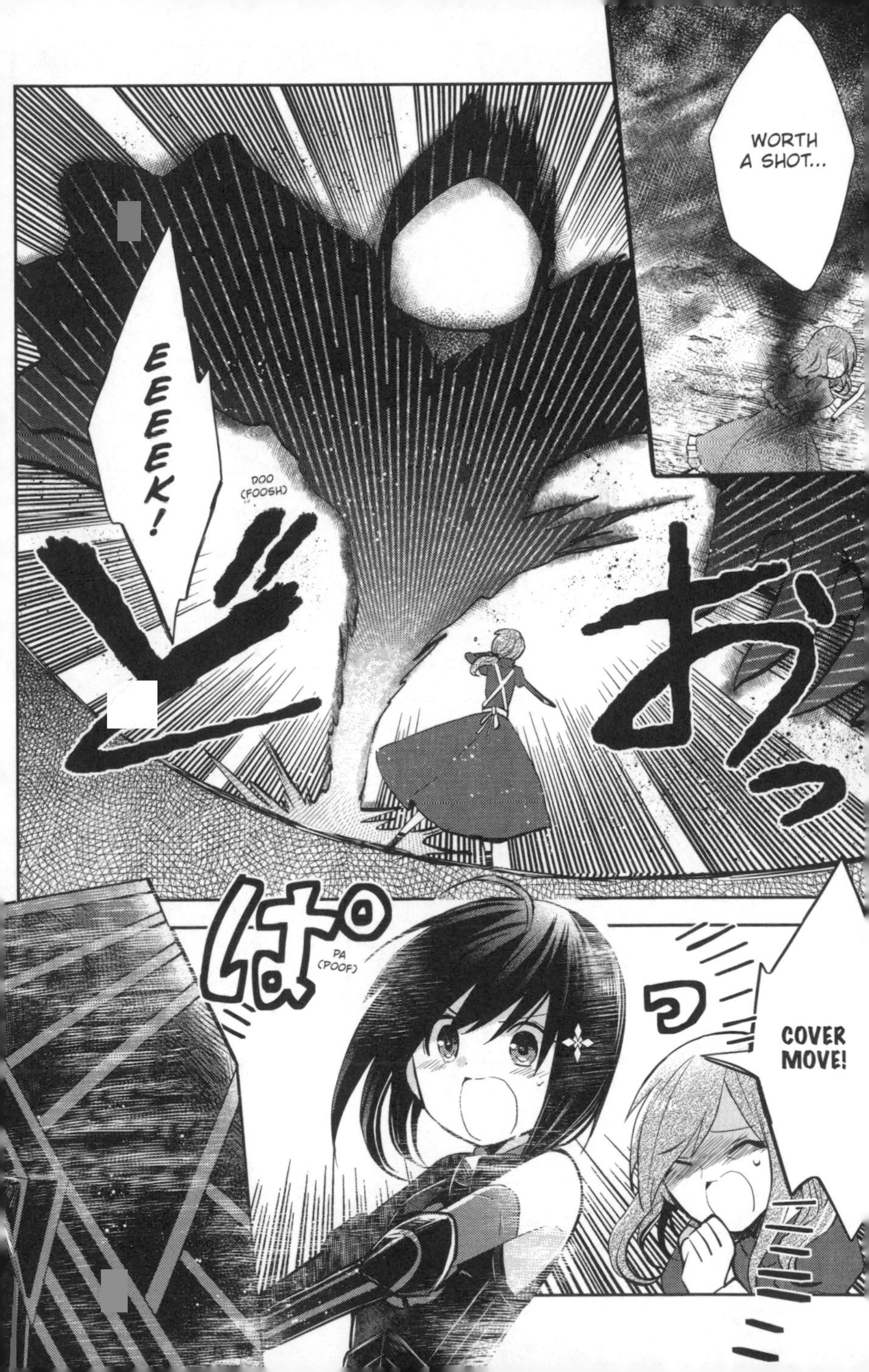
WORTH A SHOT...
EEEEK!
DOO (FOOSH)
どおっ
COVER MOVE!
ぱっ
PA (POOF)

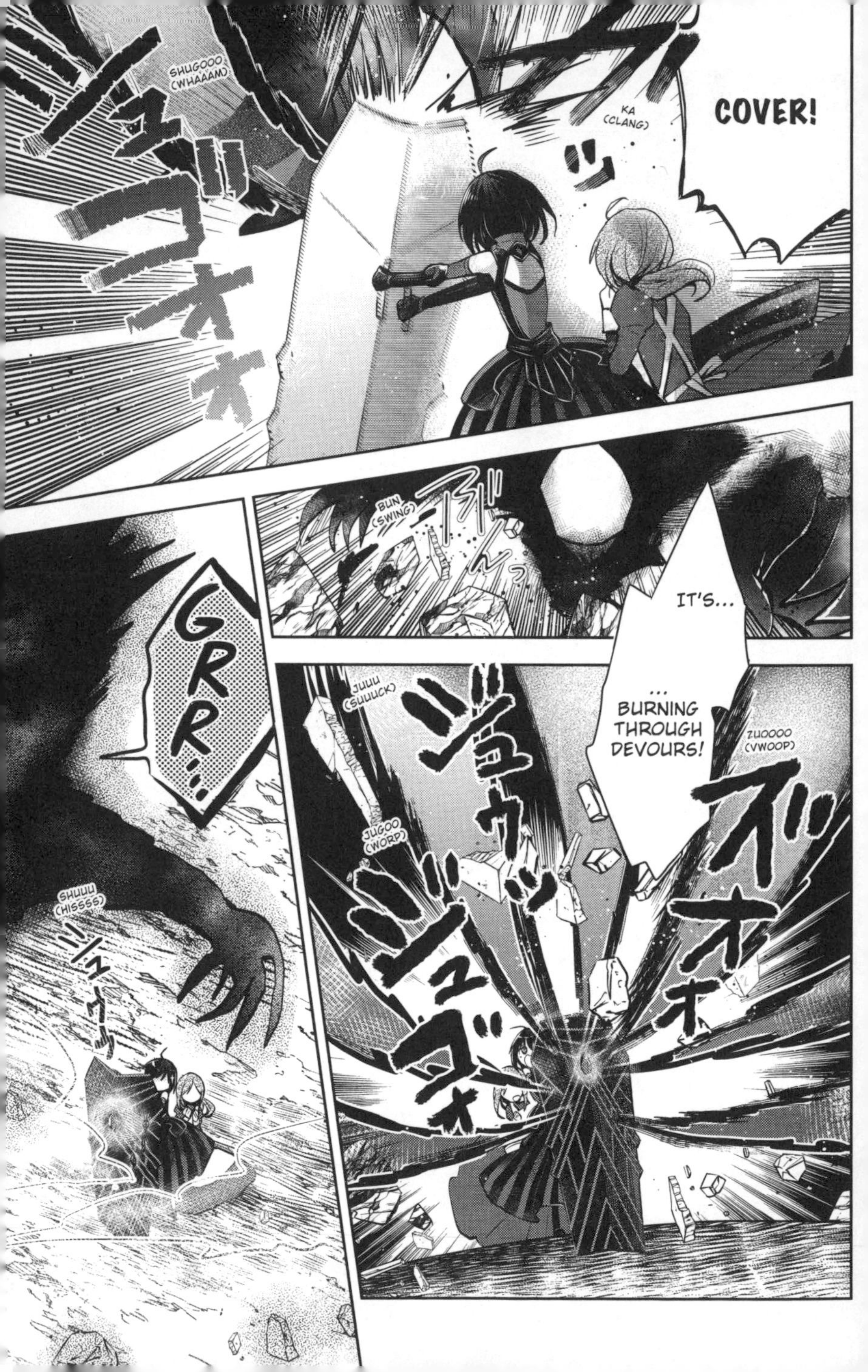
COVER!
KA (CLANG)
SHUGOOO (WHAAAM)
BUN (SWING)
IT'S...
... BURNING THROUGH DEVOURS!
ZUOOOO (VWOOP)
JUUU (SUUUCK)
JUGOO (WORP)
GRR...
SHUUU (HISSSS)

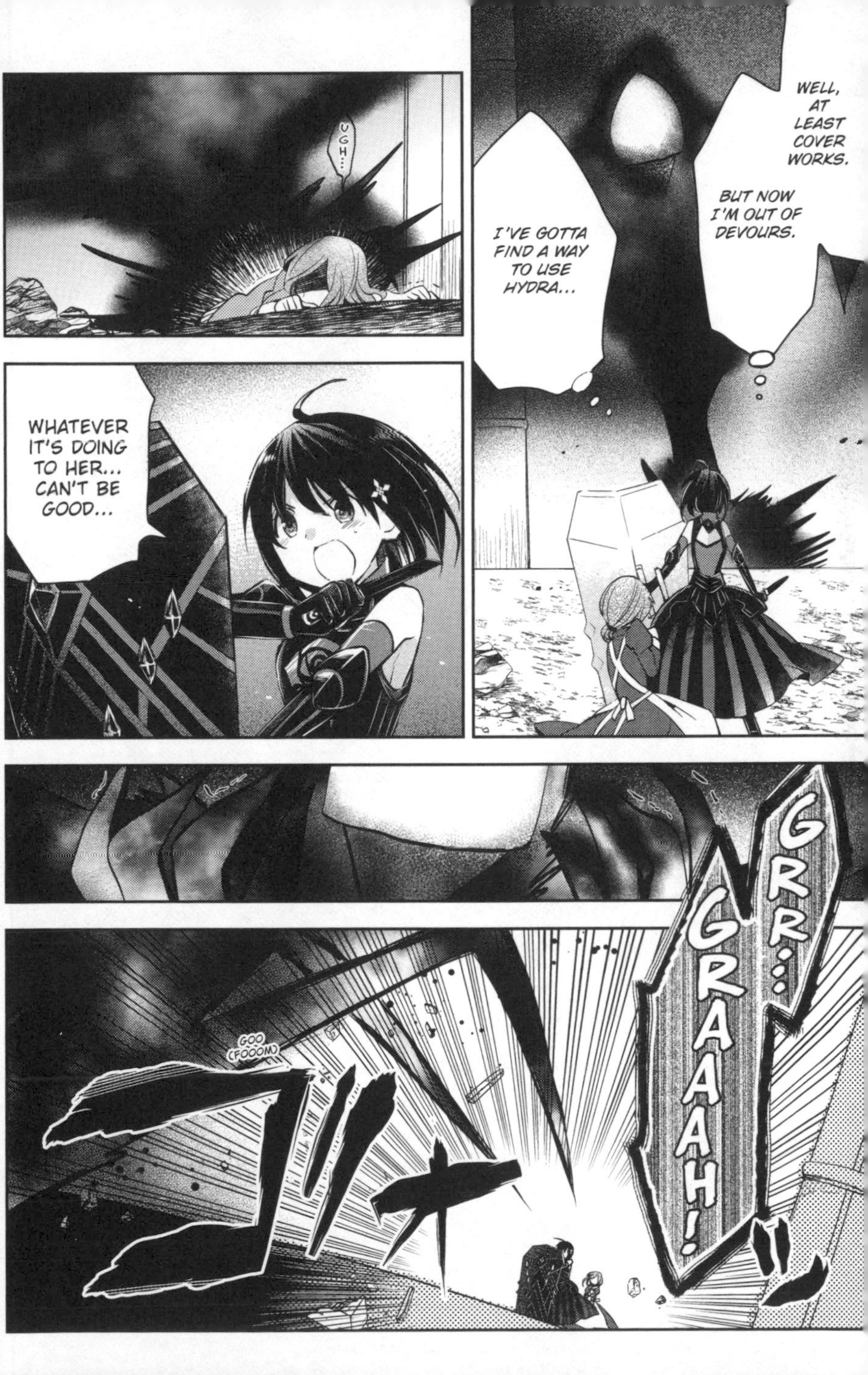
WELL, AT LEAST COVER WORKS.
BUT NOW I'M OUT OF DEVOURS.
I'VE GOTTA FIND A WAY TO USE HYDRA...
UGH...
WHATEVER IT'S DOING TO HER... CAN'T BE GOOD...
GRR...
GRAAAH!
GOO (FOOOM)

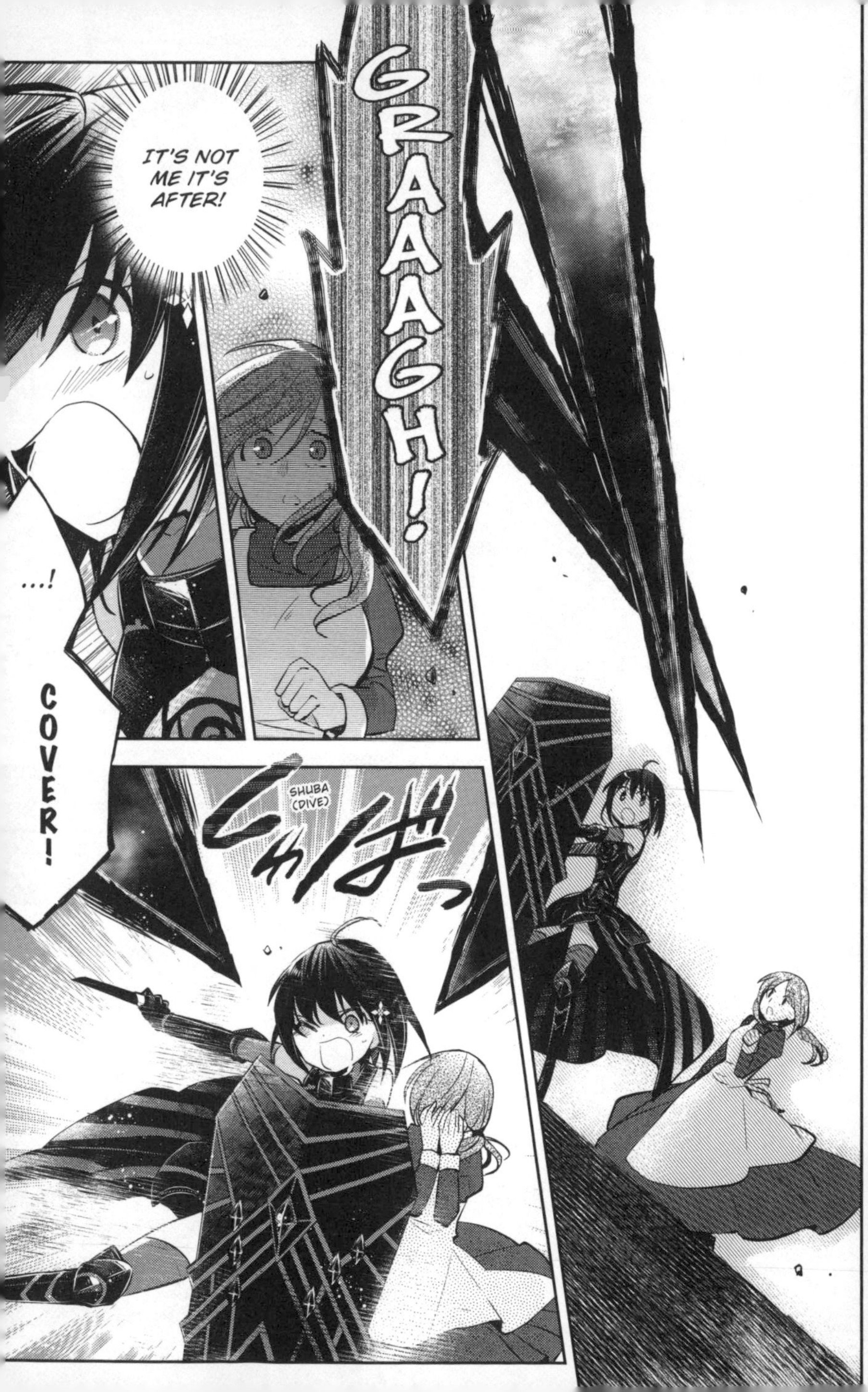

GRAAAGH!
IT'S NOT ME IT'S AFTER!
...!
しゅばっ
SHUBA (DIVE)
COVER!

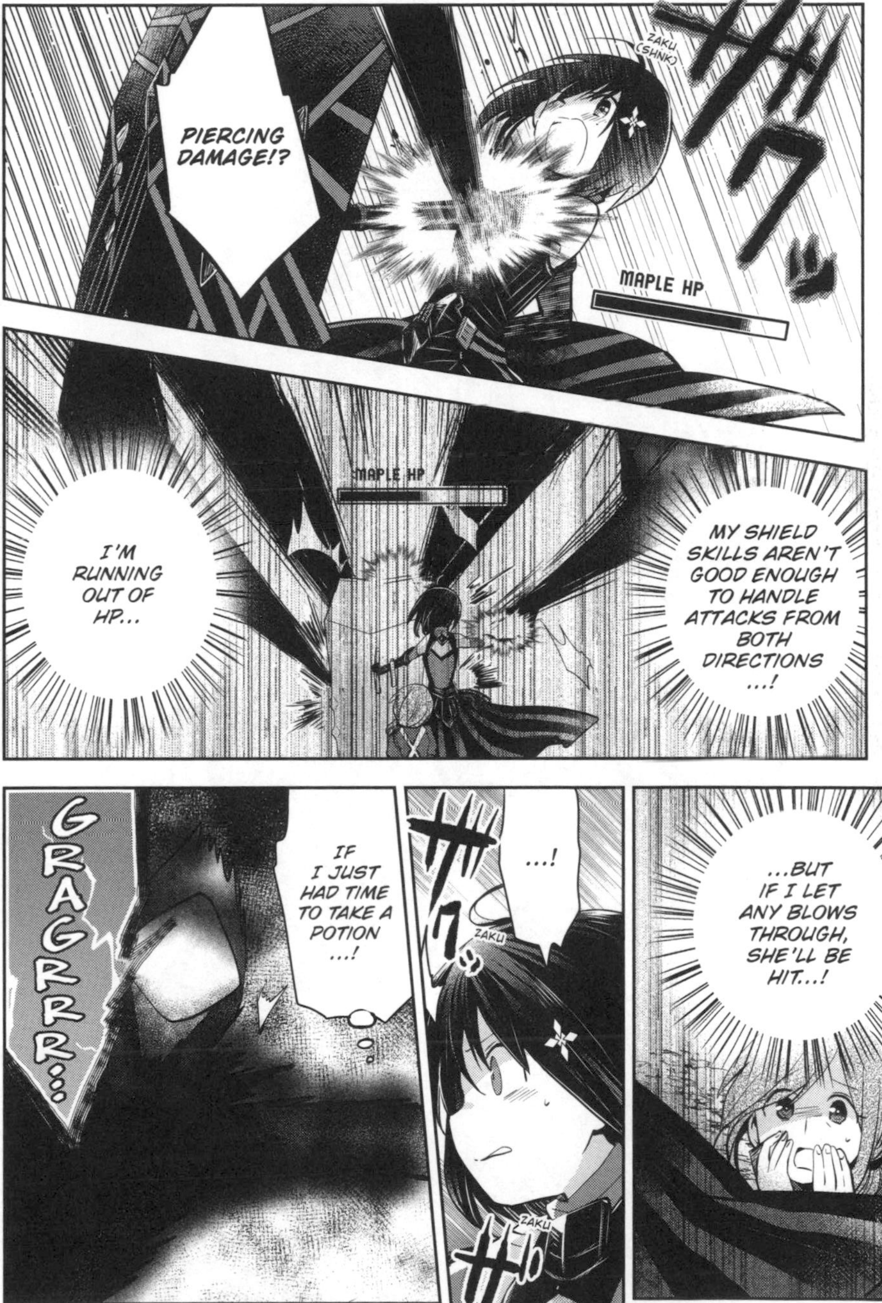
ZAKU (SHNK)
PIERCING DAMAGE!?
MAPLE HP
MAPLE HP
MY SHIELD SKILLS AREN'T GOOD ENOUGH TO HANDLE ATTACKS FROM BOTH DIRECTIONS ...!
I'M RUNNING OUT OF HP...
...BUT IF I LET ANY BLOWS THROUGH, SHE'LL BE HIT...!
...!
ZAKU
ZAKU
IF I JUST HAD TIME TO TAKE A POTION ...!
GRAGRRR..

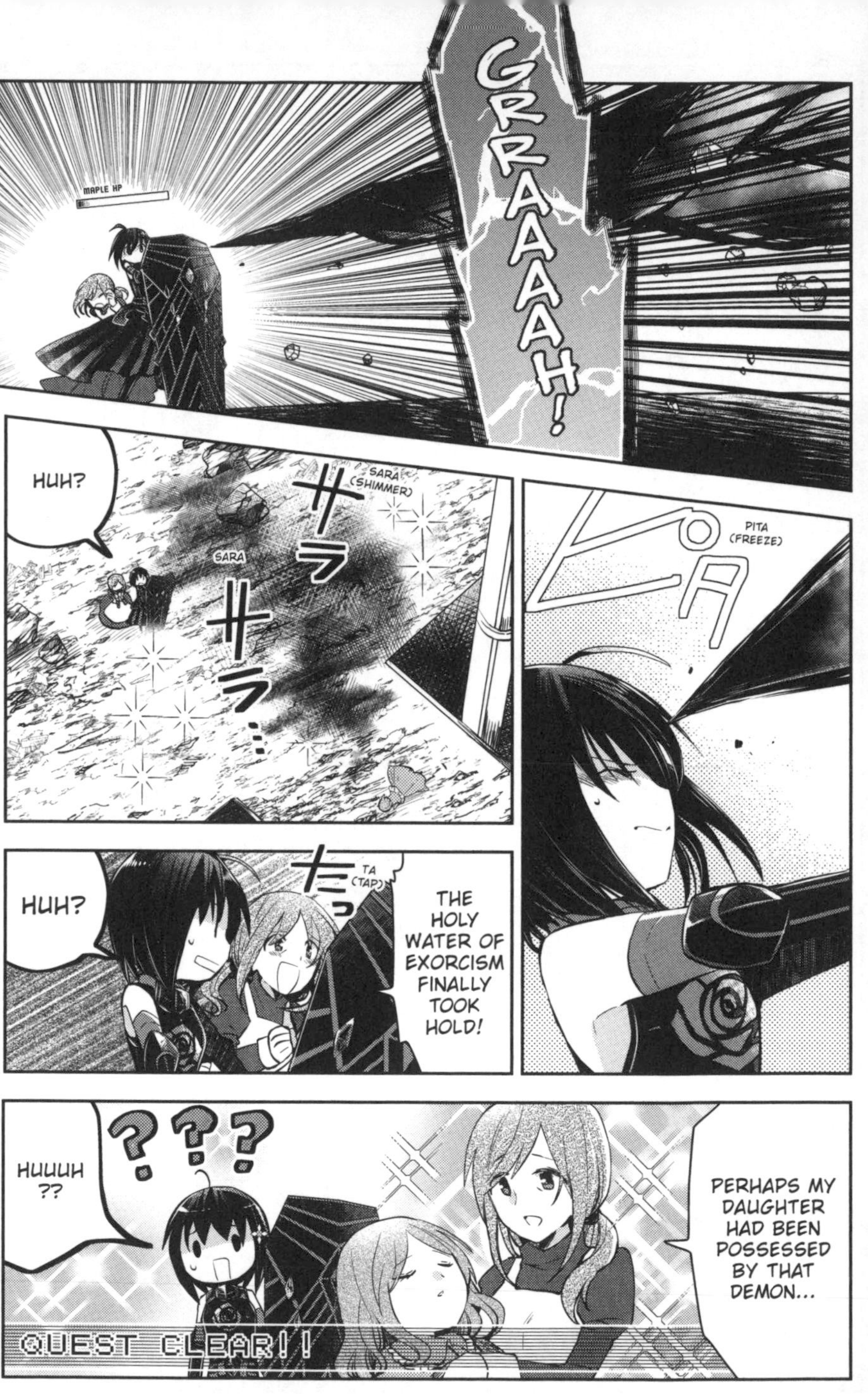
GRRAAAAH!
MAPLE HP
PITA (FREEZE)
SARA (SHIMMER)
SARA
HUH?
TA (TAP)
THE HOLY WATER OF EXORCISM FINALLY TOOK HOLD!
HUH?
PERHAPS MY DAUGHTER HAD BEEN POSSESSED BY THAT DEMON...
???
HUUUH ??
QUEST CLEAR!!

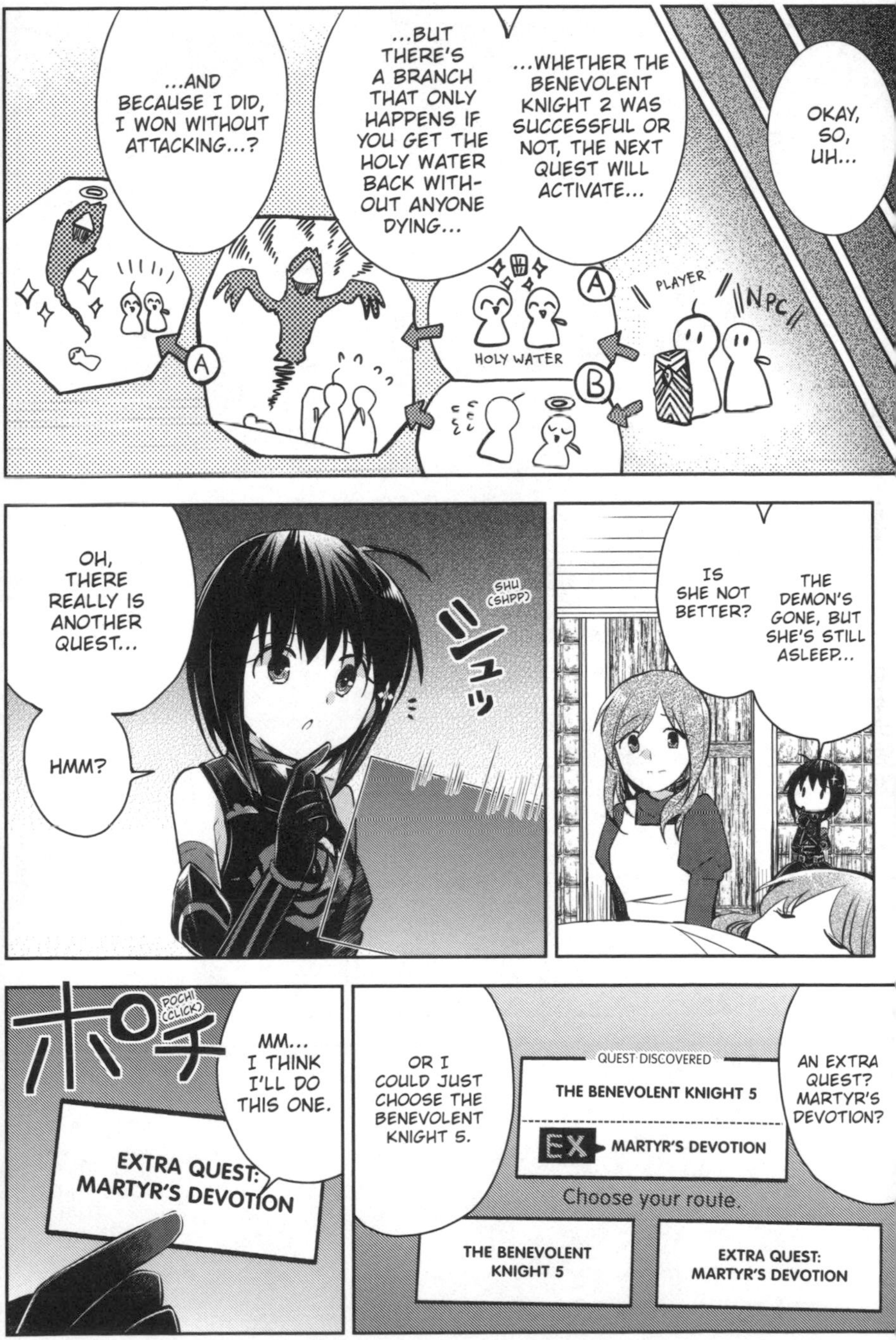
OKAY, SO, UH...
...WHETHER THE BENEVOLENT KNIGHT 2 WAS SUCCESSFUL OR NOT, THE NEXT QUEST WILL ACTIVATE...
PLAYER
NPC
A
B
HOLY WATER
...BUT THERE'S A BRANCH THAT ONLY HAPPENS IF YOU GET THE HOLY WATER BACK WITH-OUT ANYONE DYING...
A
...AND BECAUSE I DID, I WON WITHOUT ATTACKING...?
THE DEMON'S GONE, BUT SHE'S STILL ASLEEP...
IS SHE NOT BETTER?
OH, THERE REALLY IS ANOTHER QUEST...
SHU (SHPP)
HMM?
AN EXTRA QUEST? MARTYR'S DEVOTION?
QUEST DISCOVERED
THE BENEVOLENT KNIGHT 5
EX MARTYR'S DEVOTION
Choose your route.
THE BENEVOLENT KNIGHT 5
EXTRA QUEST: MARTYR'S DEVOTION
OR I COULD JUST CHOOSE THE BENEVOLENT KNIGHT 5.
MM... I THINK I'LL DO THIS ONE.
POCHI (CLICK)
EXTRA QUEST: MARTYR'S DEVOTION

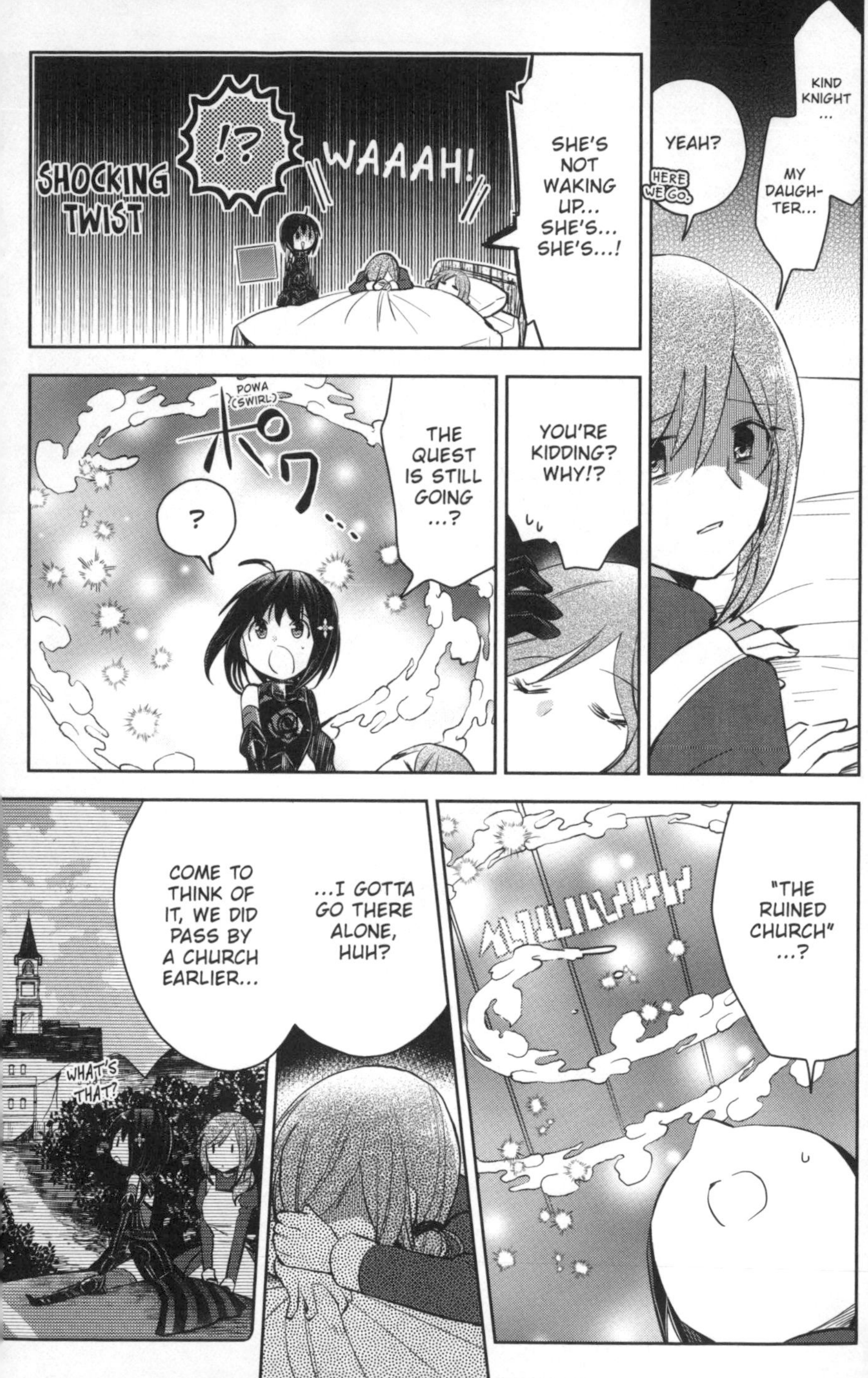
KIND KNIGHT...
MY DAUGH-TER...
YEAH?
HERE WE GO.
SHE'S NOT WAKING UP... SHE'S... SHE'S...!
WAAAH!
!?
SHOCKING TWIST
YOU'RE KIDDING? WHY!?
THE QUEST IS STILL GOING ...?
POWA (SWIRL)
?
"THE RUINED CHURCH" ...?
...I GOTTA GO THERE ALONE, HUH?
COME TO THINK OF IT, WE DID PASS BY A CHURCH EARLIER...
WHAT'S THAT?

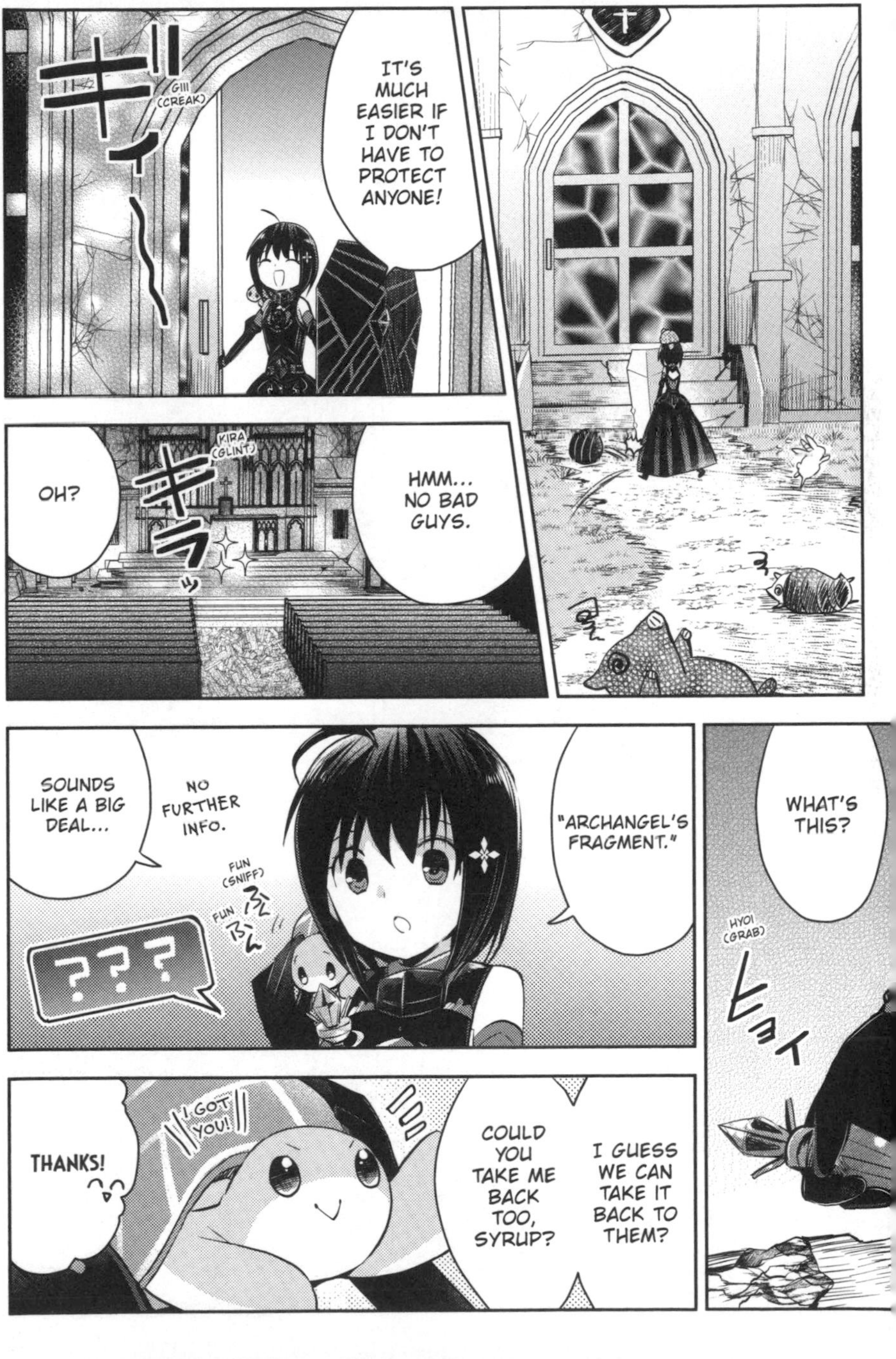
GIII (CREAK)
IT'S MUCH EASIER IF I DON'T HAVE TO PROTECT ANYONE!
HMM... NO BAD GUYS.
KIRA (GLINT)
OH?
WHAT'S THIS?
HYOI (GRAB)
"ARCHANGEL'S FRAGMENT."
NO FURTHER INFO.
SOUNDS LIKE A BIG DEAL...
FUN (SNIFF)
FUN
???
I GUESS WE CAN TAKE IT BACK TO THEM?
COULD YOU TAKE ME BACK TOO, SYRUP?
I GOT YOU!
THANKS!

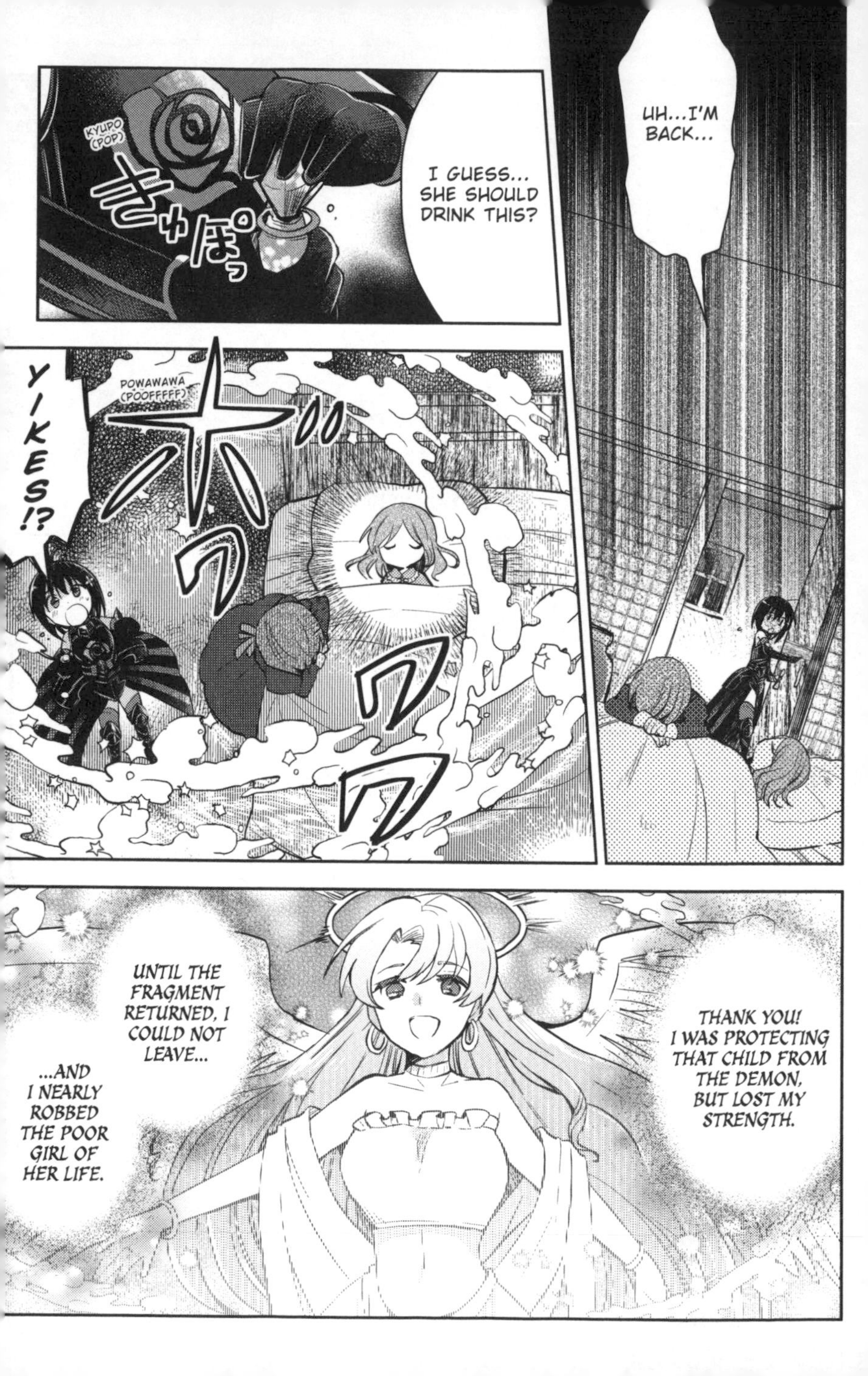
UH...I'M BACK...
I GUESS... SHE SHOULD DRINK THIS?
KYUPO (POP)
きゅぽっ
POWAWAWA (POOFFFFF)
YIKES!?
THANK YOU! I WAS PROTECTING THAT CHILD FROM THE DEMON, BUT LOST MY STRENGTH.
UNTIL THE FRAGMENT RETURNED, I COULD NOT LEAVE...
...AND I NEARLY ROBBED THE POOR GIRL OF HER LIFE.

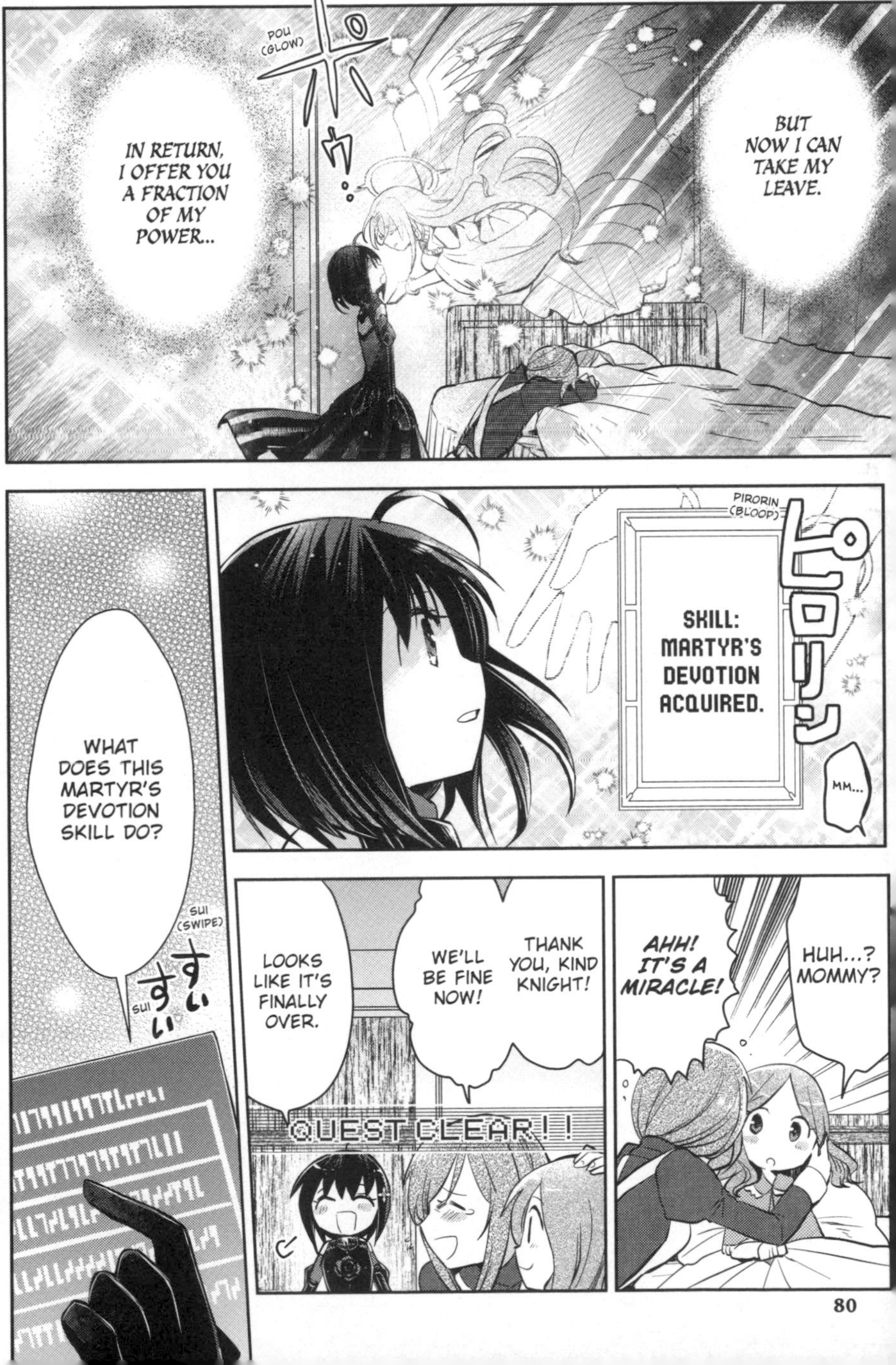
BUT NOW I CAN TAKE MY LEAVE.
POU (GLOW)
IN RETURN, I OFFER YOU A FRACTION OF MY POWER...
PIRORIN (BLOOP)
SKILL: MARTYR'S DEVOTION ACQUIRED.
MM...
HUH...? MOMMY?
AHH! IT'S A MIRACLE!
THANK YOU, KIND KNIGHT!
WE'LL BE FINE NOW!
LOOKS LIKE IT'S FINALLY OVER.
QUEST CLEAR!!
WHAT DOES THIS MARTYR'S DEVOTION SKILL DO?
SUI (SWIPE)
SUI

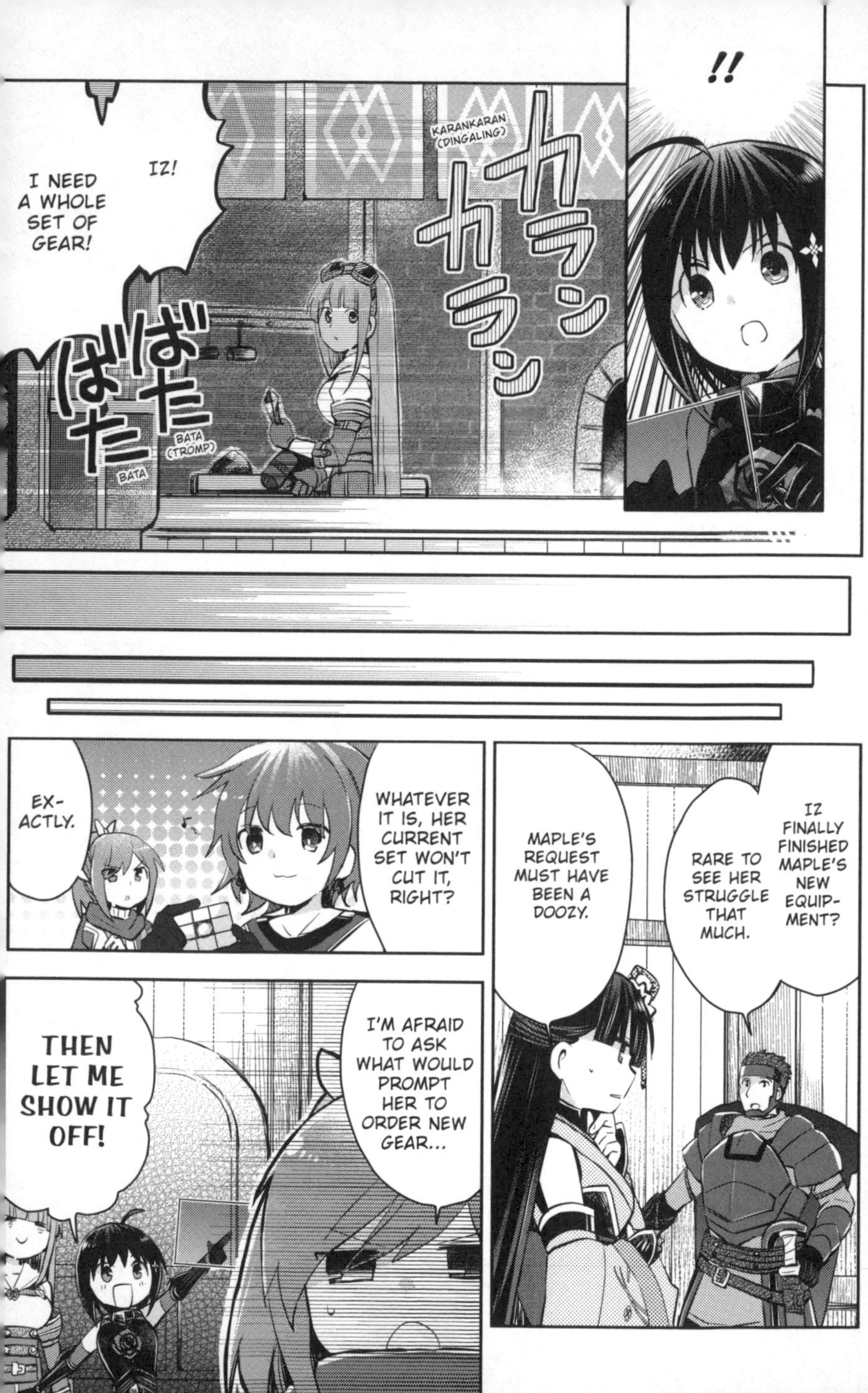
!!
カランカラン
KARANKARAN (DINGALING)
IZ!
I NEED A WHOLE SET OF GEAR!
ばたばた
BATA (TROMP)
BATA
IZ FINALLY FINISHED MAPLE'S NEW EQUIPMENT?
RARE TO SEE HER STRUGGLE THAT MUCH.
MAPLE'S REQUEST MUST HAVE BEEN A DOOZY.
WHATEVER IT IS, HER CURRENT SET WON'T CUT IT, RIGHT?
EX-ACTLY.
I'M AFRAID TO ASK WHAT WOULD PROMPT HER TO ORDER NEW GEAR...
THEN LET ME SHOW IT OFF!

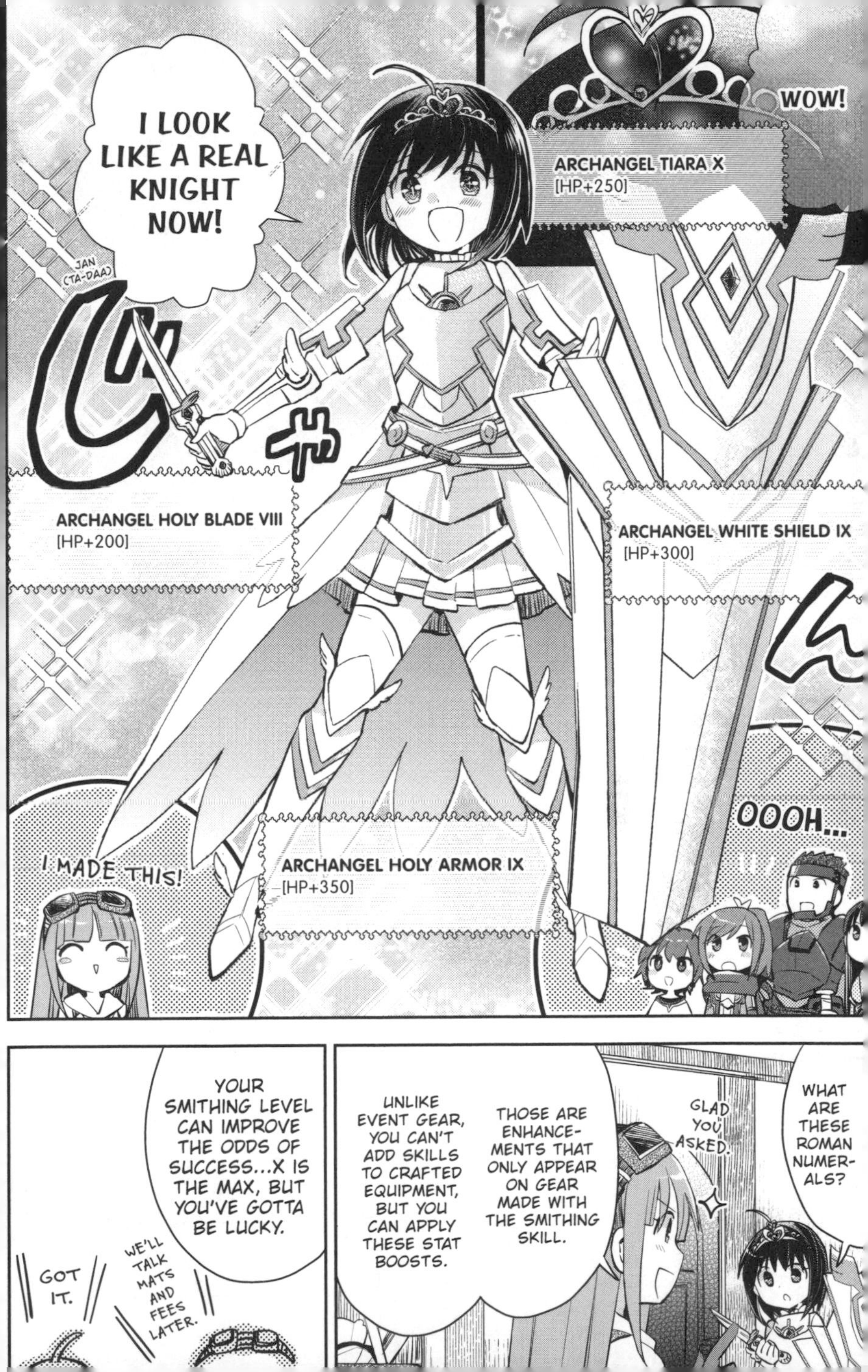
WOW!
ARCHANGEL TIARA X
[HP+250]
I LOOK LIKE A REAL KNIGHT NOW!
JAN (TA-DAA)
ARCHANGEL WHITE SHIELD IX
[HP+300]
ARCHANGEL HOLY BLADE VIII
[HP+200]
OOOH...
ARCHANGEL HOLY ARMOR IX
[HP+350]
I MADE THIS!
WHAT ARE THESE ROMAN NUMERALS?
GLAD YOU ASKED.
THOSE ARE ENHANCEMENTS THAT ONLY APPEAR ON GEAR MADE WITH THE SMITHING SKILL.
UNLIKE EVENT GEAR, YOU CAN'T ADD SKILLS TO CRAFTED EQUIPMENT, BUT YOU CAN APPLY THESE STAT BOOSTS.
YOUR SMITHING LEVEL CAN IMPROVE THE ODDS OF SUCCESS...X IS THE MAX, BUT YOU'VE GOTTA BE LUCKY.
WE'LL TALK MATS AND FEES LATER.
GOT IT.

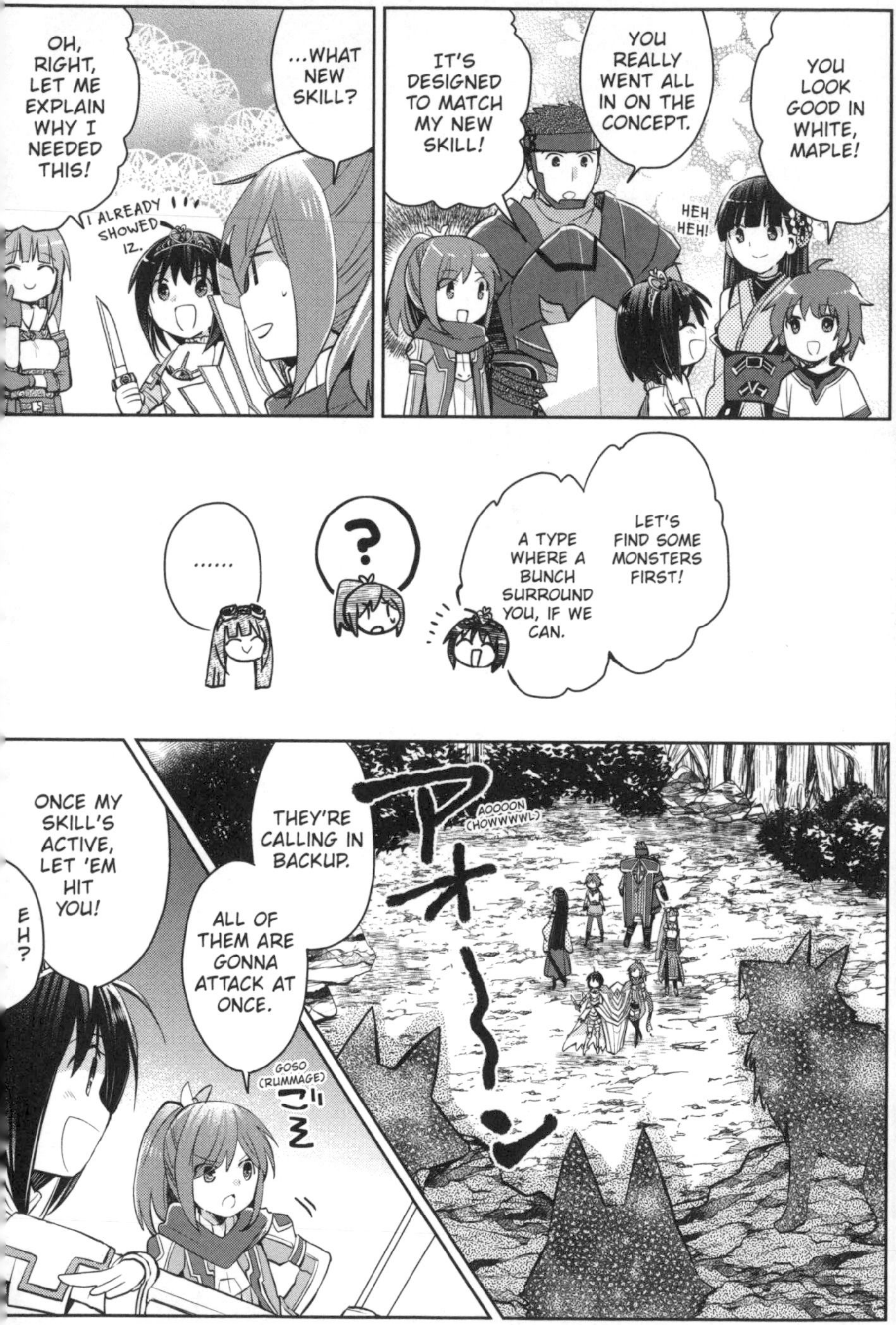
YOU LOOK GOOD IN WHITE, MAPLE!
HEH HEH!
YOU REALLY WENT ALL IN ON THE CONCEPT.
IT'S DESIGNED TO MATCH MY NEW SKILL!
...WHAT NEW SKILL?
OH, RIGHT, LET ME EXPLAIN WHY I NEEDED THIS!
I ALREADY SHOWED IZ.
LET'S FIND SOME MONSTERS FIRST!
A TYPE WHERE A BUNCH SURROUND YOU, IF WE CAN.
?
......
アオ〜ン
AOOOON (HOWWWWL)
THEY'RE CALLING IN BACKUP.
ALL OF THEM ARE GONNA ATTACK AT ONCE.
GOSO (RUMMAGE)
ごそ
ONCE MY SKILL'S ACTIVE, LET 'EM HIT YOU!
EH?

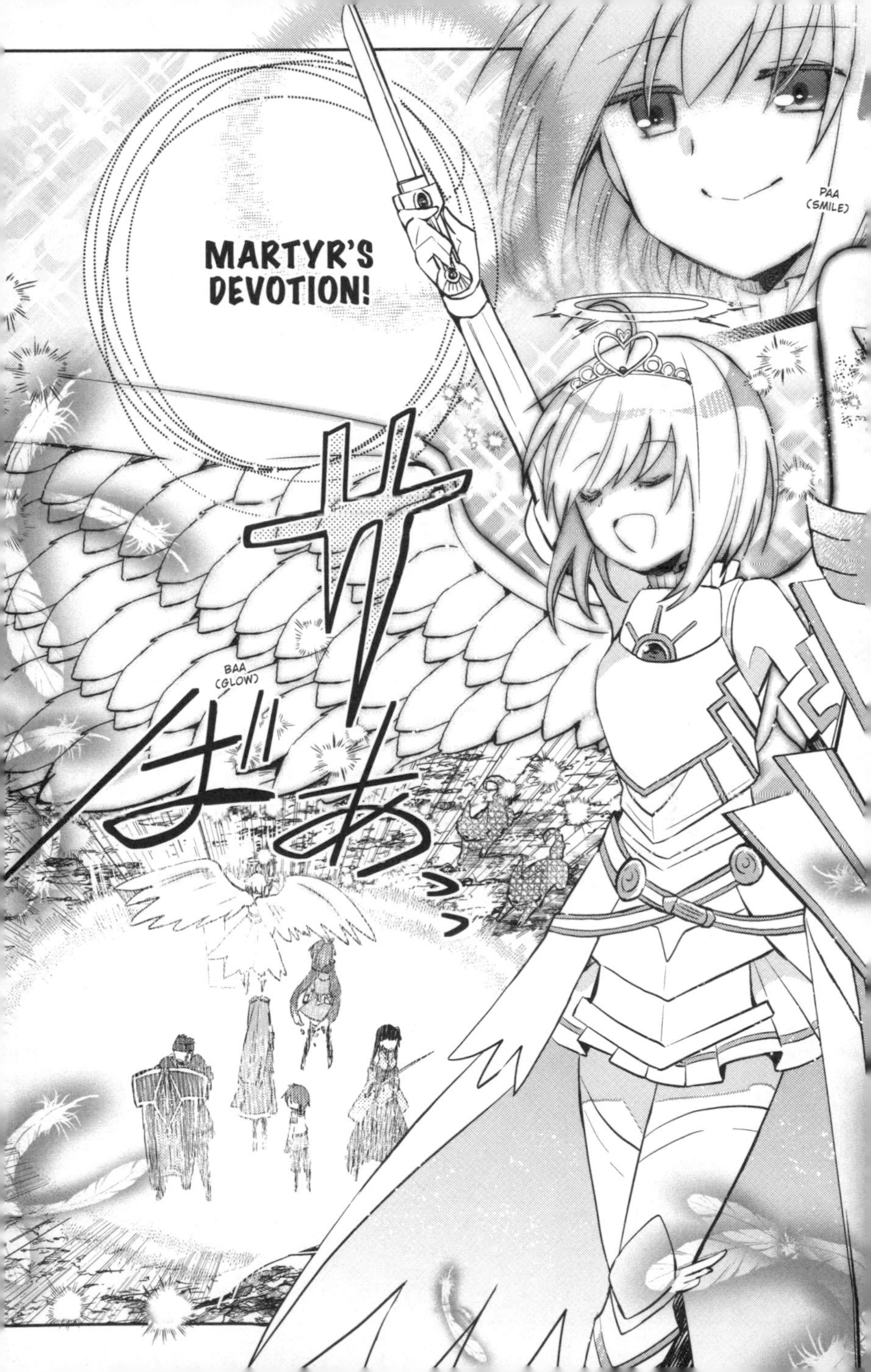
PAA (SMILE)
MARTYR'S DEVOTION!
BAA (GLOW)
ばあっ

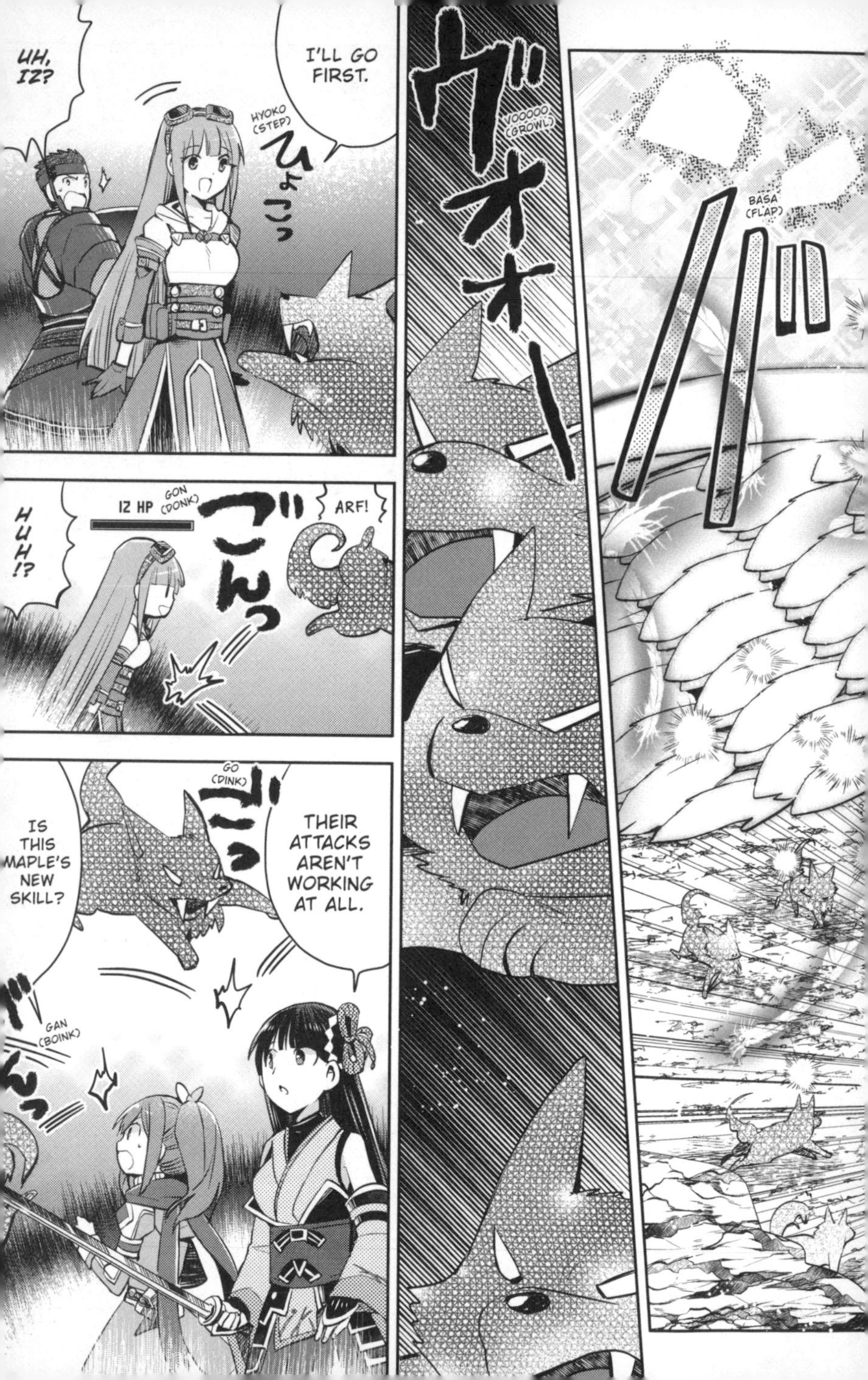
BASA (FLAP)
VOOOOO (GROWL)
I'LL GO FIRST.
HYOKO (STEP)
UH, IZ?
ARF!
GON (DONK)
IZ HP
HUH!?
GO (DINK)
THEIR ATTACKS AREN'T WORKING AT ALL.
IS THIS MAPLE'S NEW SKILL?
GAN (BOINK)

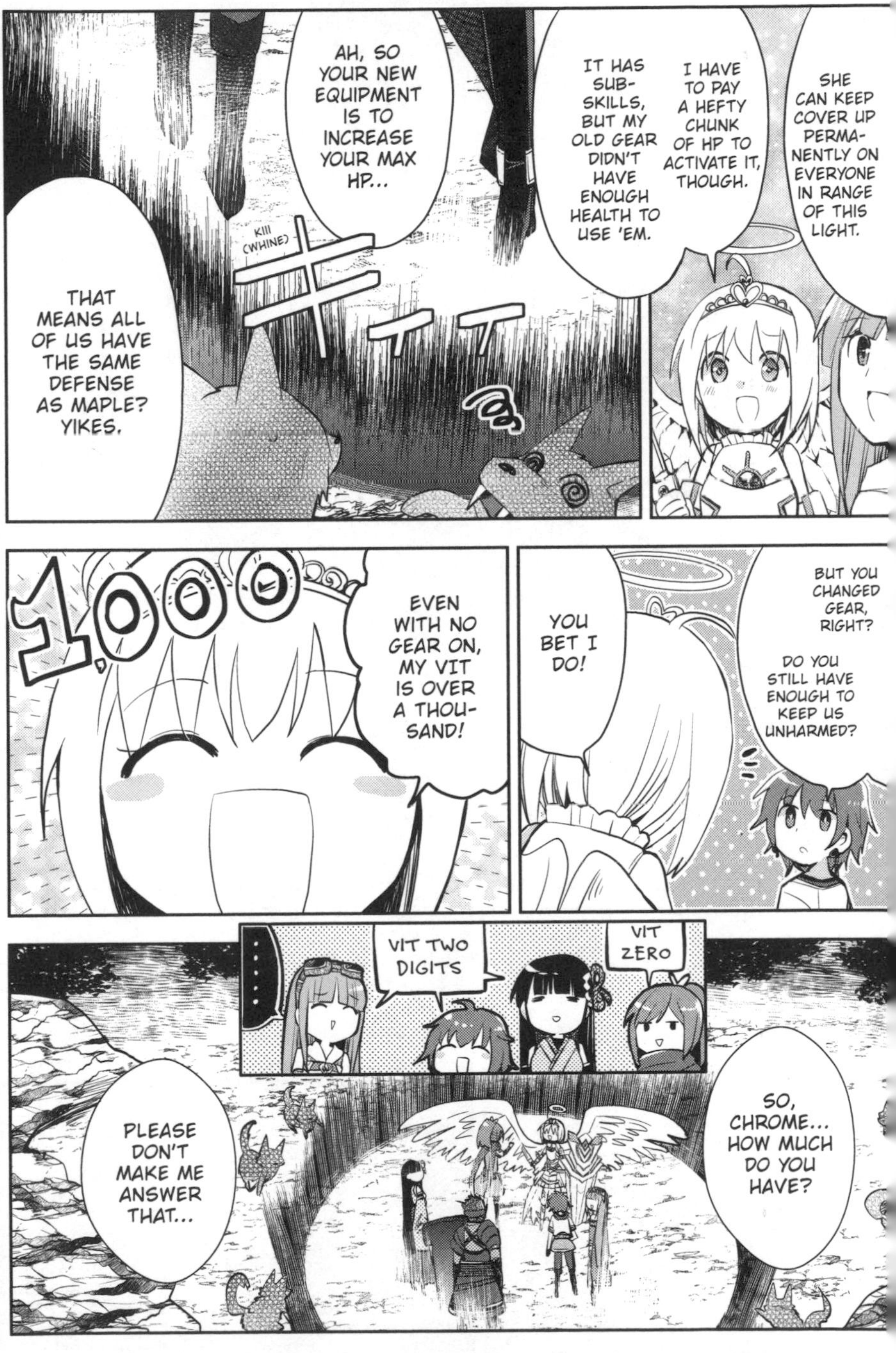
SHE CAN KEEP COVER UP PERMANENTLY ON EVERYONE IN RANGE OF THIS LIGHT.
I HAVE TO PAY A HEFTY CHUNK OF HP TO ACTIVATE IT, THOUGH.
IT HAS SUB-SKILLS, BUT MY OLD GEAR DIDN'T HAVE ENOUGH HEALTH TO USE 'EM.
AH, SO YOUR NEW EQUIPMENT IS TO INCREASE YOUR MAX HP...
KIII (WHINE)
THAT MEANS ALL OF US HAVE THE SAME DEFENSE AS MAPLE? YIKES.
BUT YOU CHANGED GEAR, RIGHT?
DO YOU STILL HAVE ENOUGH TO KEEP US UNHARMED?
YOU BET I DO!
EVEN WITH NO GEAR ON, MY VIT IS OVER A THOUSAND!
1,000
VIT ZERO
VIT TWO DIGITS
......
SO, CHROME... HOW MUCH DO YOU HAVE?
PLEASE DON'T MAKE ME ANSWER THAT...

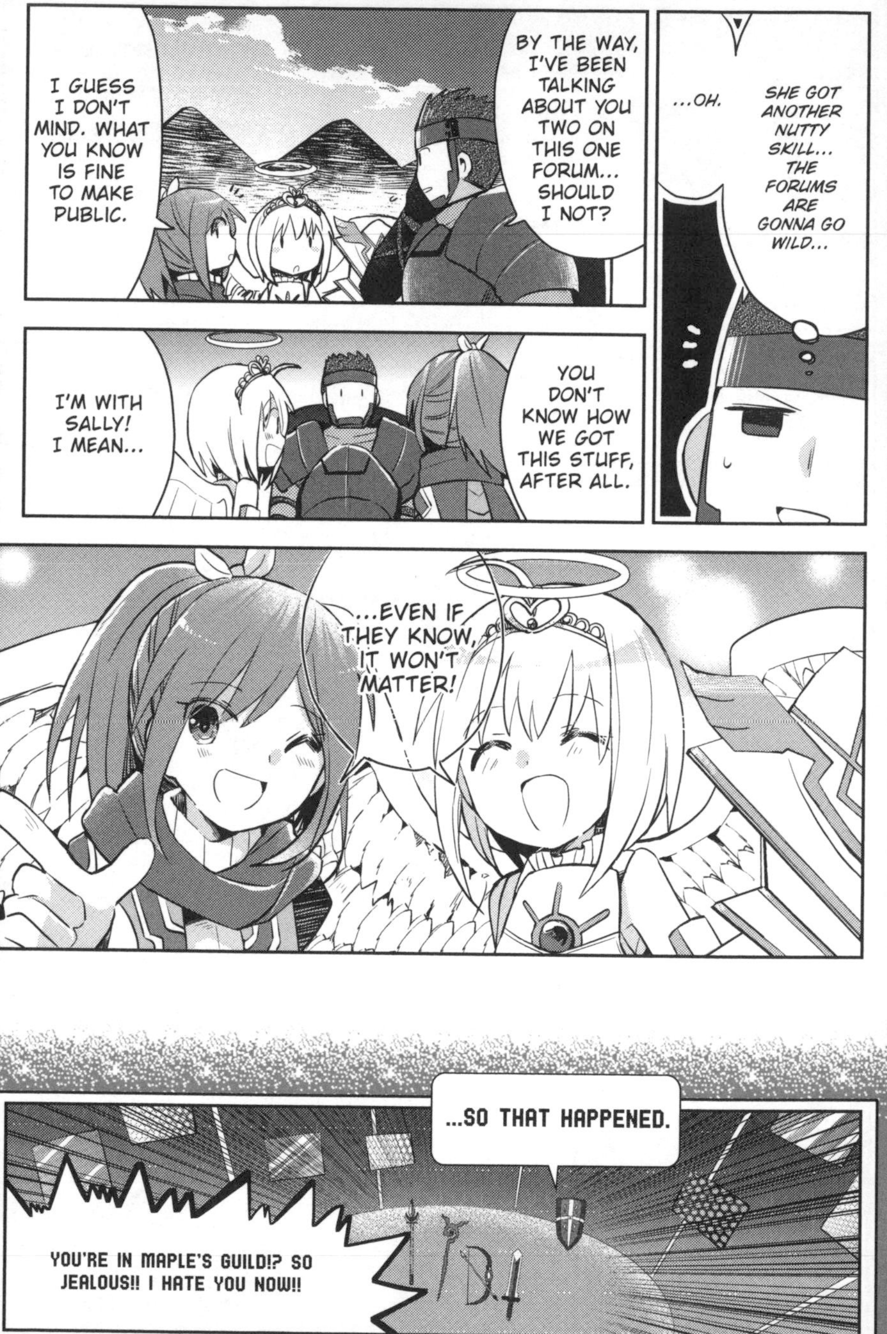
...OH.
SHE GOT ANOTHER NUTTY SKILL... THE FORUMS ARE GONNA GO WILD...
BY THE WAY, I'VE BEEN TALKING ABOUT YOU TWO ON THIS ONE FORUM... SHOULD I NOT?
I GUESS I DON'T MIND. WHAT YOU KNOW IS FINE TO MAKE PUBLIC.
YOU DON'T KNOW HOW WE GOT THIS STUFF, AFTER ALL.
I'M WITH SALLY! I MEAN...
...EVEN IF THEY KNOW, IT WON'T MATTER!
...SO THAT HAPPENED.
YOU'RE IN MAPLE'S GUILD!? SO JEALOUS!! I HATE YOU NOW!!

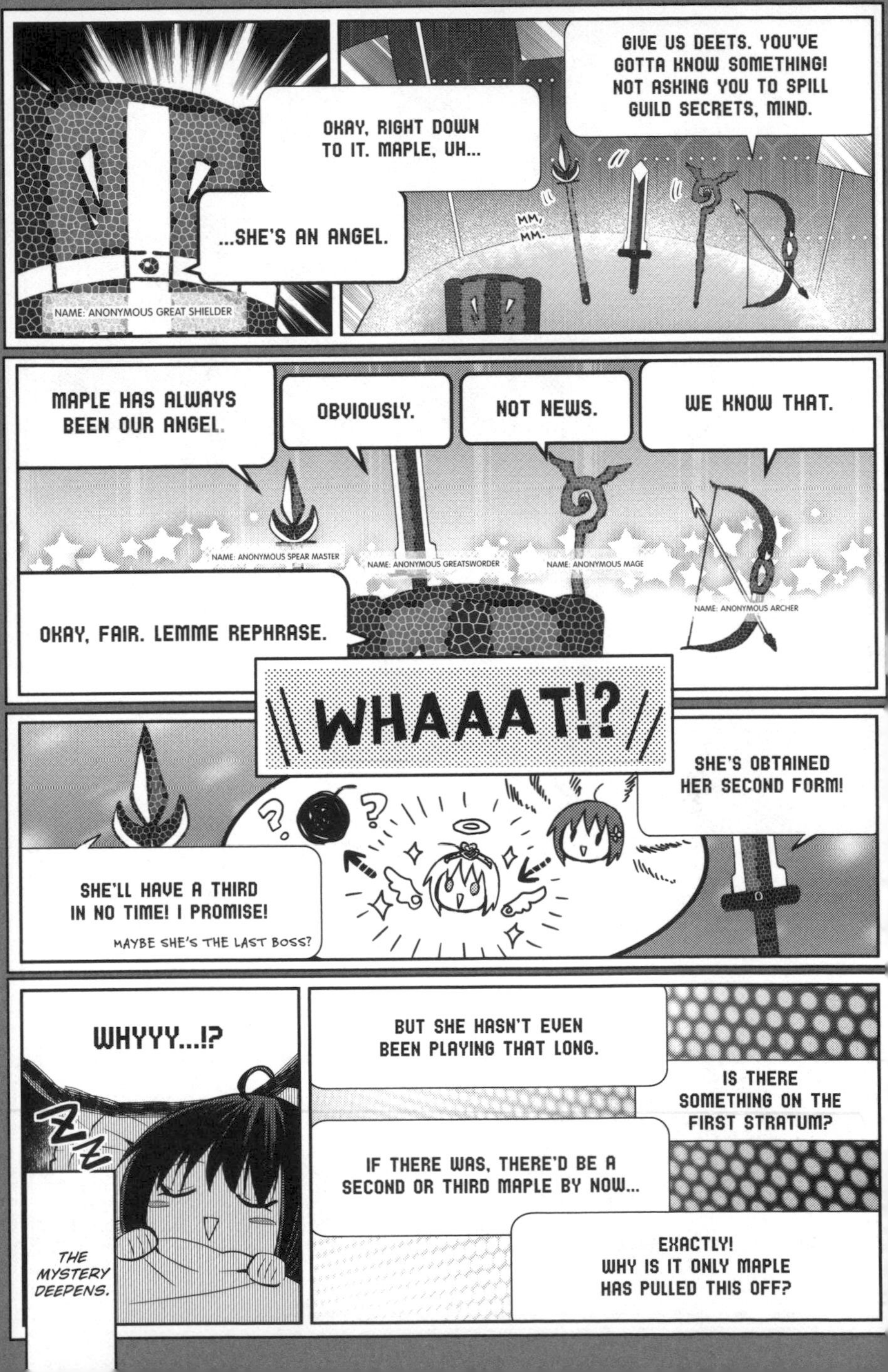
GIVE US DEETS. YOU'VE GOTTA KNOW SOMETHING! NOT ASKING YOU TO SPILL GUILD SECRETS, MIND.
MM, MM.
OKAY, RIGHT DOWN TO IT. MAPLE, UH...
...SHE'S AN ANGEL.
NAME: ANONYMOUS GREAT SHIELDER
WE KNOW THAT.
NOT NEWS.
OBVIOUSLY.
MAPLE HAS ALWAYS BEEN OUR ANGEL.
NAME: ANONYMOUS ARCHER
NAME: ANONYMOUS MAGE
NAME: ANONYMOUS GREATSWORDER
NAME: ANONYMOUS SPEAR MASTER
OKAY, FAIR. LEMME REPHRASE.
WHAAAT!?
SHE'S OBTAINED HER SECOND FORM!
SHE'LL HAVE A THIRD IN NO TIME! I PROMISE!
MAYBE SHE'S THE LAST BOSS?
BUT SHE HASN'T EVEN BEEN PLAYING THAT LONG.
IS THERE SOMETHING ON THE FIRST STRATUM?
IF THERE WAS, THERE'D BE A SECOND OR THIRD MAPLE BY NOW...
EXACTLY! WHY IS IT ONLY MAPLE HAS PULLED THIS OFF?
WHYYY...!?
THE MYSTERY DEEPENS.

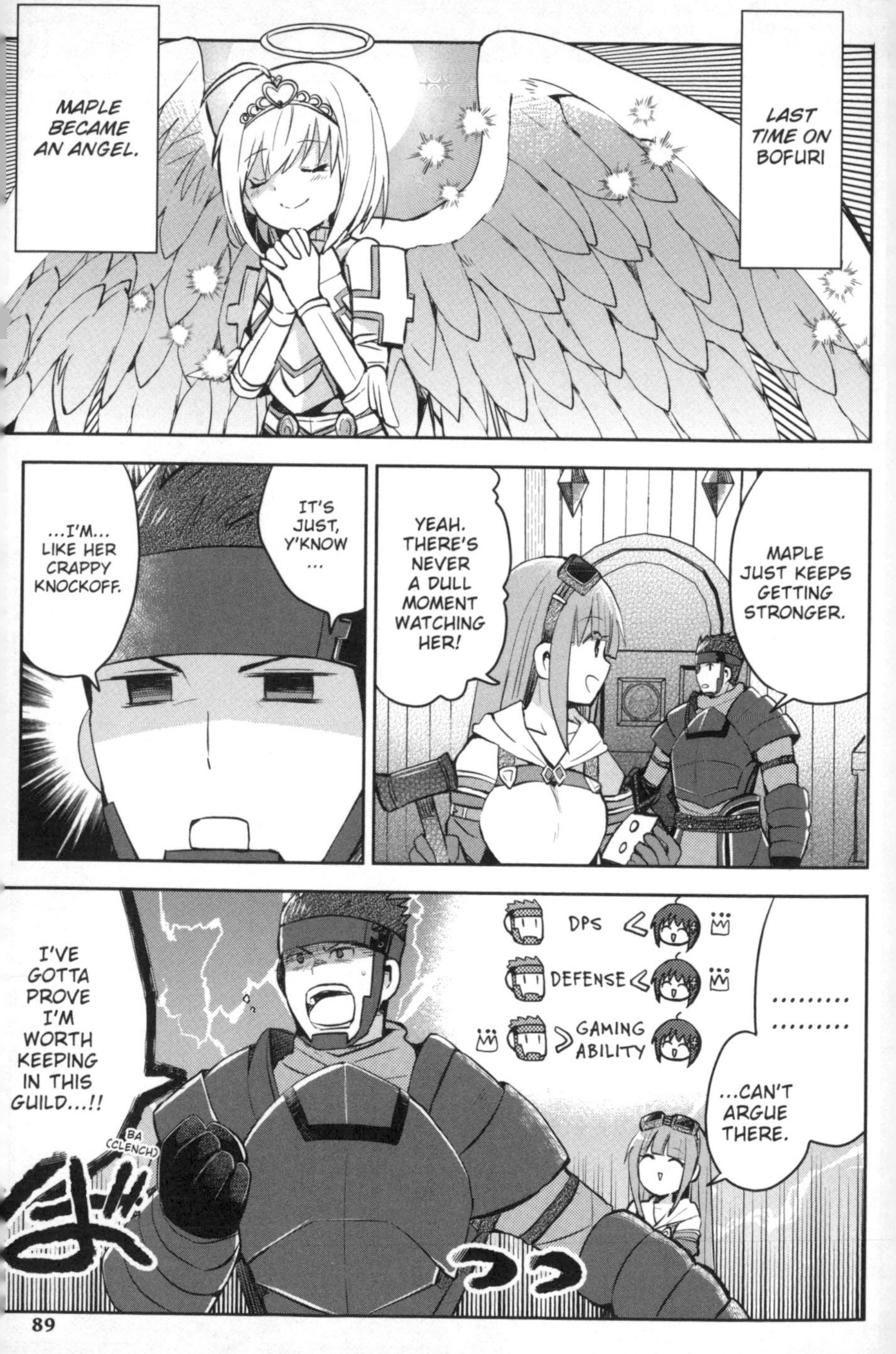
LAST TIME ON BOFURI
MAPLE BECAME AN ANGEL.
MAPLE JUST KEEPS GETTING STRONGER.
YEAH. THERE'S NEVER A DULL MOMENT WATCHING HER!
IT'S JUST, Y'KNOW ...
...I'M... LIKE HER CRAPPY KNOCKOFF.
....
....
DPS
DEFENSE
GAMING ABILITY
...CAN'T ARGUE THERE.
I'VE GOTTA PROVE I'M WORTH KEEPING IN THIS GUILD...!!
BA (CLENCH)

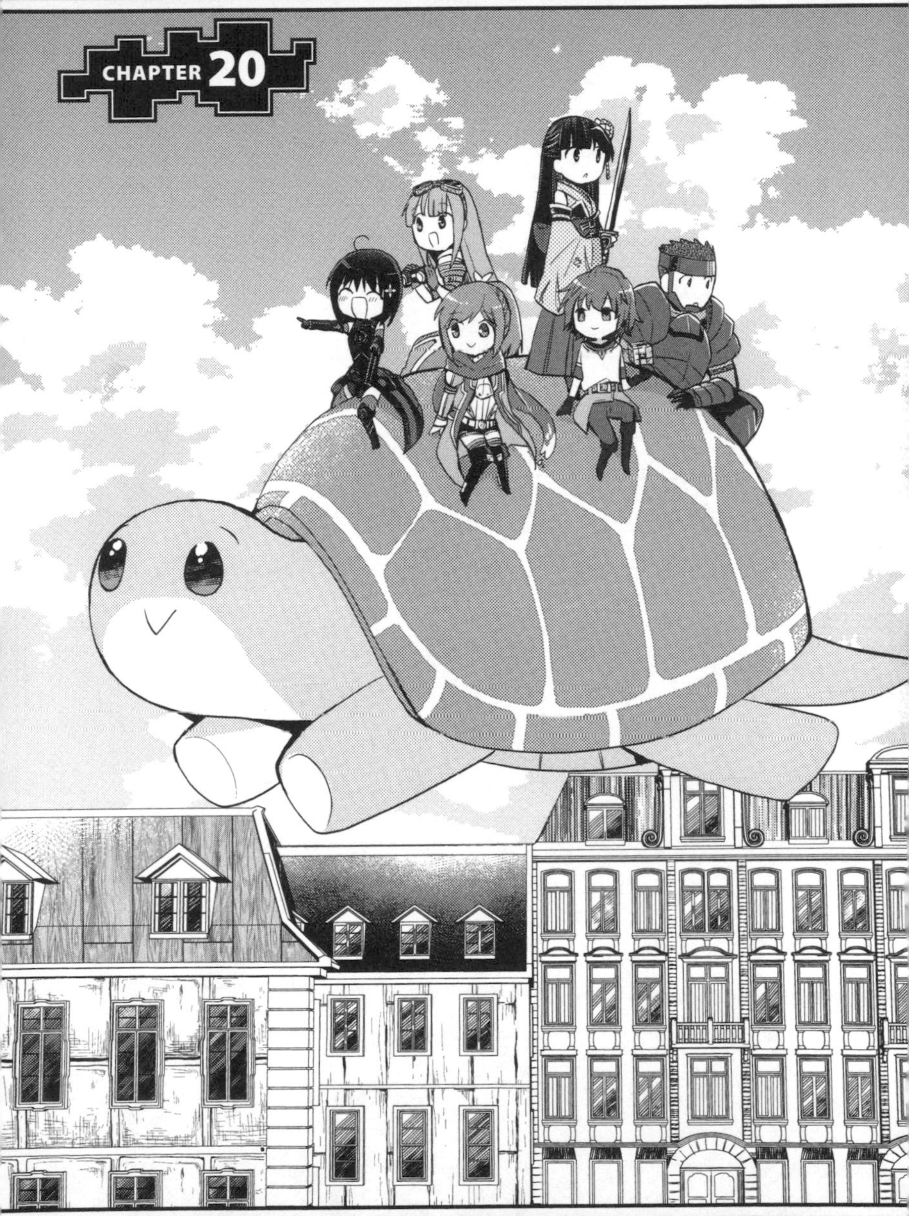
CHAPTER 20

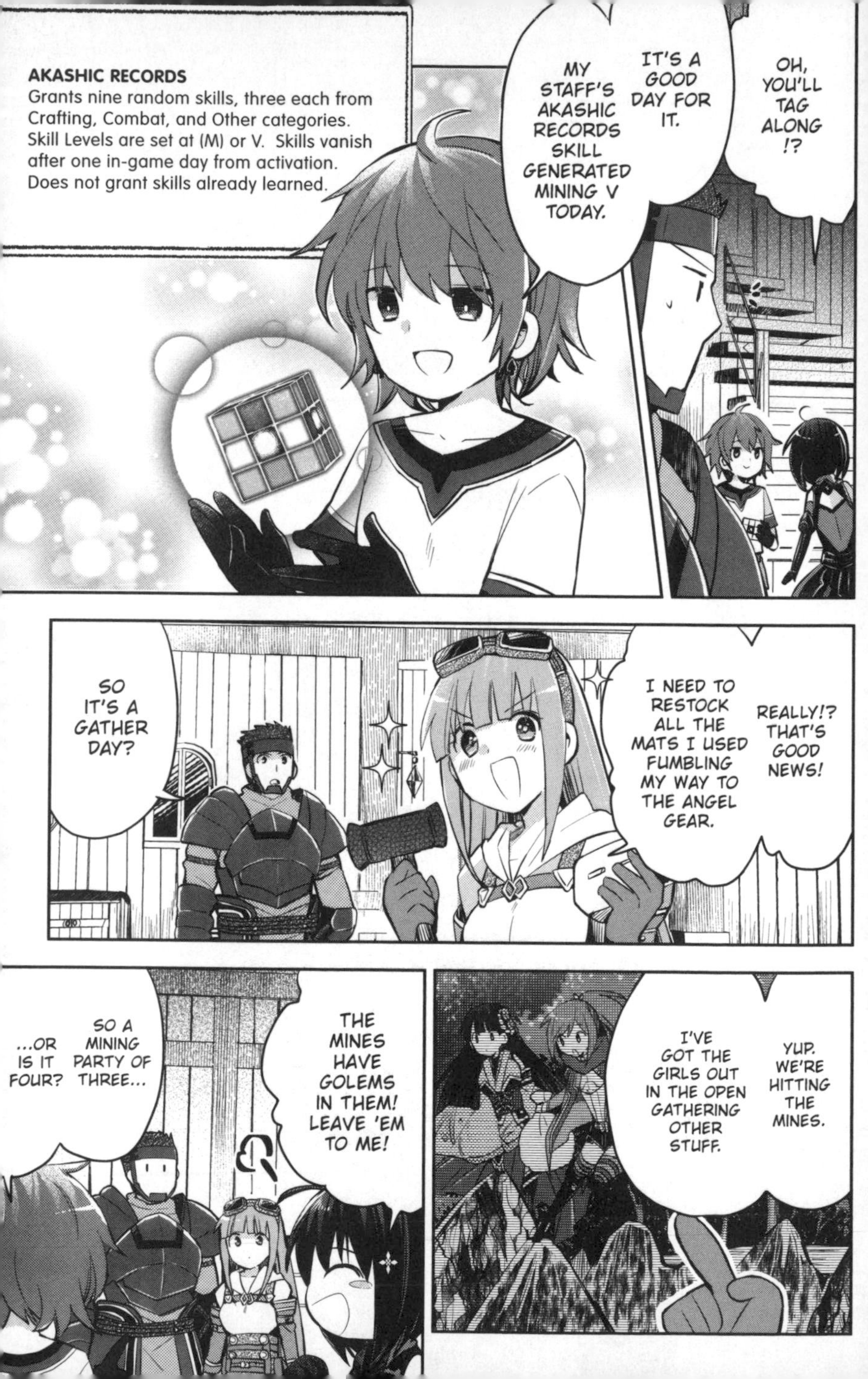
OH, YOU'LL TAG ALONG!?
IT'S A GOOD DAY FOR IT.
MY STAFF'S AKASHIC RECORDS SKILL GENERATED MINING V TODAY.
AKASHIC RECORDS
Grants nine random skills, three each from Crafting, Combat, and Other categories. Skill Levels are set at (M) or V. Skills vanish after one in-game day from activation. Does not grant skills already learned.
REALLY!? THAT'S GOOD NEWS!
I NEED TO RESTOCK ALL THE MATS I USED FUMBLING MY WAY TO THE ANGEL GEAR.
SO IT'S A GATHER DAY?
YUP. WE'RE HITTING THE MINES.
I'VE GOT THE GIRLS OUT IN THE OPEN GATHERING OTHER STUFF.
THE MINES HAVE GOLEMS IN THEM! LEAVE 'EM TO ME!
SO A MINING PARTY OF THREE...
...OR IS IT FOUR?

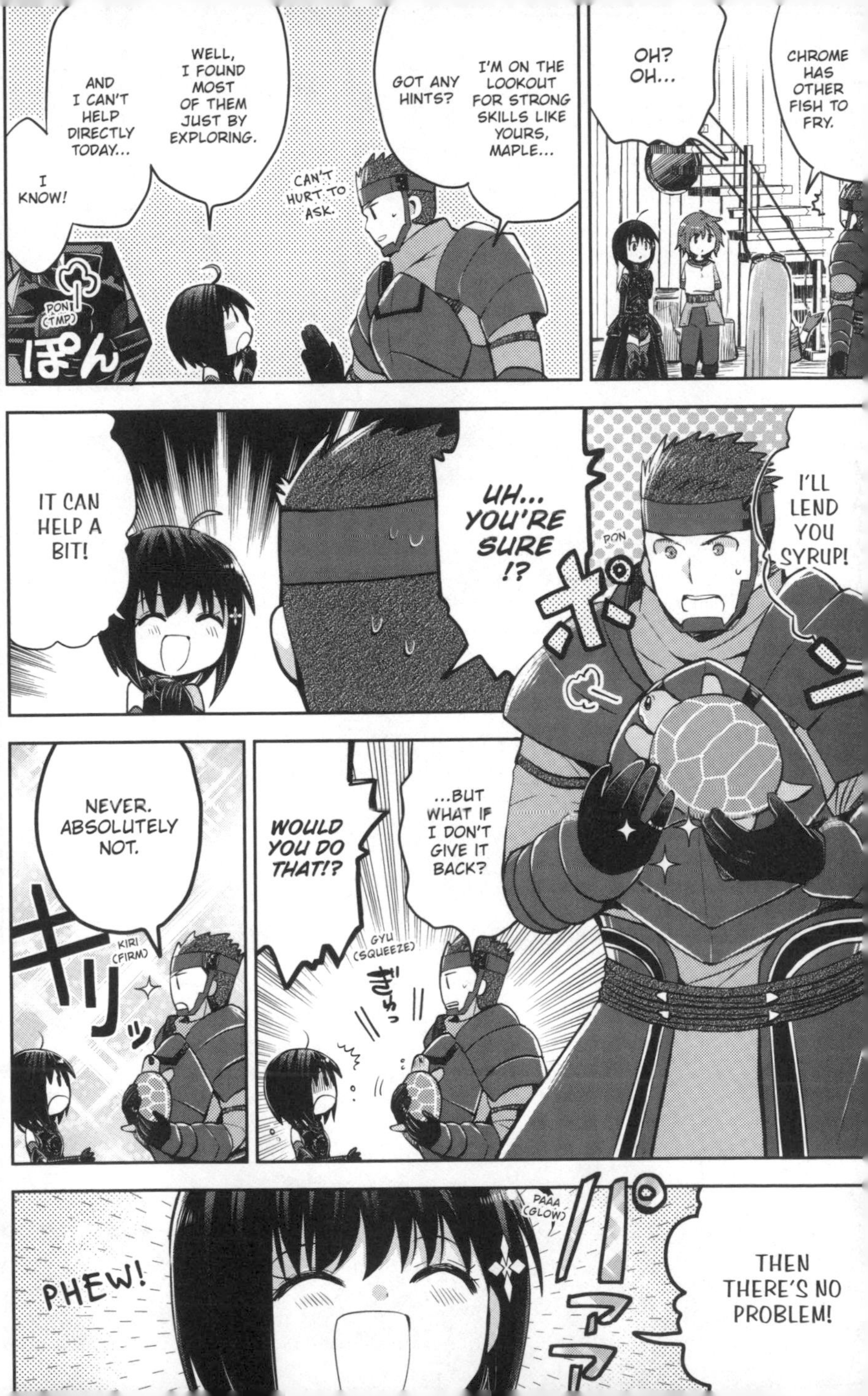
CHROME HAS OTHER FISH TO FRY.
OH? OH...
I'M ON THE LOOKOUT FOR STRONG SKILLS LIKE YOURS, MAPLE...
GOT ANY HINTS?
CAN'T HURT TO ASK.
WELL, I FOUND MOST OF THEM JUST BY EXPLORING.
AND I CAN'T HELP DIRECTLY TODAY...
I KNOW!
PON (TMP)
ぽん
I'LL LEND YOU SYRUP!
PON
ポン
UH... YOU'RE SURE!?
IT CAN HELP A BIT!
...BUT WHAT IF I DON'T GIVE IT BACK?
WOULD YOU DO THAT!?
GYU (SQUEEZE)
NEVER. ABSOLUTELY NOT.
KIRI (FIRM)
キリッ
THEN THERE'S NO PROBLEM!
PAAA (GLOW)
PHEW!

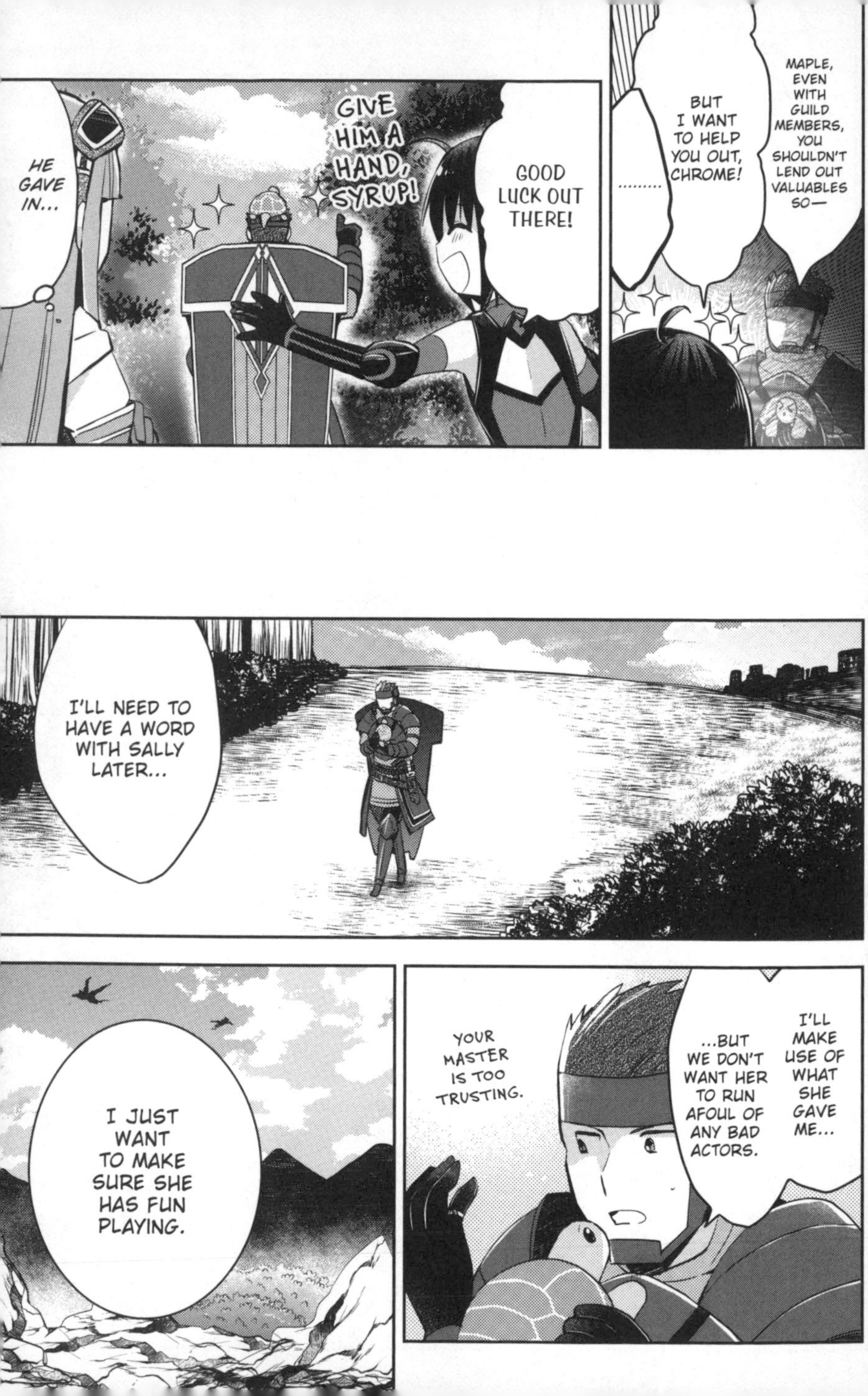
MAPLE, EVEN WITH GUILD MEMBERS, YOU SHOULDN'T LEND OUT VALUABLES SO—
BUT I WANT TO HELP YOU OUT, CHROME!
....
GOOD LUCK OUT THERE!
GIVE HIM A HAND, SYRUP!
HE GAVE IN...
I'LL NEED TO HAVE A WORD WITH SALLY LATER...
I'LL MAKE USE OF WHAT SHE GAVE ME...
...BUT WE DON'T WANT HER TO RUN AFOUL OF ANY BAD ACTORS.
YOUR MASTER IS TOO TRUSTING.
I JUST WANT TO MAKE SURE SHE HAS FUN PLAYING.

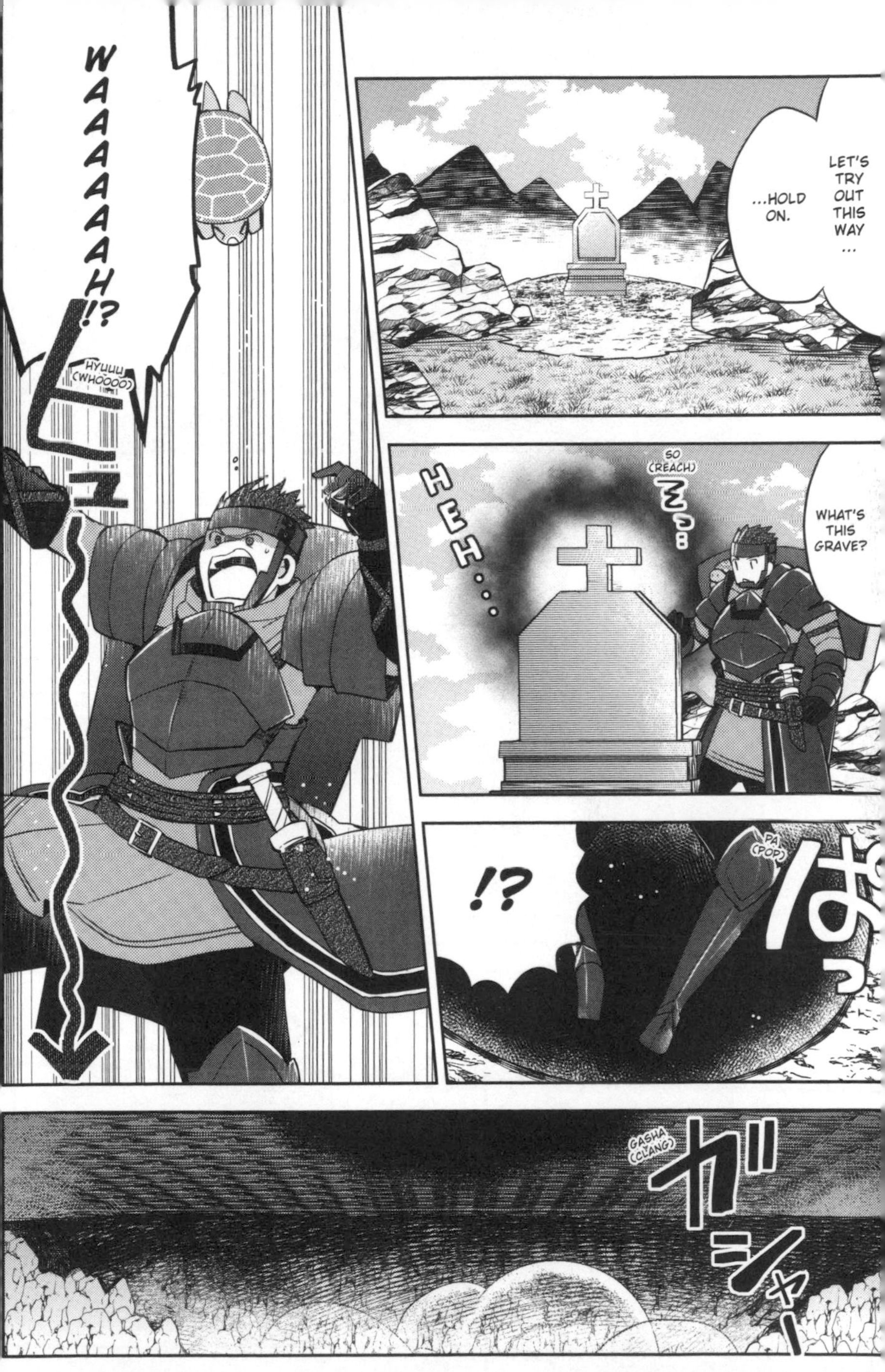
LET'S TRY OUT THIS WAY ...
...HOLD ON.
WHAT'S THIS GRAVE?
SO (REACH)
HEH...
PA (POP)
!?
WAAAAAAAAAH!?
HYUUU (WHOOOO)
GASHA (CLANG)

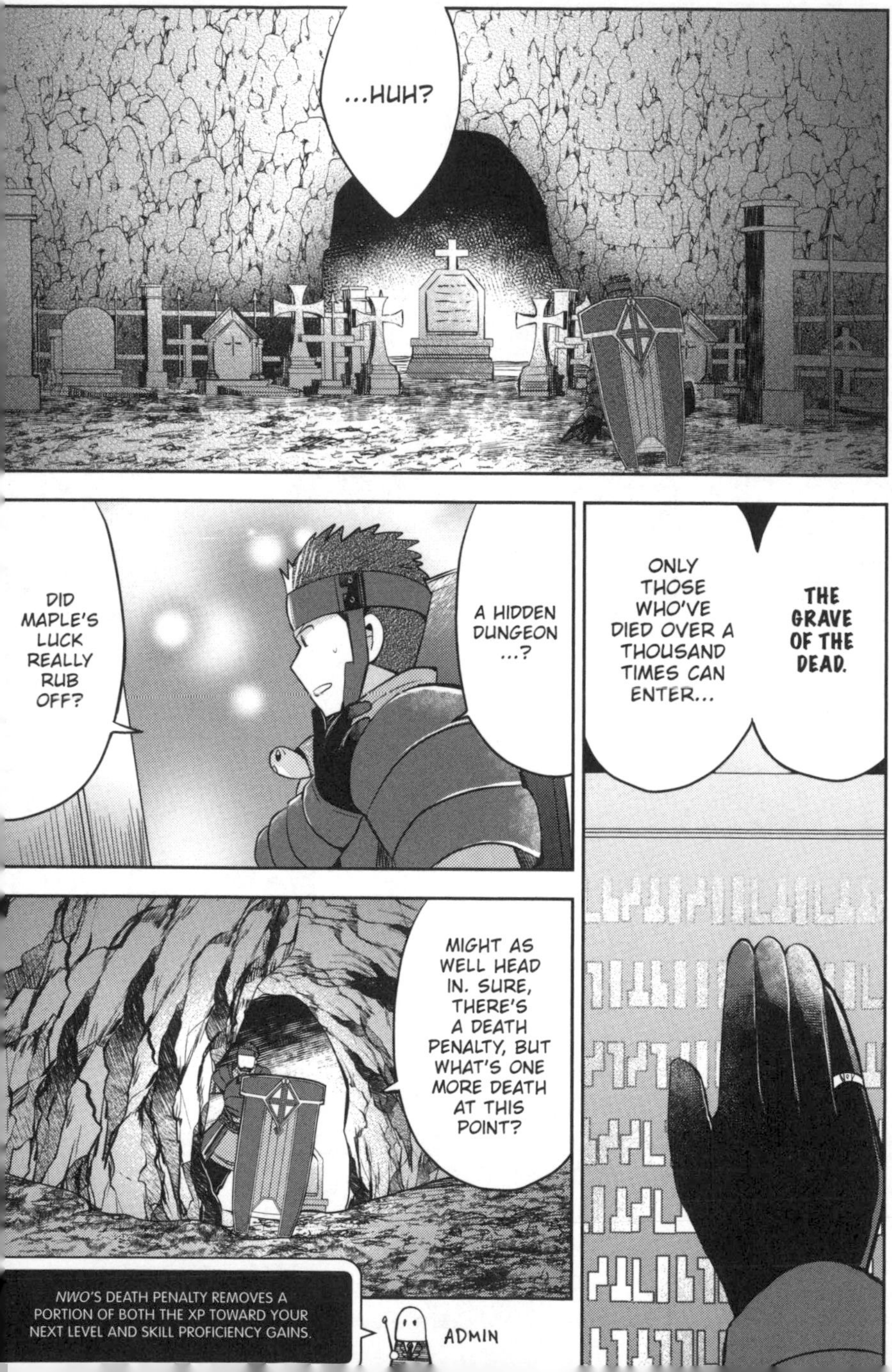
...HUH?
THE GRAVE OF THE DEAD.
ONLY THOSE WHO'VE DIED OVER A THOUSAND TIMES CAN ENTER...
A HIDDEN DUNGEON ...?
DID MAPLE'S LUCK REALLY RUB OFF?
MIGHT AS WELL HEAD IN. SURE, THERE'S A DEATH PENALTY, BUT WHAT'S ONE MORE DEATH AT THIS POINT?
NWO'S DEATH PENALTY REMOVES A PORTION OF BOTH THE XP TOWARD YOUR NEXT LEVEL AND SKILL PROFICIENCY GAINS.
ADMIN

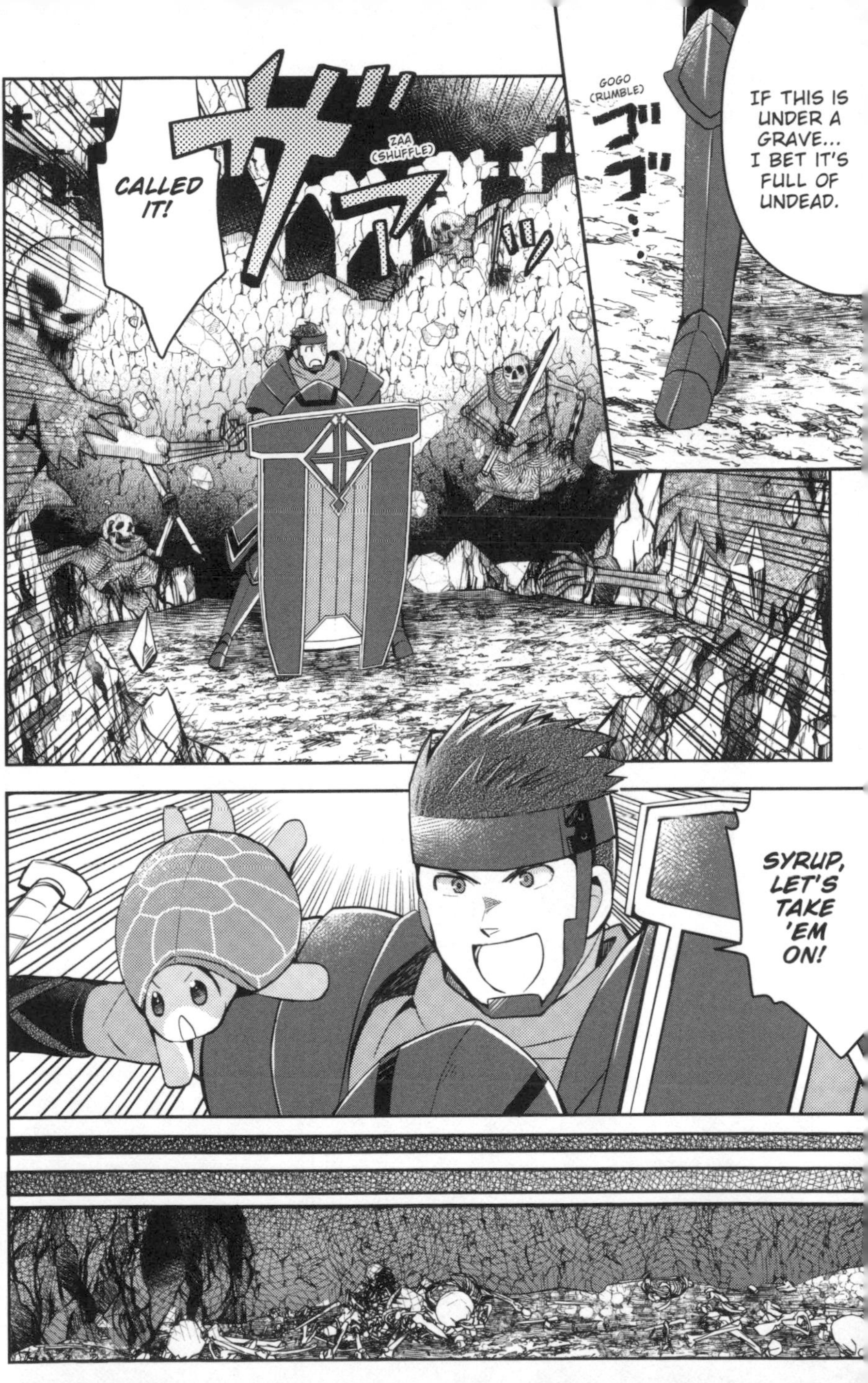
IF THIS IS UNDER A GRAVE... I BET IT'S FULL OF UNDEAD.
GOGO (RUMBLE)
ZAA (SHUFFLE)
CALLED IT!
SYRUP, LET'S TAKE 'EM ON!

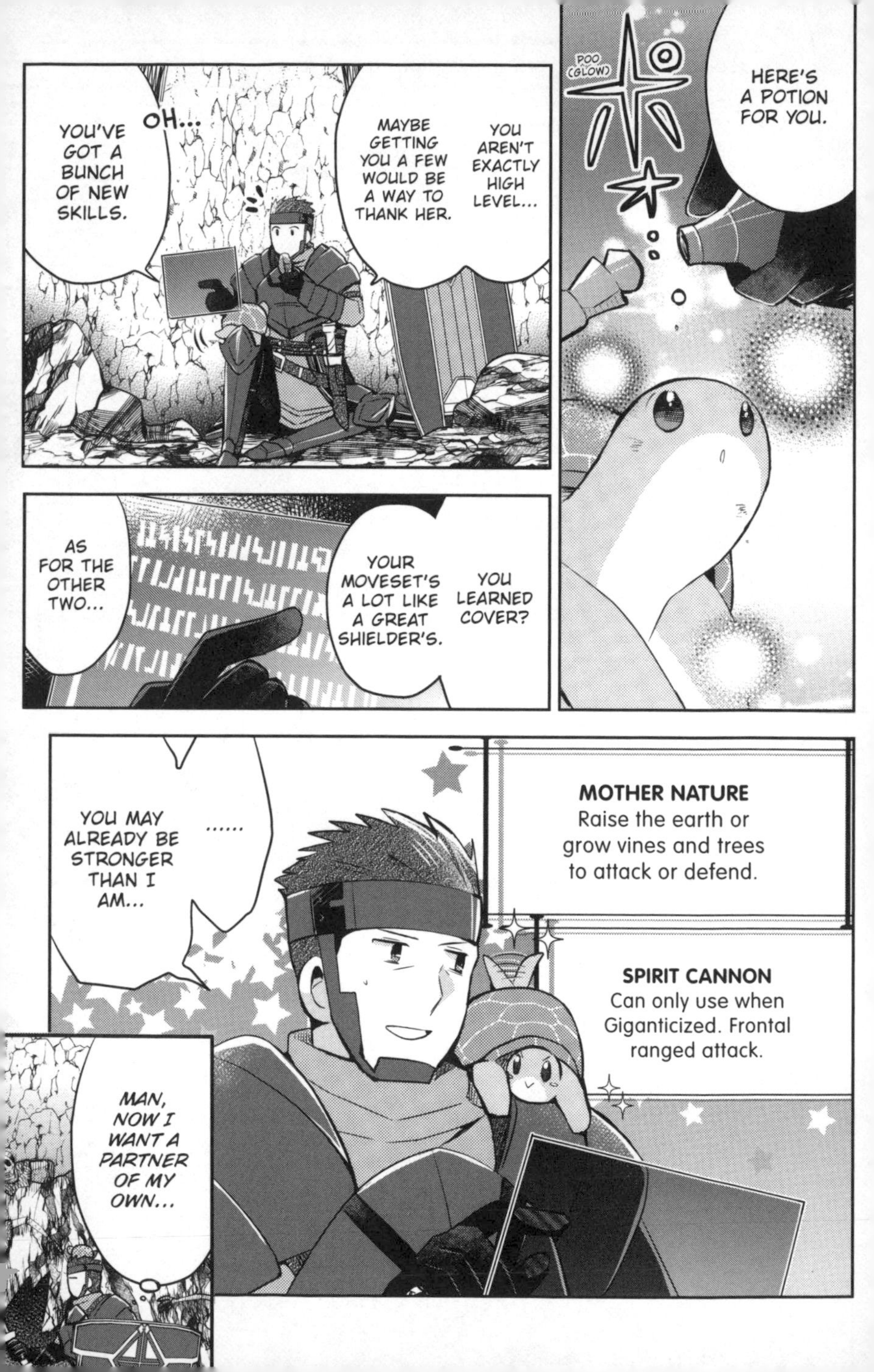
POO (GLOW)
HERE'S A POTION FOR YOU.
YOU AREN'T EXACTLY HIGH LEVEL...
MAYBE GETTING YOU A FEW WOULD BE A WAY TO THANK HER.
OH...
YOU'VE GOT A BUNCH OF NEW SKILLS.
YOU LEARNED COVER?
YOUR MOVESET'S A LOT LIKE A GREAT SHIELDER'S.
AS FOR THE OTHER TWO...
MOTHER NATURE
Raise the earth or grow vines and trees to attack or defend.
SPIRIT CANNON
Can only use when Giganticized. Frontal ranged attack.
......
YOU MAY ALREADY BE STRONGER THAN I AM...
MAN, NOW I WANT A PARTNER OF MY OWN...

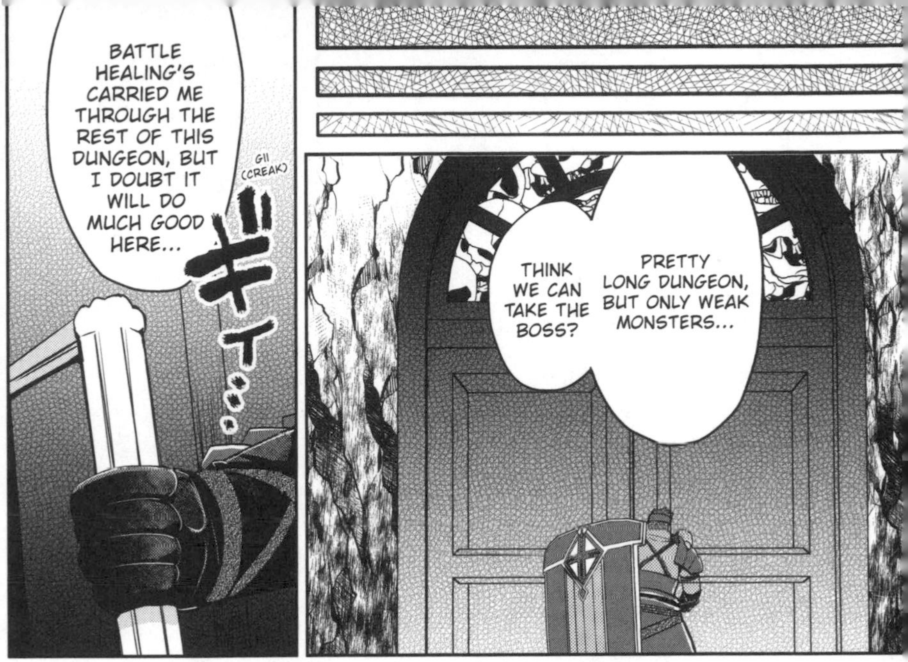
PRETTY LONG DUNGEON, BUT ONLY WEAK MONSTERS...
THINK WE CAN TAKE THE BOSS?
BATTLE HEALING'S CARRIED ME THROUGH THE REST OF THIS DUNGEON, BUT I DOUBT IT WILL DO MUCH GOOD HERE...
GII (CREAK)

★ **BATTLE HEALING:** Recover 1% HP every ten seconds during combat.

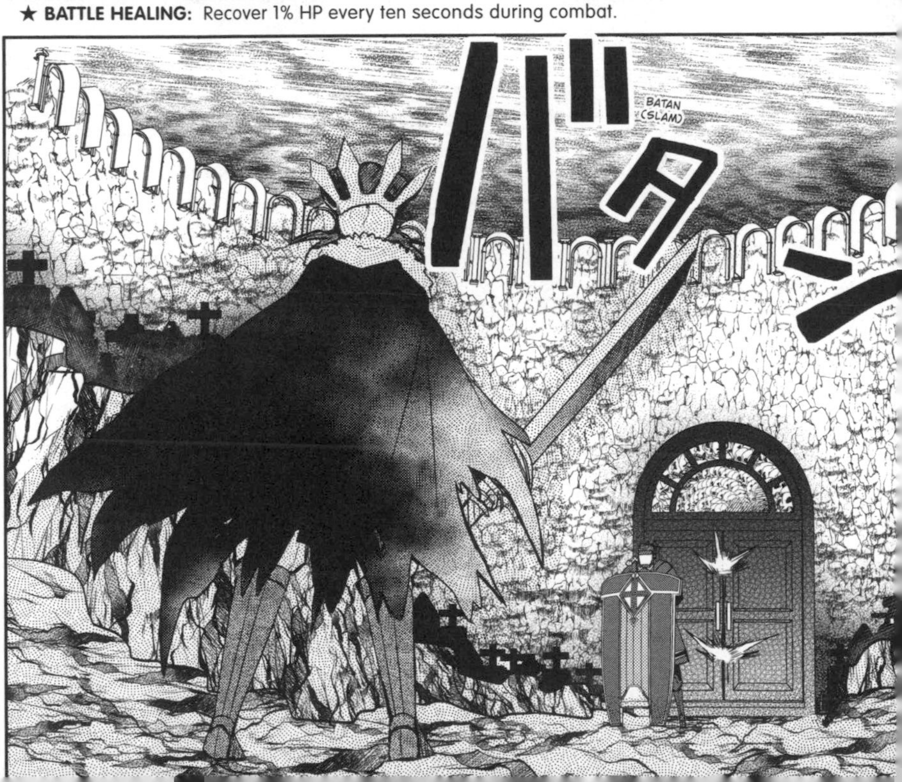
BATAN (SLAM)

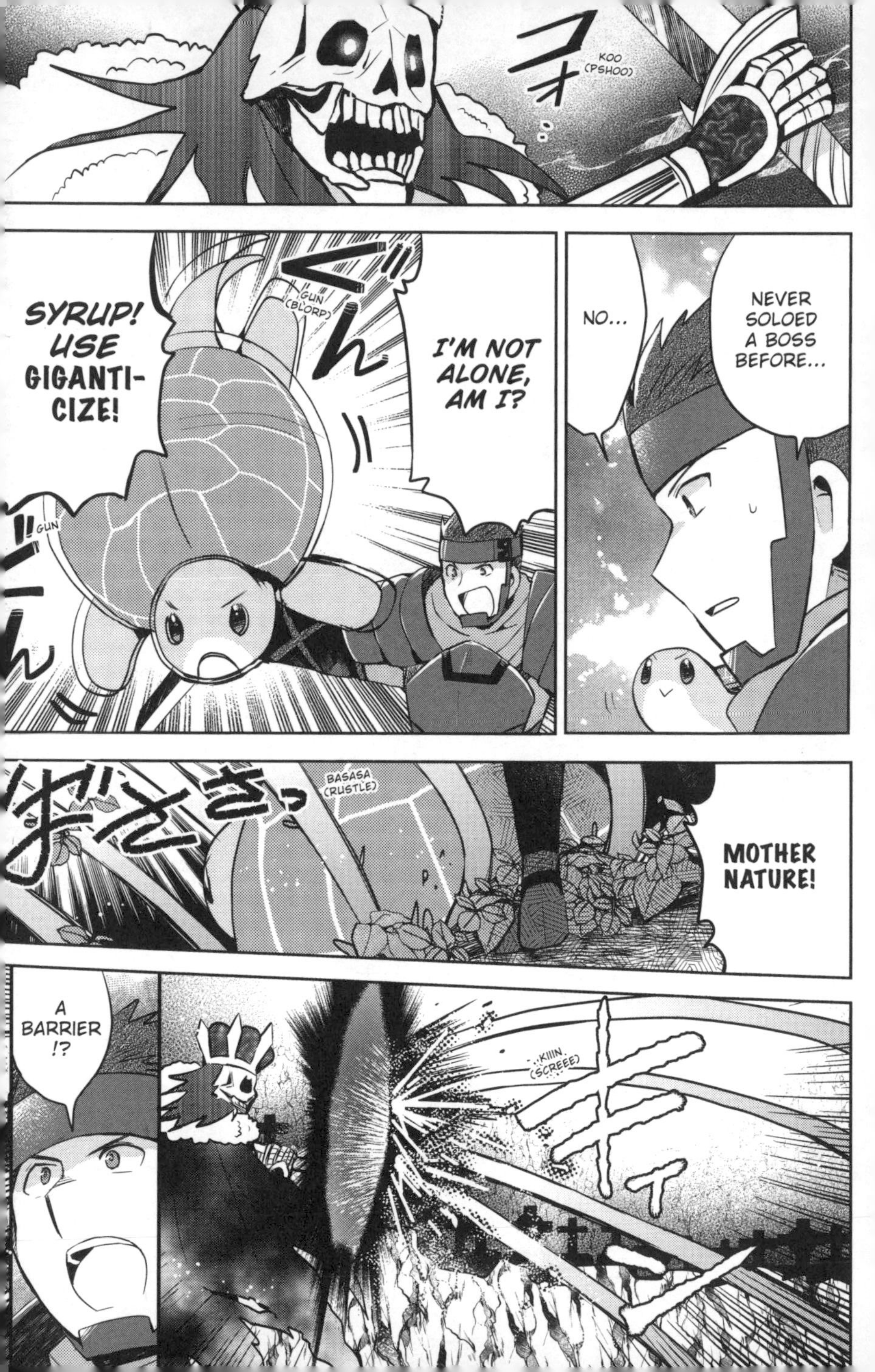
KOO (PSHOO)
NEVER SOLOED A BOSS BEFORE...
NO...
I'M NOT ALONE, AM I?
GUN (BLORP)
SYRUP! USE GIGANTI-CIZE!
GUN
MOTHER NATURE!
BASASA (RUSTLE)
KIIN (SCREEE)
A BARRIER !?

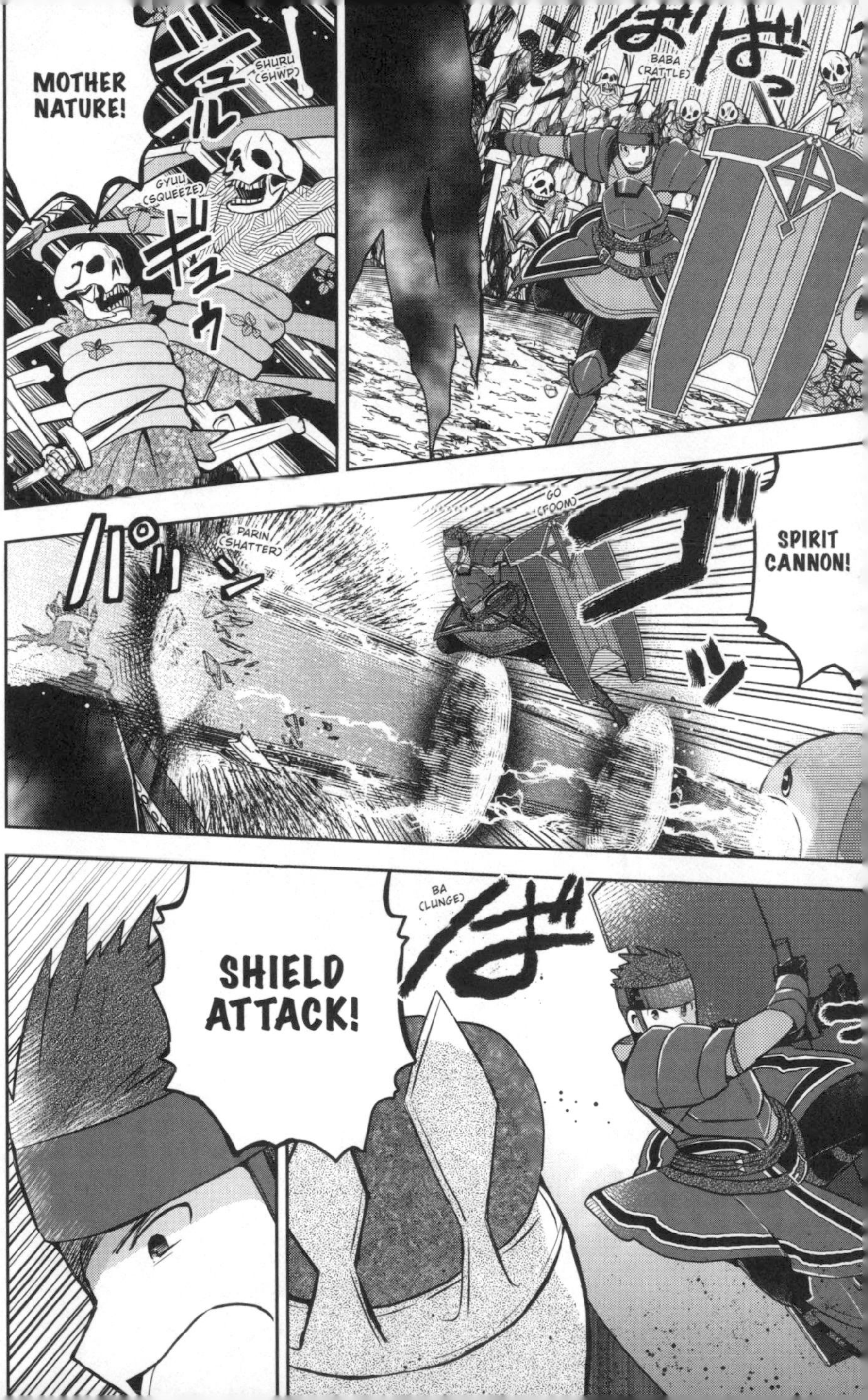
BABA (RATTLE)
MOTHER NATURE!
SHURU (SHWP)
GYUU (SQUEEZE)
SPIRIT CANNON!
GO (FOOM)
PARIN (SHATTER)
BA (LUNGE)
SHIELD ATTACK!

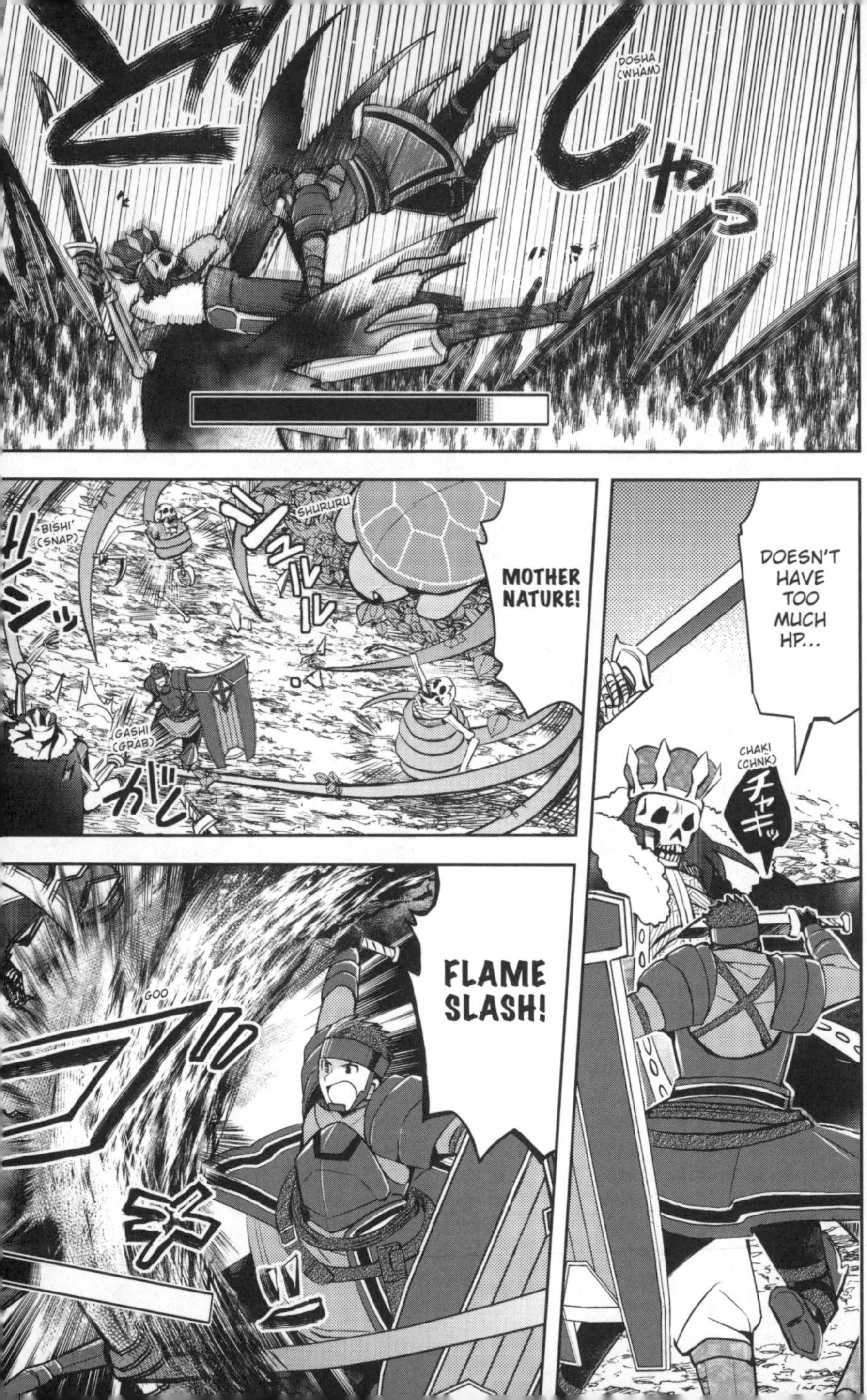
DOSHA (WHAM)
DOESN'T HAVE TOO MUCH HP...
CHAKI (CHNK)
MOTHER NATURE!
SHURURU
BISHI' (SNAP)
GASHI (GRAB)
FLAME SLASH!
GOO

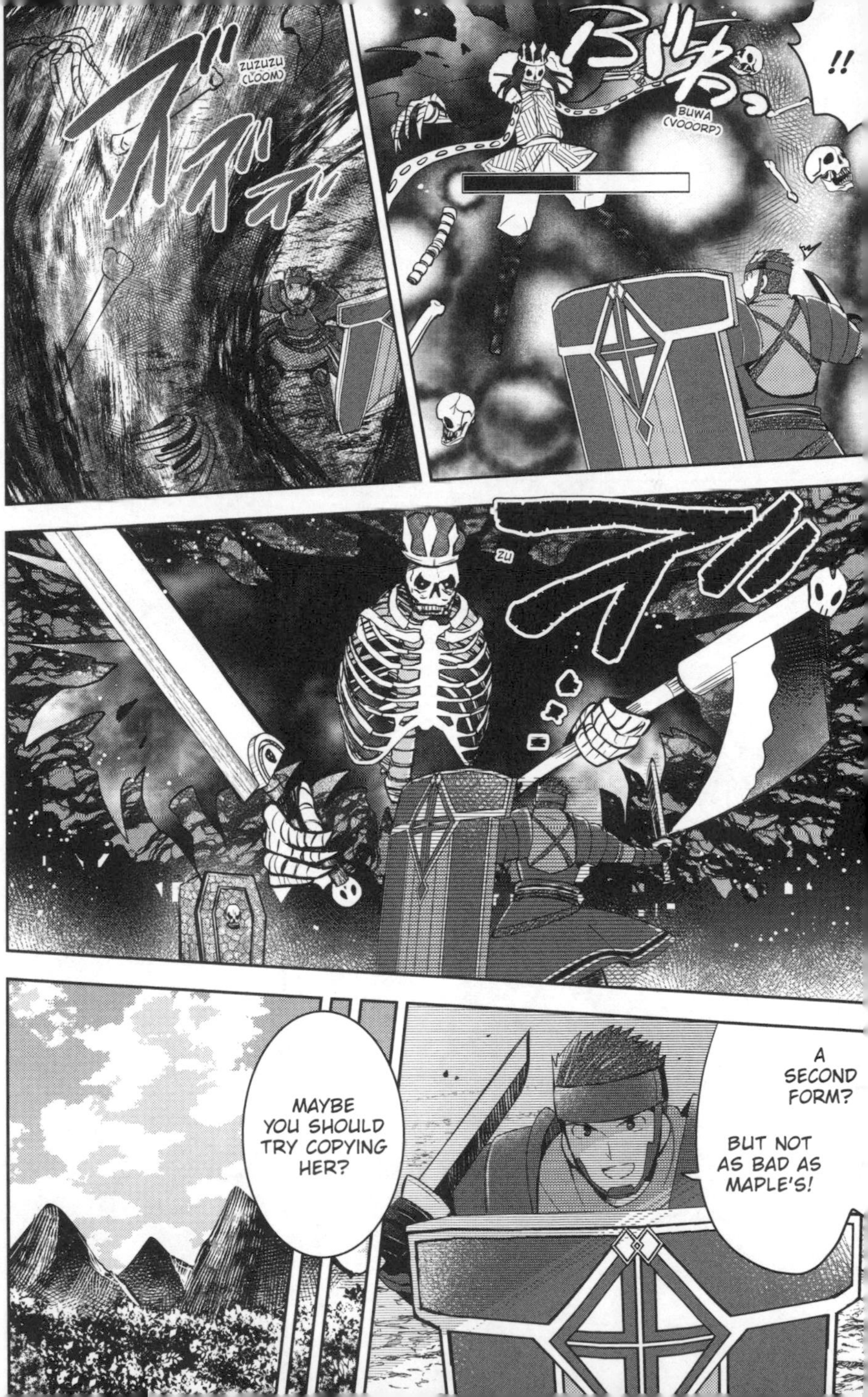
!!
BUWA (VOOORP)
ZUZUZU (LOOM)
ZU
A SECOND FORM?
BUT NOT AS BAD AS MAPLE'S!
MAYBE YOU SHOULD TRY COPYING HER?

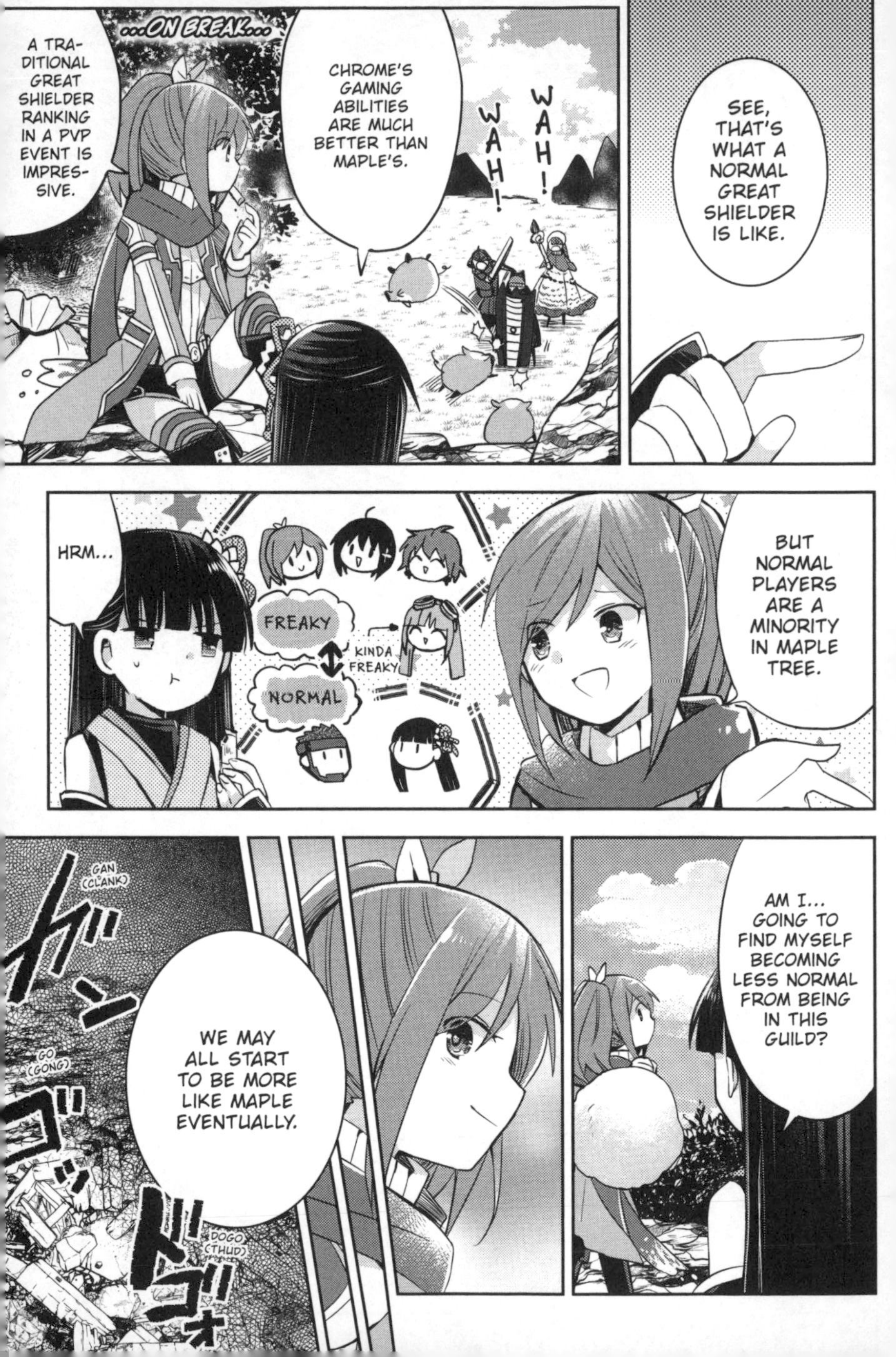
SEE, THAT'S WHAT A NORMAL GREAT SHIELDER IS LIKE.
...ON BREAK...
CHROME'S GAMING ABILITIES ARE MUCH BETTER THAN MAPLE'S.
WAH!
WAH!
A TRADITIONAL GREAT SHIELDER RANKING IN A PVP EVENT IS IMPRESSIVE.
BUT NORMAL PLAYERS ARE A MINORITY IN MAPLE TREE.
FREAKY
KINDA FREAKY
NORMAL
HRM...
AM I... GOING TO FIND MYSELF BECOMING LESS NORMAL FROM BEING IN THIS GUILD?
WE MAY ALL START TO BE MORE LIKE MAPLE EVENTUALLY.
GAN (CLANK)
GO (GONG)
DOGO (THUD)

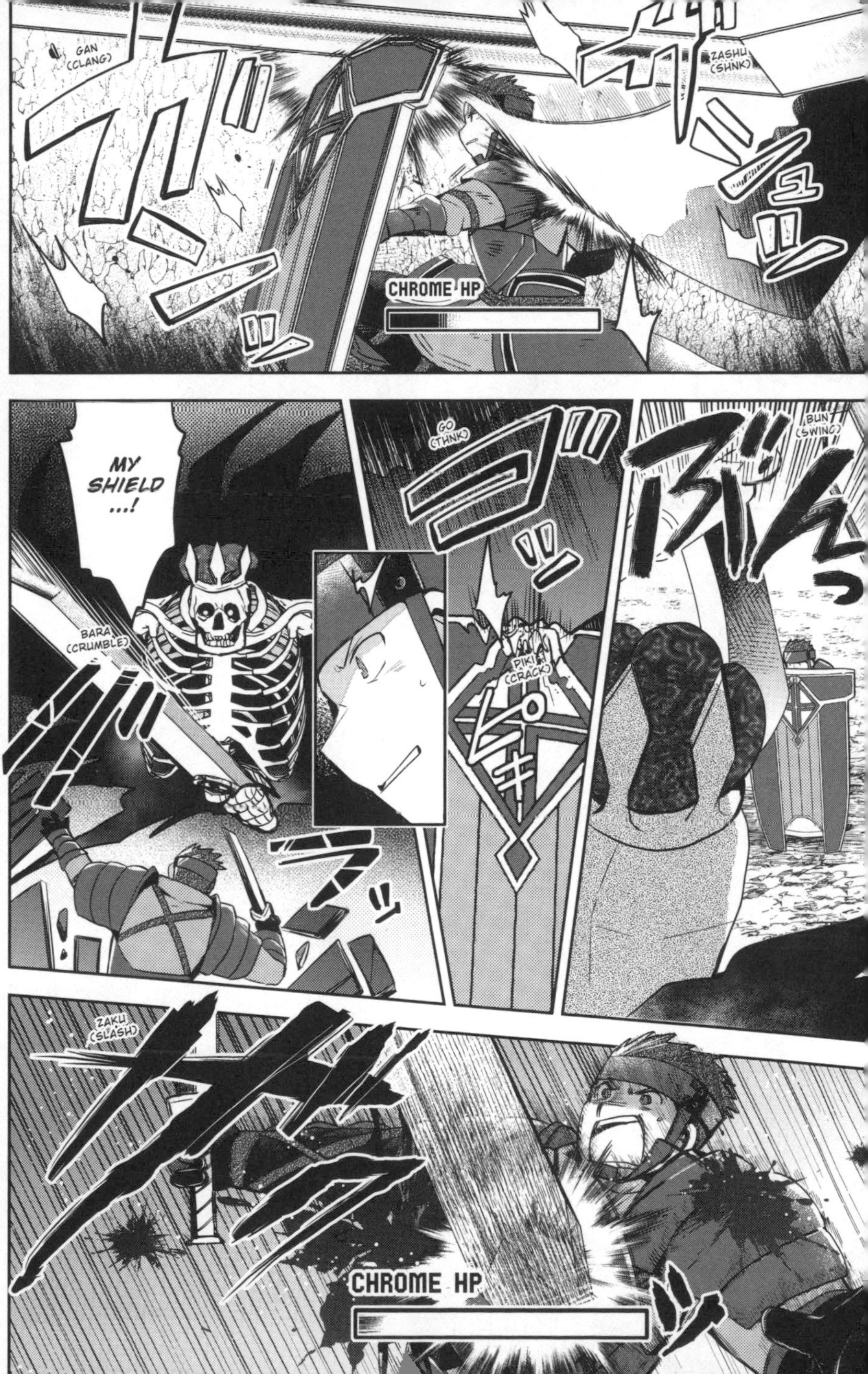
ZASHU (SHNK)
GAN (CLANG)
CHROME HP
BUN (SWING)
GO (THNK)
PIKI (CRACK)
MY SHIELD ...!
BARA (CRUMBLE)
ZAKU (SLASH)
CHROME HP

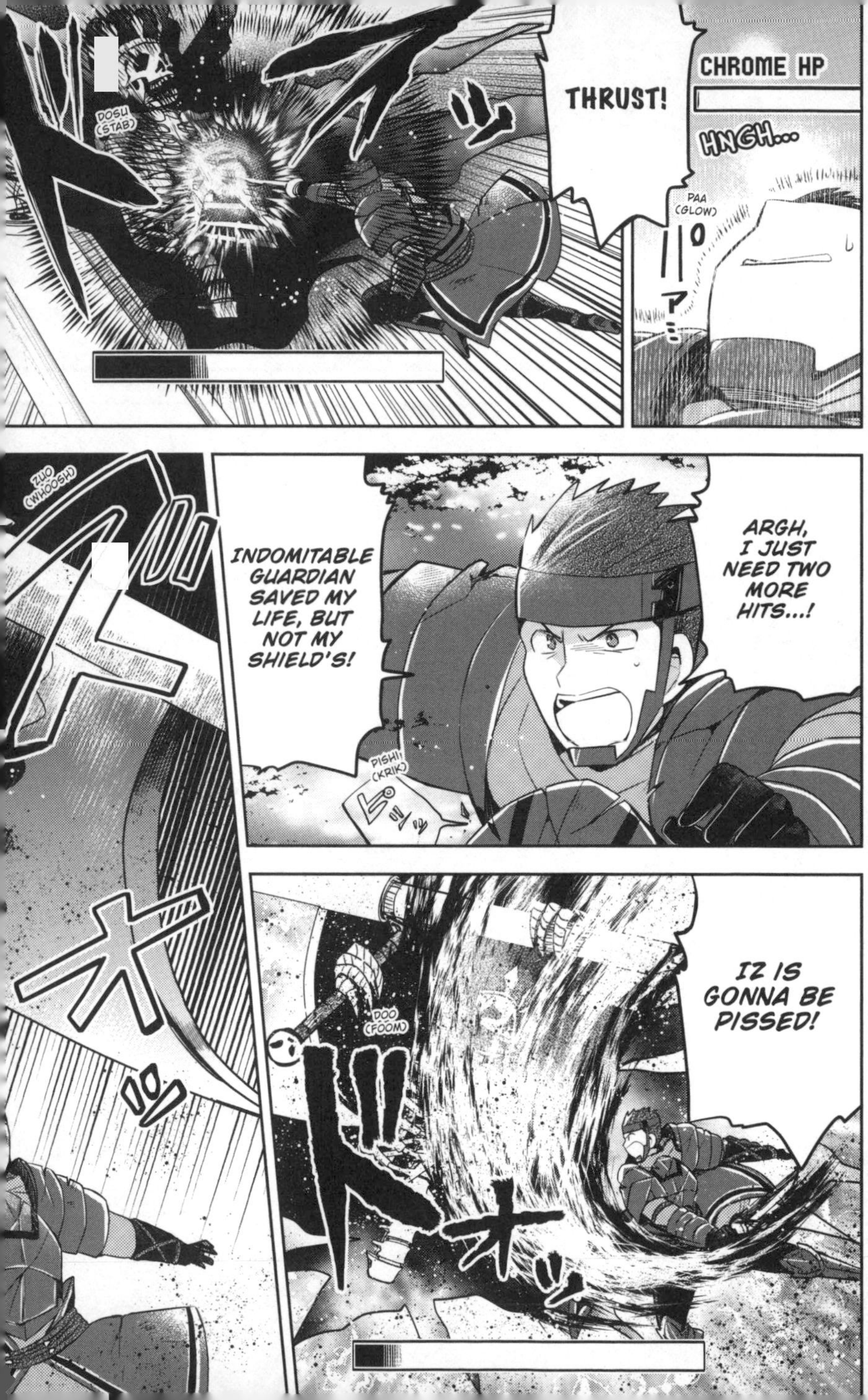
CHROME HP
HNGH...
PAA (GLOW)
THRUST!
DOSU (STAB)
ARGH, I JUST NEED TWO MORE HITS...!
INDOMITABLE GUARDIAN SAVED MY LIFE, BUT NOT MY SHIELD'S!
PISHI (KRIK)
IZ IS GONNA BE PISSED!
DOO (FOOM)
ZUO (WHOOSH)

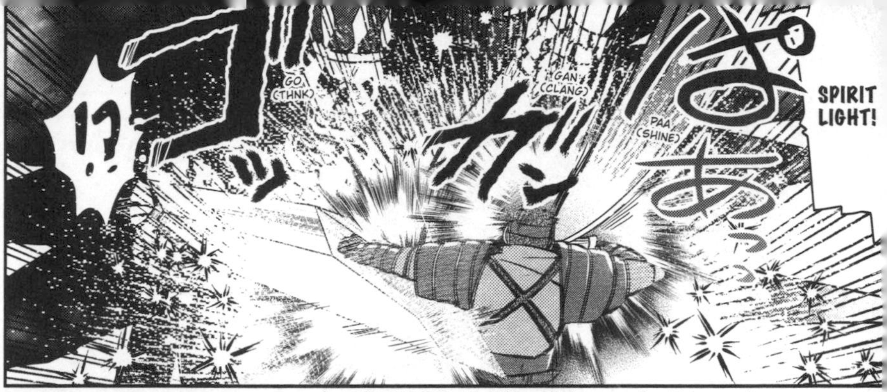
SPIRIT LIGHT!
PAA (SHINE)
GAN (CLANG)
GO (THNK)
!?

★ **SPIRIT LIGHT:** Nullifies all damage for 10 seconds.

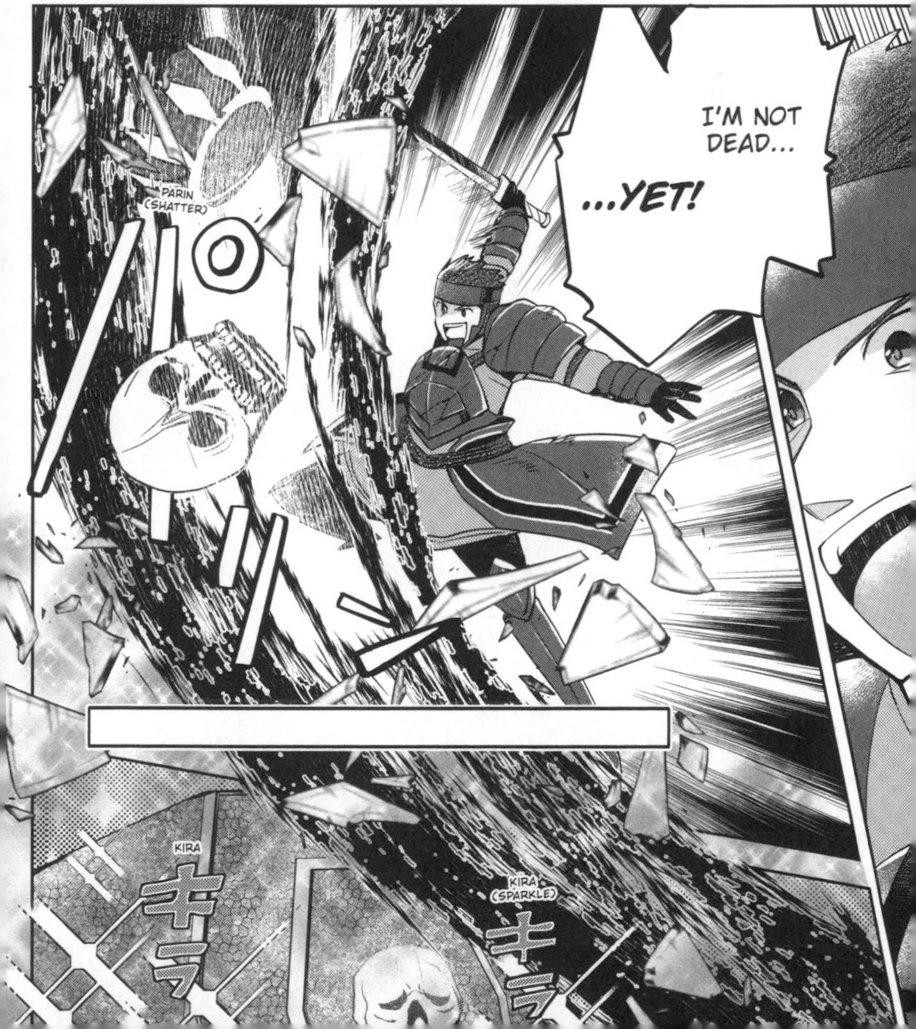
I'M NOT DEAD...
...YET!
PARIN (SHATTER)
KIRA (SPARKLE)
KIRA

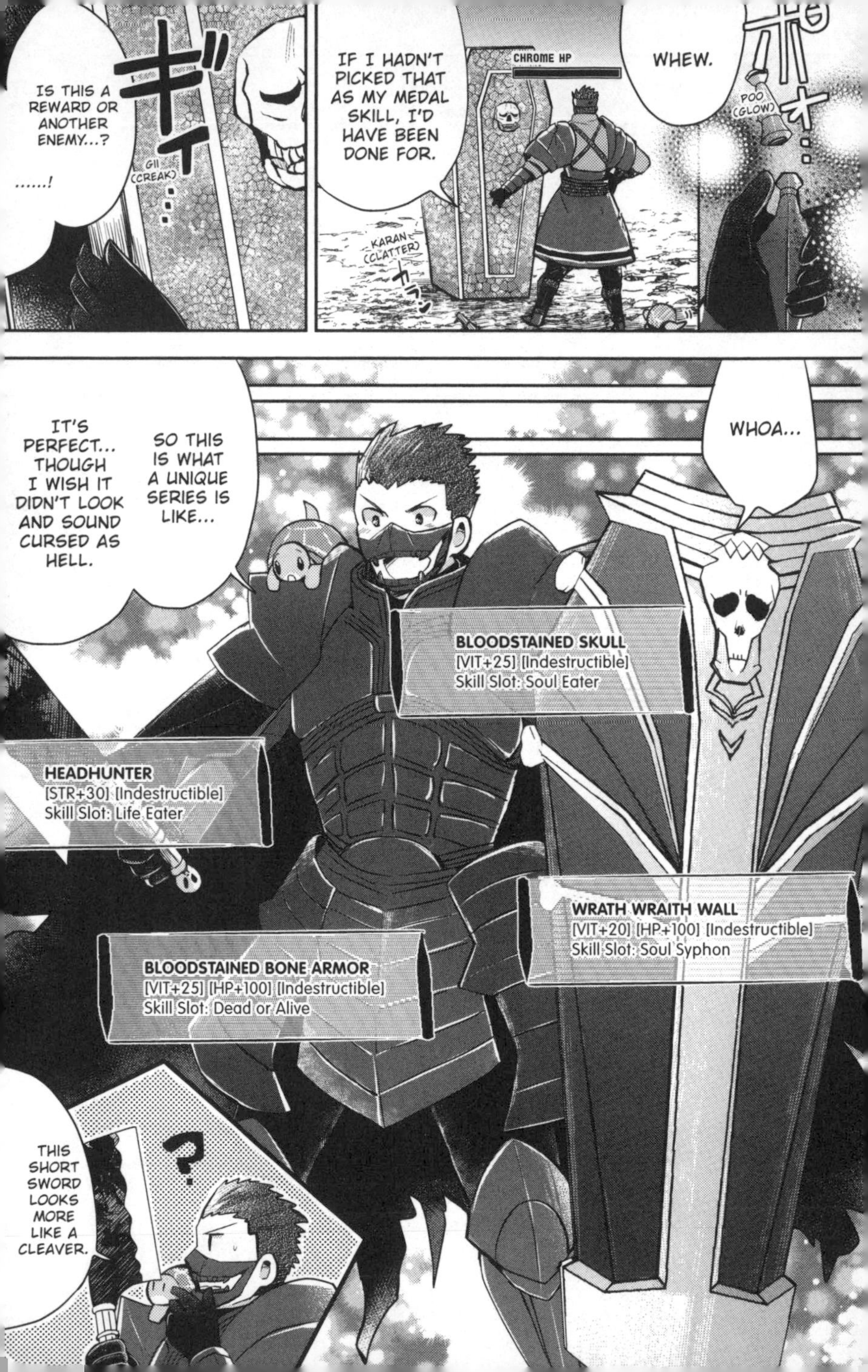
POO (GLOW)
WHEW.
CHROME HP
IF I HADN'T PICKED THAT AS MY MEDAL SKILL, I'D HAVE BEEN DONE FOR.
KARAN (CLATTER)
IS THIS A REWARD OR ANOTHER ENEMY...?
......!
GII (CREAK)
WHOA...
SO THIS IS WHAT A UNIQUE SERIES IS LIKE...
IT'S PERFECT... THOUGH I WISH IT DIDN'T LOOK AND SOUND CURSED AS HELL.
BLOODSTAINED SKULL
[VIT+25] [Indestructible]
Skill Slot: Soul Eater
HEADHUNTER
[STR+30] [Indestructible]
Skill Slot: Life Eater
WRATH WRAITH WALL
[VIT+20] [HP+100] [Indestructible]
Skill Slot: Soul Syphon
BLOODSTAINED BONE ARMOR
[VIT+25] [HP+100] [Indestructible]
Skill Slot: Dead or Alive
?
THIS SHORT SWORD LOOKS MORE LIKE A CLEAVER.

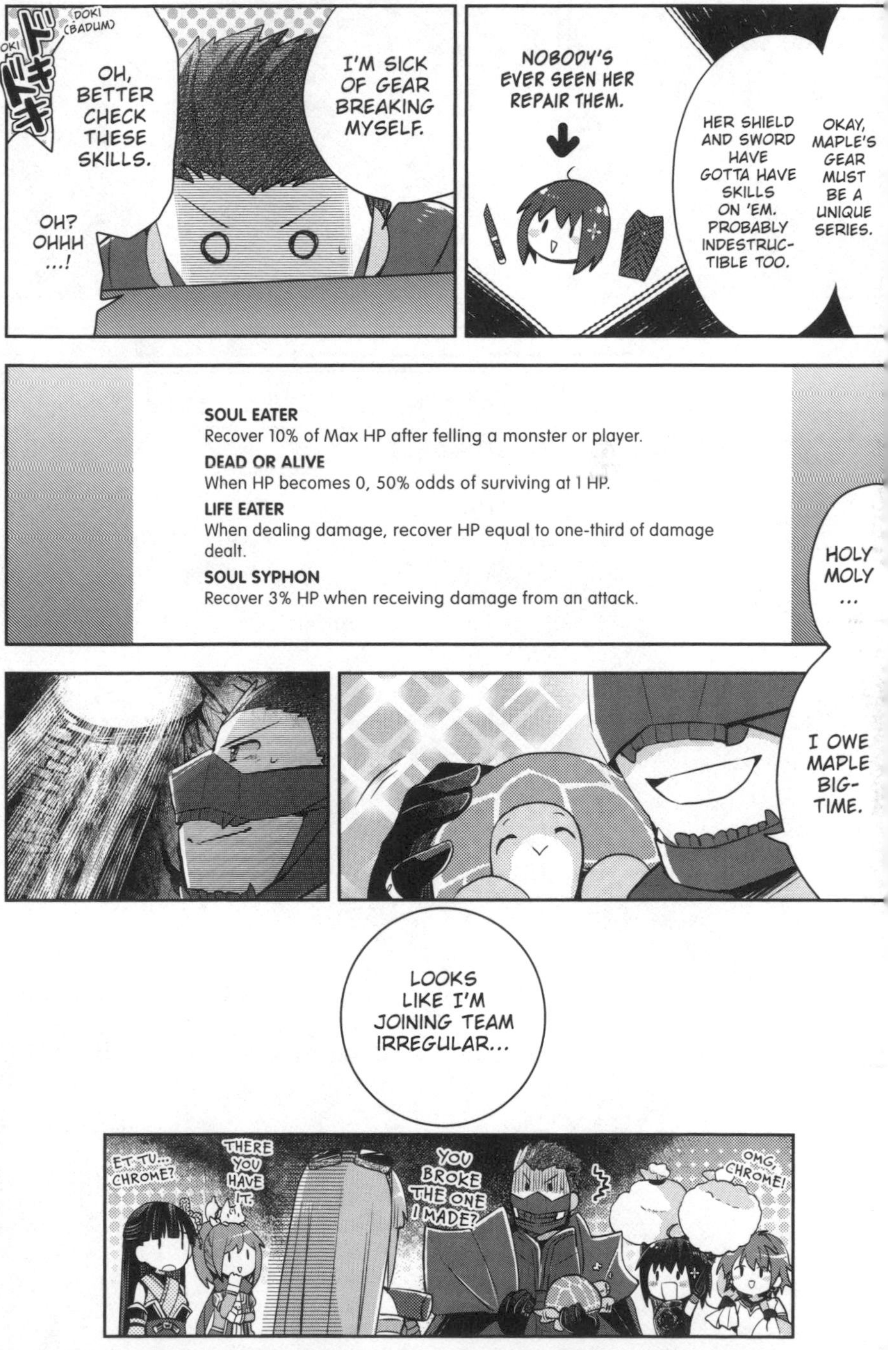
OKAY, MAPLE'S GEAR MUST BE A UNIQUE SERIES.
HER SHIELD AND SWORD HAVE GOTTA HAVE SKILLS ON 'EM. PROBABLY INDESTRUCTIBLE TOO.
NOBODY'S EVER SEEN HER REPAIR THEM.
I'M SICK OF GEAR BREAKING MYSELF.
OH, BETTER CHECK THESE SKILLS.
ドキドキ
DOKI DOKI (BADUM)
OH? OHHH ...!
HOLY MOLY ...
SOUL EATER
Recover 10% of Max HP after felling a monster or player.
DEAD OR ALIVE
When HP becomes 0, 50% odds of surviving at 1 HP.
LIFE EATER
When dealing damage, recover HP equal to one-third of damage dealt.
SOUL SYPHON
Recover 3% HP when receiving damage from an attack.
I OWE MAPLE BIG-TIME.
LOOKS LIKE I'M JOINING TEAM IRREGULAR...
OMG, CHROME!
YOU BROKE THE ONE I MADE?
THERE YOU HAVE IT.
ET TU... CHROME?

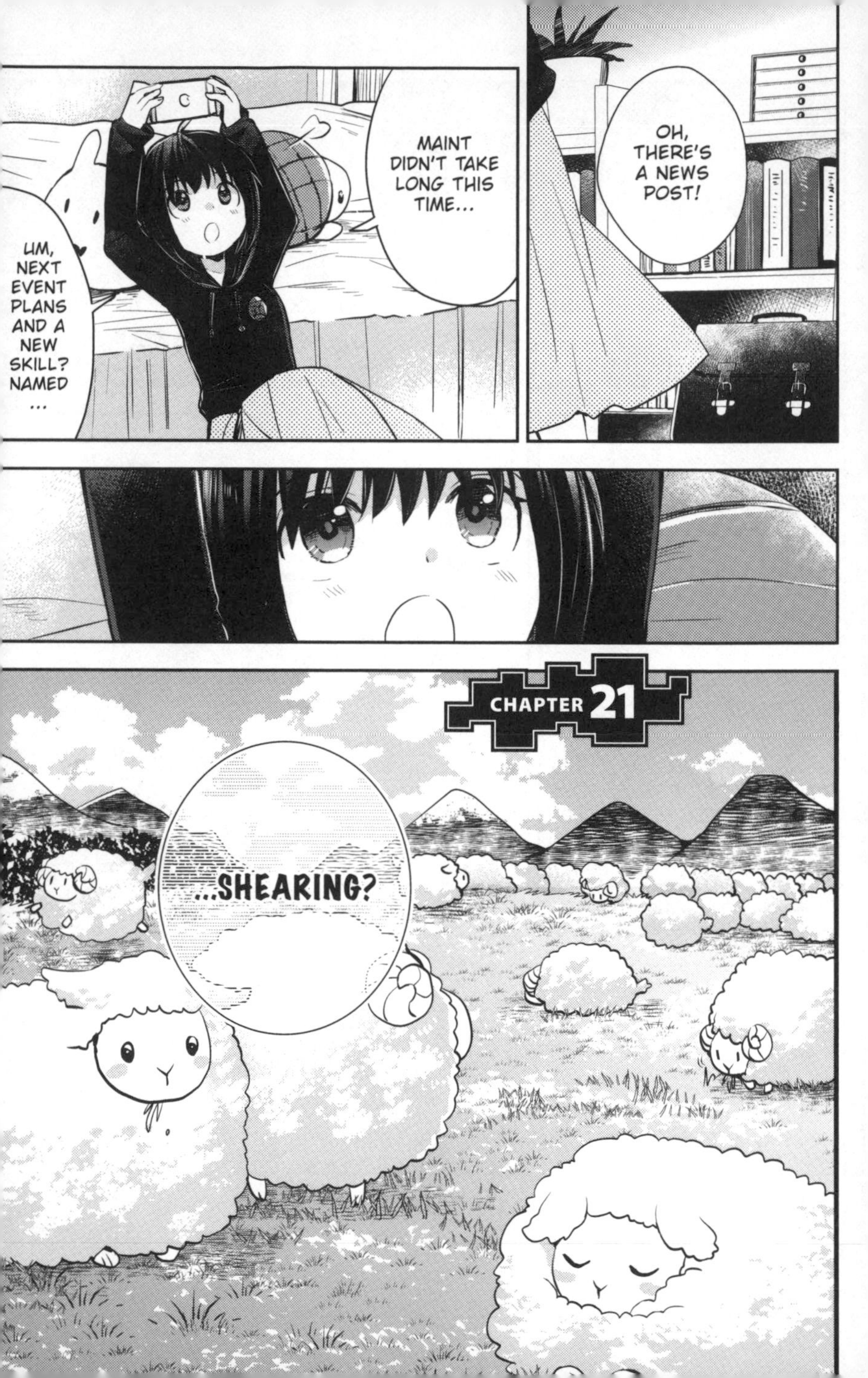
OH, THERE'S A NEWS POST!
MAINT DIDN'T TAKE LONG THIS TIME...
UM, NEXT EVENT PLANS AND A NEW SKILL? NAMED ...
CHAPTER 21
...SHEARING?

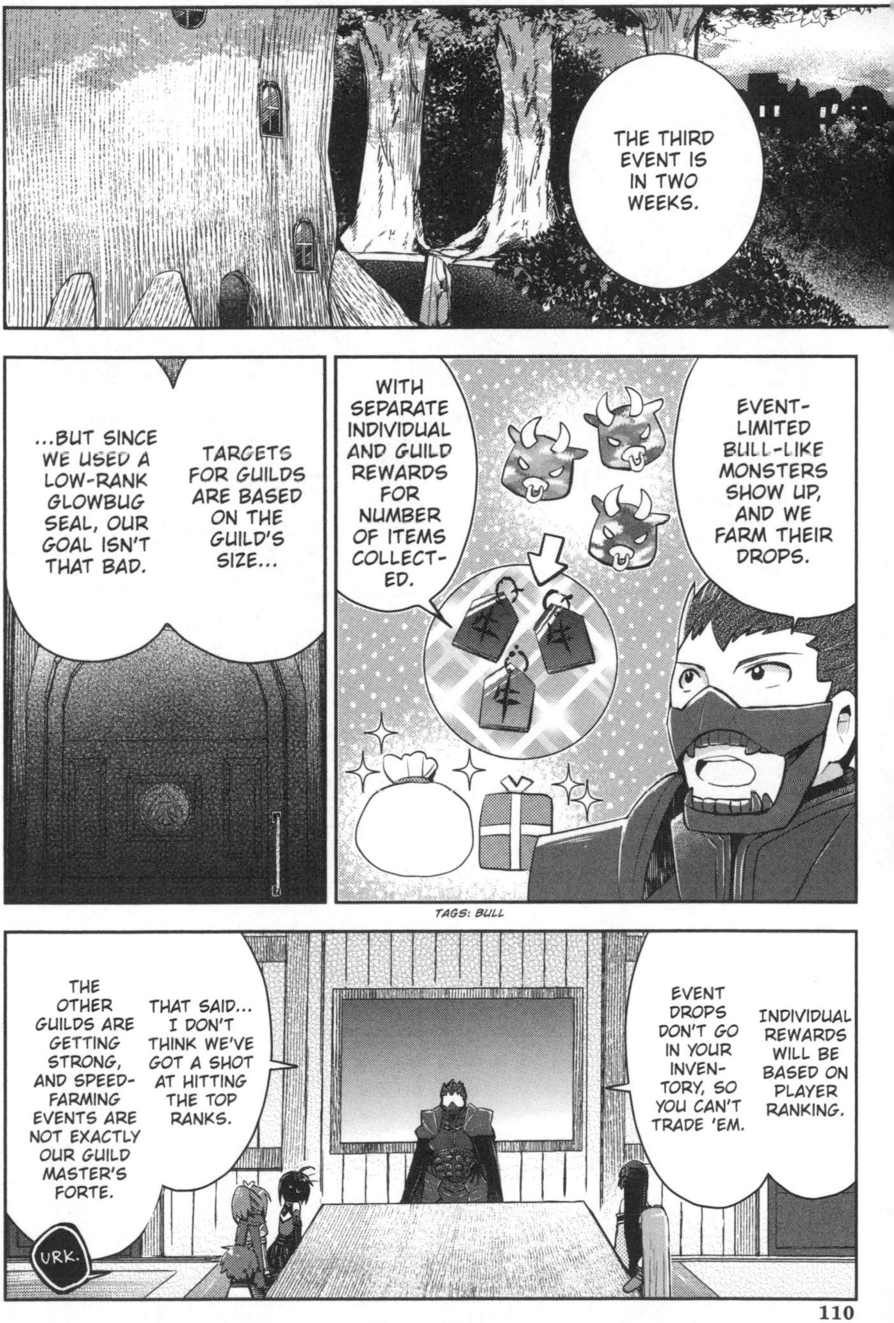
THE THIRD EVENT IS IN TWO WEEKS.
EVENT-LIMITED BULL-LIKE MONSTERS SHOW UP, AND WE FARM THEIR DROPS.
WITH SEPARATE INDIVIDUAL AND GUILD REWARDS FOR NUMBER OF ITEMS COLLECT-ED.
TAGS: BULL
TARGETS FOR GUILDS ARE BASED ON THE GUILD'S SIZE...
...BUT SINCE WE USED A LOW-RANK GLOWBUG SEAL, OUR GOAL ISN'T THAT BAD.
INDIVIDUAL REWARDS WILL BE BASED ON PLAYER RANKING.
EVENT DROPS DON'T GO IN YOUR INVEN-TORY, SO YOU CAN'T TRADE 'EM.
THAT SAID... I DON'T THINK WE'VE GOT A SHOT AT HITTING THE TOP RANKS.
THE OTHER GUILDS ARE GETTING STRONG, AND SPEED-FARMING EVENTS ARE NOT EXACTLY OUR GUILD MASTER'S FORTE.
URK.

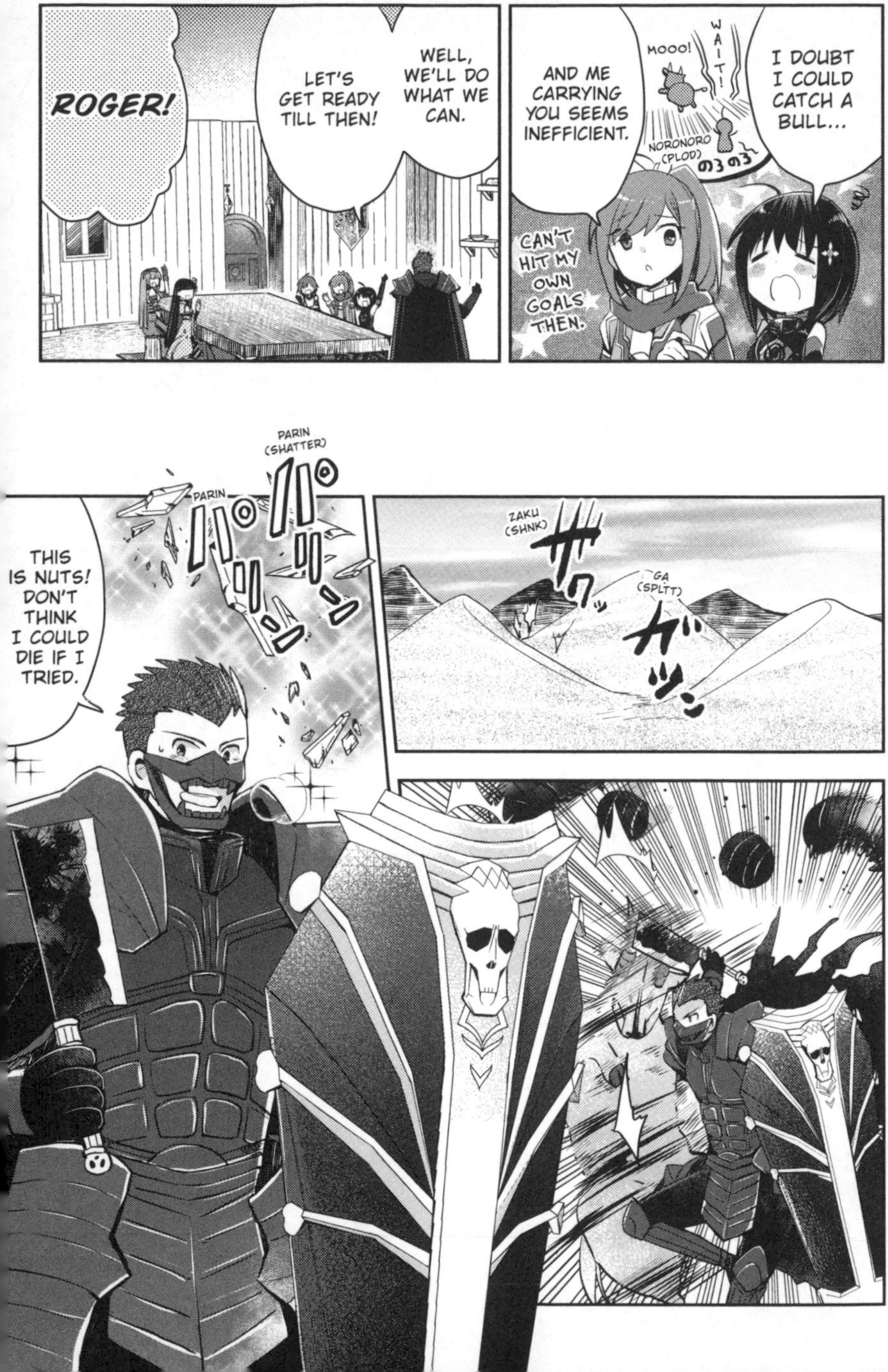

I DOUBT I COULD CATCH A BULL...
WAIT!
MOOO!
AND ME CARRYING YOU SEEMS INEFFICIENT.
NORONORO (PLOD)
のろのろ
CAN'T HIT MY OWN GOALS THEN.
WELL, WE'LL DO WHAT WE CAN.
LET'S GET READY TILL THEN!
ROGER!
ZAKU (SHNK)
GA (SPLTT)
PARIN (SHATTER)
PARIN
THIS IS NUTS! DON'T THINK I COULD DIE IF I TRIED.

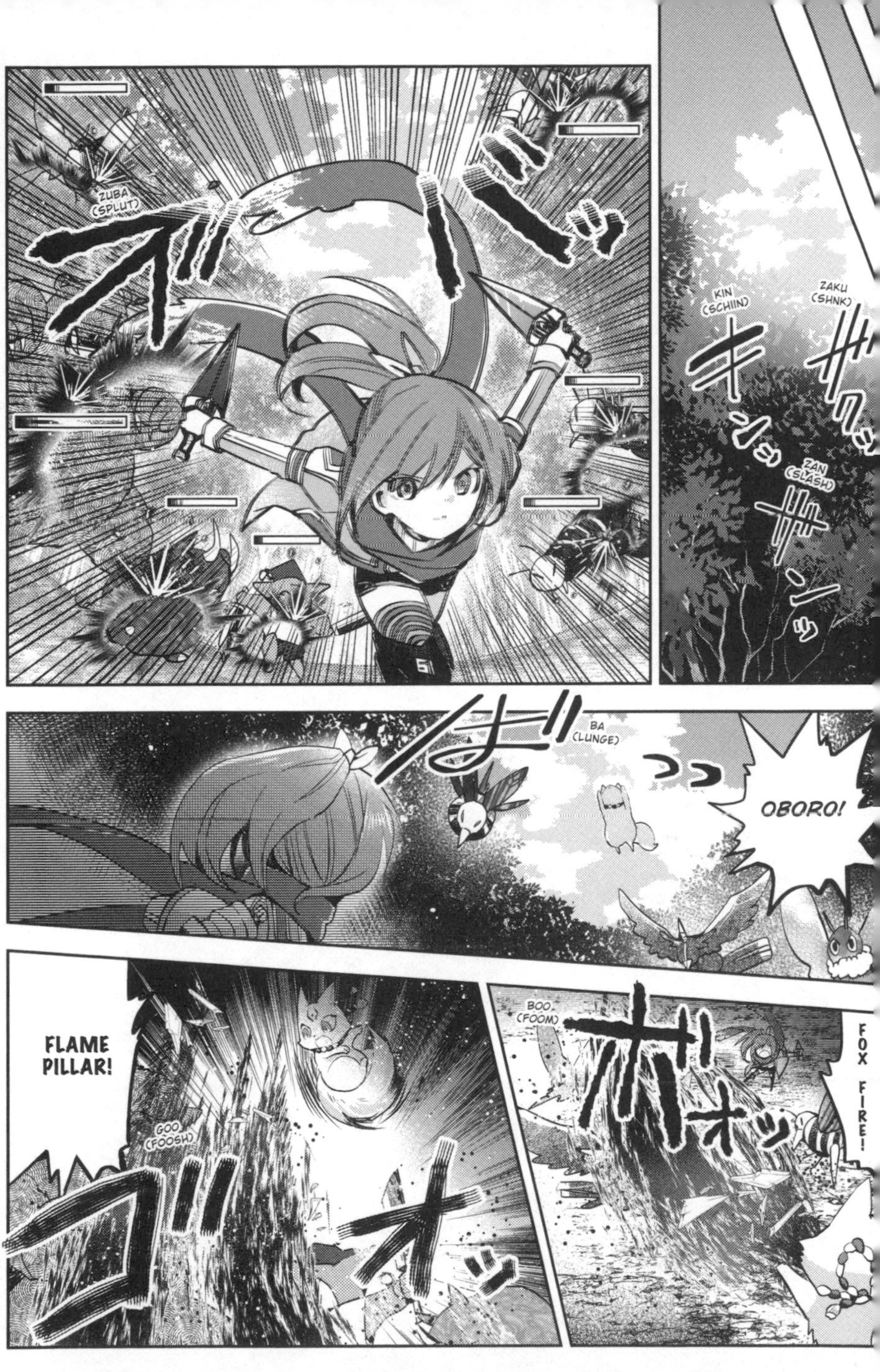
ZAKU
(SHNK)
KIN
(SCHIIN)
ZAN
(SLASH)
ZUBA
(SPLUT)
OBORO!
BA
(LUNGE)
FOX FIRE!
BOO
(FOOM)
FLAME PILLAR!
GOO
(FOOSH)

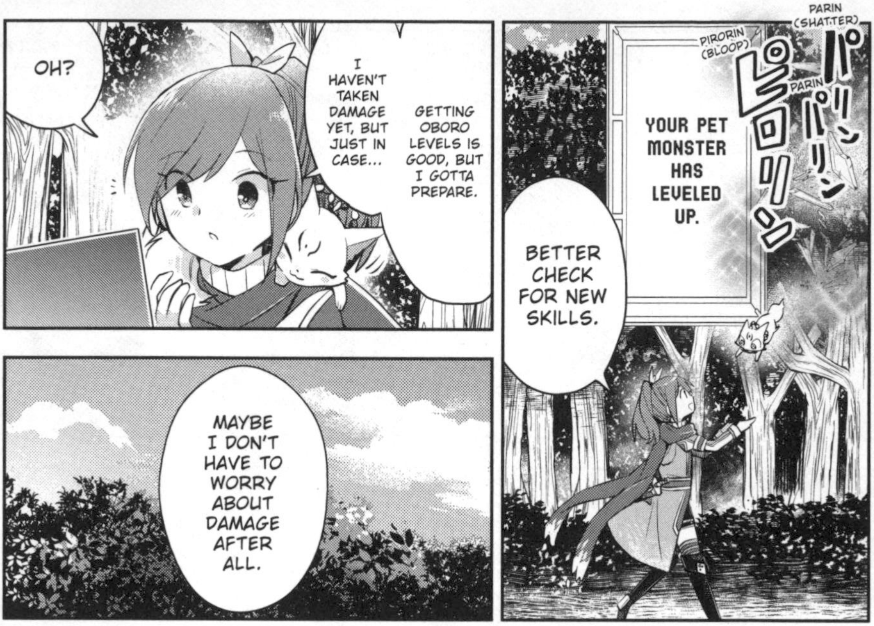
PARIN (SHATTER)
PIRORIN (BLOOP)
PARIN
YOUR PET MONSTER HAS LEVELED UP.
BETTER CHECK FOR NEW SKILLS.
GETTING OBORO LEVELS IS GOOD, BUT I GOTTA PREPARE.
I HAVEN'T TAKEN DAMAGE YET, BUT JUST IN CASE...
OH?
MAYBE I DON'T HAVE TO WORRY ABOUT DAMAGE AFTER ALL.

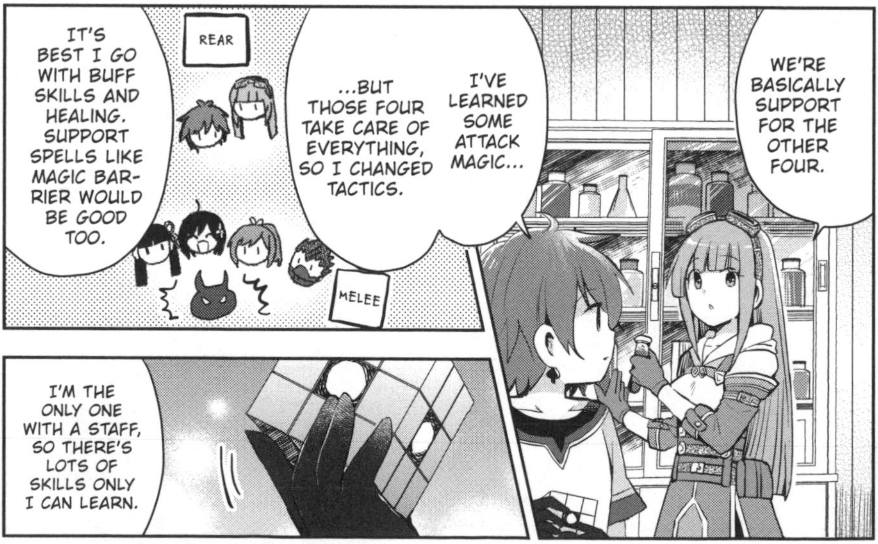
WE'RE BASICALLY SUPPORT FOR THE OTHER FOUR.
I'VE LEARNED SOME ATTACK MAGIC...
...BUT THOSE FOUR TAKE CARE OF EVERYTHING, SO I CHANGED TACTICS.
REAR
IT'S BEST I GO WITH BUFF SKILLS AND HEALING. SUPPORT SPELLS LIKE MAGIC BAR-RIER WOULD BE GOOD TOO.
MELEE
I'M THE ONLY ONE WITH A STAFF, SO THERE'S LOTS OF SKILLS ONLY I CAN LEARN.

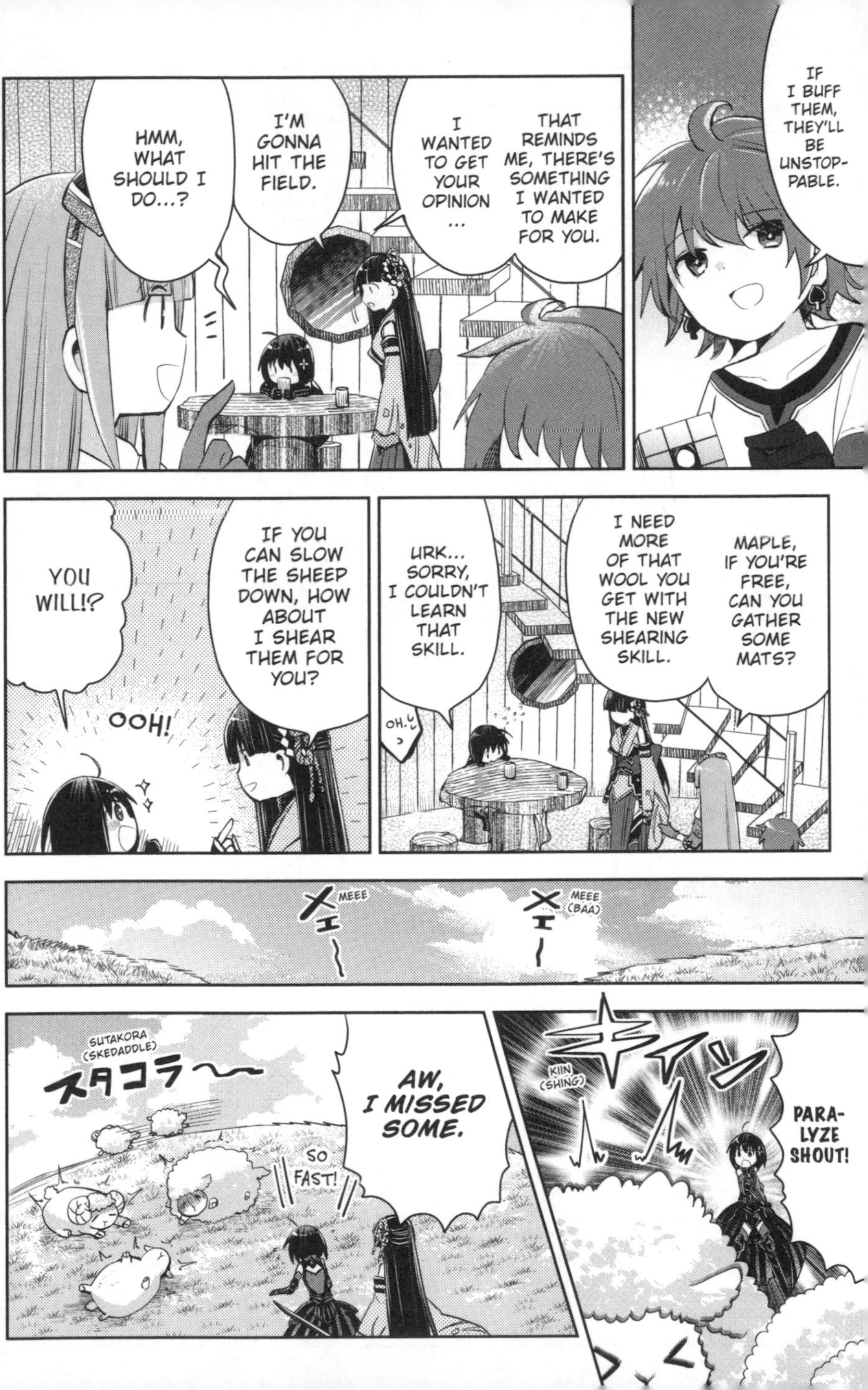
IF I BUFF THEM, THEY'LL BE UNSTOP-PABLE.
THAT REMINDS ME, THERE'S SOMETHING I WANTED TO MAKE FOR YOU.
I WANTED TO GET YOUR OPINION ...
I'M GONNA HIT THE FIELD.
HMM, WHAT SHOULD I DO...?
MAPLE, IF YOU'RE FREE, CAN YOU GATHER SOME MATS?
I NEED MORE OF THAT WOOL YOU GET WITH THE NEW SHEARING SKILL.
URK... SORRY, I COULDN'T LEARN THAT SKILL.
OH.
IF YOU CAN SLOW THE SHEEP DOWN, HOW ABOUT I SHEAR THEM FOR YOU?
YOU WILL!?
OOH!
メェ～
MEEE (BAA)
メェ～
MEEE
キィン
KIIN (SHING)
PARA-LYZE SHOUT!
AW, I MISSED SOME.
SO FAST!
スタコラ～
SUTAKORA (SKEDADDLE)

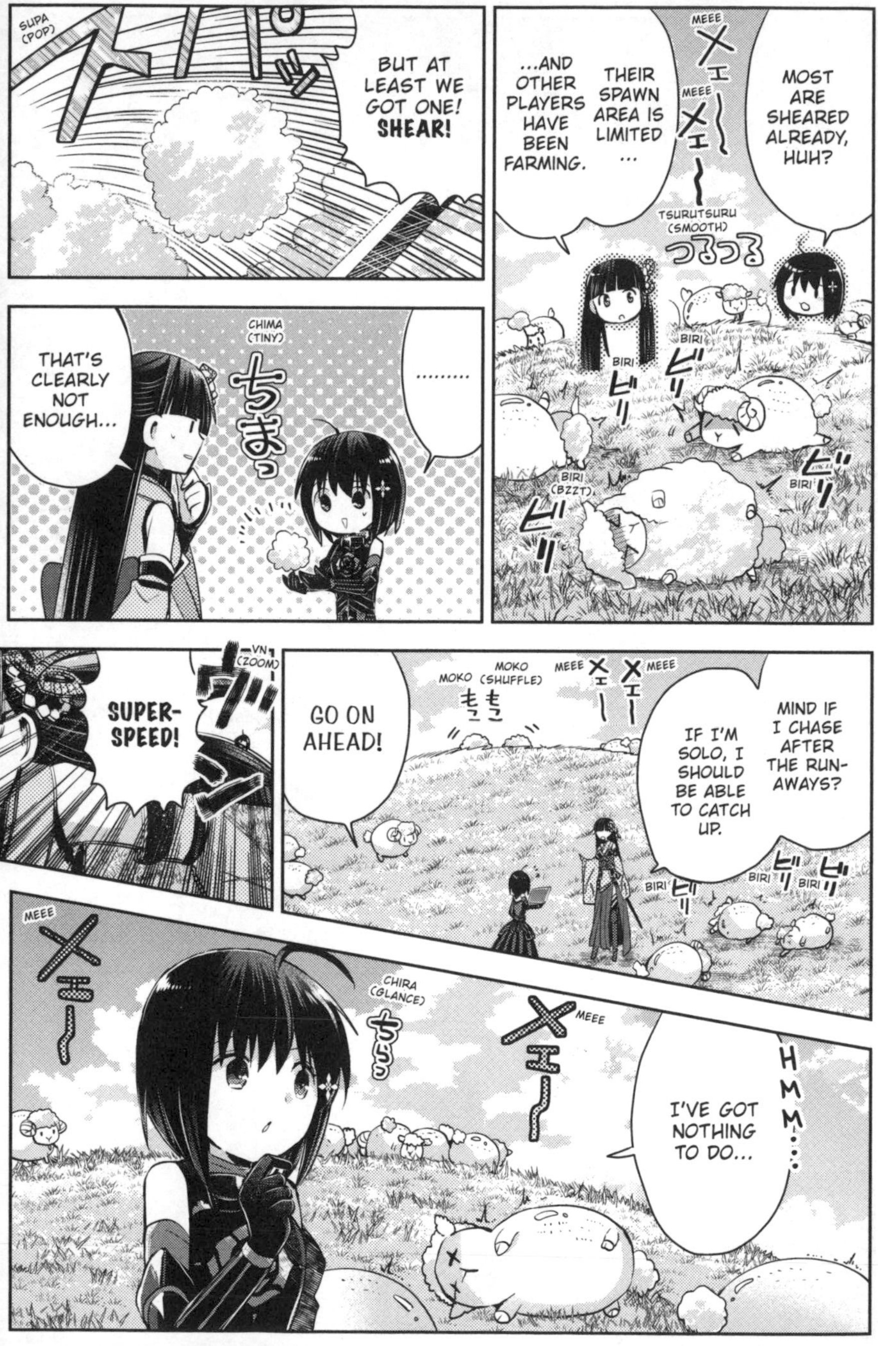
MEEE メェ～
MEEE メェ～
MOST ARE SHEARED ALREADY, HUH?
THEIR SPAWN AREA IS LIMITED...
...AND OTHER PLAYERS HAVE BEEN FARMING.
TSURUTSURU (SMOOTH) つるつる
BIRI ビリ
BIRI ビリ
BIRI ビリ
BIRI (BZZT) ビリ
SUPA (POP)
BUT AT LEAST WE GOT ONE! **SHEAR!**
....
CHIMA (TINY) ちまっ
THAT'S CLEARLY NOT ENOUGH...
MIND IF I CHASE AFTER THE RUN-AWAYS?
IF I'M SOLO, I SHOULD BE ABLE TO CATCH UP.
MEEE メェー
MEEE メェー
GO ON AHEAD!
MOKO MOKO (SHUFFLE) もこもこ
BIRI ビリ
BIRI ビリ
BIRI ビリ
VN (ZOOM)
SUPER-SPEED!
HMM...
I'VE GOT NOTHING TO DO...
MEEE メェ～
CHIRA (GLANCE) ちらっ
MEEE メェ～

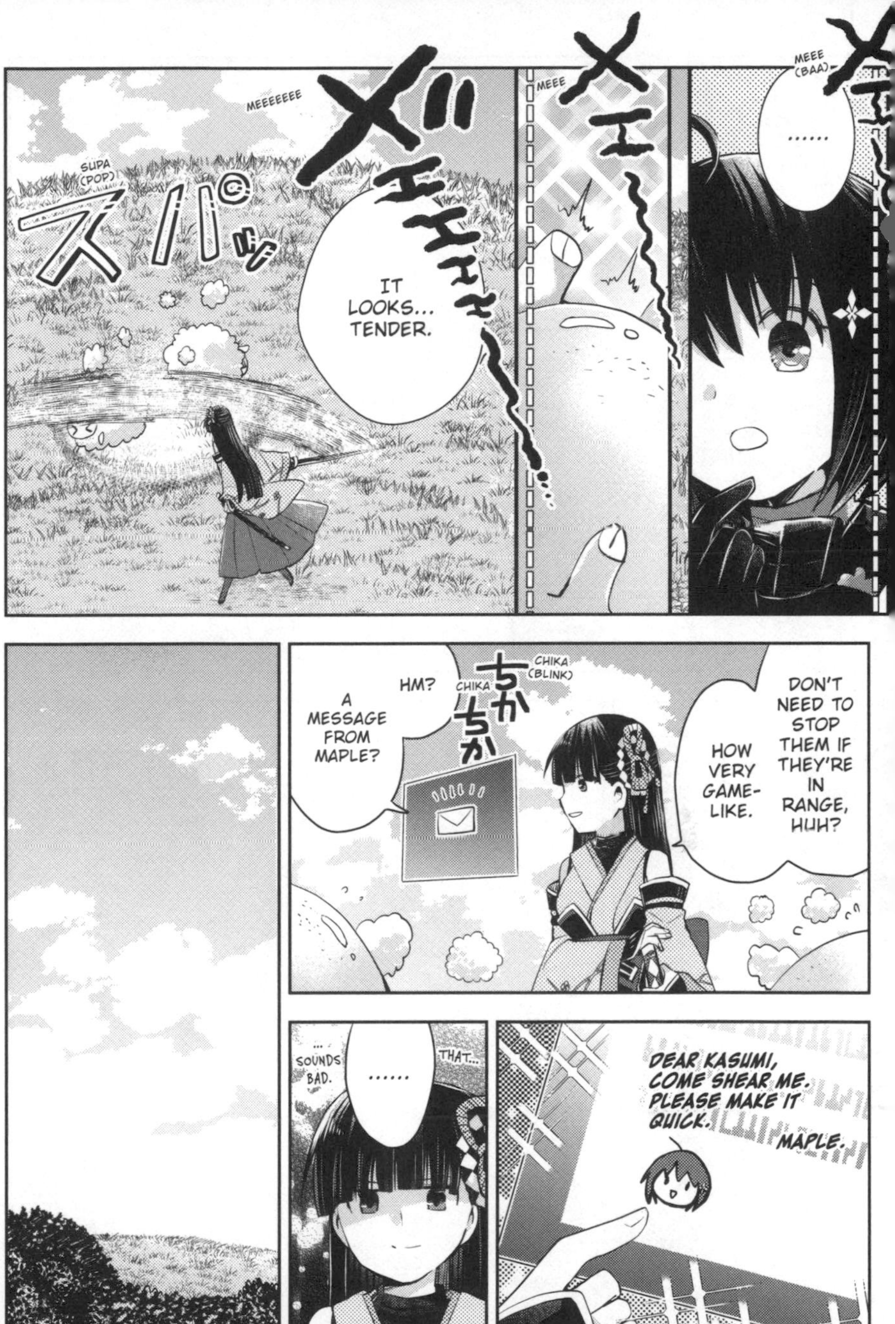
MEEE (BAA)
......
MEEE
MEEEEEEE
SUPA (POP)
IT LOOKS... TENDER.
DON'T NEED TO STOP THEM IF THEY'RE IN RANGE, HUH?
HOW VERY GAME-LIKE.
CHIKA (BLINK)
CHIKA
HM?
A MESSAGE FROM MAPLE?
DEAR KASUMI, COME SHEAR ME. PLEASE MAKE IT QUICK.
MAPLE.
......
THAT...
... SOUNDS BAD.

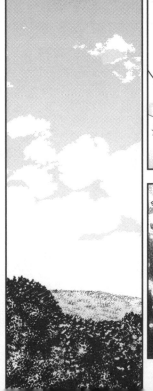

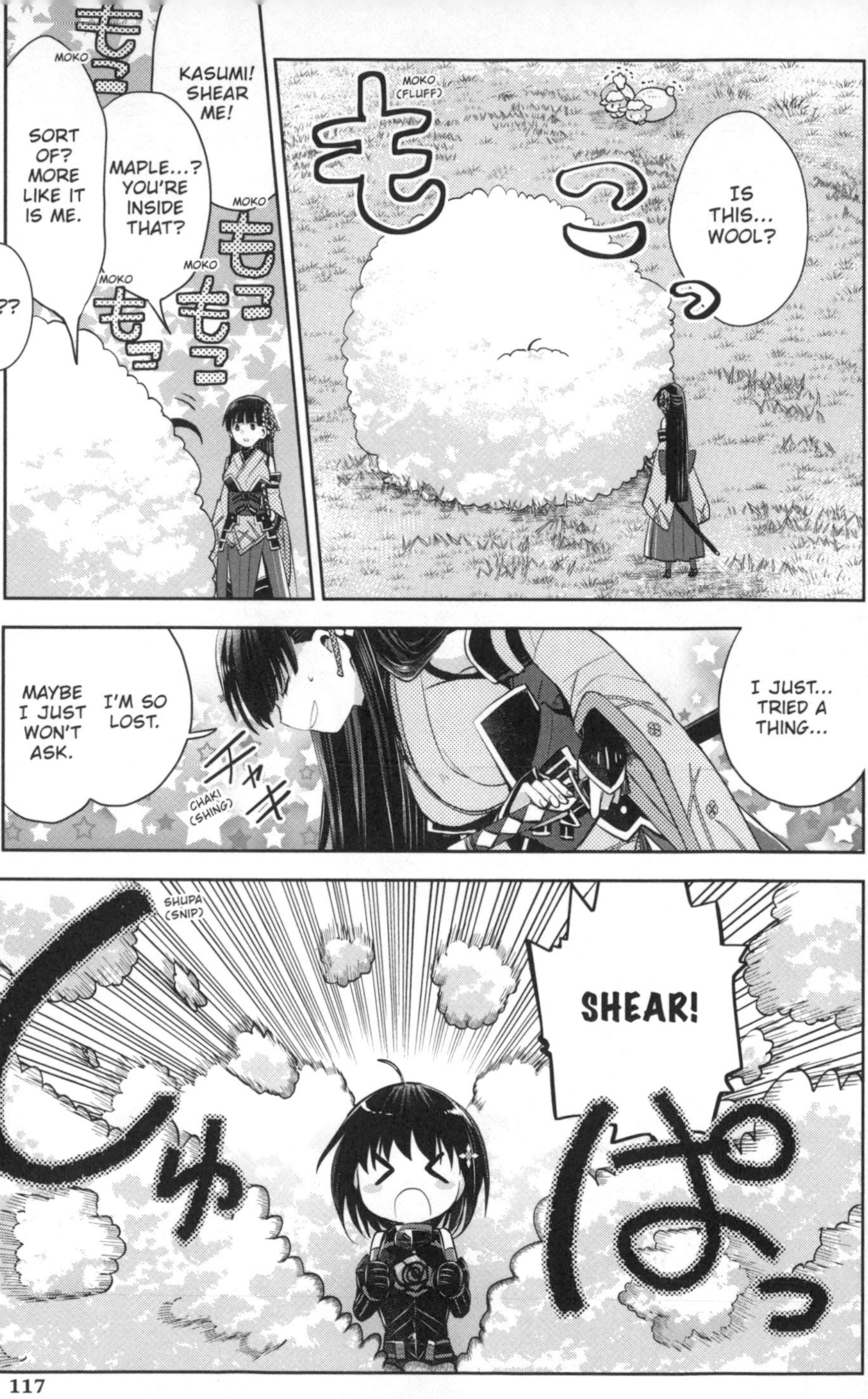
MOKO (FLUFF)
もっ
IS THIS... WOOL?
MOKO
KASUMI! SHEAR ME!
MAPLE...? YOU'RE INSIDE THAT?
MOKO
MOKO
MOKO
SORT OF? MORE LIKE IT IS ME.
???
I JUST... TRIED A THING...
CHAKI (SHING)
I'M SO LOST.
MAYBE I JUST WON'T ASK.
SHEAR!
SHUPA (SNIP)
しゅぱっ

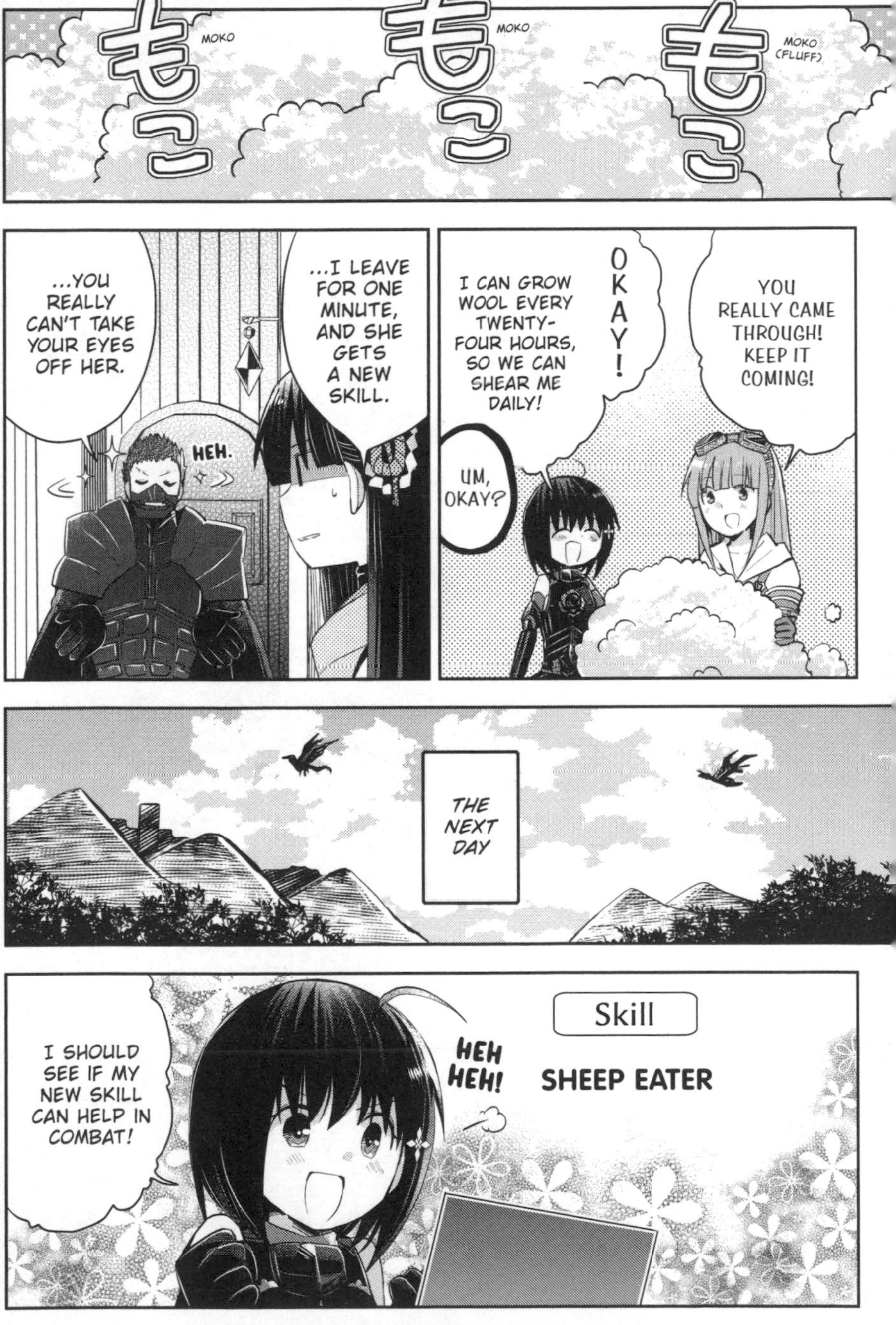
もこっ
MOKO (FLUFF)
もこっ
MOKO
もこっ
MOKO
YOU REALLY CAME THROUGH! KEEP IT COMING!
OKAY!
I CAN GROW WOOL EVERY TWENTY-FOUR HOURS, SO WE CAN SHEAR ME DAILY!
UM, OKAY?
...I LEAVE FOR ONE MINUTE, AND SHE GETS A NEW SKILL.
HEH.
...YOU REALLY CAN'T TAKE YOUR EYES OFF HER.
THE NEXT DAY
Skill
SHEEP EATER
HEH HEH!
I SHOULD SEE IF MY NEW SKILL CAN HELP IN COMBAT!

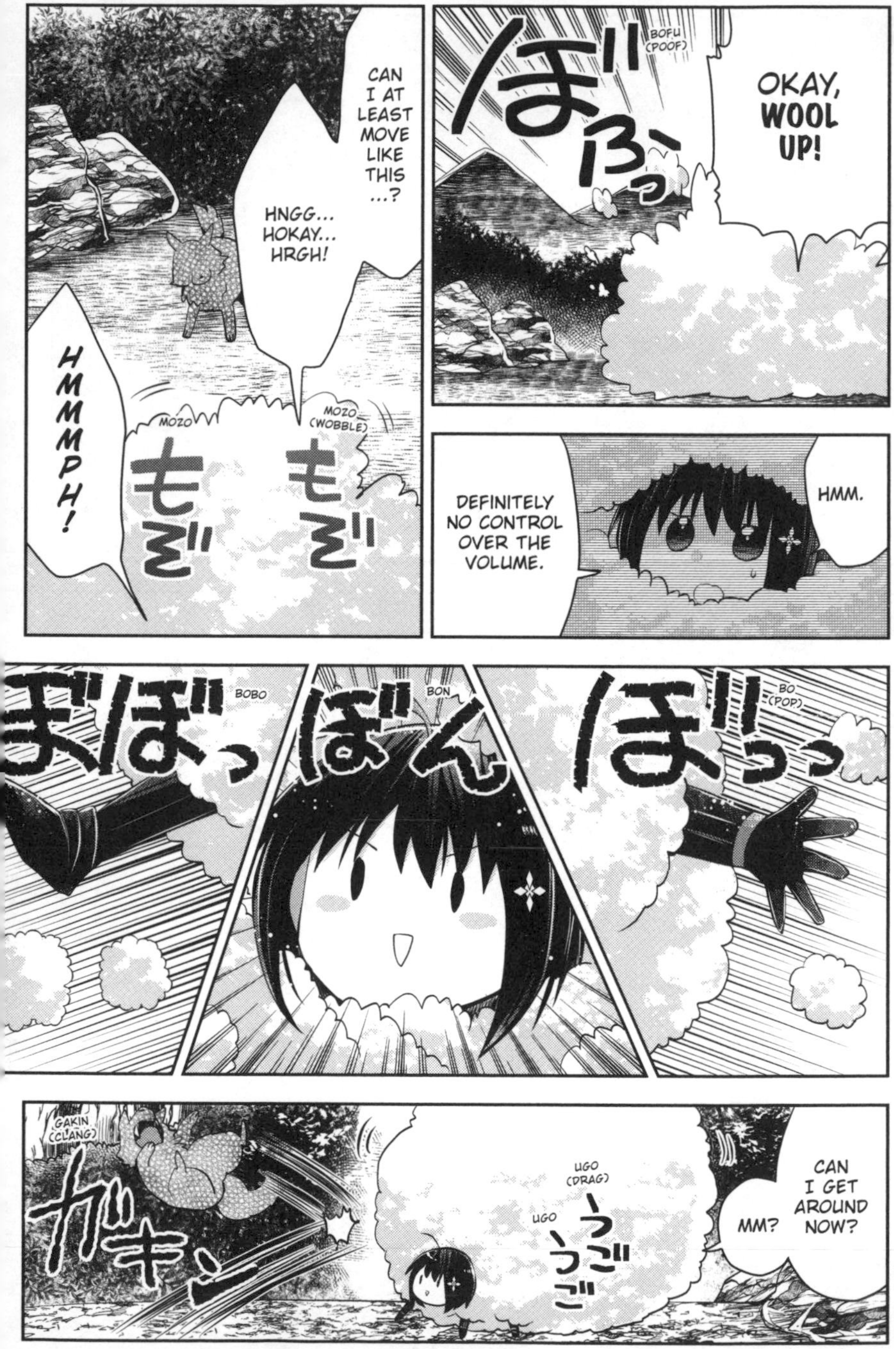
BOFU (POOF)
ぼふっ
OKAY, WOOL UP!
HMM.
DEFINITELY NO CONTROL OVER THE VOLUME.
CAN I AT LEAST MOVE LIKE THIS ...?
HNGG... HOKAY... HRGH!
MOZO (WOBBLE)
もぞ
MOZO
もぞ
HMMMMPH!
BO (POP)
ぼっっ
BON
ぼん
BOBO
ぼぼっ
CAN I GET AROUND NOW?
MM?
UGO (DRAG)
うご
UGO
うご
GAKIN (CLANG)
がきん

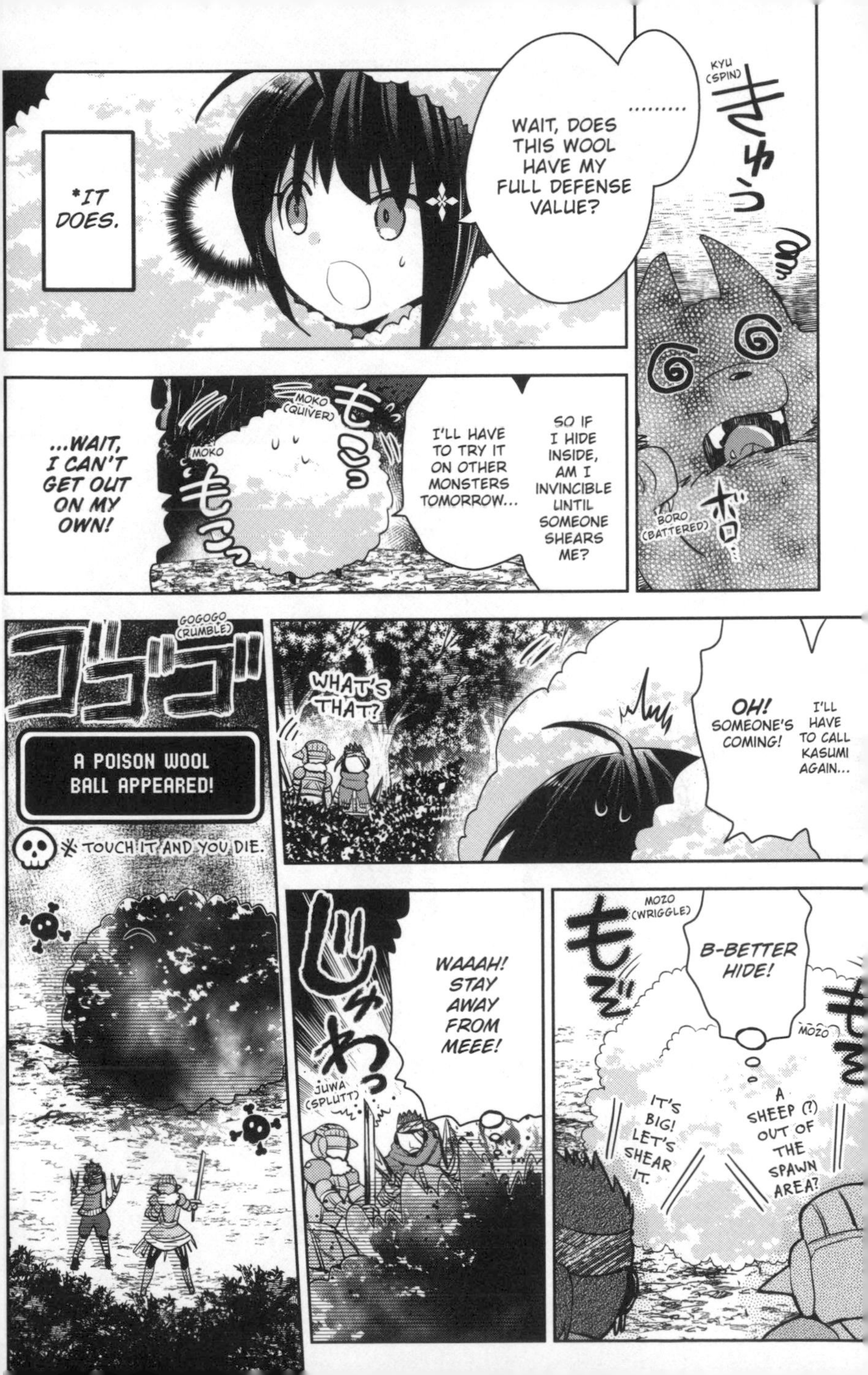
KYU (SPIN)
BORO (BATTERED)
....
WAIT, DOES THIS WOOL HAVE MY FULL DEFENSE VALUE?
*IT DOES.
SO IF I HIDE INSIDE, AM I INVINCIBLE UNTIL SOMEONE SHEARS ME?
I'LL HAVE TO TRY IT ON OTHER MONSTERS TOMORROW...
MOKO (QUIVER)
MOKO
...WAIT, I CAN'T GET OUT ON MY OWN!
OH! SOMEONE'S COMING!
I'LL HAVE TO CALL KASUMI AGAIN...
WHAT'S THAT?
MOZO (WRIGGLE)
B-BETTER HIDE!
MOZO
A SHEEP (?) OUT OF THE SPAWN AREA?
IT'S BIG! LET'S SHEAR IT.
JUWA (SPLUTT)
WAAAH! STAY AWAY FROM MEEE!
GOGOGO (RUMBLE)
A POISON WOOL BALL APPEARED!
* TOUCH IT AND YOU DIE.

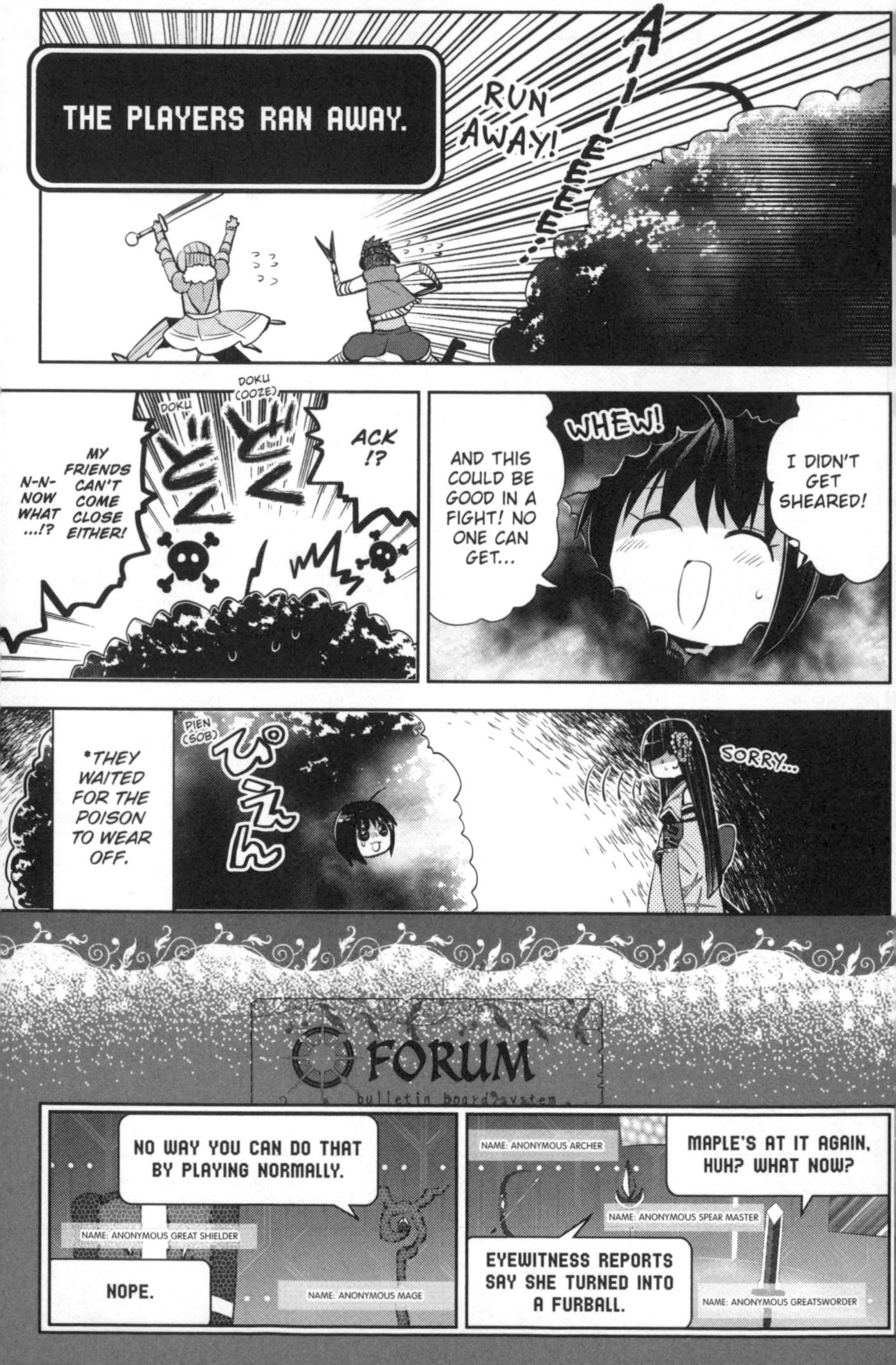
AIIIEEEEEE...!
RUN AWAY!
THE PLAYERS RAN AWAY.
WHEW!
I DIDN'T GET SHEARED!
AND THIS COULD BE GOOD IN A FIGHT! NO ONE CAN GET...
ACK!?
DOKU (COOZE)
DOKU
MY FRIENDS CAN'T COME CLOSE EITHER!
N-N-NOW WHAT...!?
SORRY...
PIEN (SOB)
*THEY WAITED FOR THE POISON TO WEAR OFF.
FORUM
bulletin board system
MAPLE'S AT IT AGAIN, HUH? WHAT NOW?
NAME: ANONYMOUS ARCHER
NAME: ANONYMOUS SPEAR MASTER
EYEWITNESS REPORTS SAY SHE TURNED INTO A FURBALL.
NAME: ANONYMOUS GREATSWORDER
NO WAY YOU CAN DO THAT BY PLAYING NORMALLY.
NAME: ANONYMOUS GREAT SHIELDER
NOPE.
NAME: ANONYMOUS MAGE

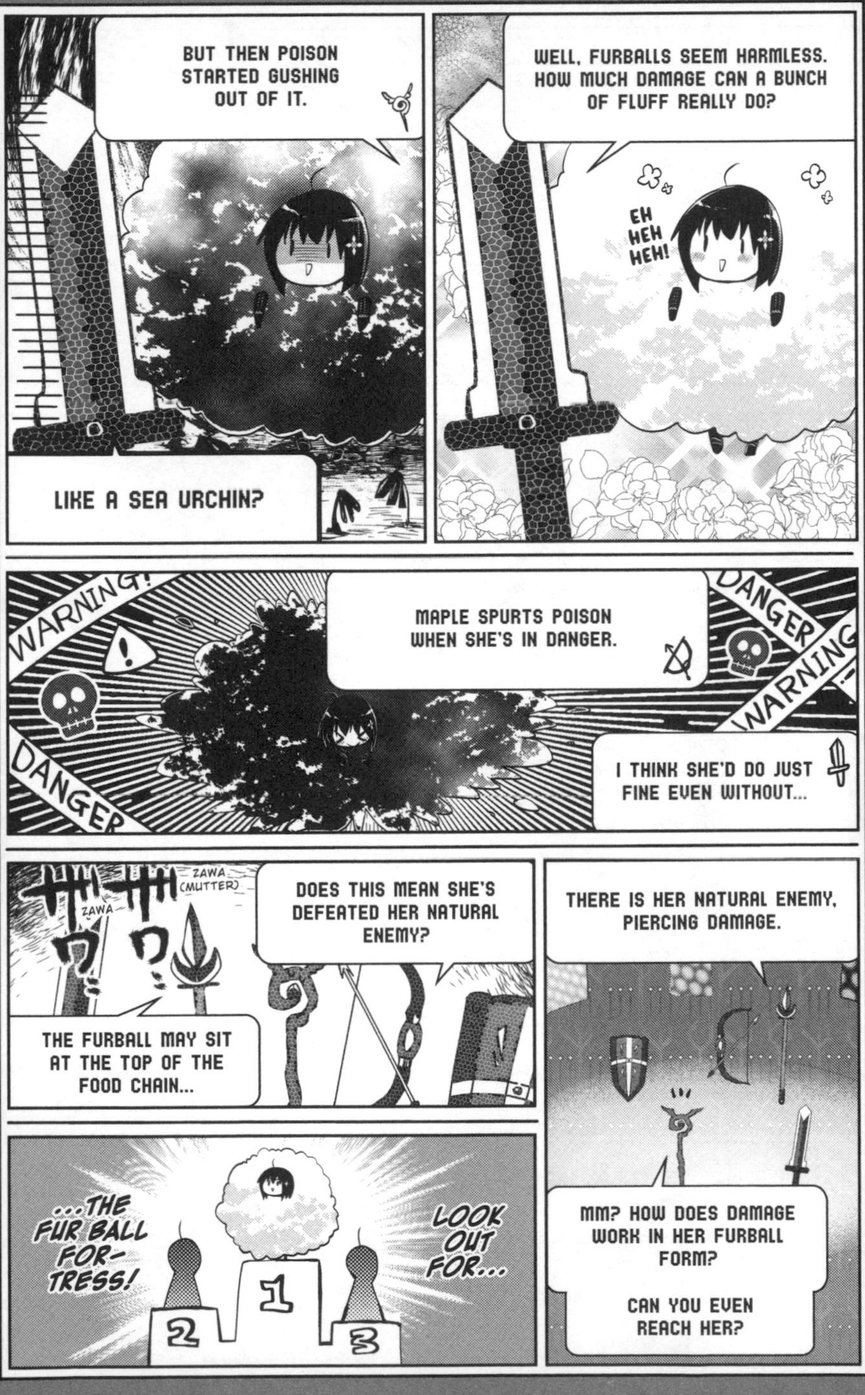
WELL, FURBALLS SEEM HARMLESS. HOW MUCH DAMAGE CAN A BUNCH OF FLUFF REALLY DO?
EH HEH HEH!
BUT THEN POISON STARTED GUSHING OUT OF IT.
LIKE A SEA URCHIN?
DANGER
WARNING
MAPLE SPURTS POISON WHEN SHE'S IN DANGER.
WARNING!
DANGER
I THINK SHE'D DO JUST FINE EVEN WITHOUT...
THERE IS HER NATURAL ENEMY, PIERCING DAMAGE.
MM? HOW DOES DAMAGE WORK IN HER FURBALL FORM?
CAN YOU EVEN REACH HER?
DOES THIS MEAN SHE'S DEFEATED HER NATURAL ENEMY?
ZAWA (MUTTER)
ZAWA
THE FURBALL MAY SIT AT THE TOP OF THE FOOD CHAIN...
LOOK OUT FOR...
...THE FUR BALL FOR-TRESS!
1
2
3

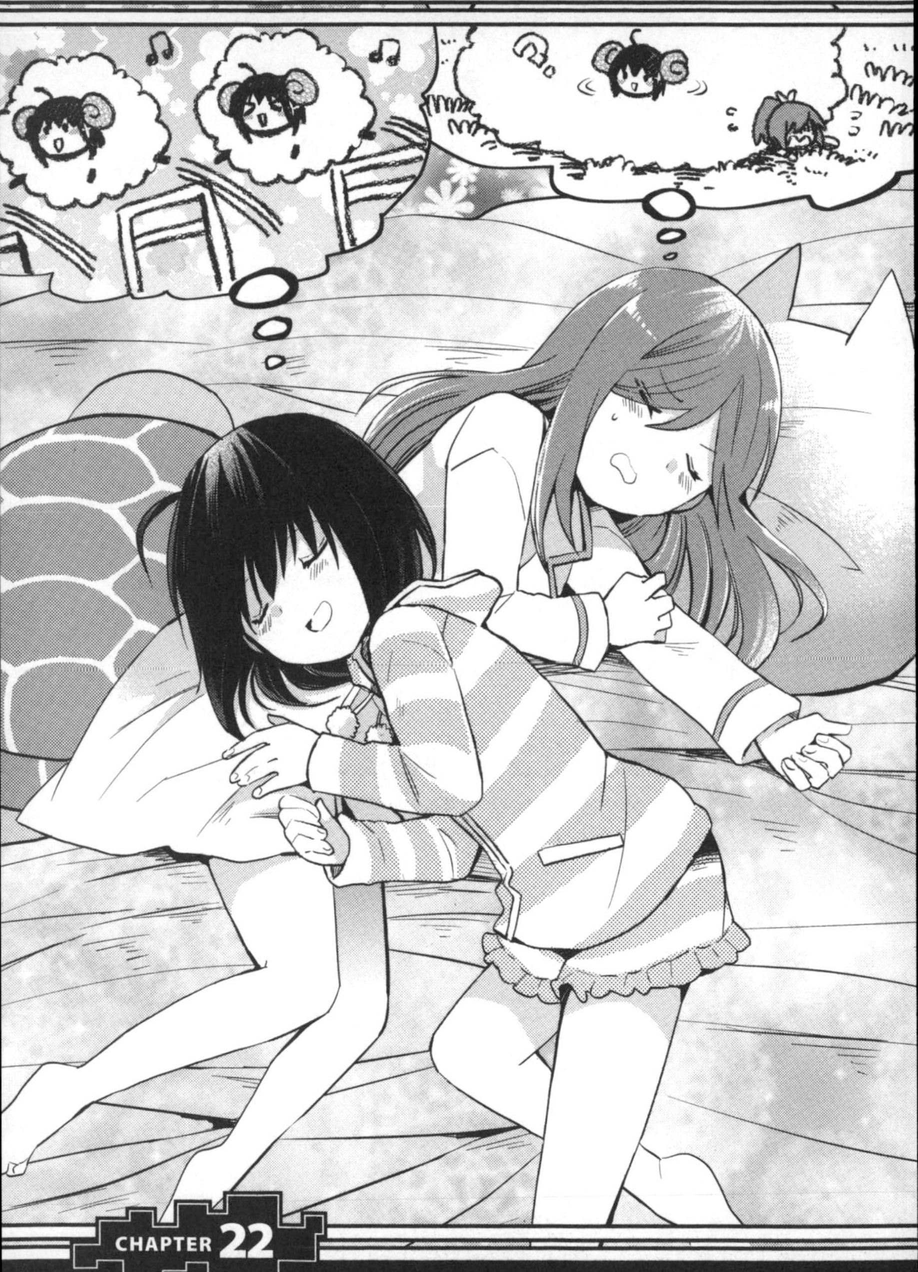
CHAPTER 22

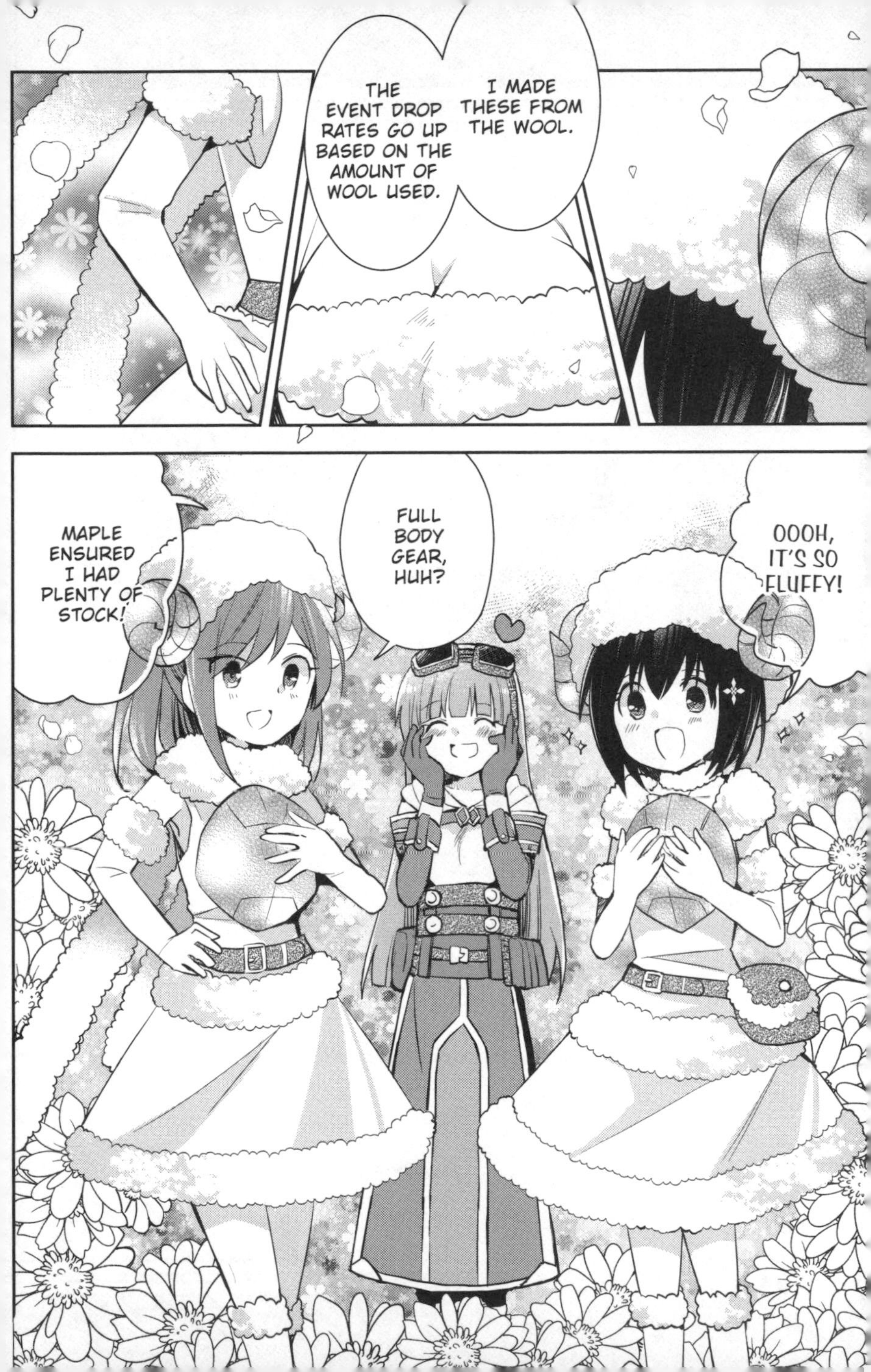
I MADE THESE FROM THE WOOL.
THE EVENT DROP RATES GO UP BASED ON THE AMOUNT OF WOOL USED.
OOOH, IT'S SO FLUFFY!
FULL BODY GEAR, HUH?
MAPLE ENSURED I HAD PLENTY OF STOCK!

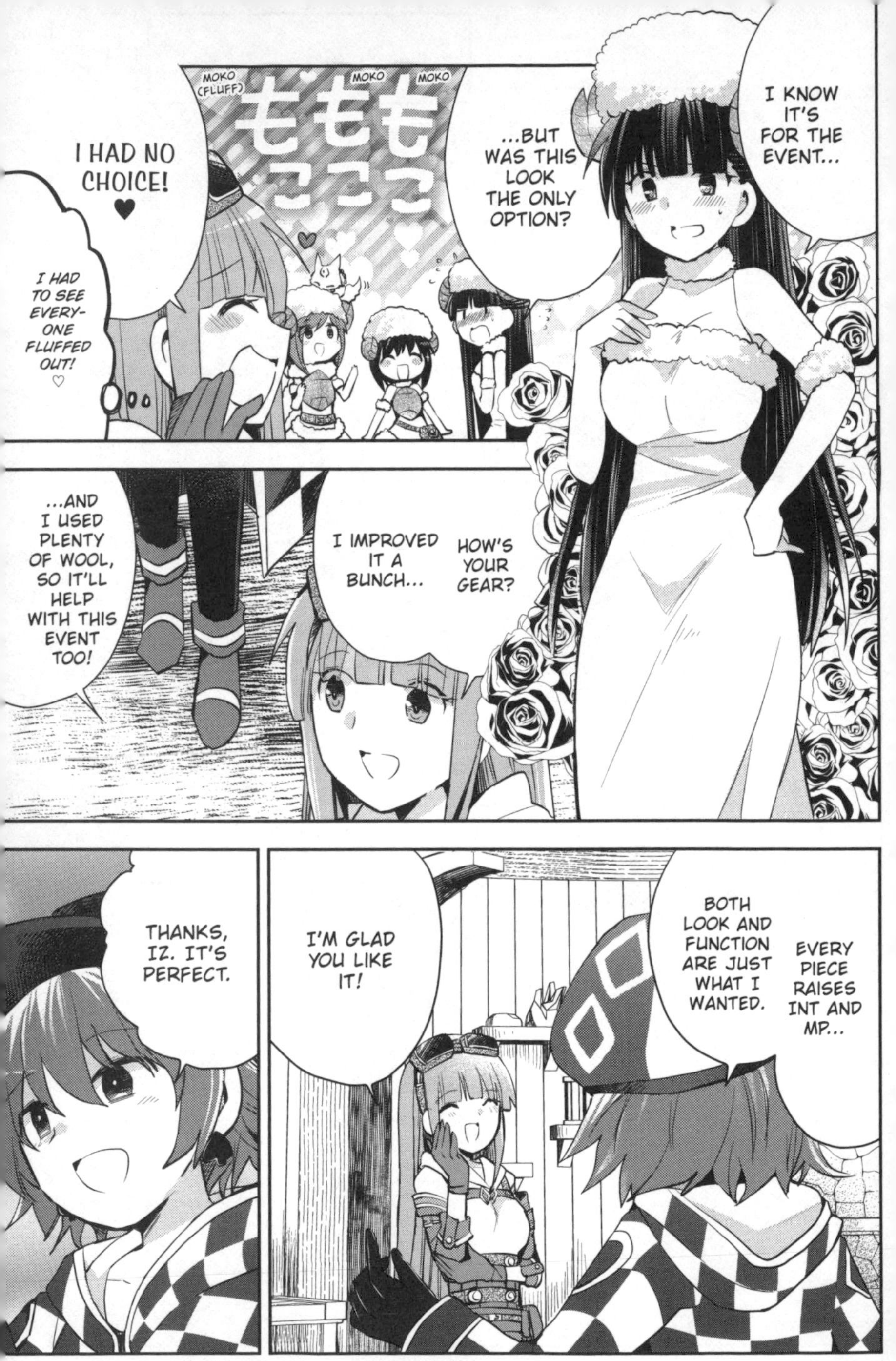
I KNOW IT'S FOR THE EVENT...
...BUT WAS THIS LOOK THE ONLY OPTION?
もこもこもこ
MOKO (FLUFF) MOKO MOKO
I HAD NO CHOICE! ♥
I HAD TO SEE EVERY-ONE FLUFFED OUT! ♡
HOW'S YOUR GEAR?
I IMPROVED IT A BUNCH...
...AND I USED PLENTY OF WOOL, SO IT'LL HELP WITH THIS EVENT TOO!
EVERY PIECE RAISES INT AND MP...
BOTH LOOK AND FUNCTION ARE JUST WHAT I WANTED.
I'M GLAD YOU LIKE IT!
THANKS, IZ. IT'S PERFECT.

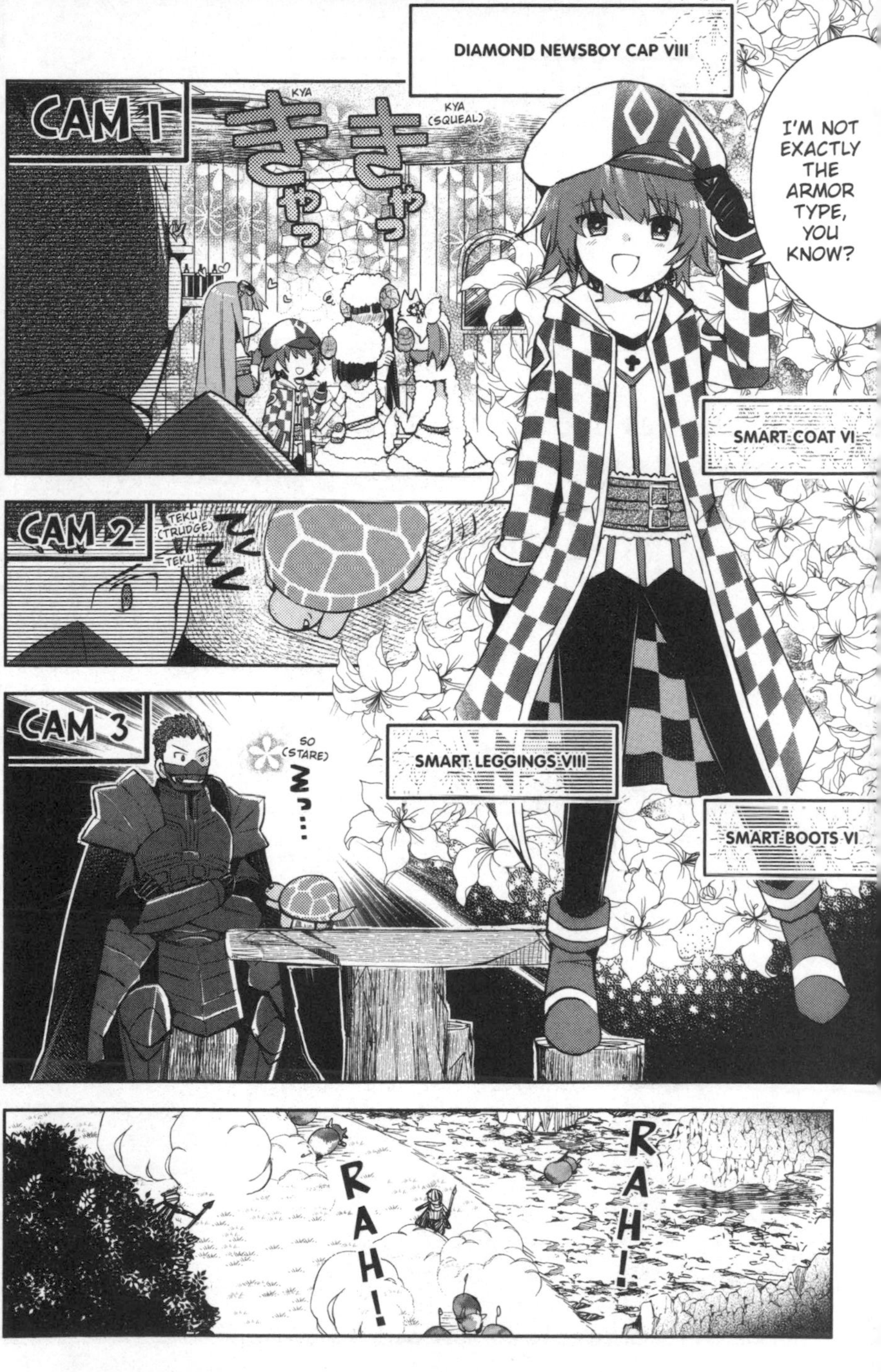
DIAMOND NEWSBOY CAP VIII
I'M NOT EXACTLY THE ARMOR TYPE, YOU KNOW?
SMART COAT VI
SMART LEGGINGS VIII
SMART BOOTS VI
CAM 1
KYA (SQUEAL)
KYA
きゃっきゃっ
CAM 2
TEKU (TRUDGE)
TEKU
てくてく
CAM 3
SO (STARE)
じっ…
RAH!
RAH!

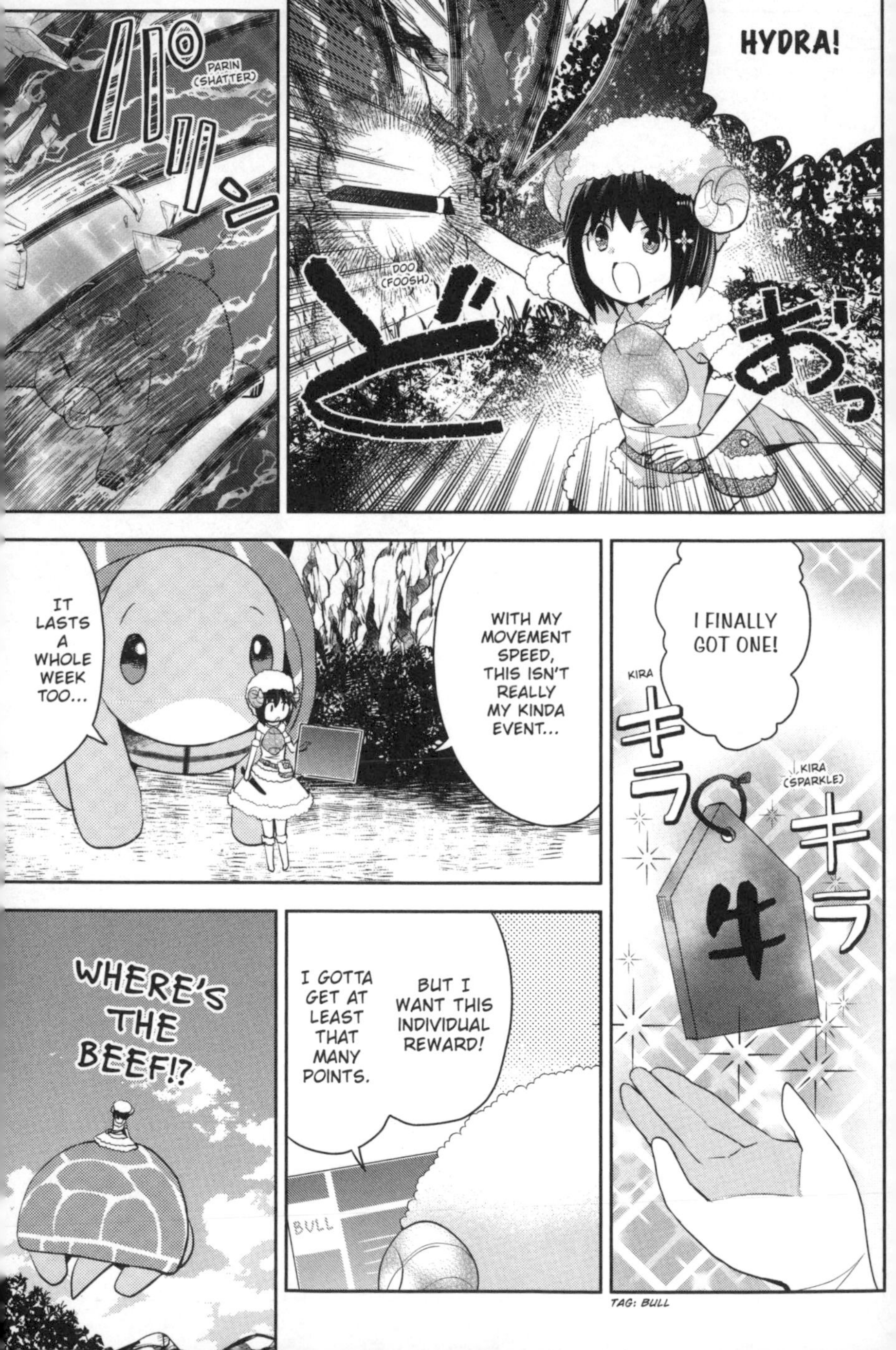
HYDRA!
DOO (FOOSH)
PARIN (SHATTER)
I FINALLY GOT ONE!
KIRA
KIRA (SPARKLE)
WITH MY MOVEMENT SPEED, THIS ISN'T REALLY MY KINDA EVENT...
IT LASTS A WHOLE WEEK TOO...
BUT I WANT THIS INDIVIDUAL REWARD!
I GOTTA GET AT LEAST THAT MANY POINTS.
BULL
WHERE'S THE BEEF!?

TAG: BULL

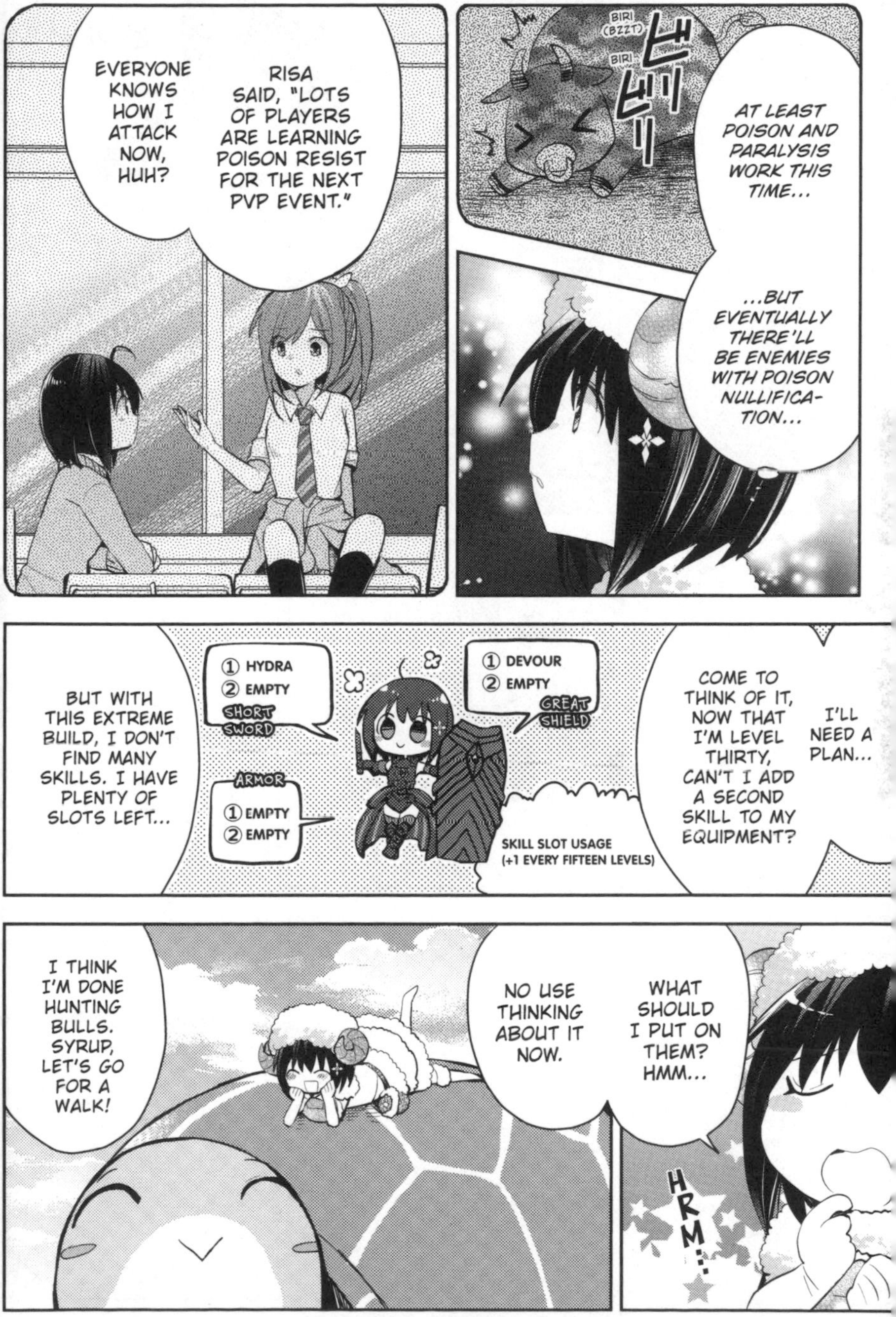
BIRI (BZZT) BIRI
AT LEAST POISON AND PARALYSIS WORK THIS TIME...
...BUT EVENTUALLY THERE'LL BE ENEMIES WITH POISON NULLIFICATION...
RISA SAID, "LOTS OF PLAYERS ARE LEARNING POISON RESIST FOR THE NEXT PVP EVENT."
EVERYONE KNOWS HOW I ATTACK NOW, HUH?
I'LL NEED A PLAN...
COME TO THINK OF IT, NOW THAT I'M LEVEL THIRTY, CAN'T I ADD A SECOND SKILL TO MY EQUIPMENT?
SKILL SLOT USAGE (+1 EVERY FIFTEEN LEVELS)
GREAT SHIELD
① DEVOUR
② EMPTY
SHORT SWORD
① HYDRA
② EMPTY
ARMOR
① EMPTY
② EMPTY
BUT WITH THIS EXTREME BUILD, I DON'T FIND MANY SKILLS. I HAVE PLENTY OF SLOTS LEFT...
HRM...
WHAT SHOULD I PUT ON THEM? HMM...
NO USE THINKING ABOUT IT NOW.
I THINK I'M DONE HUNTING BULLS. SYRUP, LET'S GO FOR A WALK!

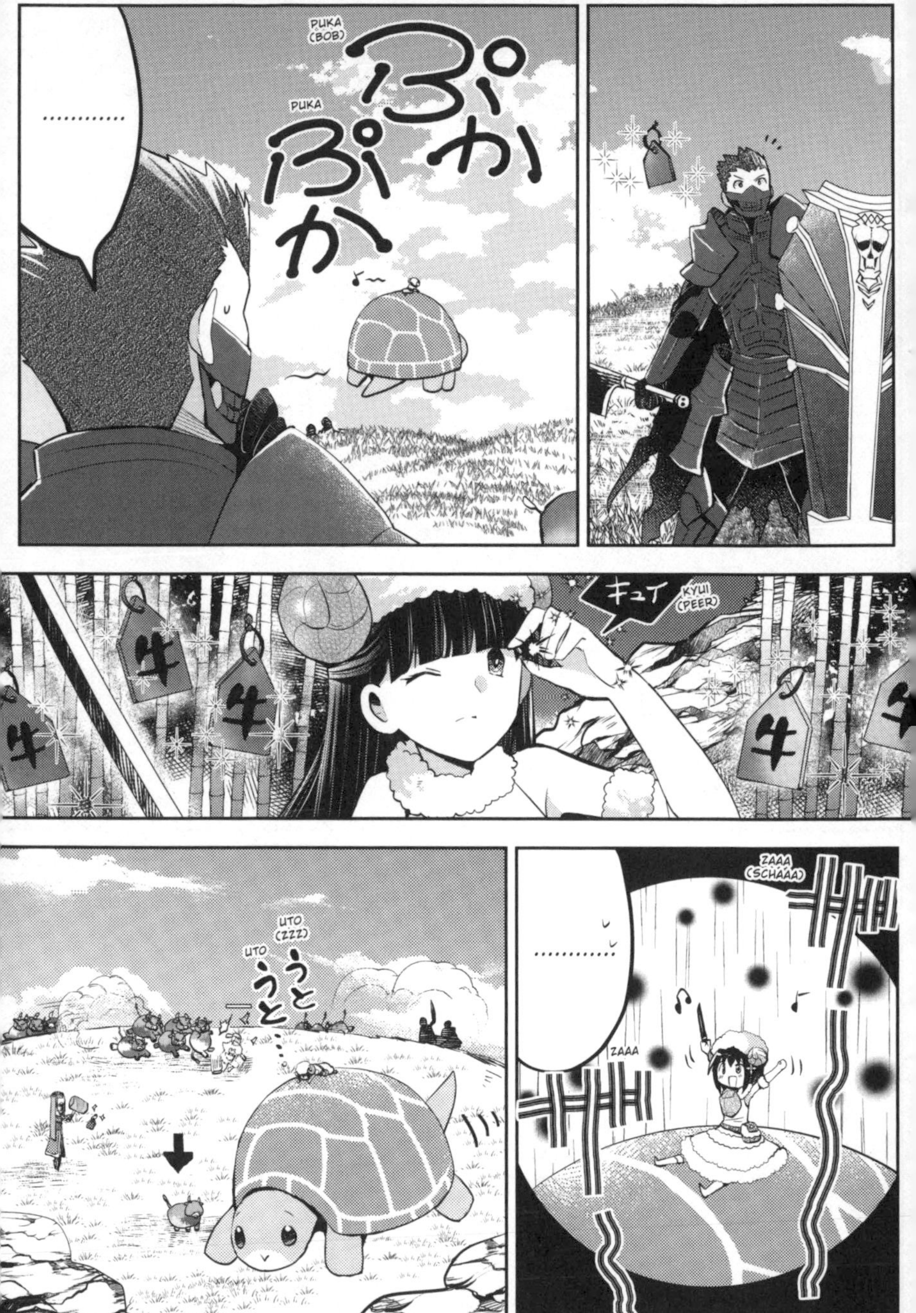
....
ぷかぷか
PUKA (BOB)
PUKA
キュイ
KYUI (PEER)
ZAAA (SCHAAA)
............!
ZAAA
うとうと
UTO (ZZZ)
UTO

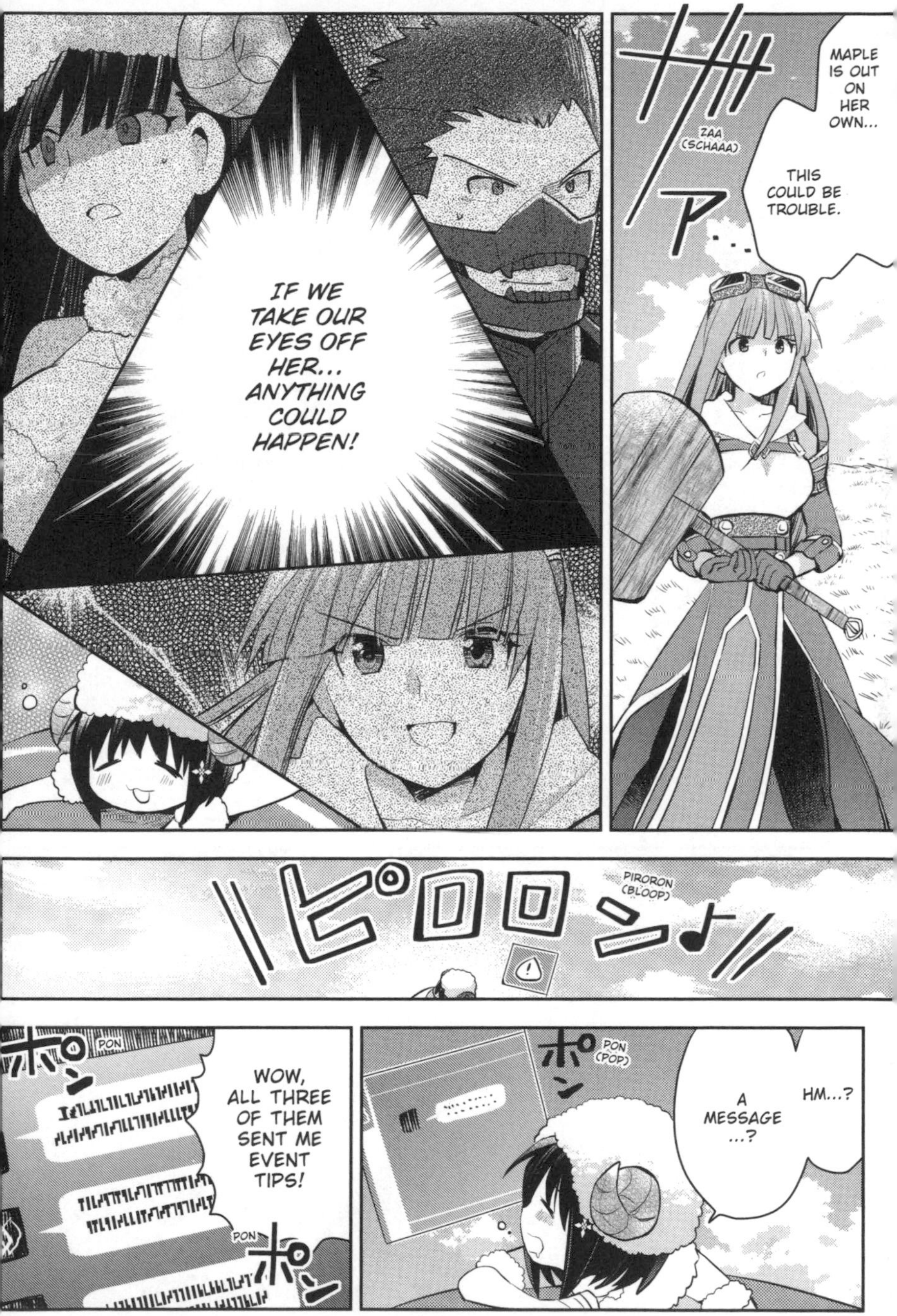
ZAA (SCHAAA)
MAPLE IS OUT ON HER OWN...
THIS COULD BE TROUBLE.
IF WE TAKE OUR EYES OFF HER... ANYTHING COULD HAPPEN!
PIRORON (BLOOP)
PON (POP)
HM...?
A MESSAGE ...?
PON
WOW, ALL THREE OF THEM SENT ME EVENT TIPS!
PON

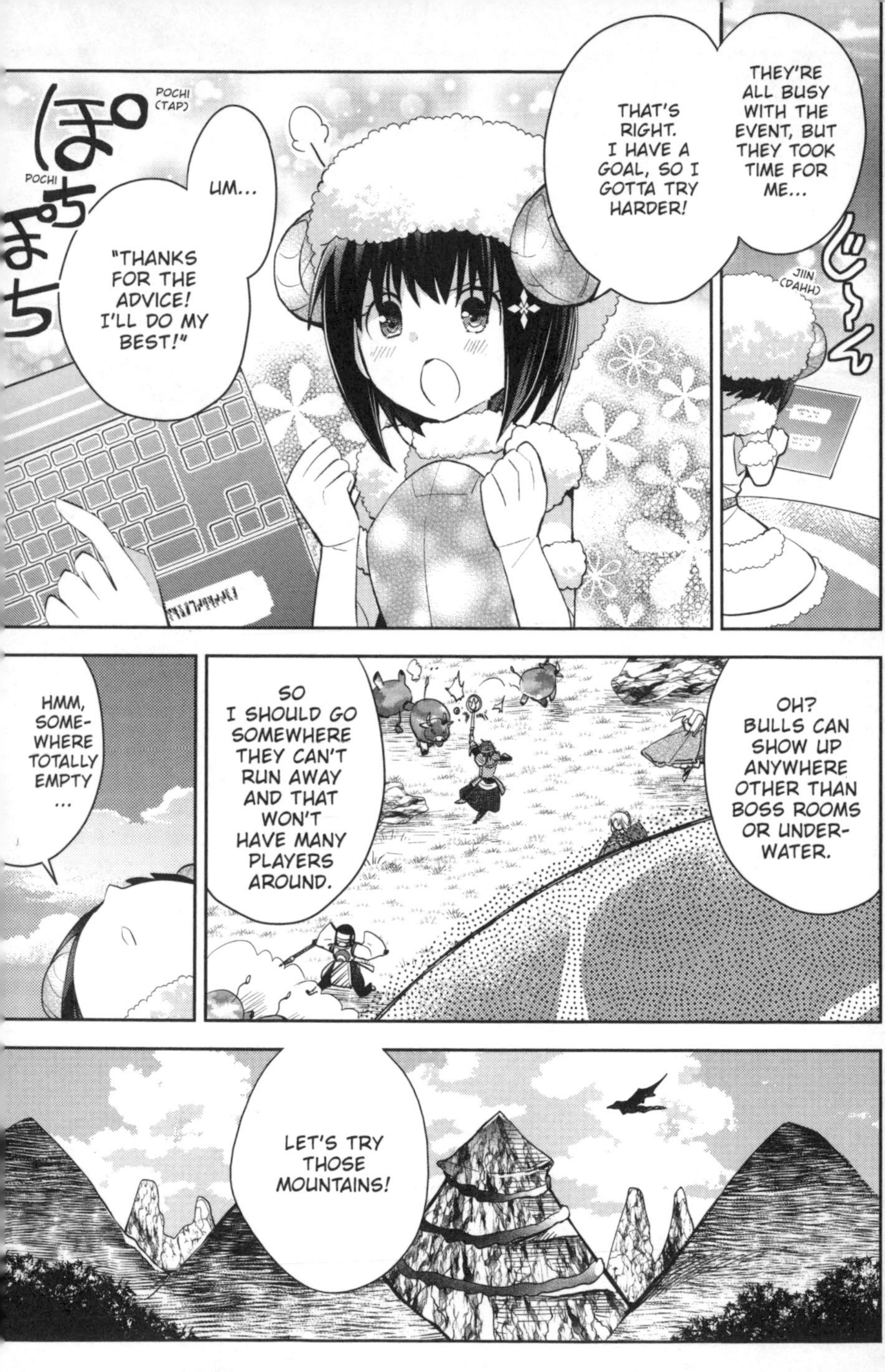
THEY'RE ALL BUSY WITH THE EVENT, BUT THEY TOOK TIME FOR ME...
じ〜ん
JIIN (DAHH)
THAT'S RIGHT. I HAVE A GOAL, SO I GOTTA TRY HARDER!
ぽち
POCHI (TAP)
UM...
"THANKS FOR THE ADVICE! I'LL DO MY BEST!"
ぽちぽち
POCHI
OH? BULLS CAN SHOW UP ANYWHERE OTHER THAN BOSS ROOMS OR UNDER-WATER.
SO I SHOULD GO SOMEWHERE THEY CAN'T RUN AWAY AND THAT WON'T HAVE MANY PLAYERS AROUND.
HMM, SOME-WHERE TOTALLY EMPTY...
LET'S TRY THOSE MOUNTAINS!

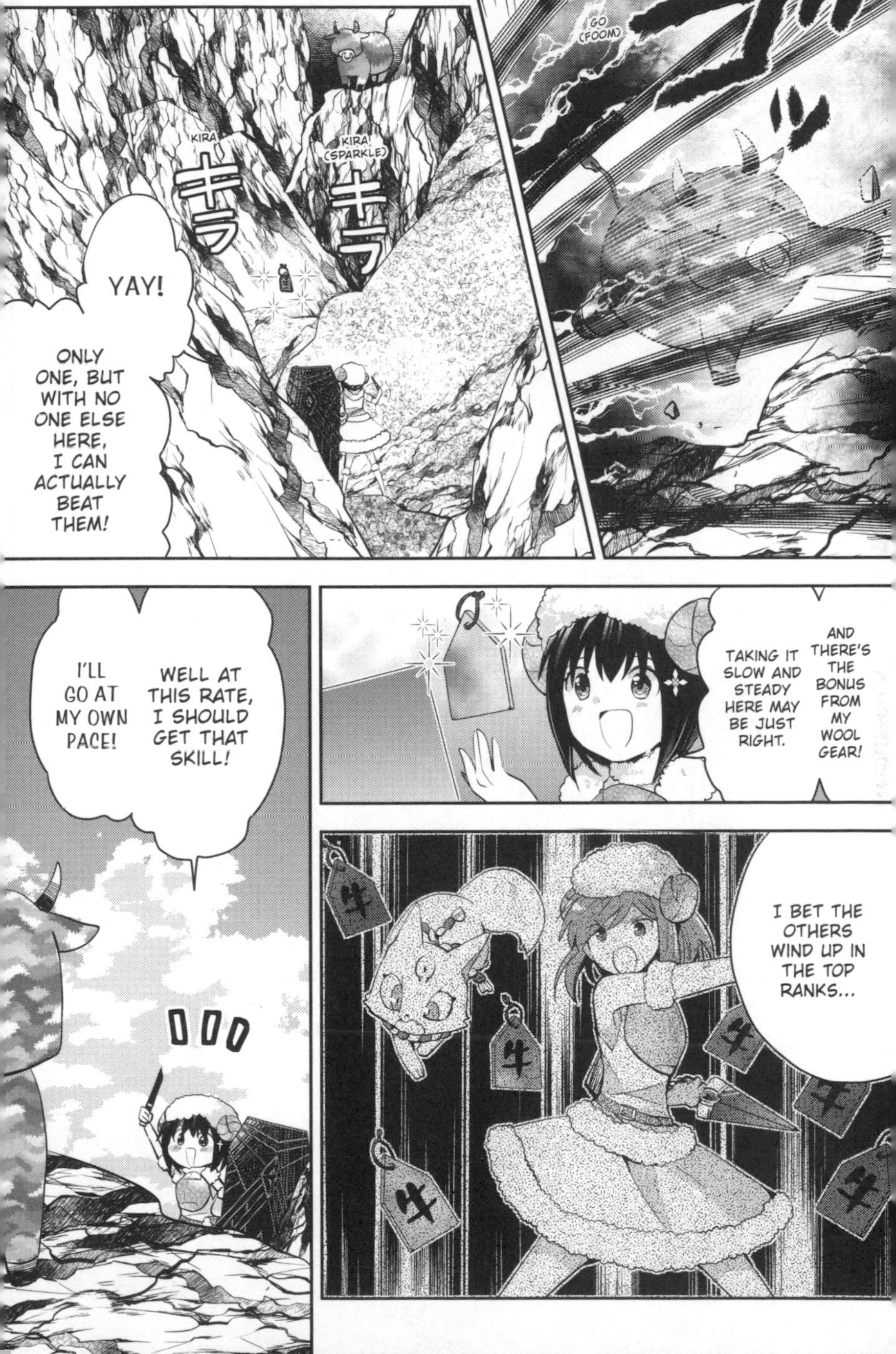
GO (FOOM)
KIRA (SPARKLE)
KIRA
YAY!
ONLY ONE, BUT WITH NO ONE ELSE HERE, I CAN ACTUALLY BEAT THEM!
AND THERE'S THE BONUS FROM MY WOOL GEAR!
TAKING IT SLOW AND STEADY HERE MAY BE JUST RIGHT.
I BET THE OTHERS WIND UP IN THE TOP RANKS…
WELL AT THIS RATE, I SHOULD GET THAT SKILL!
I'LL GO AT MY OWN PACE!

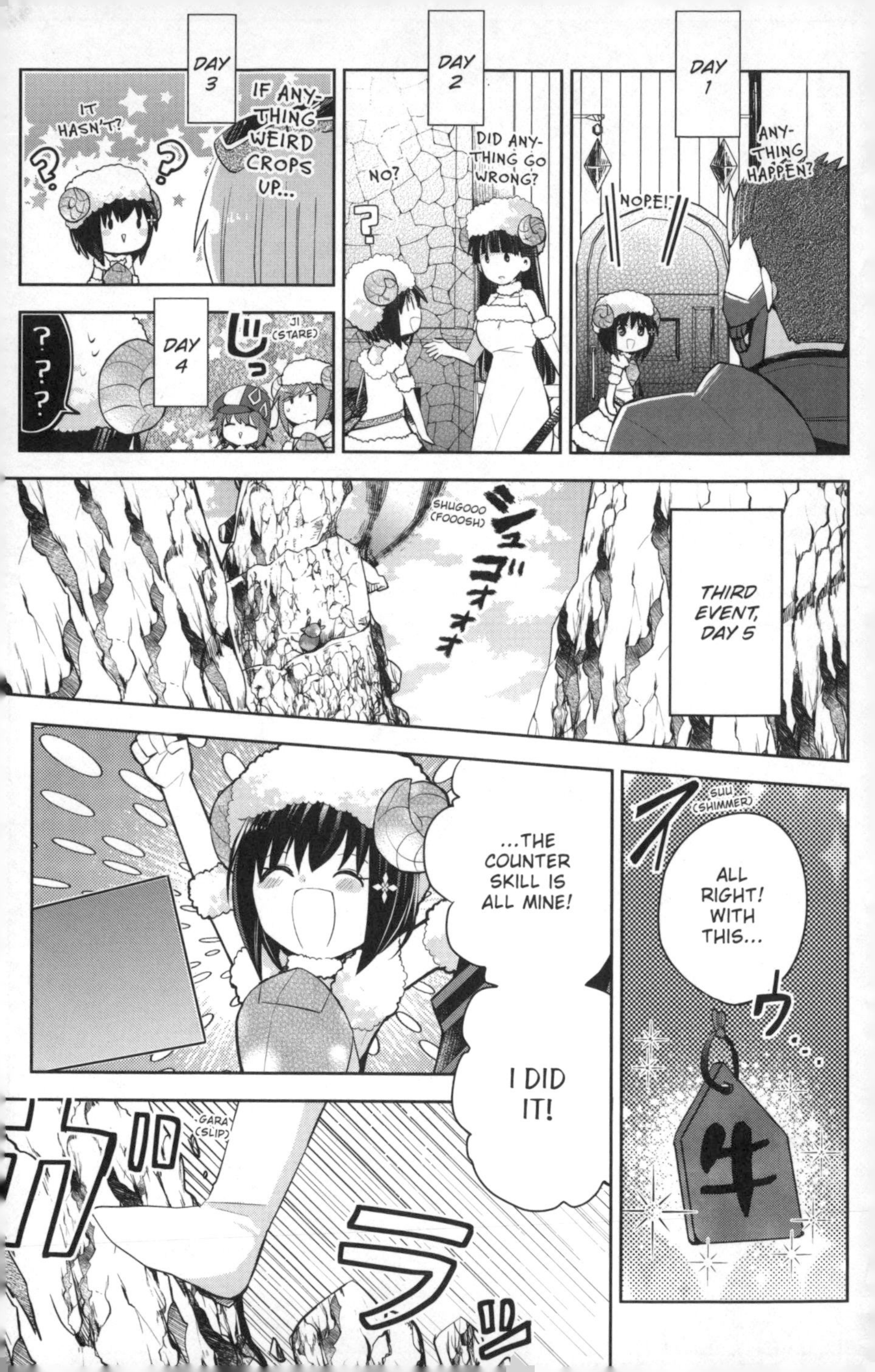
DAY 1
ANY-THING HAPPEN?
NOPE!
DAY 2
DID ANY-THING GO WRONG?
NO?
?
DAY 3
IF ANY-THING WEIRD CROPS UP...
IT HASN'T?
? ?
DAY 4
じっ
JI (STARE)
? ? ?
THIRD EVENT, DAY 5
シュゴオオオ
SHUGOOO (FOOOSH)
イ
SUU (SHIMMER)
ALL RIGHT! WITH THIS...
ウ...
牛
...THE COUNTER SKILL IS ALL MINE!
I DID IT!
ガラッ
GARA (SLIP)

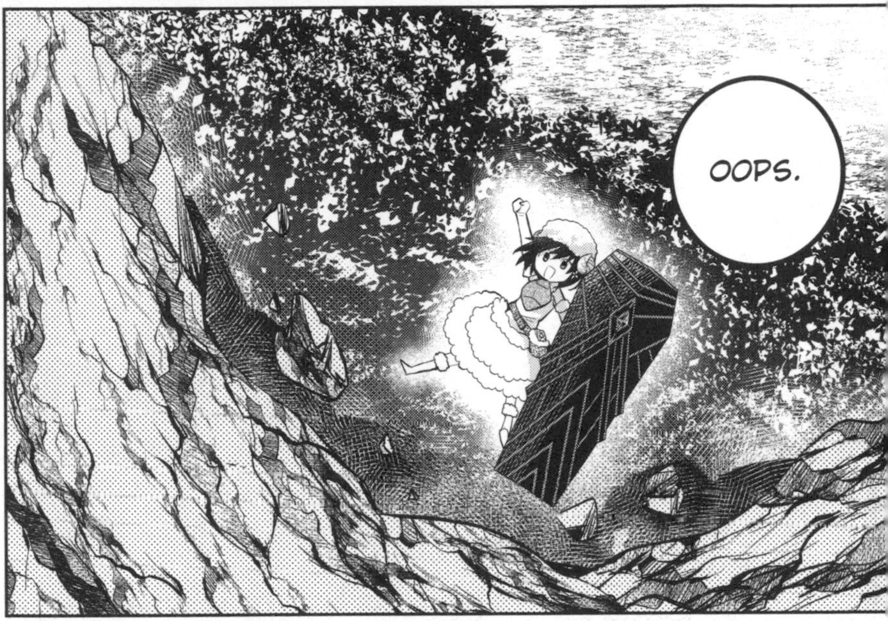
OOPS.

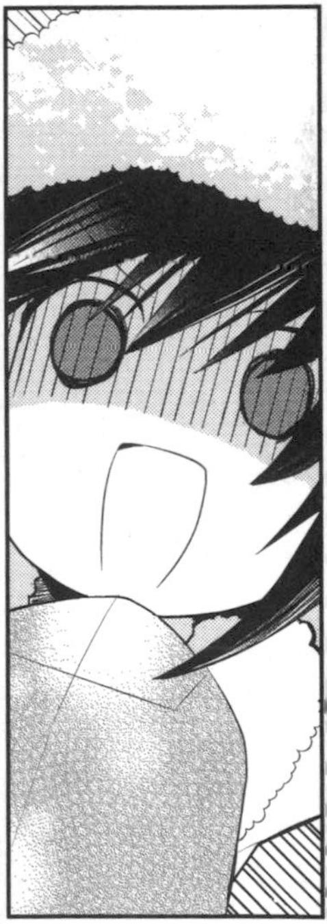

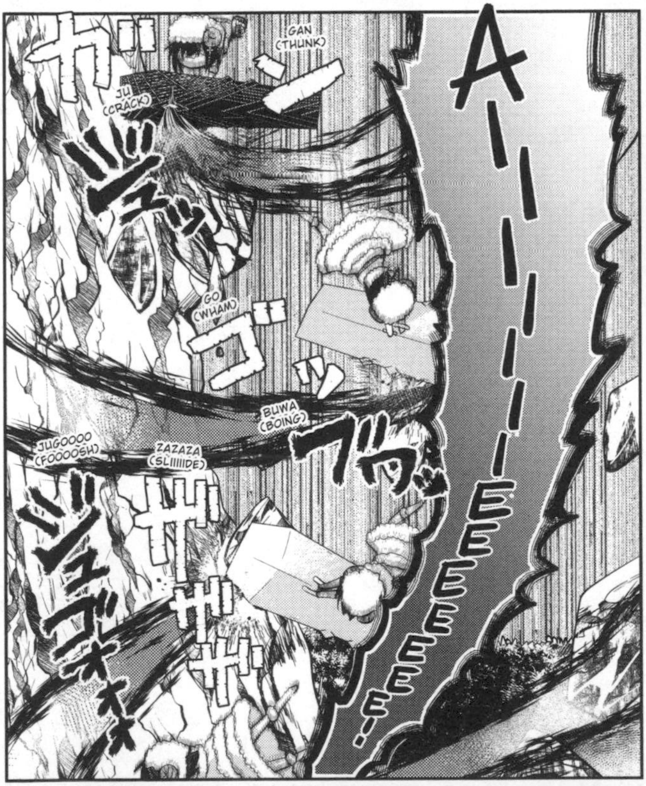
A------EEEEEEEE-!
GAN (THUNK)
JU (CRACK)
GO (WHAM)
BUWA (BOING)
ZAZAZA (SLIIIIIDE)
JUGOOOO (FOOOOSH)

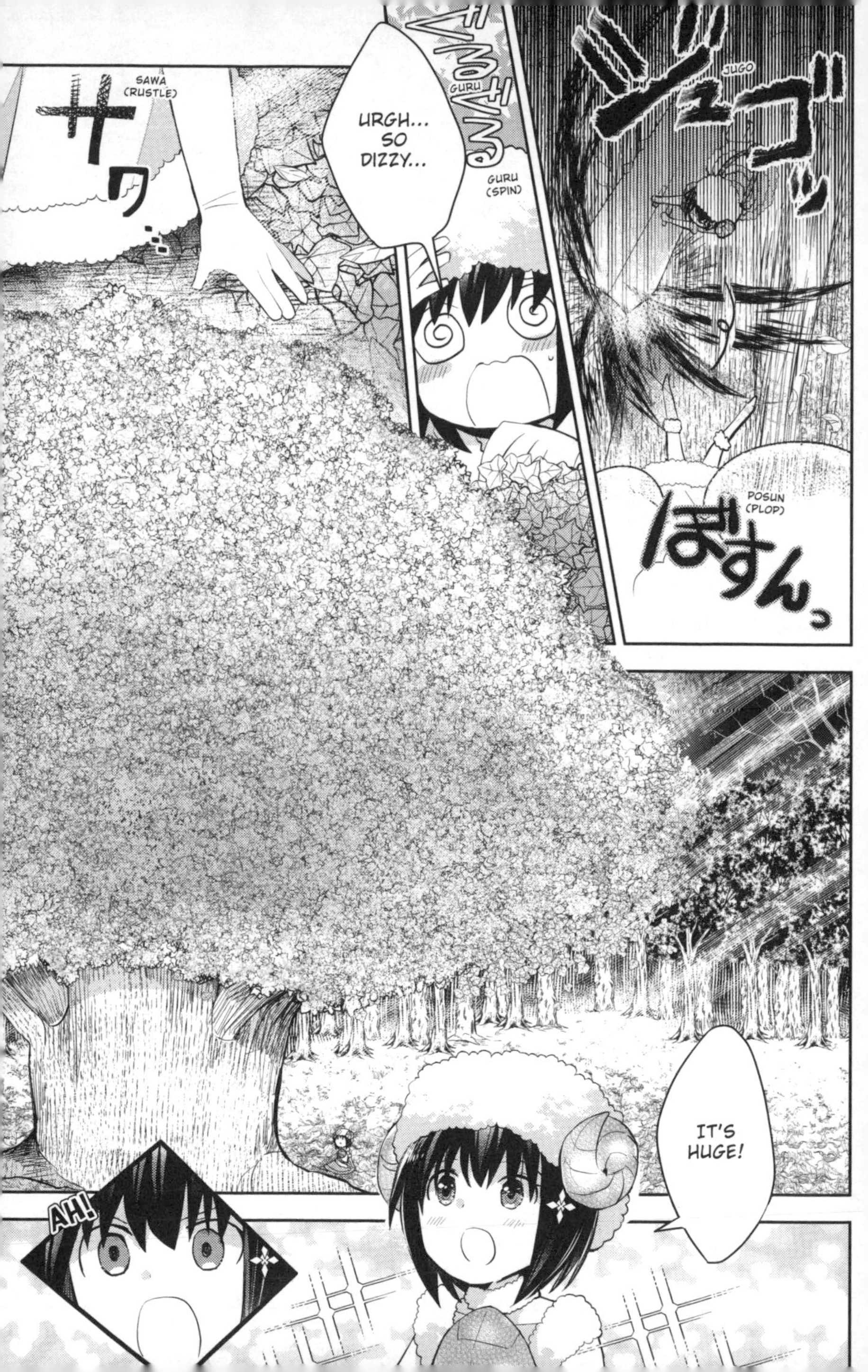
ジュゴッ
JUGO
ぽすんっ
POSUN (PLOP)
ぐるぐる
GURU
GURU (SPIN)
URGH... SO DIZZY...
サワ
SAWA (RUSTLE)
IT'S HUGE!
AH!

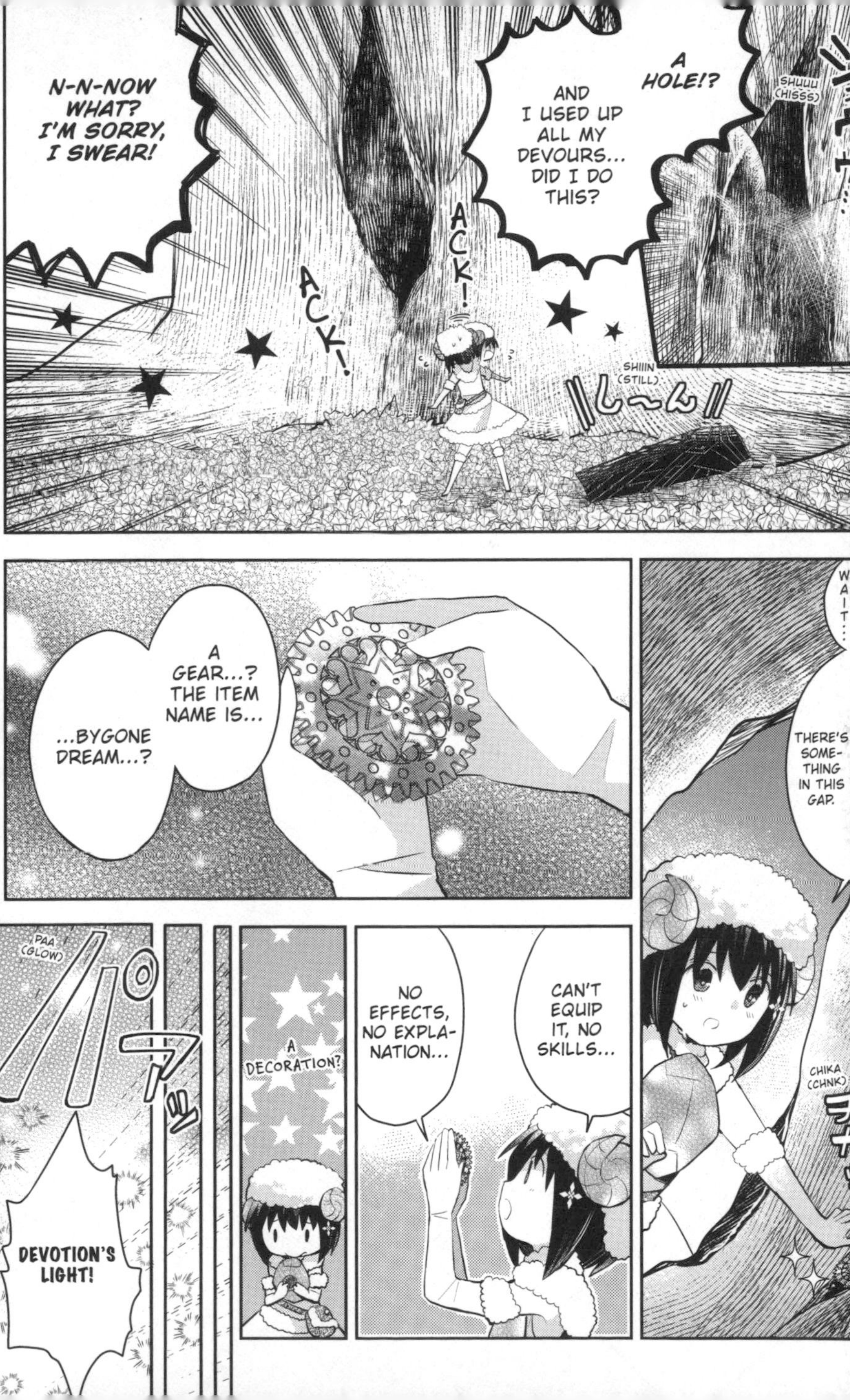
SHUUU (HISSS)
A HOLE!?
AND I USED UP ALL MY DEVOURS... DID I DO THIS?
ACK!
ACK!
N-N-NOW WHAT? I'M SORRY, I SWEAR!
SHIIN (STILL)
WAIT...
THERE'S SOME-THING IN THIS GAP.
CHIKA (CHNK)
A GEAR...? THE ITEM NAME IS...
...BYGONE DREAM...?
CAN'T EQUIP IT, NO SKILLS...
NO EFFECTS, NO EXPLA-NATION...
A DECORATION?
PAA (GLOW)
DEVOTION'S LIGHT!

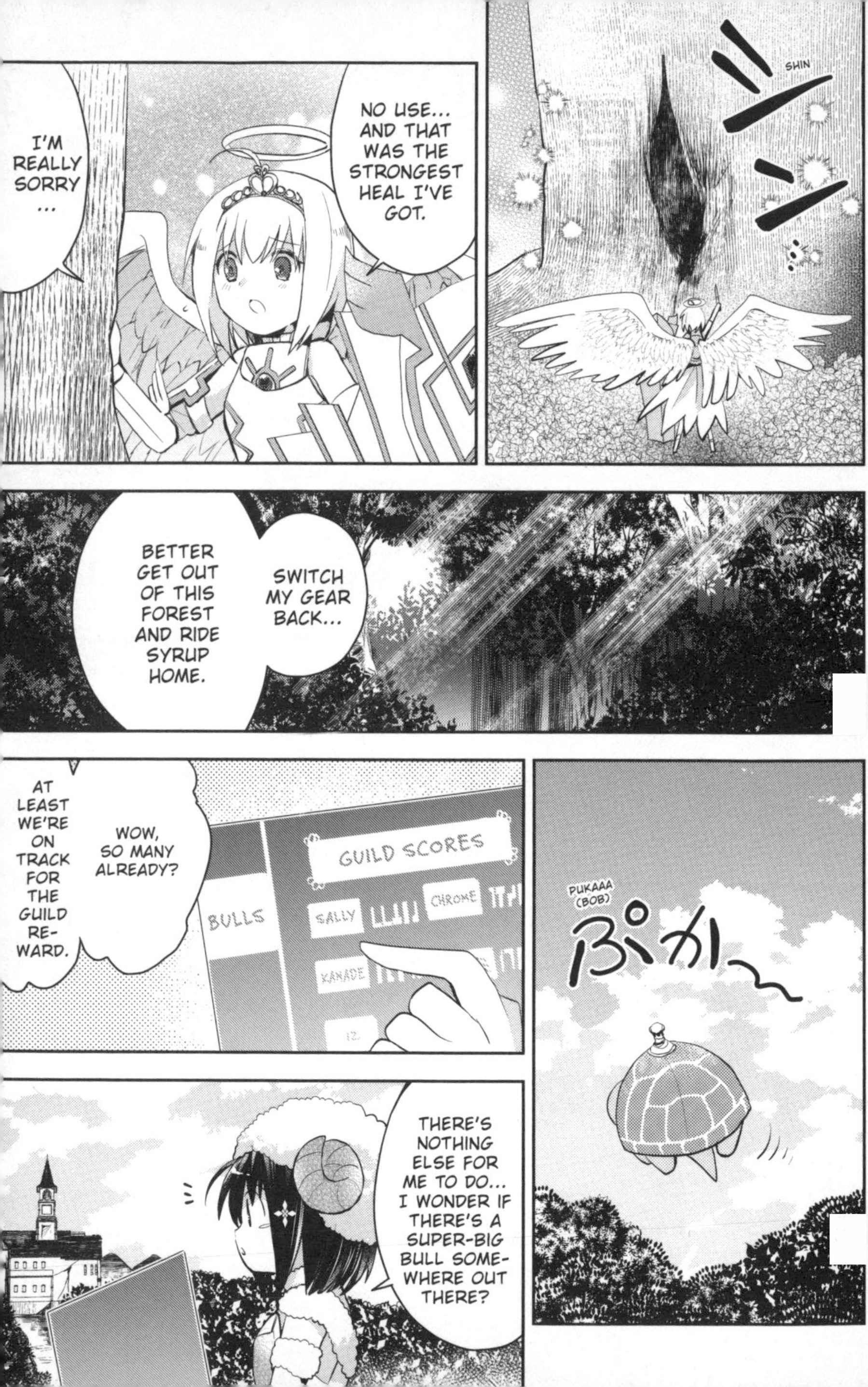
SHIN
NO USE... AND THAT WAS THE STRONGEST HEAL I'VE GOT.
I'M REALLY SORRY...
SWITCH MY GEAR BACK...
BETTER GET OUT OF THIS FOREST AND RIDE SYRUP HOME.
PUKAAA (BOB)
ぷかー
WOW, SO MANY ALREADY?
AT LEAST WE'RE ON TRACK FOR THE GUILD RE-WARD.
GUILD SCORES
BULLS
SALLY
CHROME
KANADE
THERE'S NOTHING ELSE FOR ME TO DO... I WONDER IF THERE'S A SUPER-BIG BULL SOME-WHERE OUT THERE?

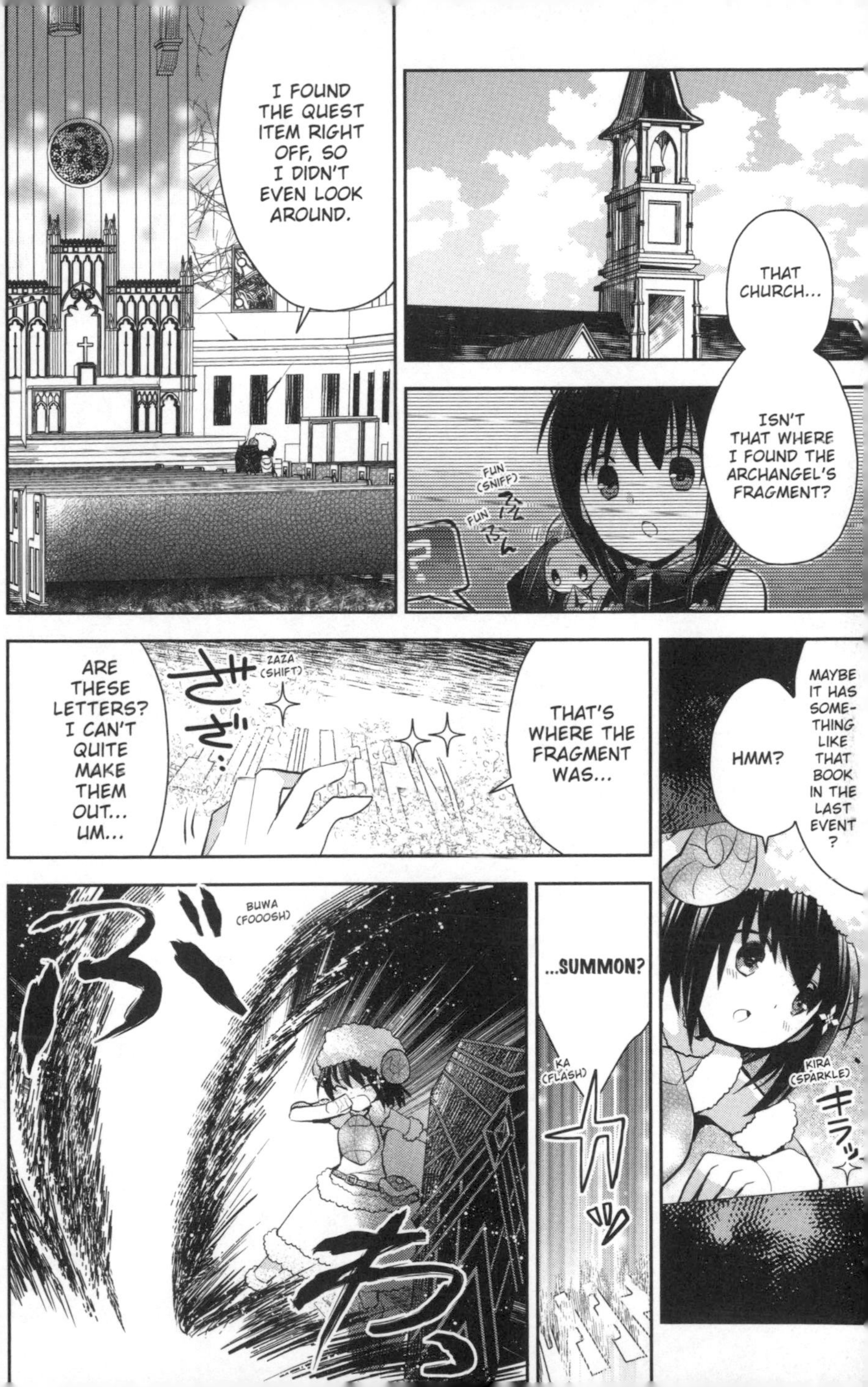
THAT CHURCH...
ISN'T THAT WHERE I FOUND THE ARCHANGEL'S FRAGMENT?
FUN (SNIFF)
FUN
I FOUND THE QUEST ITEM RIGHT OFF, SO I DIDN'T EVEN LOOK AROUND.
MAYBE IT HAS SOME-THING LIKE THAT BOOK IN THE LAST EVENT?
HMM?
KIRA (SPARKLE)
THAT'S WHERE THE FRAGMENT WAS...
ARE THESE LETTERS? I CAN'T QUITE MAKE THEM OUT... UM...
ZAZA (SHIFT)
...SUMMON?
KA (FLASH)
BUWA (FOOOSH)

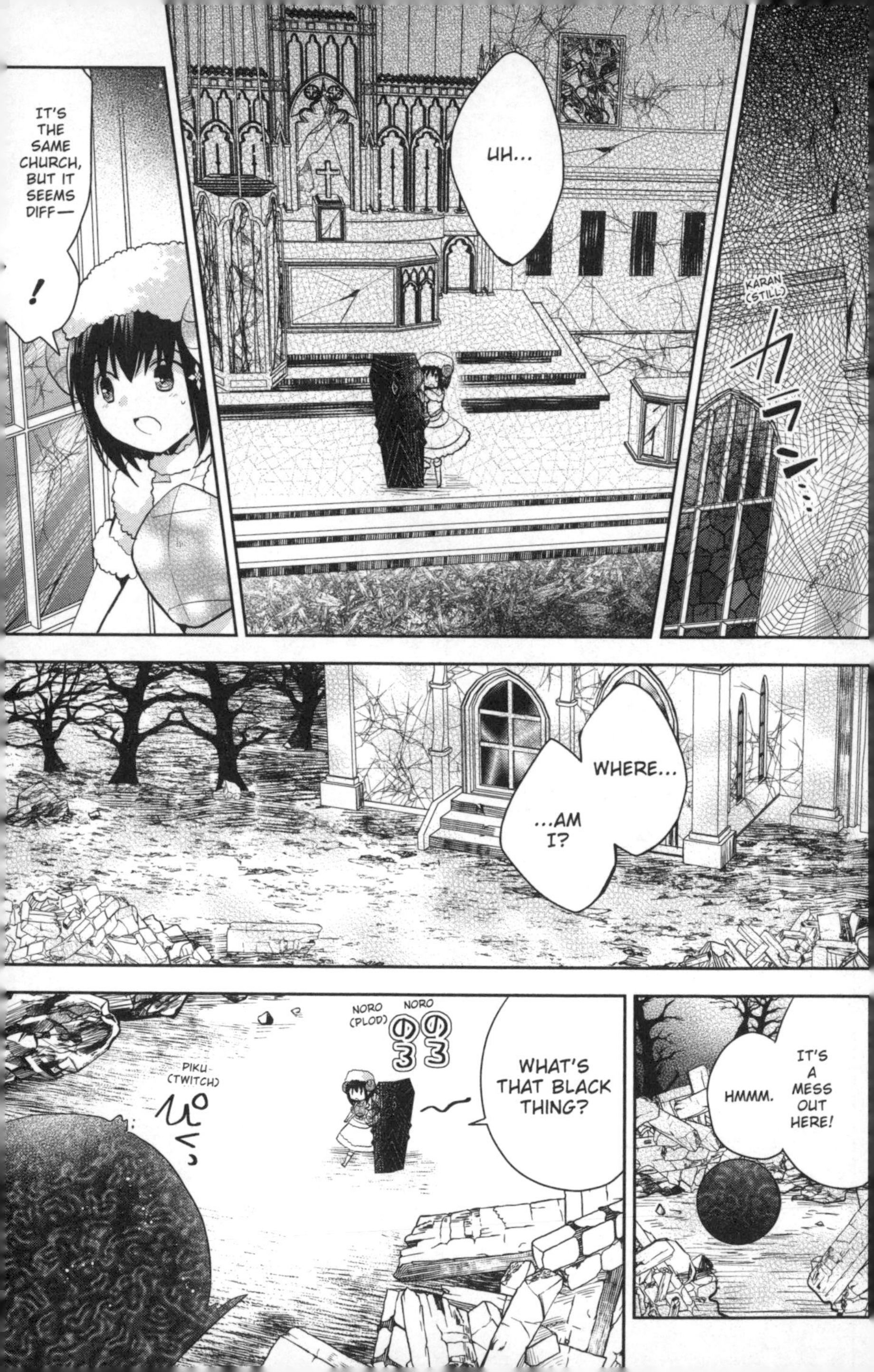
KARAN (STILL)
カラン…
UH...
IT'S THE SAME CHURCH, BUT IT SEEMS DIFF—
!
WHERE...
...AM I?
IT'S A MESS OUT HERE!
HMMM.
WHAT'S THAT BLACK THING?
NORO NORO (PLOD)
のろのろ
PIKU (TWITCH)
ぴく

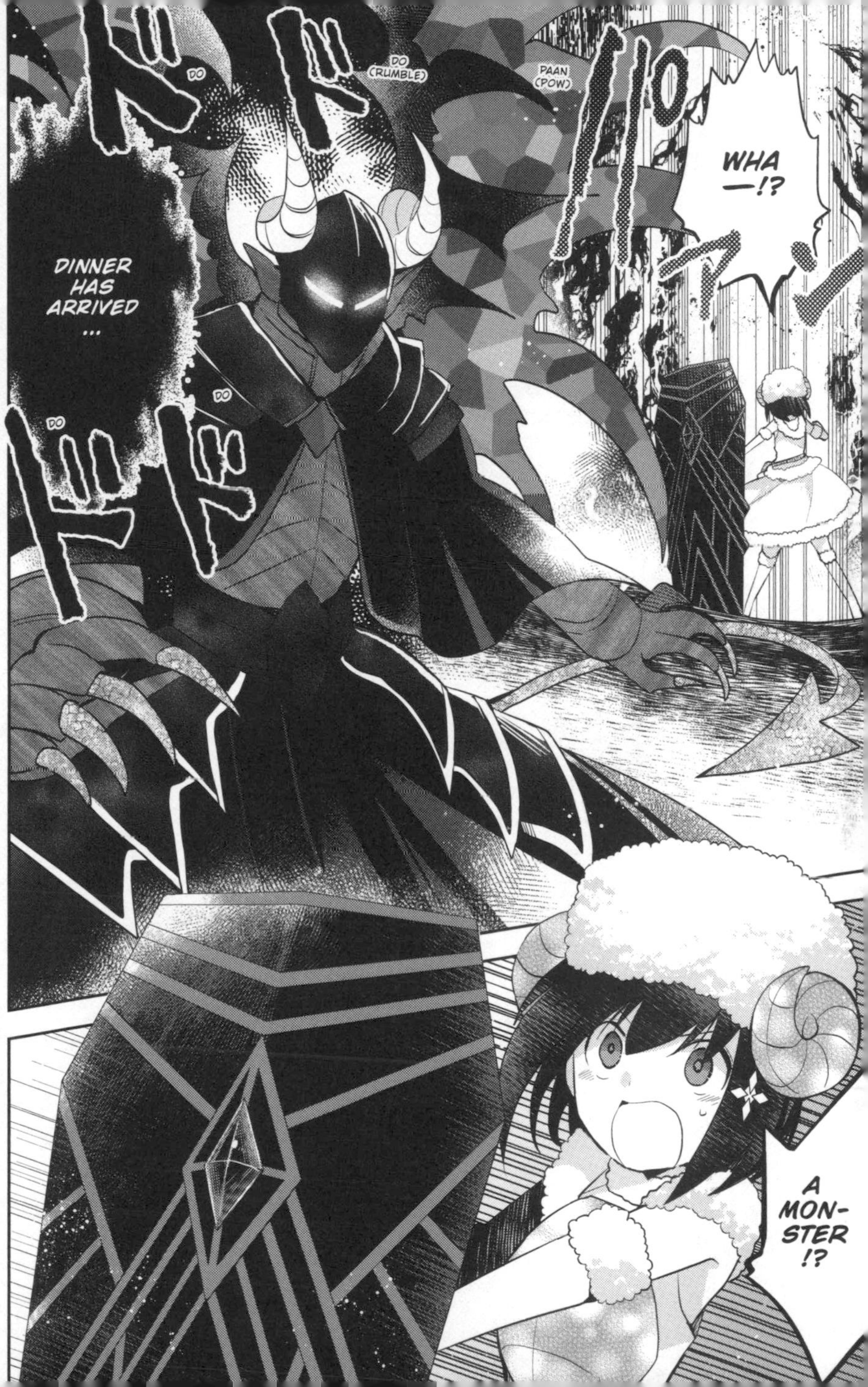
WHA—!?
PAAN (POW)
DO (RUMBLE)
DO
DINNER HAS ARRIVED ...
DO
DO
A MON-STER !?

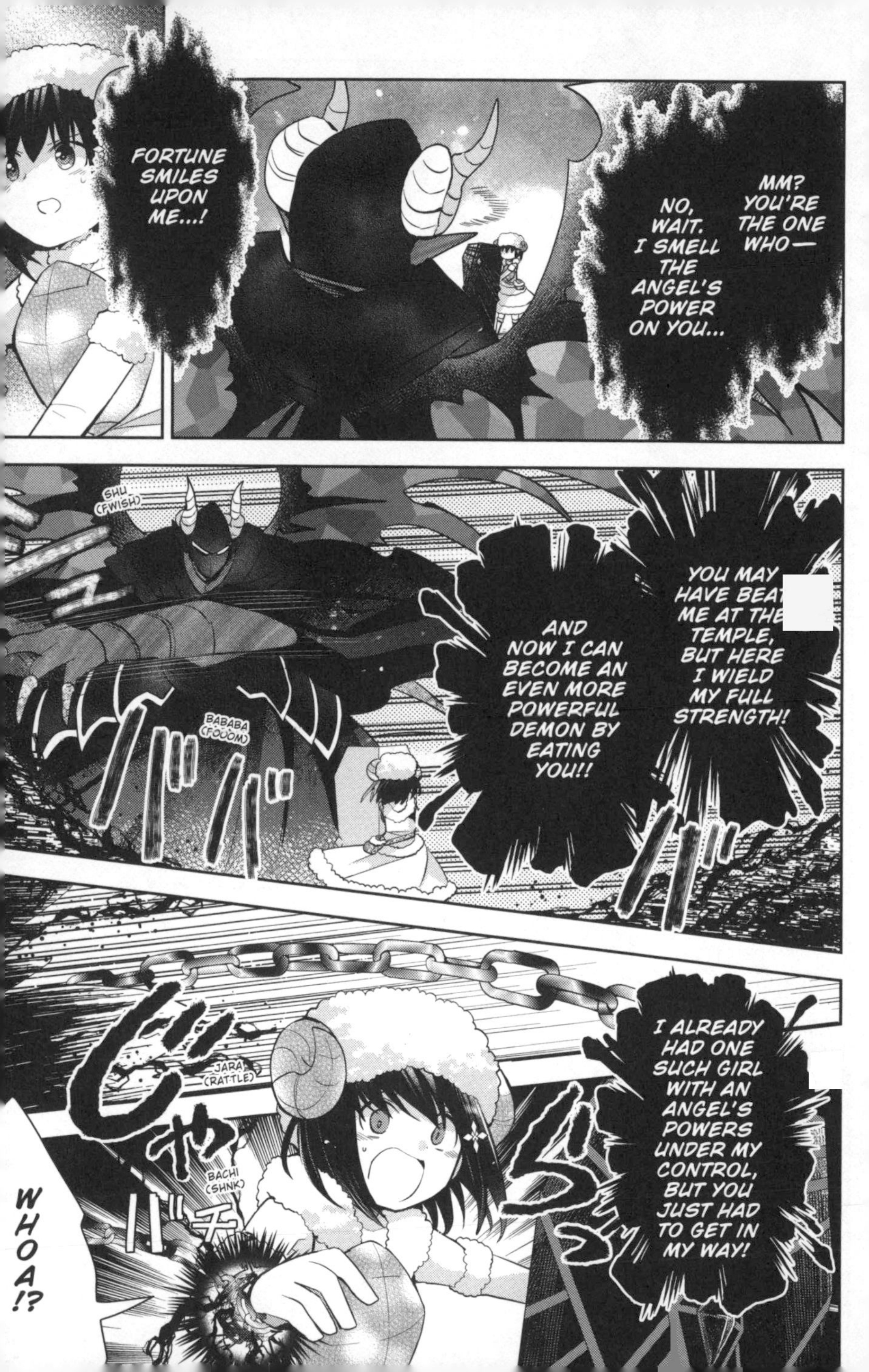
MM? YOU'RE THE ONE WHO—
NO, WAIT. I SMELL THE ANGEL'S POWER ON YOU...
FORTUNE SMILES UPON ME...!
YOU MAY HAVE BEAT ME AT THE TEMPLE, BUT HERE I WIELD MY FULL STRENGTH!
AND NOW I CAN BECOME AN EVEN MORE POWERFUL DEMON BY EATING YOU!!
SHU (FWISH)
BABABA (FOOOM)
I ALREADY HAD ONE SUCH GIRL WITH AN ANGEL'S POWERS UNDER MY CONTROL, BUT YOU JUST HAD TO GET IN MY WAY!
JARA (RATTLE)
BACHI (SHNK)
WHOA!?

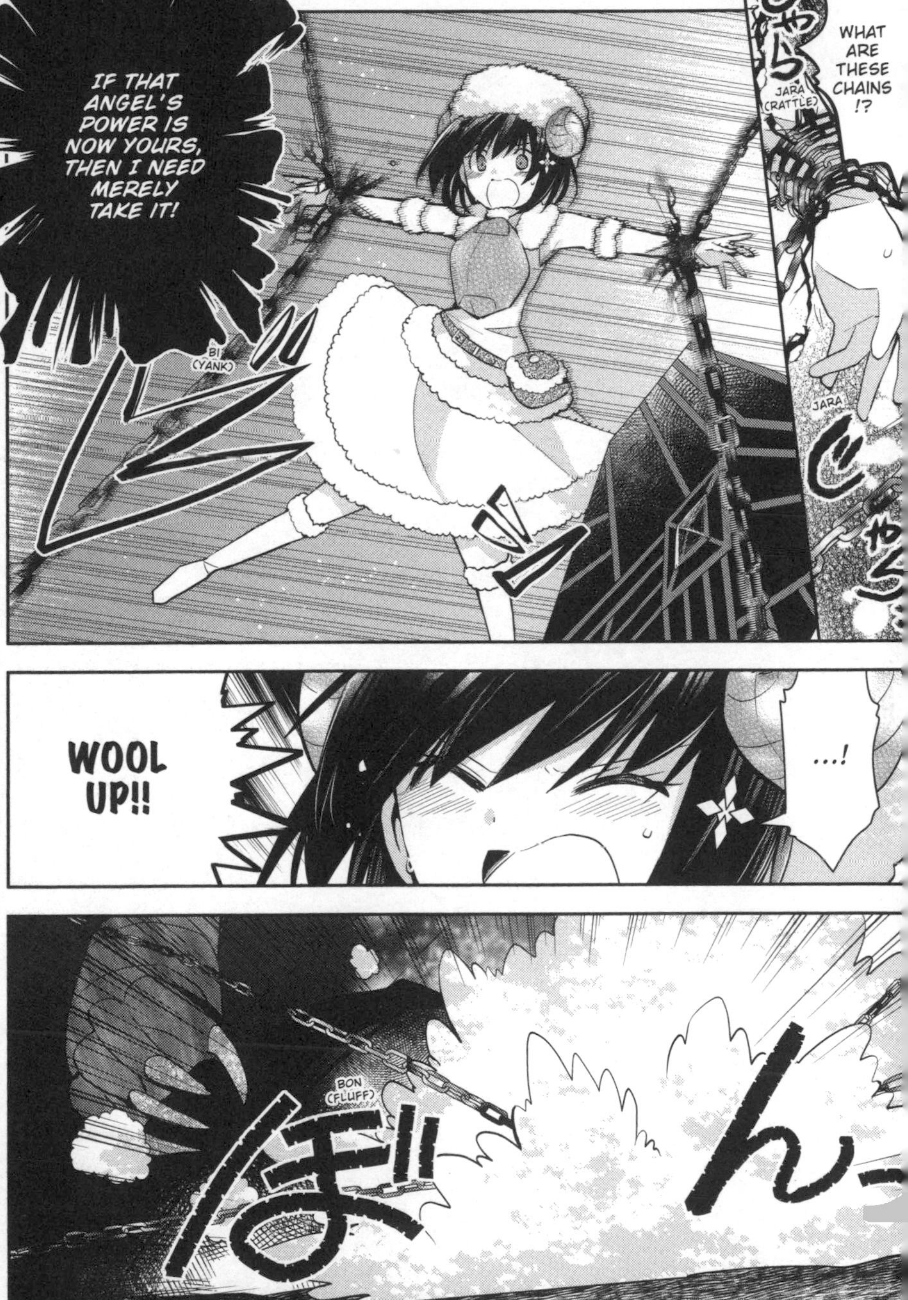
WHAT ARE THESE CHAINS !?
JARA (RATTLE)
JARA
IF THAT ANGEL'S POWER IS NOW YOURS, THEN I NEED MERELY TAKE IT!
BI (YANK)
...!
WOOL UP!!
BON (FLUFF)

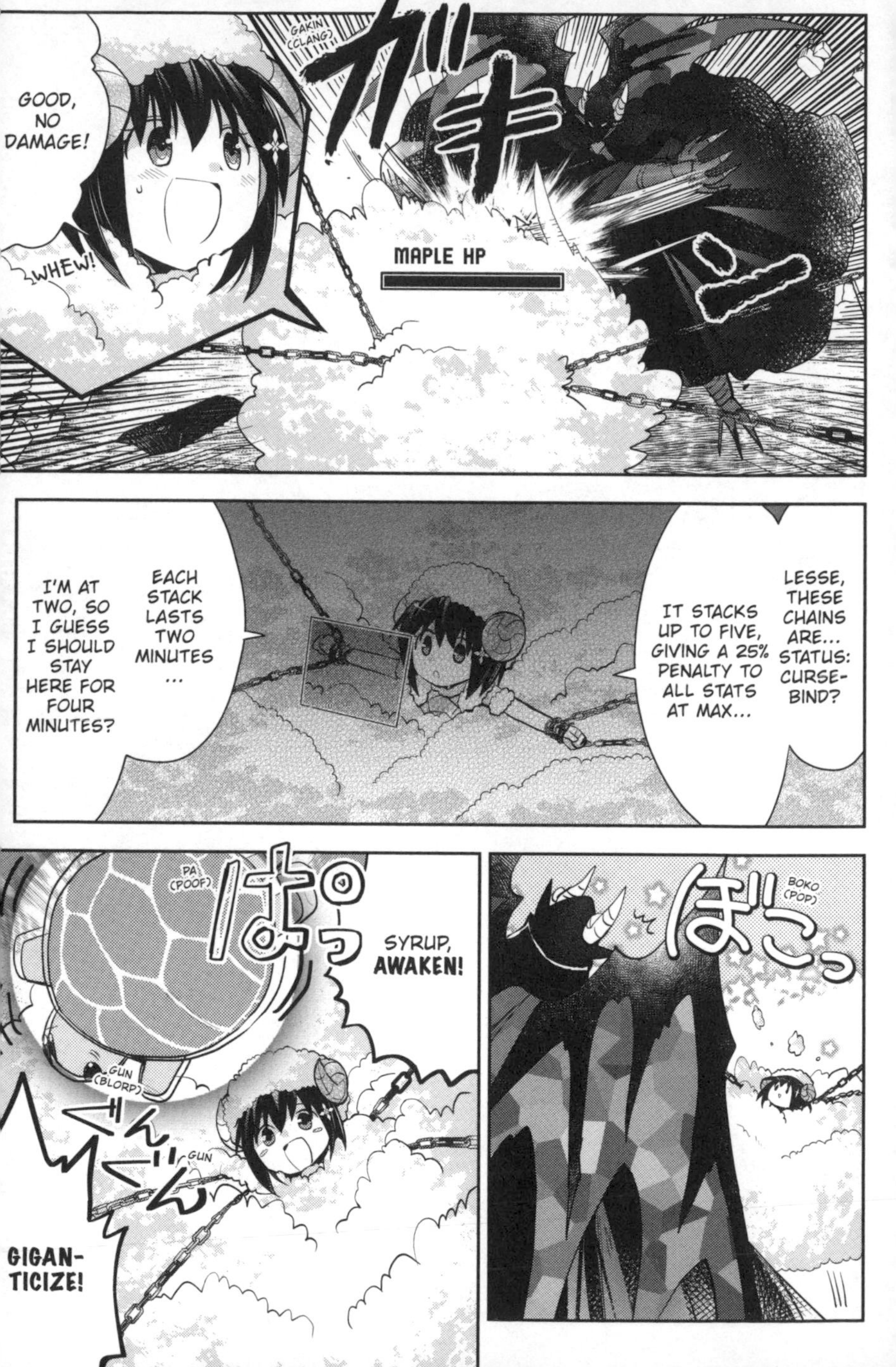
GAKIN (CLANG)
MAPLE HP
GOOD, NO DAMAGE!
WHEW!
LESSE, THESE CHAINS ARE... STATUS: CURSE-BIND?
IT STACKS UP TO FIVE, GIVING A 25% PENALTY TO ALL STATS AT MAX...
EACH STACK LASTS TWO MINUTES...
I'M AT TWO, SO I GUESS I SHOULD STAY HERE FOR FOUR MINUTES?
BOKO (POP)
PA (POOF)
SYRUP, AWAKEN!
GUN (BLORP)
GUN
GIGAN-TICIZE!

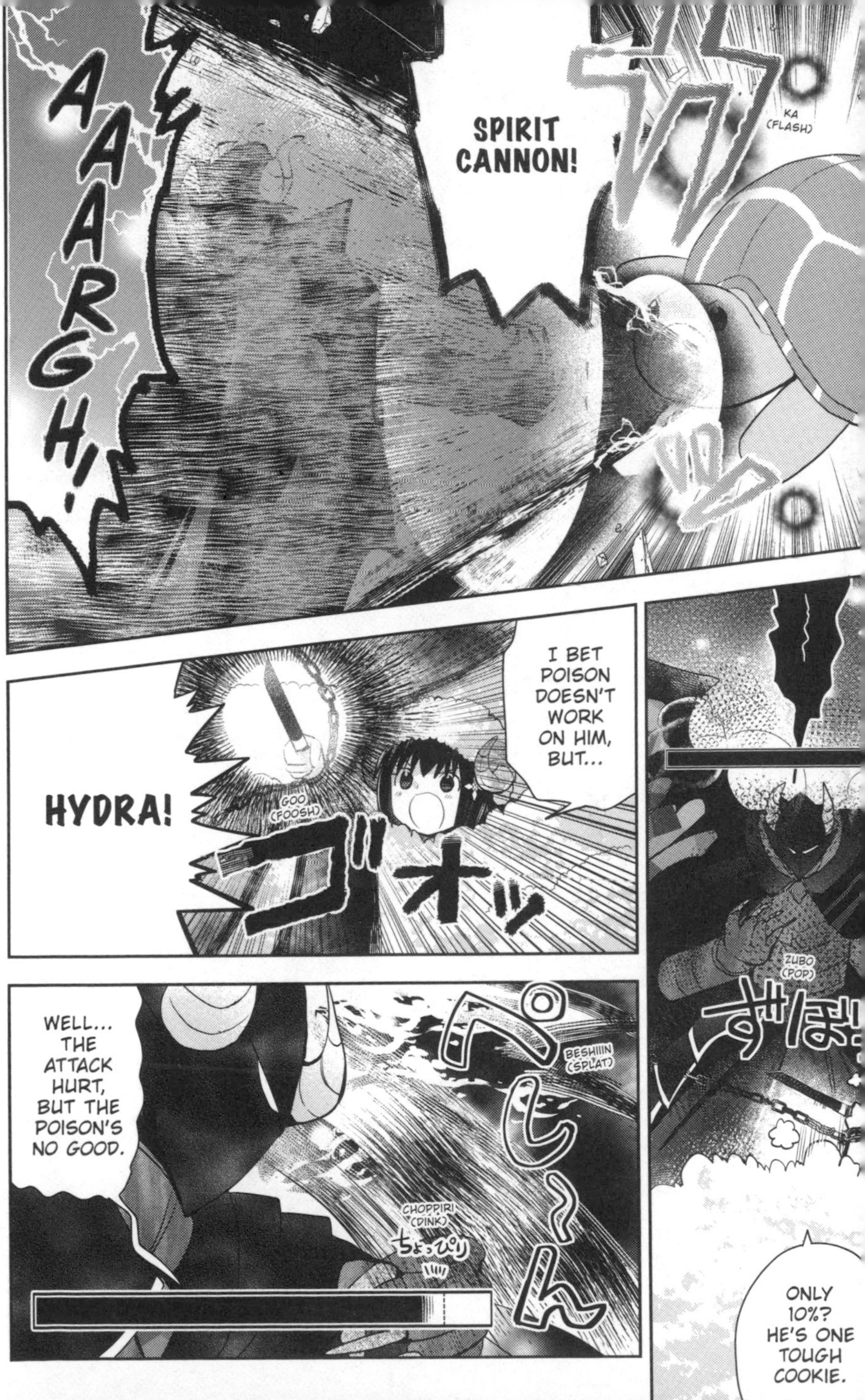
KA (FLASH)
SPIRIT CANNON!
AAAARGH!
ZUBO (POP)
ずぽ
ONLY 10%? HE'S ONE TOUGH COOKIE.
I BET POISON DOESN'T WORK ON HIM, BUT...
HYDRA!
GOO (FOOSH)
ゴオッ
BESHIIIN (SPLAT)
ぺしーん
WELL... THE ATTACK HURT, BUT THE POISON'S NO GOOD.
CHOPPIRI (DINK)
ちょっぴり

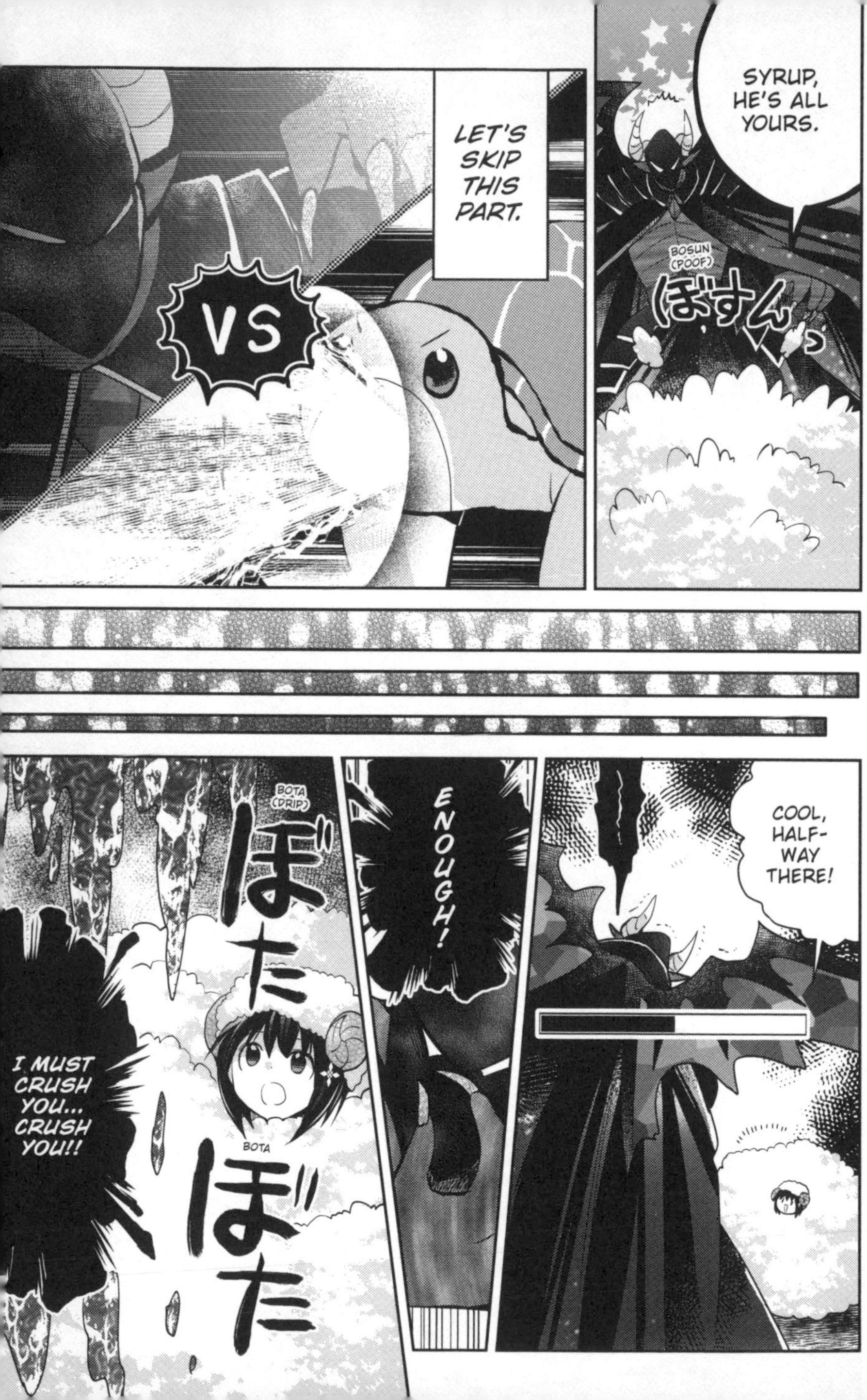
SYRUP, HE'S ALL YOURS.
BOSUN (POOF)
ぼすんっ
LET'S SKIP THIS PART.
VS
COOL, HALF-WAY THERE!
ENOUGH!
BOTA (DRIP)
ぼた
BOTA
ぼた
I MUST CRUSH YOU... CRUSH YOU!!

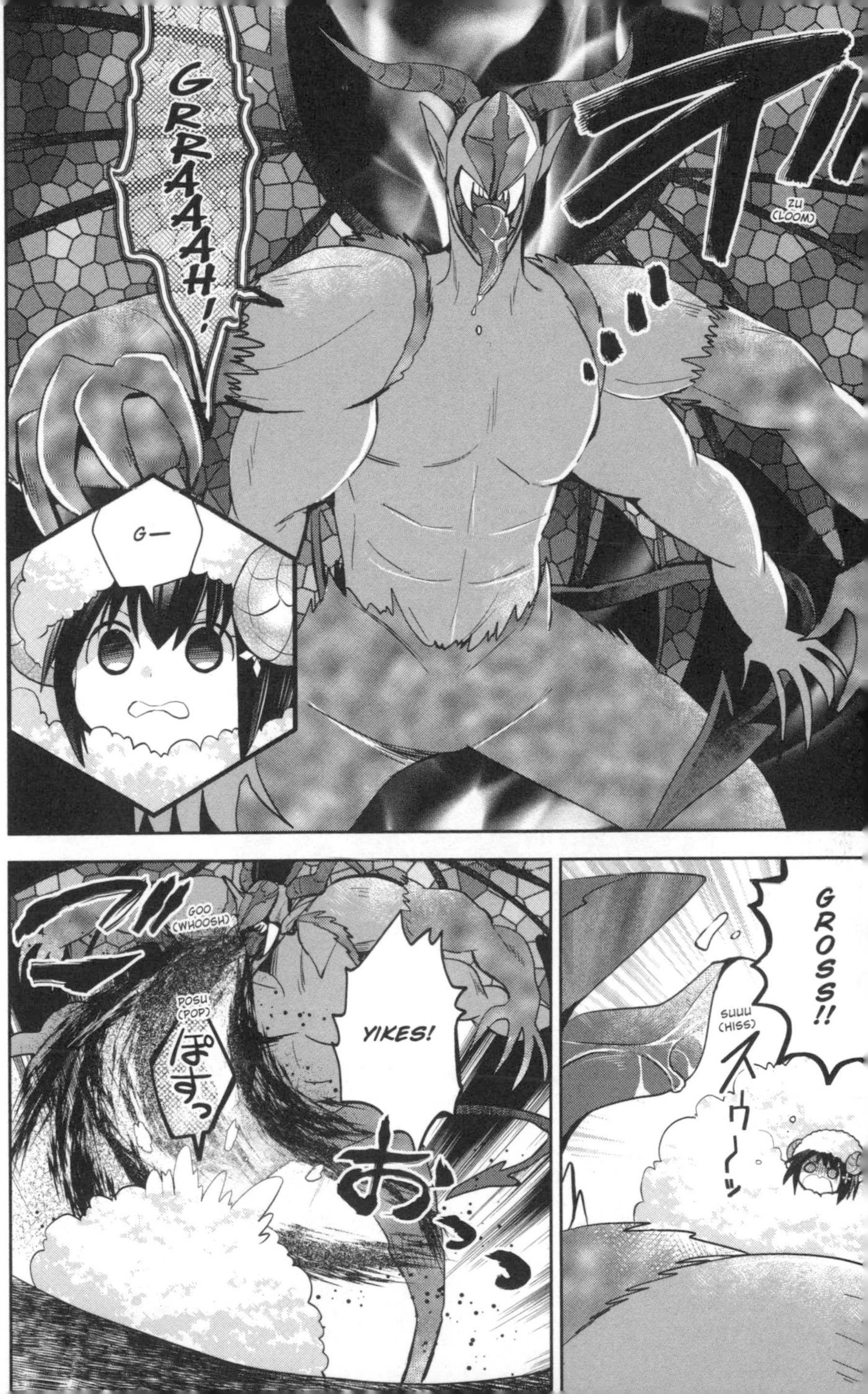
GRRAAAH!
ZU (LOOM)
G—
GROSS!!
SUUU (HISS)
スウ～ッ
GOO (WHOOSH)
POSU (POP)
ぽすっ
YIKES!
おっっ

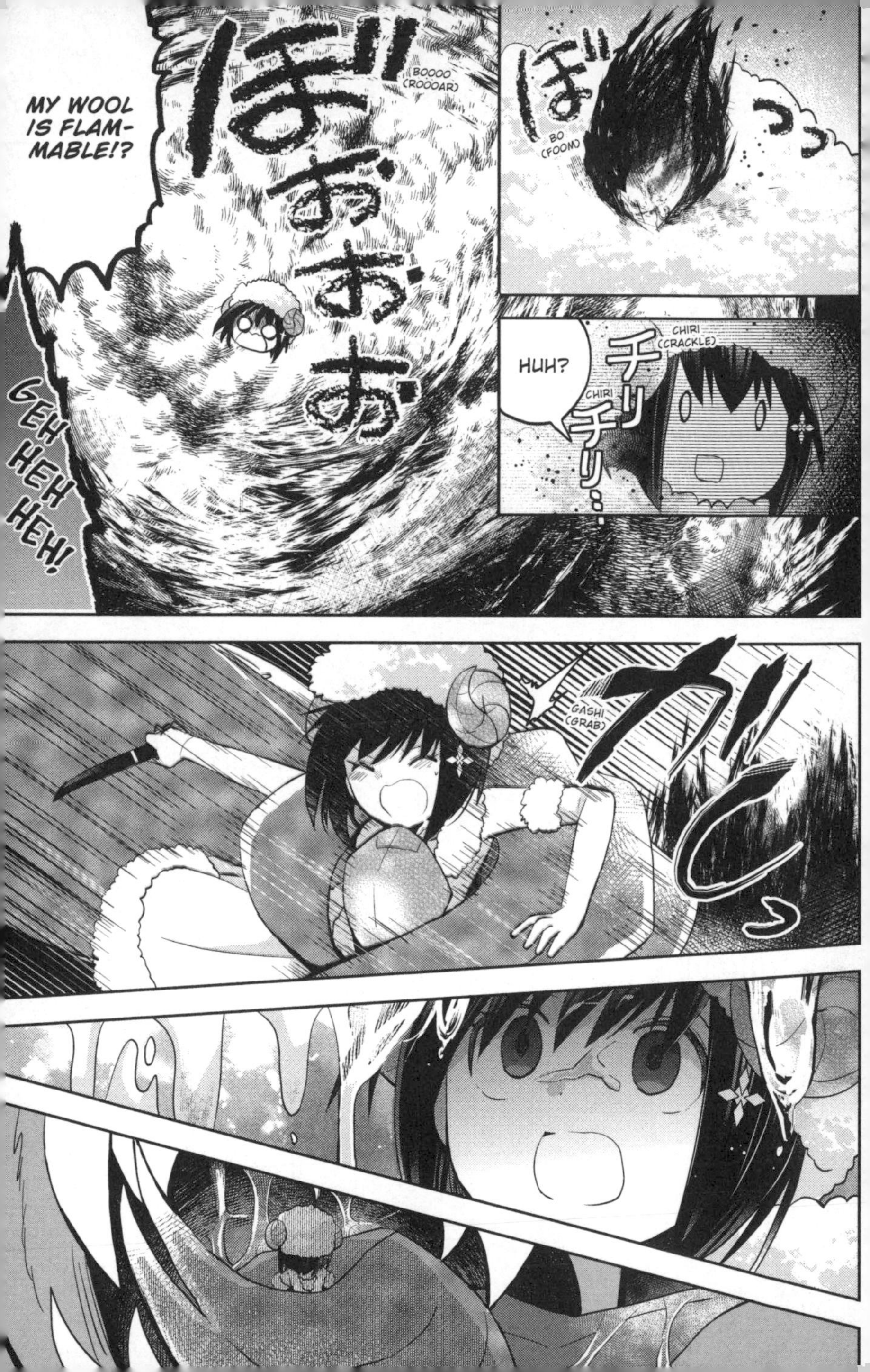
ぼっ
BO (FOOM)
CHIRI (CRACKLE)
チリチリッ
HUH?
CHIRI
ぼぉぉぉ
BOOOO (ROOOAR)
MY WOOL IS FLAM-MABLE!?
GEH HEH HEH HEH!
ガシッ
GASHI (GRAB)

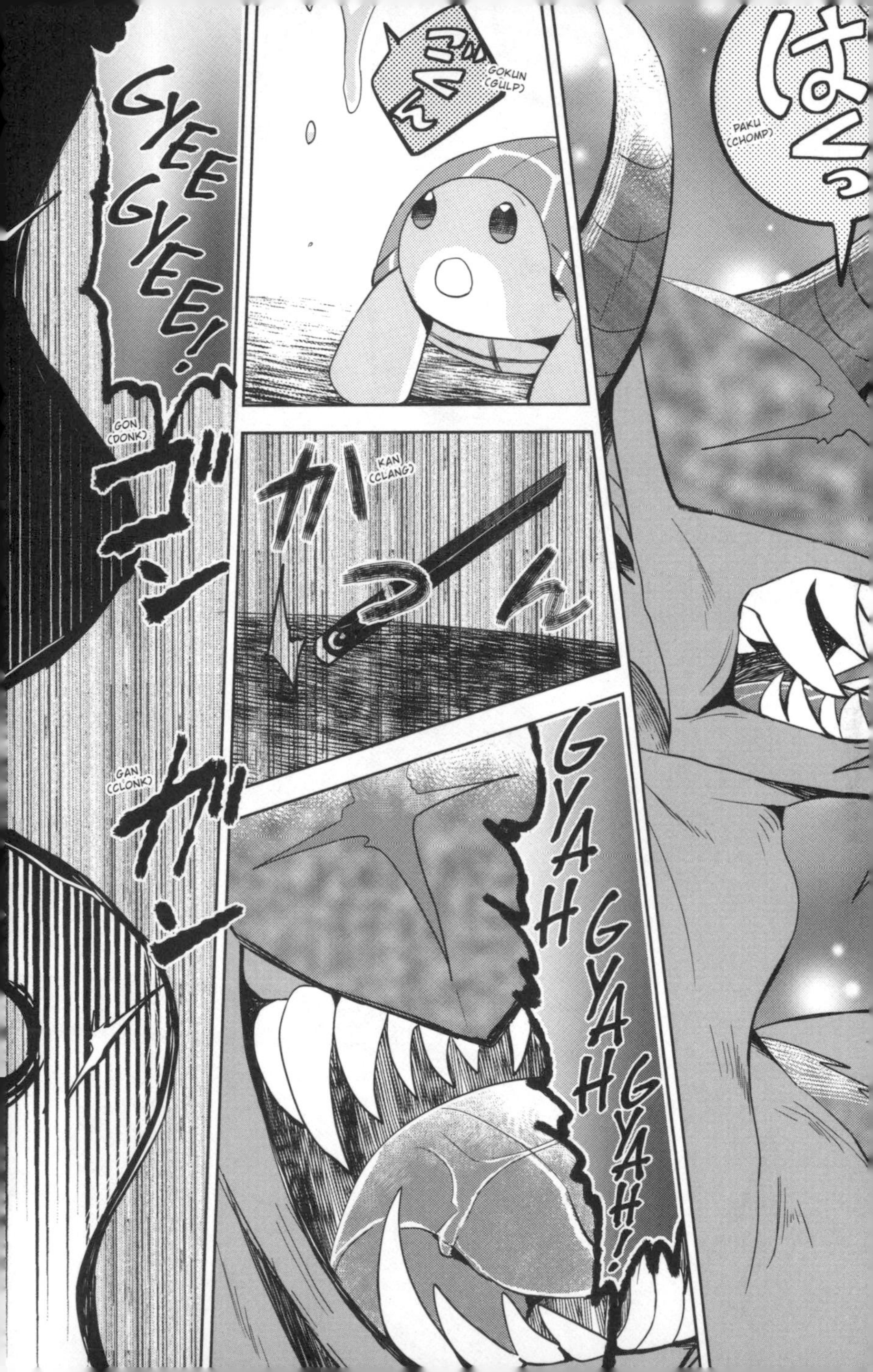
はくっ
PAKU (CHOMP)
ごくん
GOKUN (GULP)
かーん
KAN (CLANG)
GYAH GYAH GYAH!
GYEE GYEE!
ゴン
GON (DONK)
ガン
GAN (CLONK)

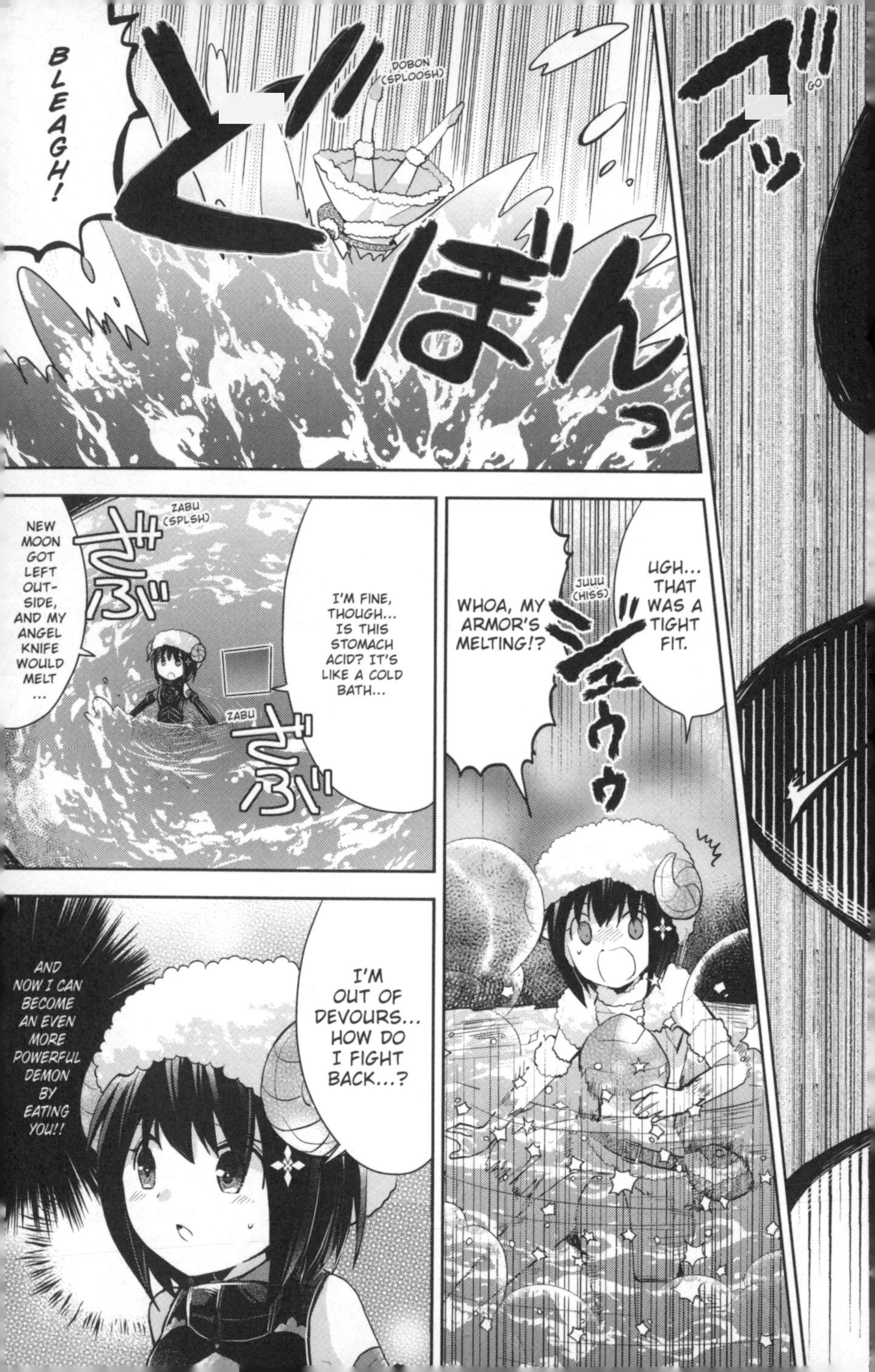
GO
DOBON (SPLOOSH)
BLEAGH!
UGH... THAT WAS A TIGHT FIT.
JUUU (HISS)
WHOA, MY ARMOR'S MELTING!?
ZABU (SPLSH)
I'M FINE, THOUGH... IS THIS STOMACH ACID? IT'S LIKE A COLD BATH...
NEW MOON GOT LEFT OUT-SIDE, AND MY ANGEL KNIFE WOULD MELT...
ZABU
I'M OUT OF DEVOURS... HOW DO I FIGHT BACK...?
AND NOW I CAN BECOME AN EVEN MORE POWERFUL DEMON BY EATING YOU!!

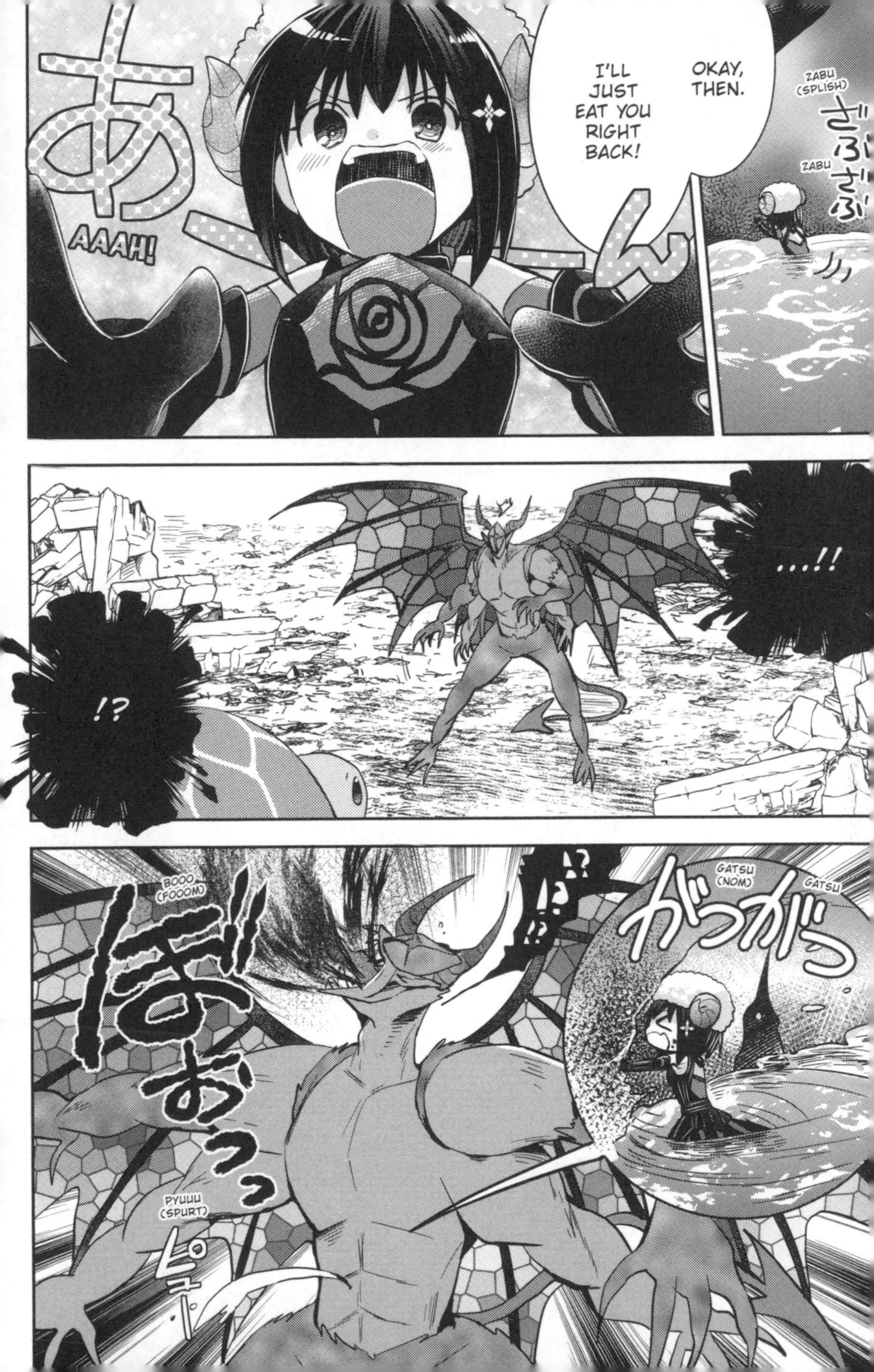

ZABU (SPLISH)
ざぶざぶ
ZABU
OKAY, THEN.
I'LL JUST EAT YOU RIGHT BACK!
AAAH!
...!!
!?
GATSU (NOM)
がつがつ
GATSU
!?
BOOO (FOOOM)
PYUUU (SPURT)

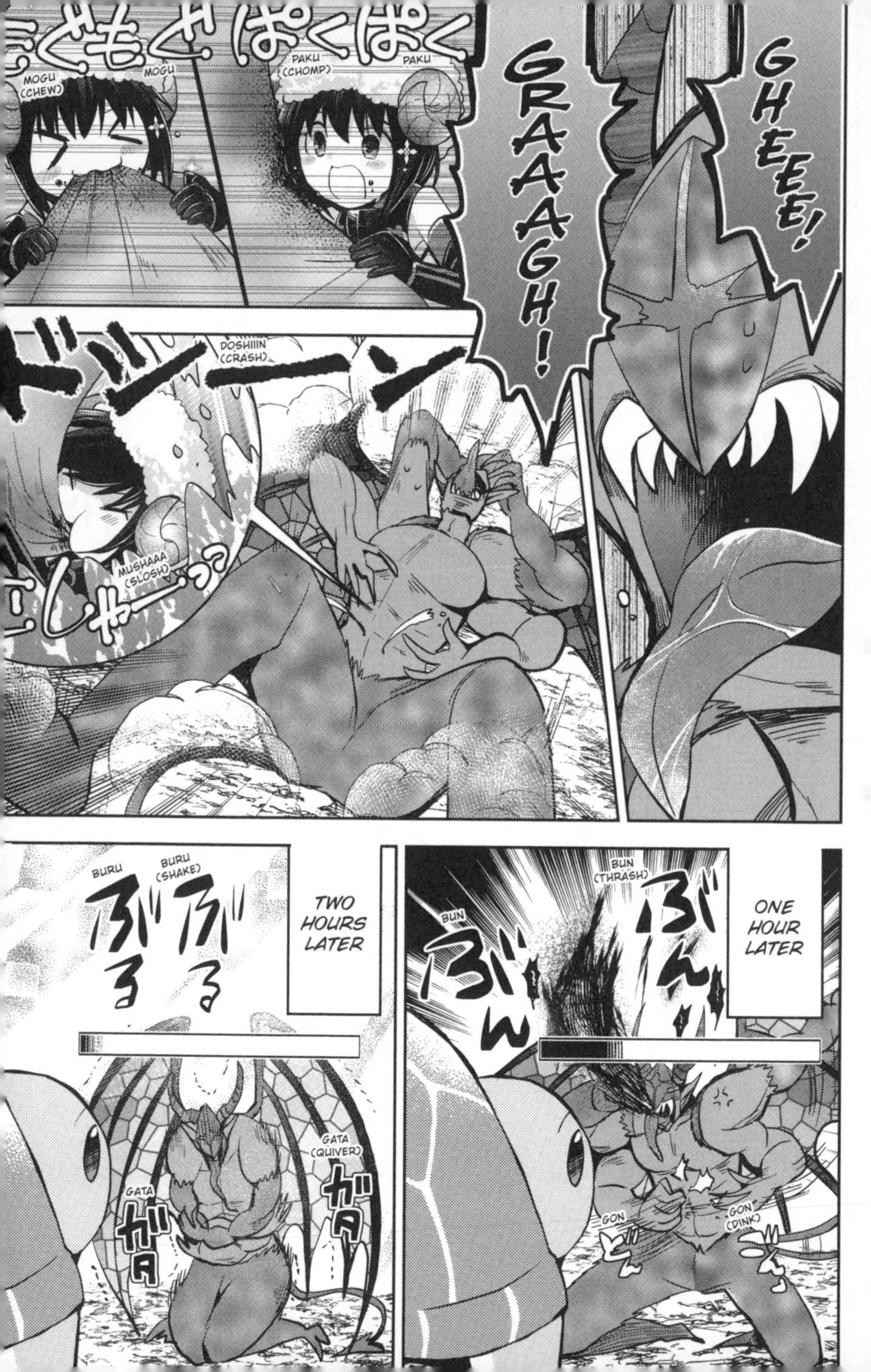
GHEEEE!
GRAAAGH!
もぐもぐ ぱくぱく
MOGU (CHEW) MOGU
PAKU (CHOMP) PAKU
DOSHIIIN (CRASH)
MUSHAAA (SLOSH)
ONE HOUR LATER
BUN (THRASH) BUN
ぶん ぶん
GON (DINK) GON
TWO HOURS LATER
BURU (SHAKE) BURU
ぶる ぶる
GATA (QUIVER) GATA
ガタ ガタ

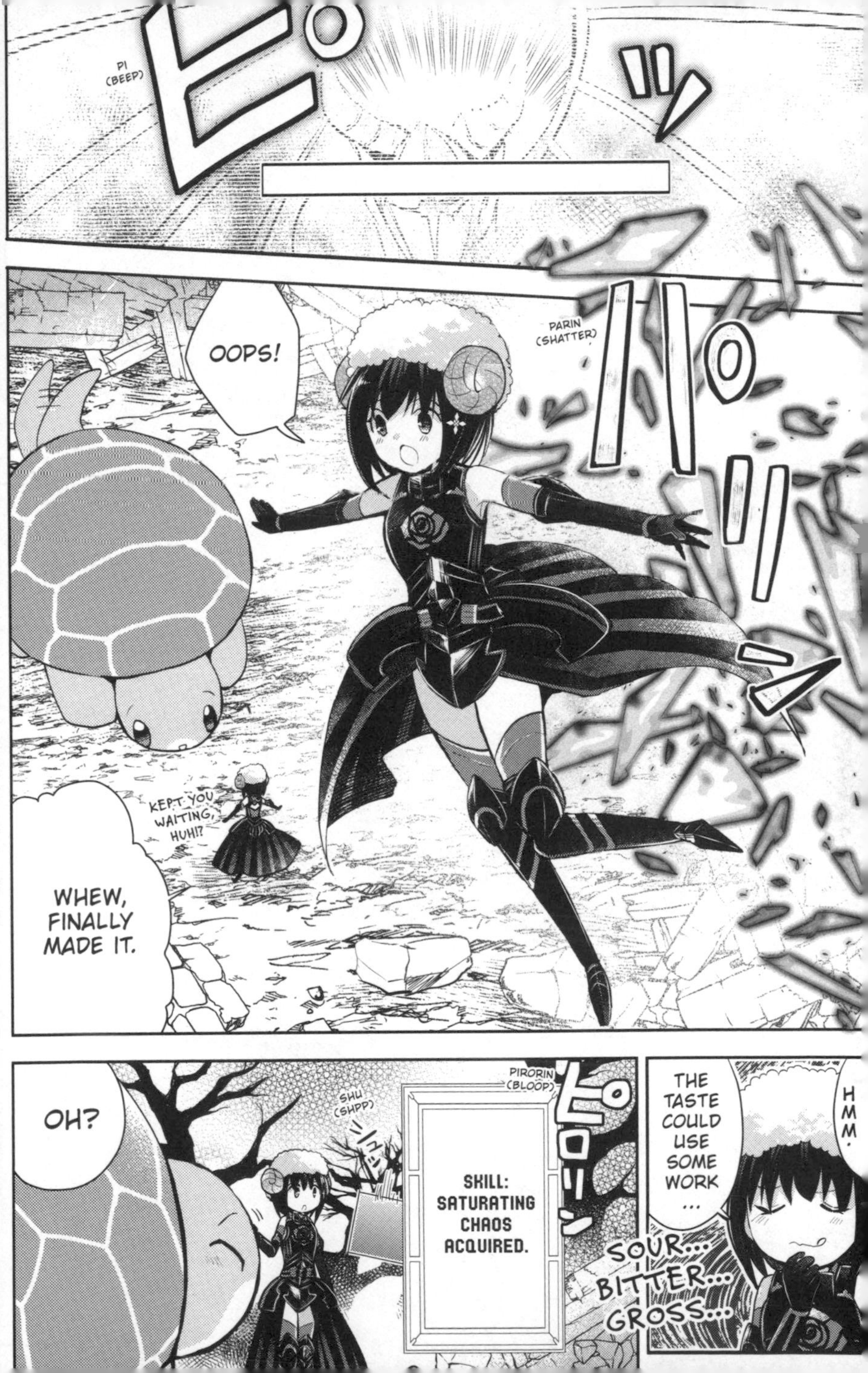
PI (BEEP)
PARIN (SHATTER)
OOPS!
KEPT YOU WAITING, HUH!?
WHEW, FINALLY MADE IT.
HMM.
THE TASTE COULD USE SOME WORK...
SOUR... BITTER... GROSS...
PIRORIN (BLOOP)
SKILL: SATURATING CHAOS ACQUIRED.
SHU (SHPP)
OH?

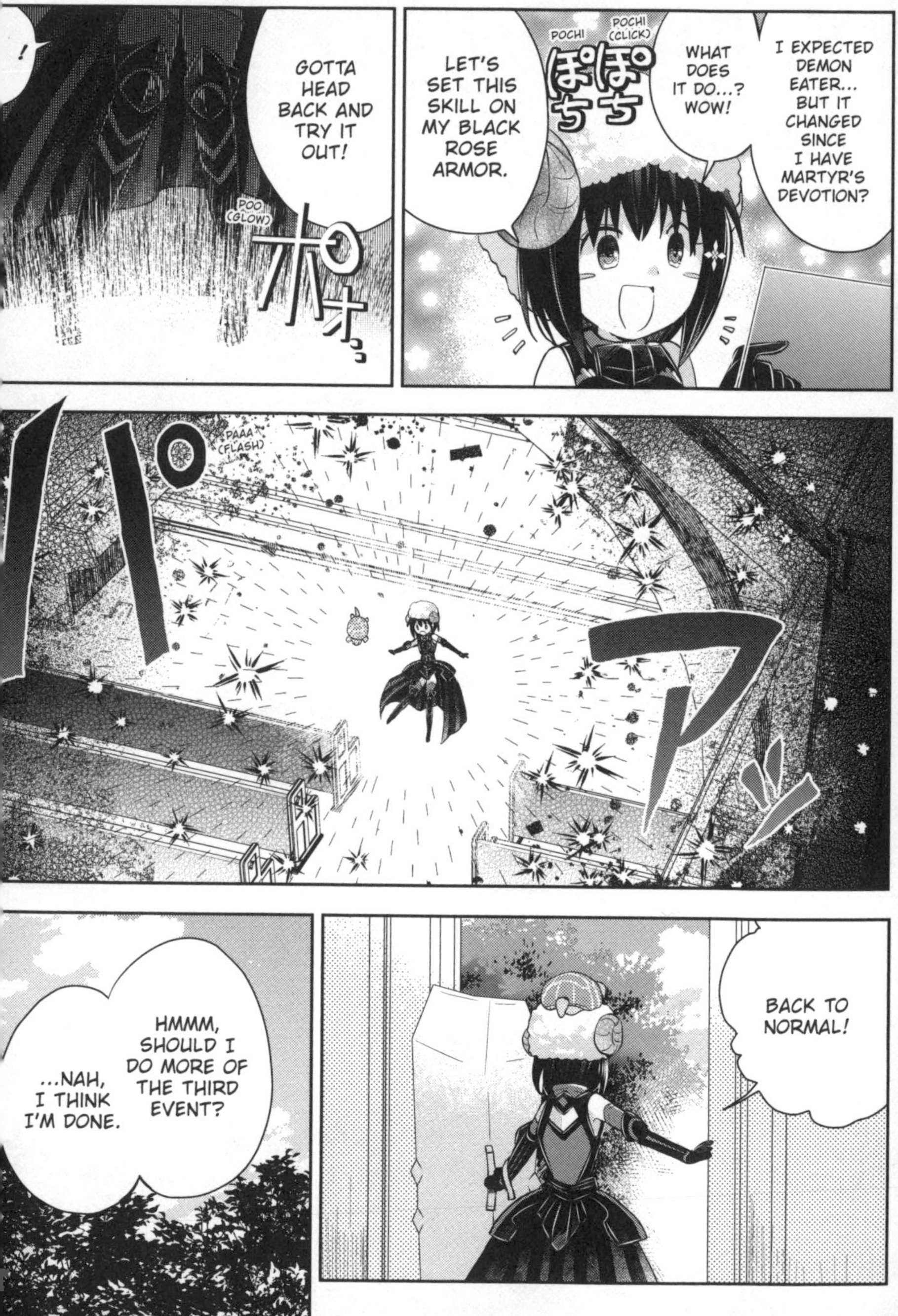
I EXPECTED DEMON EATER... BUT IT CHANGED SINCE I HAVE MARTYR'S DEVOTION?
WHAT DOES IT DO...? WOW!
POCHI POCHI (CLICK)
ぽちぽち
LET'S SET THIS SKILL ON MY BLACK ROSE ARMOR.
GOTTA HEAD BACK AND TRY IT OUT!
POO (GLOW)
ポオっ
!
PAAA (FLASH)
パアッ
BACK TO NORMAL!
HMMM, SHOULD I DO MORE OF THE THIRD EVENT?
...NAH, I THINK I'M DONE.

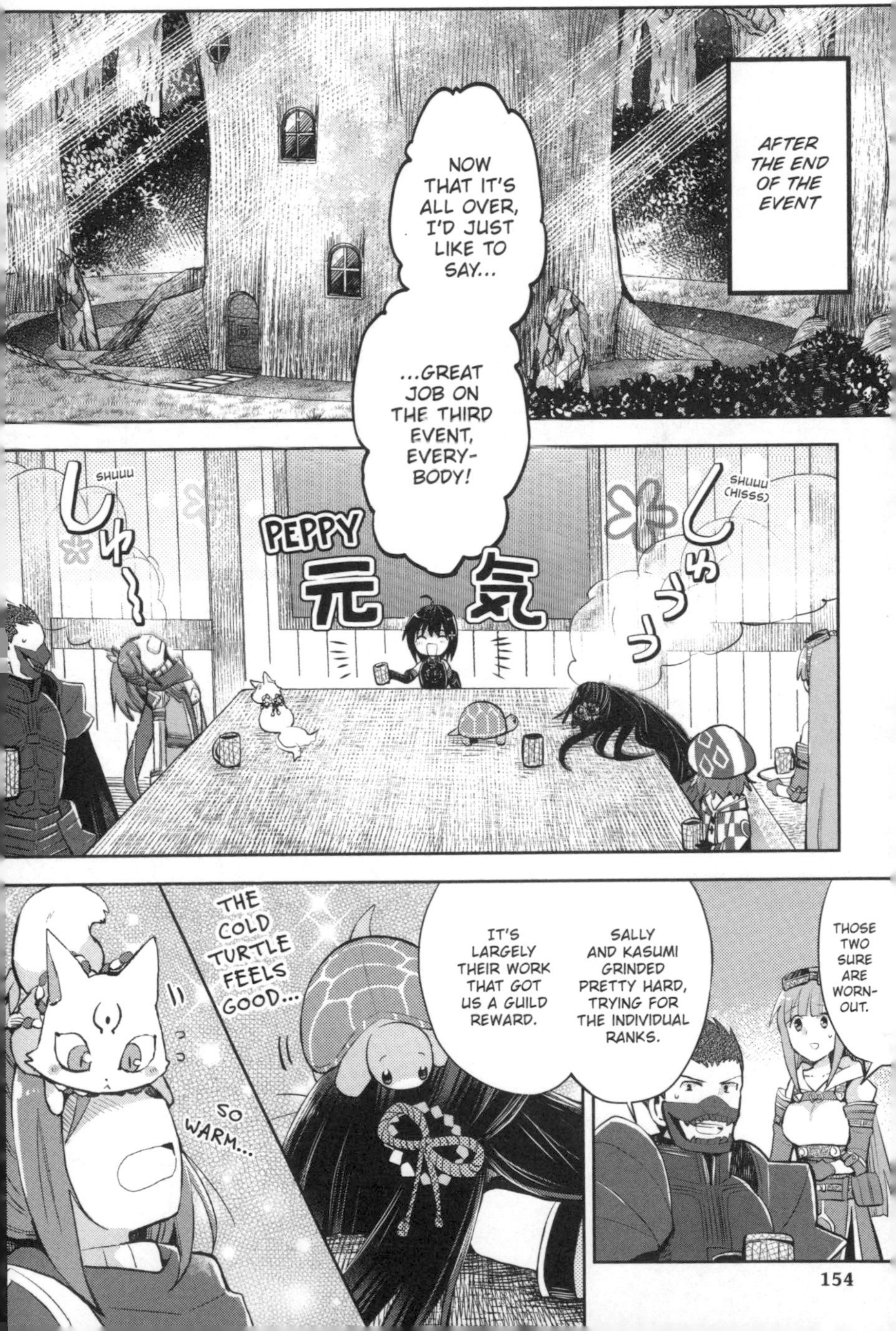
AFTER THE END OF THE EVENT
NOW THAT IT'S ALL OVER, I'D JUST LIKE TO SAY...
...GREAT JOB ON THE THIRD EVENT, EVERY-BODY!
SHUUU (HISSS)
PEPPY
元気
SHUUU
THOSE TWO SURE ARE WORN-OUT.
SALLY AND KASUMI GRINDED PRETTY HARD, TRYING FOR THE INDIVIDUAL RANKS.
IT'S LARGELY THEIR WORK THAT GOT US A GUILD REWARD.
THE COLD TURTLE FEELS GOOD...
SO WARM...

AND THE GUILD MASTER'S OVER LEVEL SIXTY, THE GAME'S TOP PLAYER.

THAT GUILD GATHERED THE TOP PERFORMERS FROM THE FIRST EVENT.

THE ORDER TOPPED THE GUILD RANKINGS?

3rd Event Rankings

1st The Order of the Holy Sword	♛	👑
2nd Flame Empire		👑 2
3rd The Hiking Horde		👑
4th 'Rainbow Wings'		
5th BamBOOs		
6th Clear Crime		
7th Rapid Fire		
8th Line Wars!		
9th Rose Dualists		
10th Thunder Storm		

...WE JUST DON'T HAVE THE NUMBERS TO COMPETE...

FLAME EMPIRE? THEY'VE BEEN EXPANDING BIG-TIME.

I'VE SEEN THE SECOND GUILD MAKING SPEECHES IN TOWN.

RUMOR IS THEY'RE ALREADY ONE OF THE BIGGEST GUILDS AROUND.

APPARENTLY, IT'S BASED PURELY ON THE GUILD MASTER'S FORCE OF PERSONALITY.

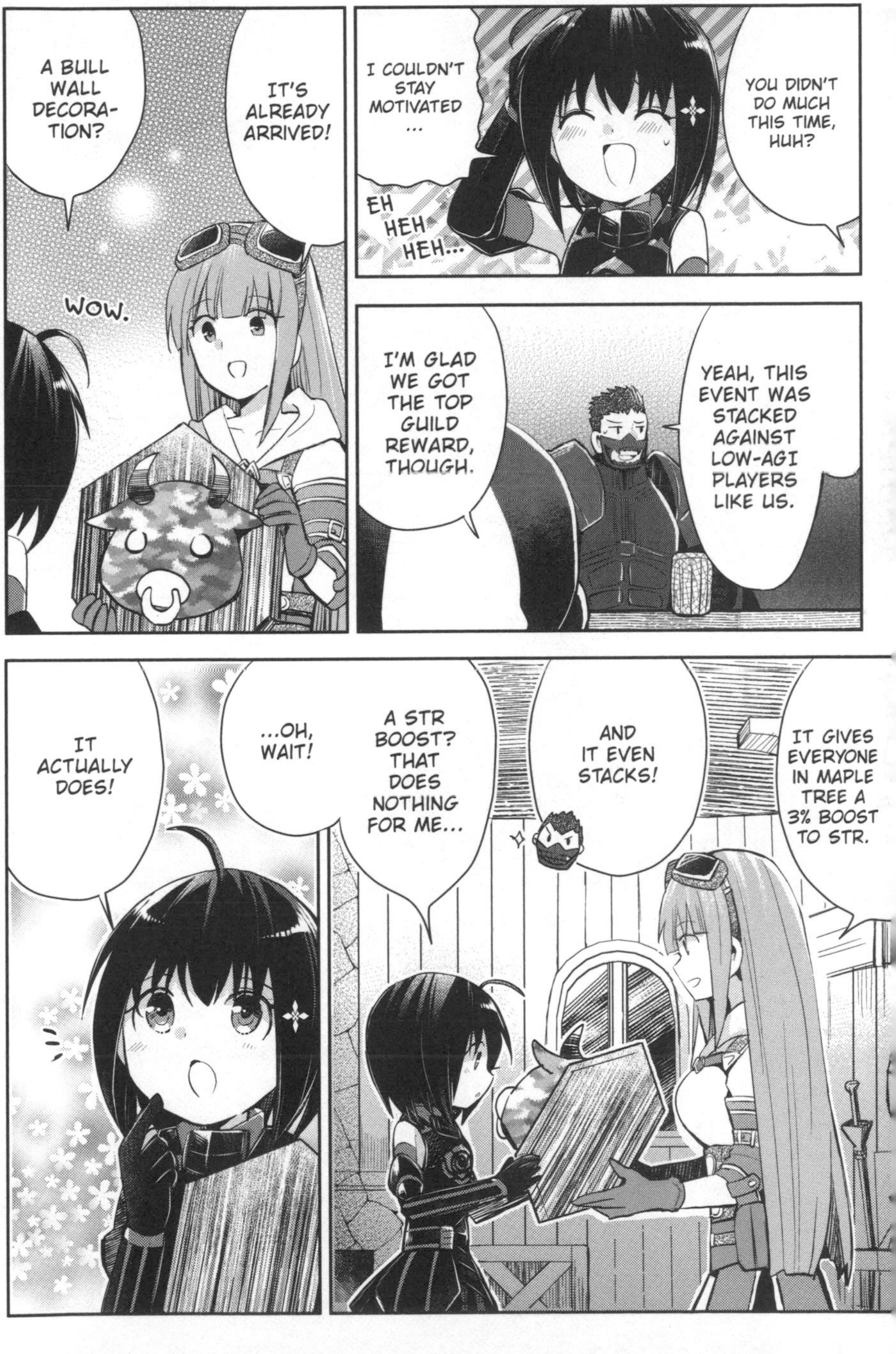
YOU DIDN'T DO MUCH THIS TIME, HUH?
I COULDN'T STAY MOTIVATED ...
EH HEH HEH...
YEAH, THIS EVENT WAS STACKED AGAINST LOW-AGI PLAYERS LIKE US.
I'M GLAD WE GOT THE TOP GUILD REWARD, THOUGH.
IT'S ALREADY ARRIVED!
A BULL WALL DECORATION?
WOW.
IT GIVES EVERYONE IN MAPLE TREE A 3% BOOST TO STR.
AND IT EVEN STACKS!
A STR BOOST? THAT DOES NOTHING FOR ME...
...OH, WAIT!
IT ACTUALLY DOES!

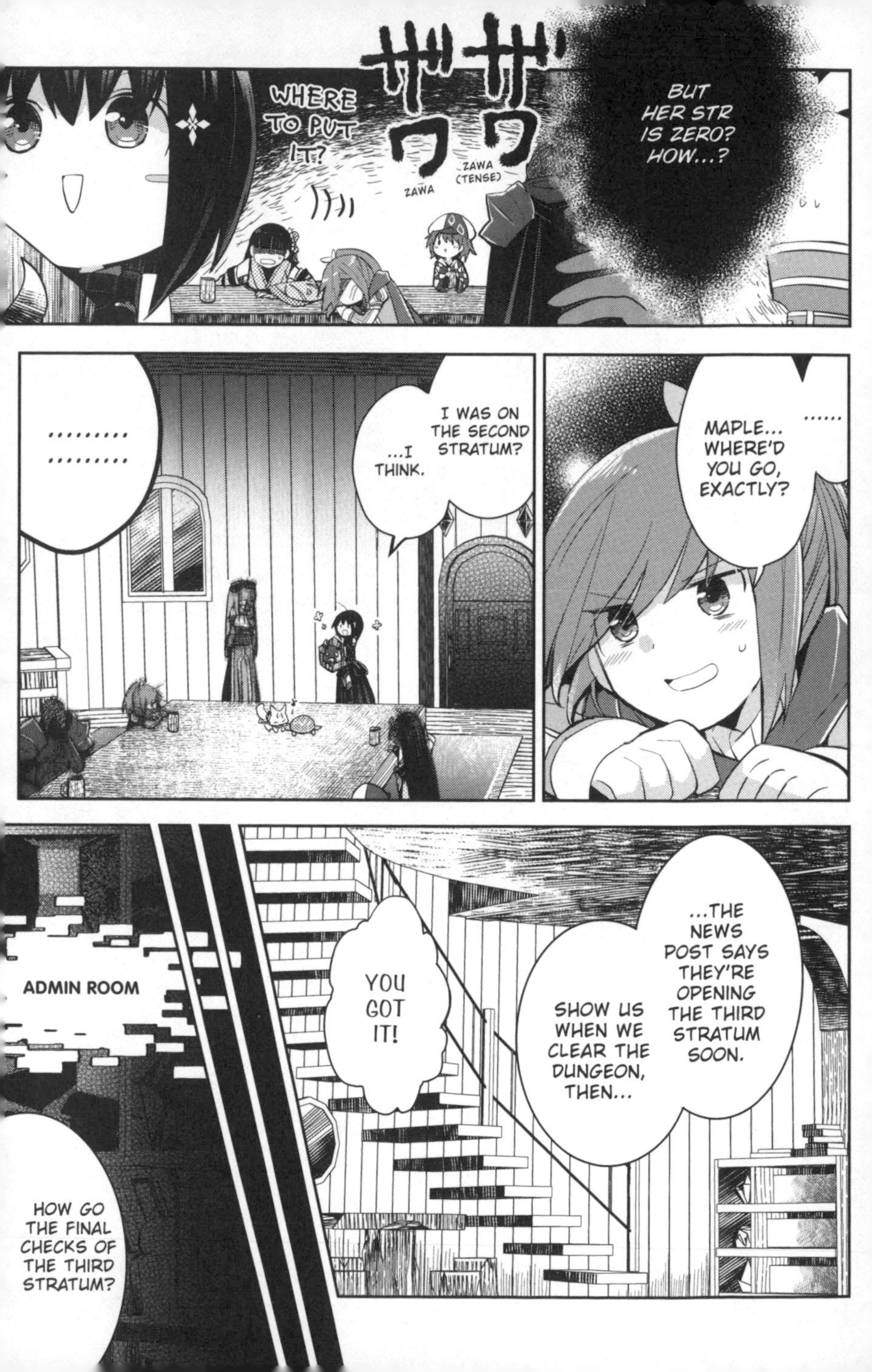
BUT HER STR IS ZERO? HOW...?
ザワ
ZAWA (TENSE)
ザワ
ZAWA
WHERE TO PUT IT?
......
MAPLE... WHERE'D YOU GO, EXACTLY?
I WAS ON THE SECOND STRATUM?
...I THINK.
....
....
...THE NEWS POST SAYS THEY'RE OPENING THE THIRD STRATUM SOON.
SHOW US WHEN WE CLEAR THE DUNGEON, THEN...
YOU GOT IT!
ADMIN ROOM
HOW GO THE FINAL CHECKS OF THE THIRD STRATUM?

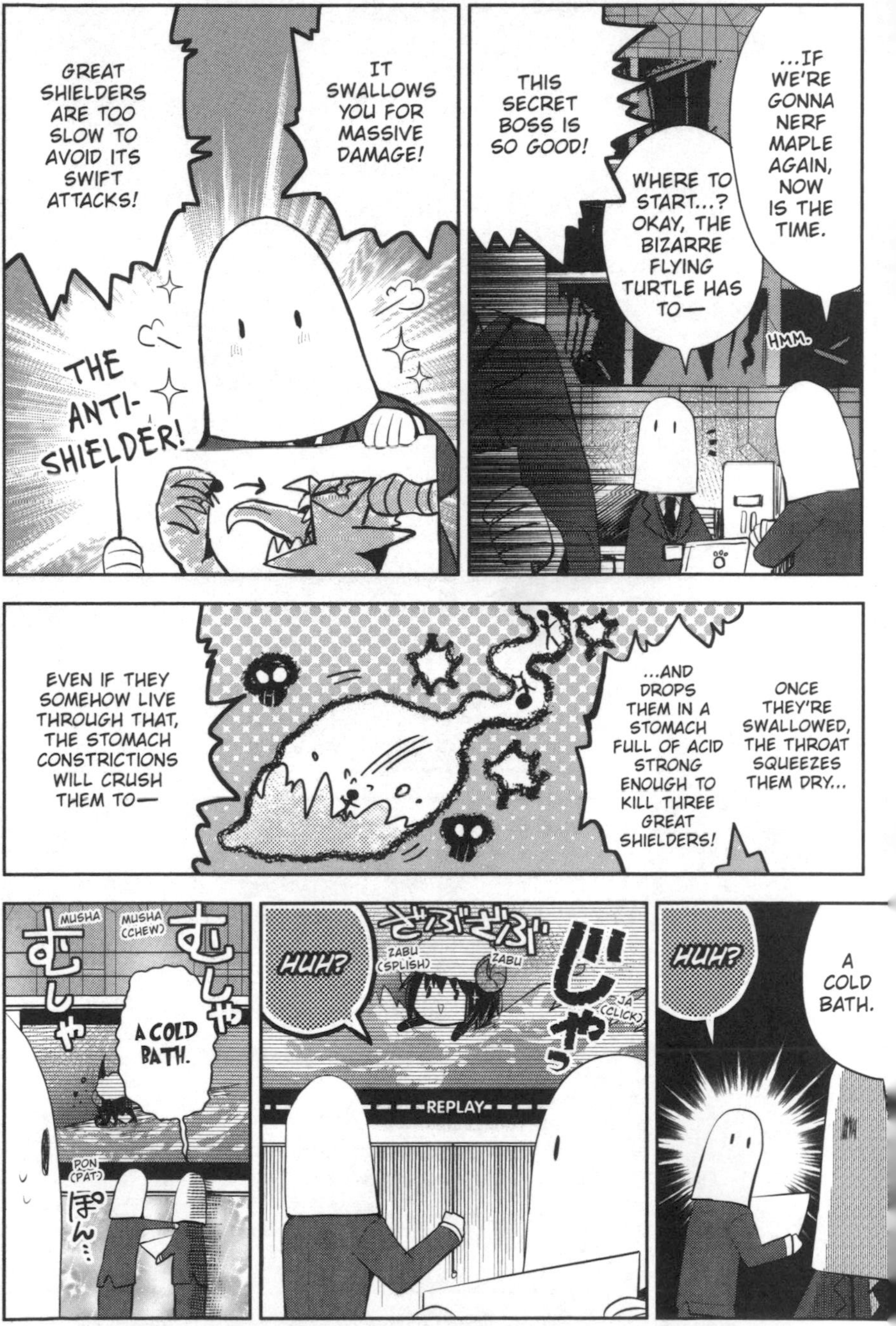

...IF WE'RE GONNA NERF MAPLE AGAIN, NOW IS THE TIME.
THIS SECRET BOSS IS SO GOOD!
WHERE TO START...? OKAY, THE BIZARRE FLYING TURTLE HAS TO—
HMM.
IT SWALLOWS YOU FOR MASSIVE DAMAGE!
GREAT SHIELDERS ARE TOO SLOW TO AVOID ITS SWIFT ATTACKS!
THE ANTI-SHIELDER!
ONCE THEY'RE SWALLOWED, THE THROAT SQUEEZES THEM DRY...
...AND DROPS THEM IN A STOMACH FULL OF ACID STRONG ENOUGH TO KILL THREE GREAT SHIELDERS!
EVEN IF THEY SOMEHOW LIVE THROUGH THAT, THE STOMACH CONSTRICTIONS WILL CRUSH THEM TO—
A COLD BATH.
HUH?
じゃっ
JA (CLICK)
ざぶざぶ
ZABU (SPLISH) ZABU
HUH?
REPLAY
むしゃむしゃ
MUSHA (CHEW) MUSHA
A COLD BATH.
ぽん...
PON (PAT)

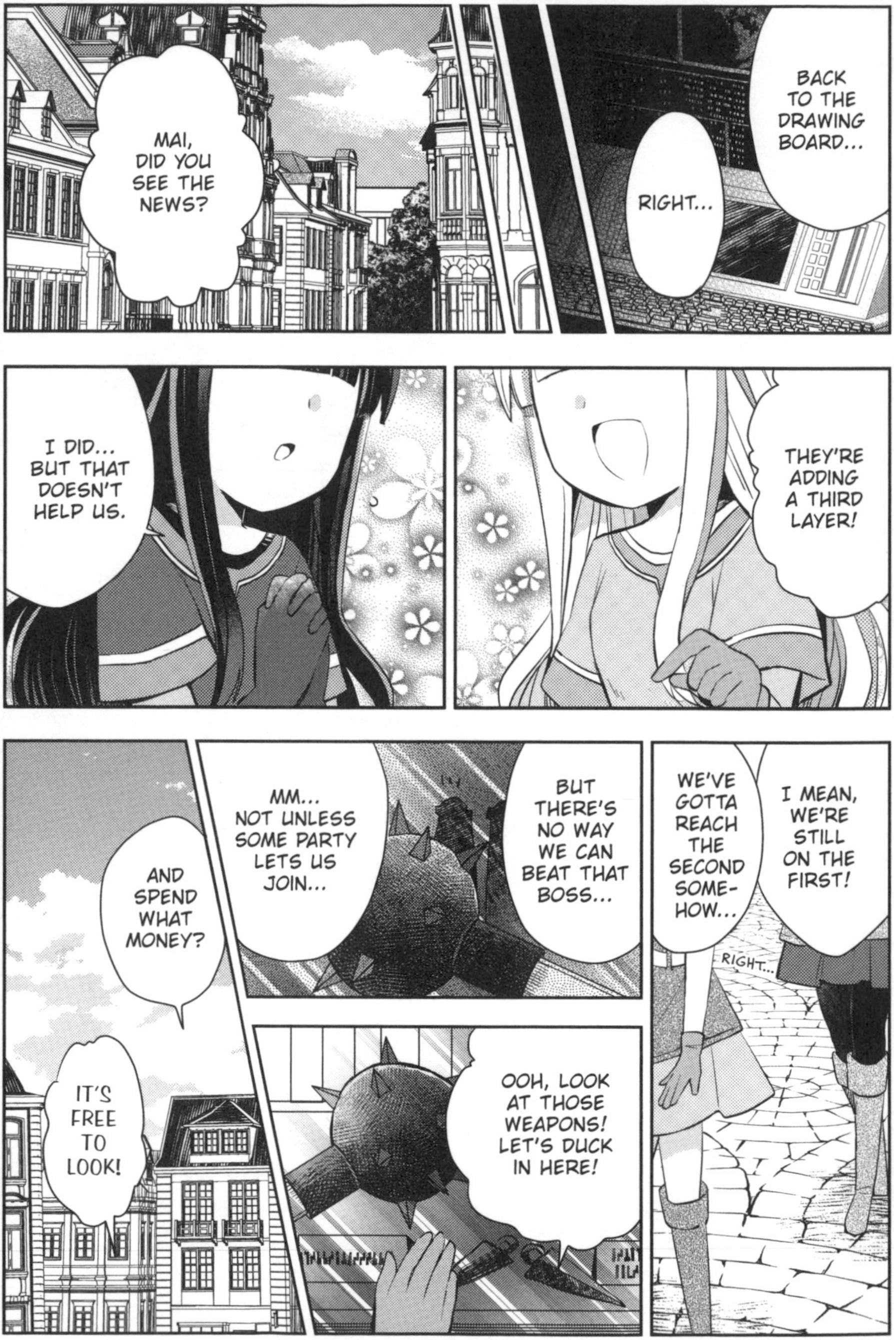
BACK TO THE DRAWING BOARD...
RIGHT...
MAI, DID YOU SEE THE NEWS?
THEY'RE ADDING A THIRD LAYER!
I DID... BUT THAT DOESN'T HELP US.
I MEAN, WE'RE STILL ON THE FIRST!
WE'VE GOTTA REACH THE SECOND SOME-HOW...
RIGHT...
BUT THERE'S NO WAY WE CAN BEAT THAT BOSS...
MM... NOT UNLESS SOME PARTY LETS US JOIN...
OOH, LOOK AT THOSE WEAPONS! LET'S DUCK IN HERE!
AND SPEND WHAT MONEY?
IT'S FREE TO LOOK!

Welcome to *NewWorld Online*.

I Don't Want to Get Hurt, so I'll Max Out My Defense.

presented by: **JIROU OIMOTO & YUUMIKAN**

THE MANGA IS MOSTLY BASED ON THE SOURCE NOVELS BUT TAKES SOME CUES FROM THE ANIME.

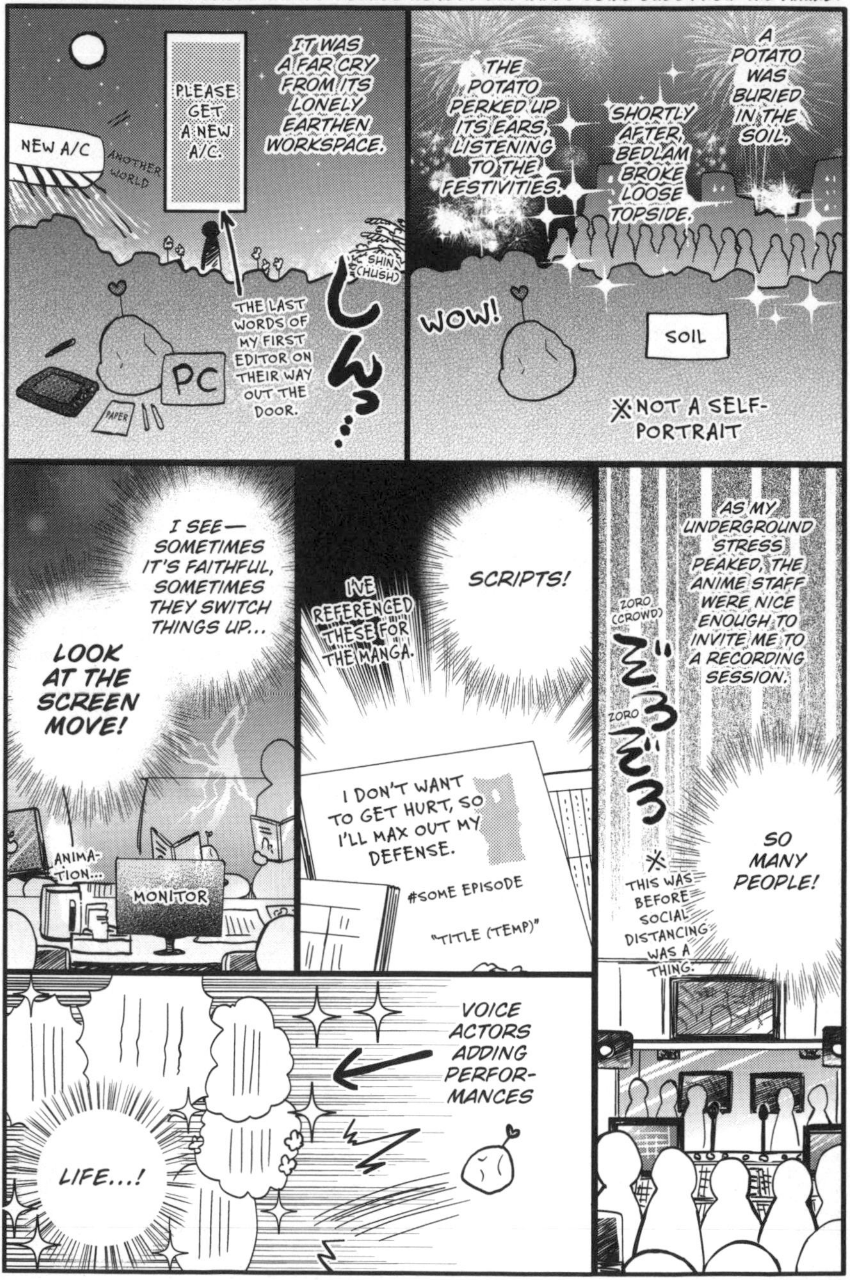
A POTATO WAS BURIED IN THE SOIL.
SHORTLY AFTER, BEDLAM BROKE LOOSE TOPSIDE.
THE POTATO PERKED UP ITS EARS, LISTENING TO THE FESTIVITIES.
SOIL
WOW!
※NOT A SELF-PORTRAIT
IT WAS A FAR CRY FROM ITS LONELY EARTHEN WORKSPACE.
PLEASE GET A NEW A/C.
NEW A/C
ANOTHER WORLD
SHIN (HUSH)
しん…
THE LAST WORDS OF MY FIRST EDITOR ON THEIR WAY OUT THE DOOR.
PC
PAPER
AS MY UNDERGROUND STRESS PEAKED, THE ANIME STAFF WERE NICE ENOUGH TO INVITE ME TO A RECORDING SESSION.
ZORO (CROWD)
ぞろぞろ
ZORO
SO MANY PEOPLE!
※THIS WAS BEFORE SOCIAL DISTANCING WAS A THING.
SCRIPTS!
I'VE REFERENCED THESE FOR THE MANGA.
I DON'T WANT TO GET HURT, SO I'LL MAX OUT MY DEFENSE.
#SOME EPISODE
"TITLE (TEMP)"
I SEE—SOMETIMES IT'S FAITHFUL, SOMETIMES THEY SWITCH THINGS UP...
LOOK AT THE SCREEN MOVE!
ANIMATION...
MONITOR
VOICE ACTORS ADDING PERFORMANCES
LIFE...!

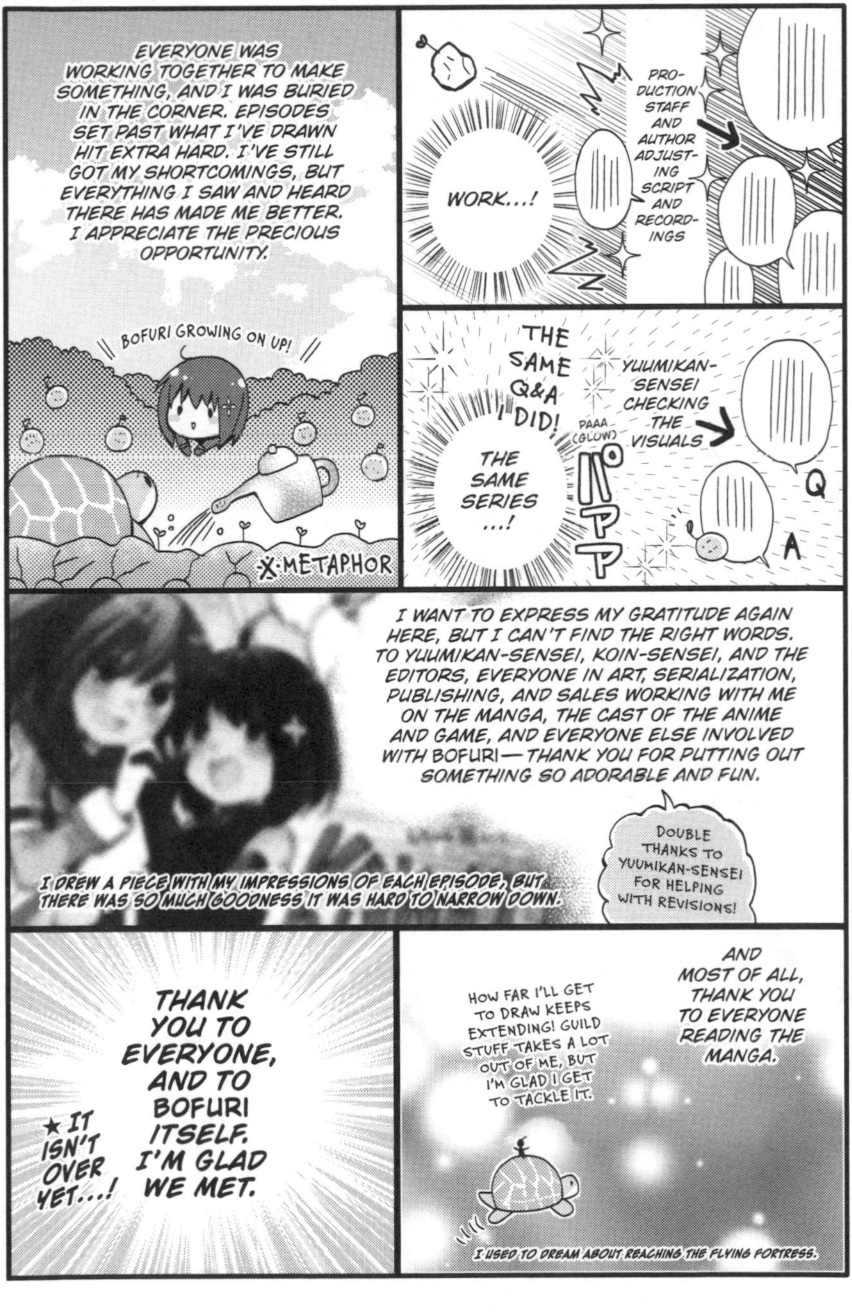
PRO-DUCTION STAFF AND AUTHOR ADJUST-ING SCRIPT AND RECORD-INGS
WORK...!
YUUMIKAN-SENSEI CHECKING THE VISUALS
Q
A
THE SAME Q&A I DID!
PAAA (GLOW)
THE SAME SERIES...!
EVERYONE WAS WORKING TOGETHER TO MAKE SOMETHING, AND I WAS BURIED IN THE CORNER. EPISODES SET PAST WHAT I'VE DRAWN HIT EXTRA HARD. I'VE STILL GOT MY SHORTCOMINGS, BUT EVERYTHING I SAW AND HEARD THERE HAS MADE ME BETTER. I APPRECIATE THE PRECIOUS OPPORTUNITY.
BOFURI GROWING ON UP!
※METAPHOR
I WANT TO EXPRESS MY GRATITUDE AGAIN HERE, BUT I CAN'T FIND THE RIGHT WORDS. TO YUUMIKAN-SENSEI, KOIN-SENSEI, AND THE EDITORS, EVERYONE IN ART, SERIALIZATION, PUBLISHING, AND SALES WORKING WITH ME ON THE MANGA, THE CAST OF THE ANIME AND GAME, AND EVERYONE ELSE INVOLVED WITH BOFURI—THANK YOU FOR PUTTING OUT SOMETHING SO ADORABLE AND FUN.
DOUBLE THANKS TO YUUMIKAN-SENSEI FOR HELPING WITH REVISIONS!
I DREW A PIECE WITH MY IMPRESSIONS OF EACH EPISODE, BUT THERE WAS SO MUCH GOODNESS IT WAS HARD TO NARROW DOWN.
AND MOST OF ALL, THANK YOU TO EVERYONE READING THE MANGA.
HOW FAR I'LL GET TO DRAW KEEPS EXTENDING! GUILD STUFF TAKES A LOT OUT OF ME, BUT I'M GLAD I GET TO TACKLE IT.
I USED TO DREAM ABOUT REACHING THE FLYING FORTRESS.
THANK YOU TO EVERYONE, AND TO BOFURI ITSELF. I'M GLAD WE MET.
★IT ISN'T OVER YET...!

Bofuri

I Don't Want to Get Hurt, so I'll Max Out My Defense.

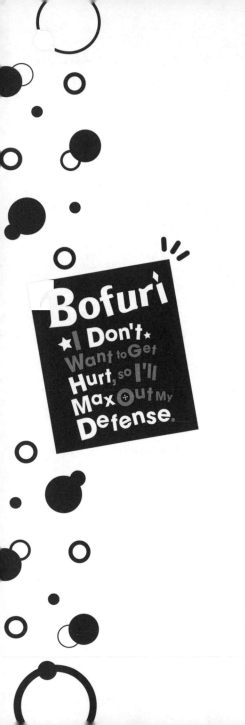

Bofuri ★ I Don't Want to Get Hurt, so I'll Max Out My Defense.

[4]

[Art] **JIROU OIMOTO**
[Original Story] **YUUMIKAN**
[Character Design] **KOIN**

Translation: **Andrew Cunningham** ★ Lettering: **Phil Christie**

This book is a work of fiction. Names, characters, places, and incidents are the product of the author's imagination or are used fictitiously. Any resemblance to actual events, locales, or persons, living or dead, is coincidental.

ITAINO WA IYA NANODE BOGYORYOKU NI KYOKUFURI SHITAITO OMOIMASU Vol. 4
©Jirou Oimoto 2021 ©Yuumikan 2021 ©Koin 2021
First published in Japan in 2021 by KADOKAWA CORPORATION, Tokyo. English translation rights arranged with KADOKAWA CORPORATION, Tokyo through TUTTLE-MORI AGENCY, INC., Tokyo.

English translation © 2022 by Yen Press, LLC

Yen Press
150 West 30th Street, 19th Floor
New York, NY 10001

Visit us!
yenpress.com • facebook.com/yenpress • twitter.com/yenpress
yenpress.tumblr.com • instagram.com/yenpress

First Yen Press Edition: May 2022

Yen Press is an imprint of Yen Press, LLC.
The Yen Press name and logo are trademarks of Yen Press, LLC.

The publisher is not responsible for websites (or their content) that are not owned by the publisher.

Library of Congress Control Number: 2020953028

ISBNs: 978-1-9753-4274-6 (paperback)
978-1-9753-4275-3 (ebook)

10 9 8 7 6 5 4 3 2 1

LSC-C

Printed in the United States of America

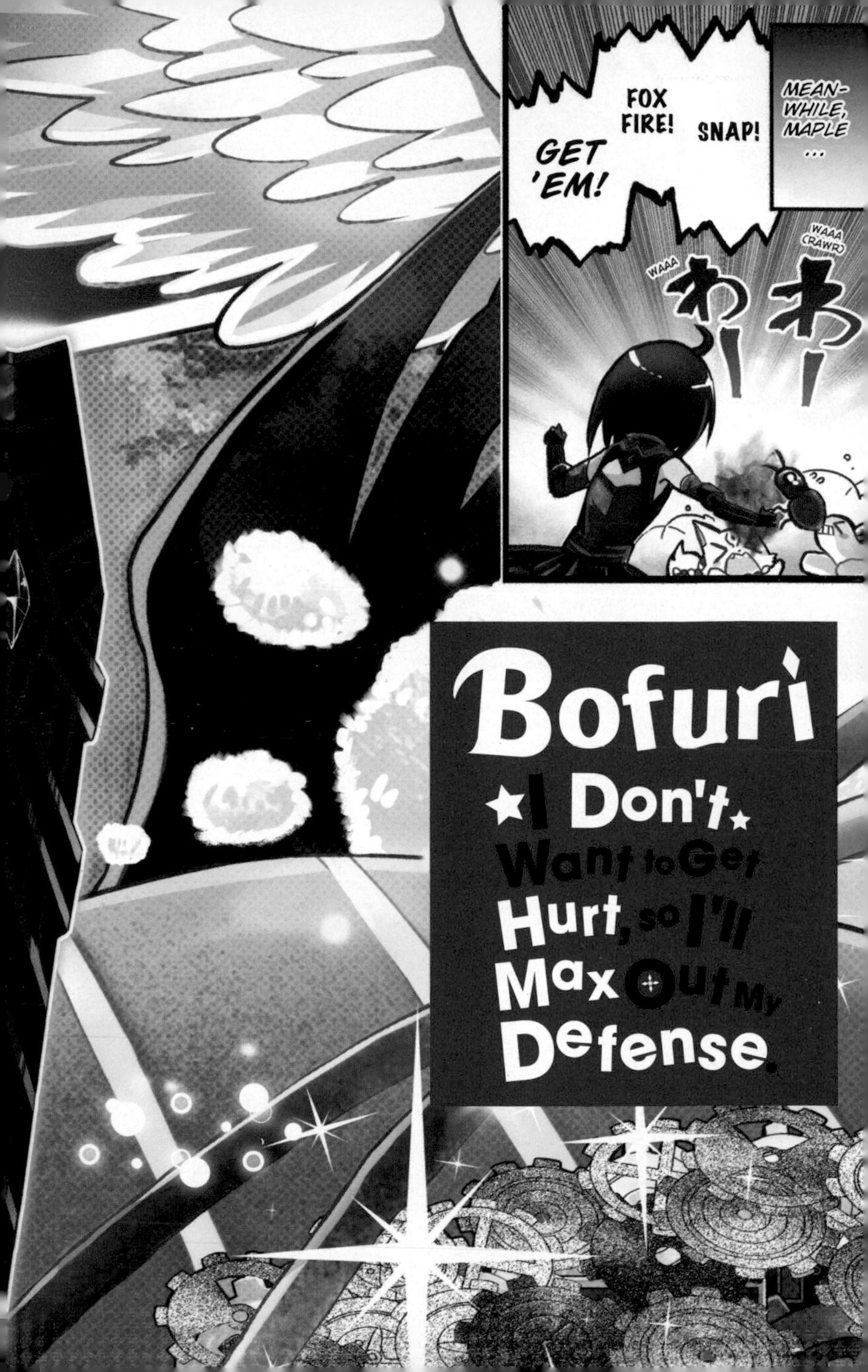
MEAN-WHILE, MAPLE...
SNAP!
FOX FIRE!
GET 'EM!
WAAA (RAWR)
WAAA
Bofuri
I Don't Want to Get Hurt, so I'll Max Out My Defense.

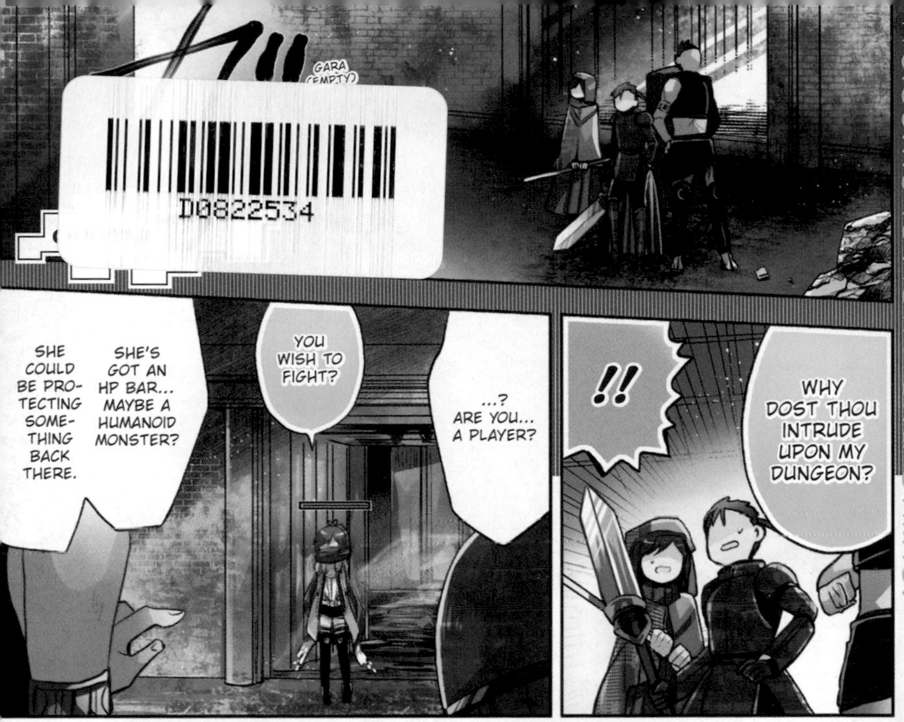
GARA (EMPTY)
!!
WHY DOST THOU INTRUDE UPON MY DUNGEON?
...? ARE YOU... A PLAYER?
YOU WISH TO FIGHT?
SHE'S GOT AN HP BAR... MAYBE A HUMANOID MONSTER?
SHE COULD BE PROTECTING SOMETHING BACK THERE.

presented by: JIROU OIMOTO & YUUMIKAN

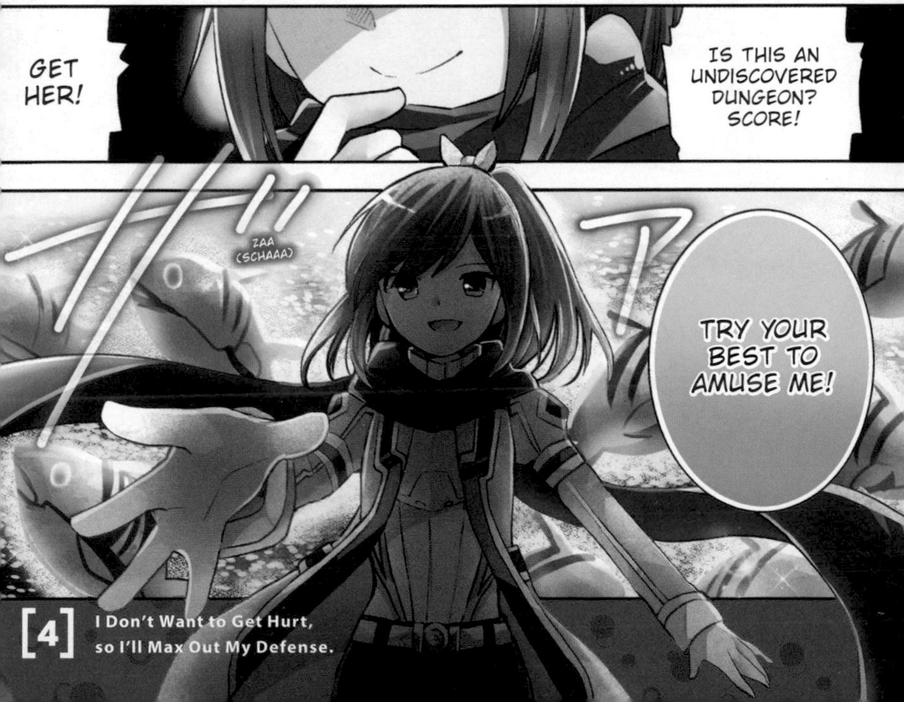
IS THIS AN UNDISCOVERED DUNGEON? SCORE!
GET HER!
TRY YOUR BEST TO AMUSE ME!
ZAA (SCHAAA)

[4] I Don't Want to Get Hurt, so I'll Max Out My Defense.